WARTIME DIARY

Simone de Beauvoir

WARTIME DIARY

Translation and Notes by
Anne Deing Cordero
Edited by Margaret A. Simons
and Sylvie Le Bon de Beauvoir

Foreword by Sylvie Le Bon de Beauvoir

University of Illinois Press

Urbana and Chicago

English-language translation of *Journal de guerre:
Septembre 1939–Janvier 1941,* transcribed, edited, and
annotated by Sylvie Le Bon de Beauvoir (Paris: Gallimard,
1990). This translation includes several pages from the
end of notebook 7 of Beauvoir's handwritten diary that
were not included in the Gallimard edition. These pages
have been transcribed by Sylvie Le Bon de Beauvoir. The
footnotes in this volume were translated from Sylvie
Le Bon de Beauvoir's footnotes that appeared in the
Gallimard edition. The endnotes have been prepared for
this translation. With the exception of endnotes 11, 12, and
14 for notebook 7, which are the work of Nancy Bauer, all
other endnotes and any clarifications that appear between
brackets are the work of Anne Deing Cordero and
Margaret Simons.

Library of Congress Cataloging-in-Publication Data
Beauvoir, Simone de, 1908-1986.
[Journal de guerre. English]
Wartime diary / Simone de Beauvoir ;
edited by Margaret A. Simons and
Sylvie Le Bon de Beauvoir ; translation and
notes by Anne Deing Cordero ;
foreword by Sylvie Le Bon de Beauvoir.
p.   cm. — (The Beauvoir series)
Includes bibliographical references and index.
ISBN 978-0-252-03377-3 (cloth : alk. paper)
1. Beauvoir, Simone de, 1908-1986—Diaries.
2. Authors, French—20th century—Diaries.
I. Simons, Margaret A.
II. Le Bon de Beauvoir, Sylvie.
III. Title.
PQ2603.E362Z46   2009
848'.91403—dc22[B]   2008035333

The editors gratefully acknowledge the support of
a Collaborative Research Grant from the National
Endowment for the Humanities, an independent federal
agency; a translation grant from the French Ministry of
Culture; and a Matching Funds grant from the Illinois
Board of Higher Education.

Contents

Foreword to the Beauvoir Series   *vii*
  Sylvie Le Bon de Beauvoir

Acknowledgments   *ix*

Preface to the French Edition   *xi*
  Sylvie Le Bon de Beauvoir

Introduction   *1*
  Margaret A. Simons

NOTEBOOK 1:   September 1–October 4, 1939   37

NOTEBOOK 2:   October 5–November 14, 1939   88

NOTEBOOK 3:   November 15–December 25, 1939   156

NOTEBOOK 4:   December 26, 1939–January 19, 1940   206

NOTEBOOK 5:   January 20–February 23, 1940   233

NOTEBOOK 6:   June 9–July 18, 1940   270

NOTEBOOK 7:   September 20, 1940–January 29, 1941   315

Works Cited   *329*

Index   *333*

Contributors   *351*

Foreword to the Beauvoir Series

Sylvie Le Bon de Beauvoir

TRANSLATED BY MARYBETH TIMMERMANN

It is my pleasure to honor the monumental work of research and publication that the Beauvoir Series represents, which was undertaken and brought to fruition by Margaret A. Simons and her team. These volumes of Simone de Beauvoir's writings, concerning literature as well as philosophy and feminism, stretch from 1926 to 1979, that is to say, throughout almost her entire life. Some of them have been published before and are known, but they remain dispersed throughout time and space, in diverse editions, newspapers, or reviews. Other pieces were read by Beauvoir during conferences or radio programs and then lost from view. Some had been left completely unpublished. What gives all of them force and meaning is precisely having them gathered together, closely, as a whole. Nothing of the sort has yet been realized, except, on a much smaller scale, *Les Écrits de Simone de Beauvoir* (The Writings of Simone de Beauvoir), published in France in 1979. Here, the aim is an exhaustive corpus, as much as that is possible.

Because they cover more than fifty years, these volumes faithfully reflect the thoughts of their author, the early manifestation and permanence of certain of her preoccupations as a writer and philosopher, as a woman and feminist. What will be immediately striking, I think, is their extraordinary *coherence*. Obviously, from this point of view, *Les Cahiers de jeunesse* (The Student Diaries; the first volume, *Diary of a Philosophy Student, 1926–27*, was published in 2006), previously unpublished, constitute the star document. The very young eighteen-, nineteen-, or twenty-year-old Simone de Beauvoir who writes them is clearly already the future great Simone de Beauvoir, author of *L'Invitée* (She Came to Stay), *Pour une morale de l'ambiguïté* (The Ethics of Ambiguity), *Le Deuxième sexe* (The Second Sex), *Les Mandarins* (The Mandarins), and *Mémoires* (Memoirs of a Dutiful Daughter). Her vocation as a writer is energetically affirmed in these diaries, but one also discovers in them the roots of her later reflections. It is particularly touching to see the birth, often with hesitations, doubt, and anguish, of the fundamental choices of thought and existence that would have such an impact on so many future readers, women and men. Beauvoir expresses torments, doubt, and anguish, but also exultation and confidence in her strength and in the future. The foresight of certain passages is impressive. Take the one from June 25, 1929, for example: "Strange certitude that these riches will be welcomed, that some words will be said and heard, that this life will be a fountainhead from which many others will draw. Certitude of a vocation."

These precious *Cahiers* will cut short the unproductive and recurrent debate about the "influence" that Sartre supposedly had on Simone de Beauvoir, since they incontestably reveal to us Simone de Beauvoir *before* Sartre. Thus, the relationship of Beauvoir and Sartre will take on its true sense, and one will understand to what point Beauvoir was even more herself when she agreed with some of Sartre's themes, because all those lonely years of apprenticeship and training were leading her to a definite path and not just any path. Therefore, it is not a matter of influence but an encounter in the strong sense of the term. Beauvoir and Sartre *recognized themselves* in one another because each already existed independently and intensely. One can all the better discern the originality of Simone de Beauvoir in her ethical preoccupations, her own conception of concrete freedom, and her dramatic consciousness of the essential role of the Other, for example, because they are prefigured in the feverish meditations that occupied her youth. *Les cahiers* constitute a priceless testimony.

I will conclude by thanking Margaret A. Simons and her associates again for their magnificent series, which will constitute an irreplaceable contribution to the study and the true understanding of the thoughts and works of Simone de Beauvoir.

Acknowledgments

Anne Deing Cordero writes: It is a privilege and a challenge to translate the work of an authoritative author. One of the major challenges was to do justice to Simone de Beauvoir the literary author and Simone de Beauvoir the philosopher. I sincerely thank Margaret Simons, who always reminded me of this fact. My heartfelt thanks also go to my friends and colleagues, especially Henry P. Meyer, who helped me maneuver through the difficulties posed by the *Wartime Diary.*

Margaret Simons writes: Anne Deing Cordero has my sincere admiration for this marvelous translation; working with her has been a great pleasure. Sylvie Le Bon de Beauvoir's 1990 editions of her adoptive mother's diary and correspondence inspired us to undertake the translations that comprise the Beauvoir Series. I would like to express my deepest appreciation for her warm encouragement and continuing enthusiasm for our project.

The following persons have my profound gratitude for their generous assistance: Mauricette Berne at the Bibliothèque Nationale; Joan Catapano and Carol Betts at the University of Illinois Press; Anne-Solange Noble at Éditions Gallimard; and Janette Johnson, Jo Barnes, Steve Hansen, and Kent

Neely, at Southern Illinois University Edwardsville (SIUE). Special thanks go to Jo Kibbee, Reference Department of the University of Illinois Library, for locating the Hegel passages; to Marybeth Timmermann for her general assistance with editing; and to Nancy Bauer for editing the translation of excerpts on Descartes and Kant in notebook 7 and for providing endnotes 11, 12, and 14 for that notebook. My research for the introduction benefited from discussions with Pam Decoteau, Jeanne Marie Kusina, and audiences at the 2006 Philosophy Symposium, California State University, Fullerton; the 2006 Celebration of Women's Studies Scholarship, at SIUE; the 2006 Existential and Phenomenological Theory and Culture Conference at York University, Toronto; and a 2007 Philosophy Department Colloquium at SIUE.

Beauvoir's *Wartime Diary* and the Beauvoir Series as a whole have been made possible by the generous support of a Collaborative Research Grant from the National Endowment for the Humanities (NEH), an independent federal agency; a translation grant from the French Ministry of Culture; and a Matching Funds grant from the Illinois Board of Higher Education, allocated by the Graduate School of Southern Illinois University Edwardsville. Finally, I am very grateful to the SIUE Graduate School for the support of the Vaughnie J. Lindsay Research Professor Award, which enabled me to complete the introduction and final editing of this volume.

Preface to the French Edition

Sylvie Le Bon de Beauvoir

This diary of the declaration and the beginning of the war (seven note-books) represents only a fragment of the diary that Simone de Beauvoir kept almost since childhood and throughout her adolescence and her entire life, although with some interruptions. It must be considered a part of a much vaster whole. Its separate publication was meant to complement her correspondence with Sartre [see Beauvoir 1990, 1992], more than half of which relates to the dark period of 1939 and 1940. It seemed interesting to contrast the two contemporary versions in their subtle but significant differences. In particular, the diary fills in the gaps of the correspondence that were inevitable when the two letter writers were together, for example, Castor's [Beauvoir's nickname] clandestine visit to Brumath in November, Sartre's stay in Paris during his leave in February, and their brutal separation when all communication was cut off after Sartre was taken prisoner in June 1940. The diary makes it therefore possible to reconstitute their history in its continuity.

This specific perspective explains why the footnotes are less detailed than those of the letters, why, for example, they do not include elaborate cross-references with supporting pagination to Simone de Beauvoir's novels and autobiographical works. They only aim to make the text intelligible and to identify the various characters, in short, to facilitate the reading. If the readers desire more detailed information, they will find it in the edition of the letters to Sartre. Several expurgated excerpts of these notebooks were incorporated into *La Force de l'âge* [The Prime of Life] by Simone de Beauvoir. I shall point them out as the text moves along.

WARTIME DIARY

INTRODUCTION

Margaret A. Simons

Simone de Beauvoir's readers who saw a heterosexual ideal in her relationship with Jean-Paul Sartre must have been dismayed by the 1990 French
publication of her *Wartime Diary* (as *Journal de guerre*) and *Letters to Sartre*
(as *Lettres à Sartre*). Discovered after Beauvoir's death in 1986 and edited
for publication by her adopted daughter, Sylvie Le Bon de Beauvoir, Beauvoir's *Wartime Diary* and *Letters to Sartre* recount her sexual affairs with
several young women. In Deirdre Bair's authorized biography of Beauvoir,
also published in 1990, Bair describes the young women in question as
merely Beauvoir's friends and reports that Beauvoir denied having sexual
relationships with women (see Bair 1990, 213–15, 510). With the publication
of the wartime diary and letters, Beauvoir's readers and her biographer were
thus confronted with the uncomfortable revelation that Beauvoir had lied to
them about her sexual relationships.[1]

Given society's attitudes toward bisexuality, Beauvoir's lies about her relationships with women may be understandable. But evidence that Beauvoir
lied about her work in philosophy and her influence on Sartre—evidence
first discovered by Edward Fullbrook in Beauvoir's and Sartre's wartime
diaries and letters—is more perplexing (see Fullbrook and Fullbrook 1993;

Fullbrook 1999). Beauvoir earned a graduate *agrégation* degree in philosophy and authored numerous philosophical novels and essays. But her philosophical work, including her metaphysical novel *She Came to Stay* (published as *L'Invitée* in 1943)—the story of an unconventional solipsist who, forced to recognize the existence of other minds, resorts to murder as a solution to the problem of the Other—has traditionally been dismissed as a literary application of Sartre's philosophy in *Being and Nothingness* (1943), a view paradoxically encouraged by Beauvoir herself. While the evidence that Beauvoir lied about her work in philosophy may be disconcerting, it does open up new areas of research, as I'll suggest below, raising questions about her philosophy in *She Came to Stay*, her philosophical relationship with Sartre, and the wartime transformations in her philosophy that were foreclosed by the traditional reading of Beauvoir as Sartre's follower.

Some of the evidence that *She Came to Stay* predated—and influenced— *Being and Nothingness* is available to English readers for the first time in the present volume. Earlier English editions of the letters were flawed. The English edition of Sartre's letters, for example, most of which are addressed to Beauvoir, omits almost three hundred pages of letters to Beauvoir from 1939, including those that were part of their crucial discussions of the philosophical concept of "situation." The English translation of Beauvoir's *Letters to Sartre* is also problematic, as it deletes one-third of the French text, including thirty-eight references to Beauvoir's work on *She Came to Stay* from letters in November and December 1939 alone. There are also serious mistranslations that distort her philosophical work: Beauvoir's reference in the French edition to a "metaphysical and moral" "need" for the other (Beauvoir 1990, 1:254; translations from this work are my own) is obliterated in the English edition, which translates the adjectives, nonsensically, as nouns, "metaphysics and ethics" (Beauvoir 1992, 160), thus obscuring a point of philosophical difference between Beauvoir and Sartre; and her description of the "central subject" of her novel, "Françoise's problem with consciousnesses" (Beauvoir 1990, 1:178), is mistranslated as the "problem with consciousness" (Beauvoir 1992, 111), misconstruing a social problem as an individual one.

Beauvoir's misrepresentation of her work in philosophy seems to begin in *Memoirs of a Dutiful Daughter* (published as *Mémoires d'une jeune fille rangée* in 1958), the first volume of her autobiography. In *Memoirs* Beauvoir quotes extensively from her 1926–27 diary, written while a philosophy student at the Sorbonne, before her first meeting with Sartre in 1929. But in quoting from the diary, she deletes important passages referring to her early passion for philosophy, her methodological interest in doing philosophy in literature, and her early formulations of the concept of bad faith and the philosophical theme of "the opposition of self and other" (Beauvoir 2006, 279; see also Simons 1999a and 2006a, 39–43).

In the second volume of Beauvoir's autobiography, *The Prime of Life* (first published as *La Force de l'âge* in 1960), she continues this pattern, deleting references to philosophy in quotations from her wartime diary, for example, and omitting any discussion of her 1946 article "Literature and Metaphysics," where she defends her method of doing philosophy in literature. In *Prime*, Beauvoir draws an implausibly sharp line between philosophy and literature, identifying Sartre as the philosopher and herself as a literary writer. Beauvoir writes in *Prime* that Sartre influenced her philosophical works but did not influence her literary works, such as *She Came to Stay*, since she wrote them based on her own experience. "I would not consider myself a philosopher," Beauvoir says. "In this domain, truly creative spirits are so rare that it is silly to ask me why I didn't try to join their ranks. [. . .] Explaining, developing, [. . .] criticizing the ideas of others, no, I saw no interest in that. [. . .] I wanted to communicate that which was original in my experience. To succeed in that, I knew that it was towards literature that I had to orient myself" (1960, 254–55).[2]

That *She Came to Stay* is a philosophical work was already apparent to Hazel Barnes, the translator of *Being and Nothingness*, when she wrote in 1959 that the philosophical similarities between Sartre's essay and Beauvoir's novel were too striking to be mere coincidence. Barnes believed that the question of which author originated their shared philosophy should be left open. But her description of Beauvoir's novel as the literary application of Sartre's philosophy assumed that Sartre was the originator (Barnes 1959, 122). This assumption was undermined a year later by Beauvoir's account in *Prime* of completing *She Came to Stay* in 1941, when Sartre's essay was barely begun, and by her describing her novel as an attempt to solve a problem within her own life: the problem of the Other (see Beauvoir 1960, 385–87). But Barnes's account has prevailed, becoming the standard American account, surely in part because Beauvoir's denial in *Prime* that she was doing philosophy in her novel fails to explain its obvious philosophical content.

The fact that Beauvoir's position seems untenable, however, does not mean that she abandoned it. Indeed she defended it in interviews until her death in 1986, including discussions from 1981–86 with Bair, who quotes Beauvoir as saying that her philosophical work derived from *Being and Nothingness*, "which she accepted unquestioningly as her own *raison d'être*"

(Bair 1990, 381). The most surprising of Beauvoir's remarks quoted by Bair may be those concerning the writing of *She Came to Stay*, a new account that differs dramatically from the one in *Prime*.

Beauvoir tells Bair that she did not fully conceptualize her novel until after Sartre's military leave in February 1940, when he gave her the idea for the dramatic confrontation of self and other in the conclusion of *She Came to Stay*, when the novel's main protagonist, Françoise, murders Xavière, her younger woman rival in a love triangle. "Actually, by February 1940," Bair observes, Beauvoir "had written what would later amount to less than fifty pages of the printed text, nor did she fully conceptualize it until Sartre's first leave, in that month. She always remembered that she began the concentrated writing during the first German invasion of Western Europe, in May 1940" (Bair 1990, 228). "By the time of Sartre's February [1940] leave," Bair writes, "she was no further along with the novel than the initial conception and the development of the two women characters [Françoise and Elisabeth]" (229).

Bair also reports that Beauvoir told her that she didn't invent the character of Xavière until after Sartre's February leave, in response to his criticisms: "It seemed the only thing to do was to invent another character to become Pierre's other love object and the third angle of the triangle" (Bair 1990, 230). In Bair's account Sartre's ideas were also the source for the novel's conclusion, which Beauvoir tells Bair was not written until winter 1941. Bair writes, "What still eluded her, however, was the crux upon which her plot should turn. [. . .] Not until she read [Sartre's 'little theory about freedom and nothingness' in a December 19, 1939, letter] did she have what she needed to finish the novel. In the next few months he enlarged his initial thinking in letters, and during his leave he spent long hours explaining it" (231). According to Bair, Beauvoir "repeated" Sartre's ideas "to herself in the dismal winter of 1941 as she struggled to find a successful way out of the fictional impasse she had created." Bair adds, "The middle part of [*She Came to Stay*] came fairly quickly to her, but the conclusion, 'beyond any doubt the weakest aspect of the book,' took longer. She ground it out during some of the darkest days of her life"—in winter 1941 when Sartre was in a German prison camp and Beauvoir lived in German-occupied Paris (232).

It is ironic that Bair's biography was published in the same year as the French publication of Beauvoir's *Wartime Diary* and *Letters to Sartre*. The latter volumes both show, as *Prime* reports, that Beauvoir's concentrated writing of the novel began in October 1939 and reached its peak in the four months preceding Sartre's February 1940 leave, and that the character of Xavière (modeled on their friend and former lover, Olga Kosakievitch), the problem of consciousnesses, the murderous confrontation of self and other, and indeed the entire outline of the novel were already present in autumn 1939.

In a letter dated October 25, 1939, Beauvoir writes to Sartre, "The entire novel is so much in my mind that I'm aghast at having to stop at each chapter" (Beauvoir 1990, 1:220). In a November 28, 1939, letter, Beauvoir explicitly refers to the character of Xavière (Olga): "I began the major chapter on the consciousnesses [part 2, chapter 4, of the published novel], with Kos., who burns her hand; I blended in the Xavière-Gerbert story in a manner that I believe to be skillful" (1:309). And in a letter dated December 2, 1939, Beauvoir refers to the concluding murder: "I made a detailed outline, chapter by chapter[,] of the entire end. There is action to spare—but it is indispensable that there be a true, brutal murder at the end, without that everything is in [the realm of] 'ideas,' an idea of murder, [. . .] an idea of the relations of consciousness[es]—a real act is necessary in order for everything to be realized" (1:318). This confirms Beauvoir's account in *Prime*: "In *She Came to Stay* everything came to me as a whole, in the form of fantasies that I kept trotting out over several years" (1960, 624). "Xavière's murder might appear to be the hasty and clumsy resolution of a drama that I didn't know how to conclude," Beauvoir writes elsewhere in *Prime*. "It was, on the contrary, the driving force and the *raison d'être* of the entire novel" (388).

Beauvoir's letters to Sartre in the fall of 1939 show her working intensely and making steady progress on drafts of the unfinished chapters. On November 15, she writes to Sartre, "I'm working on the chapter about the sickness [part 1, chapter 8, of the published novel], which is immense with the grand scene where the lovers declare themselves and the trio is formed. [. . .] I'm in a hurry because I have the entire conclusion in my head, and since you are not here to see the definitive version, I'm not doing one; I'm holding myself to a second or third draft (which for me is not at all a final version) and I'm going ahead" (1990, 1:268). In her November 26 letter, Beauvoir brags to Sartre about her progress:

> [M]y work went marvelously well, it's the chapter on Gerbert [a character based on Beauvoir's younger lover, Jacques Bost; part 2, chapter 3, of the published novel] and it's so much fun to do; and then I see well the whole novel in my head, and I find that it'll be damned clever; only it will be long: I did 100 pages of revised draft already, in one month [. . .] which is to say half of what I did last year; and it seems to me that there are still at least 300 pages to do—plus everything to revise. Thus I have worked with joy. [. . .] It supports me through the days, formidably, and

more than last year because I'm giving more time to it more regularly, and because it comes in one breath. (1:304)

In her December 7, 1939, letter, Beauvoir tells Sartre that she has "had enough of rough drafts, everything is in place now and I want to write the definitive version; I find it enormously amusing and seductively easy" (1990, 1:334). "This kind of work is a joy," she writes on December 8 (1:336). She writes on December 13 that she would like to show him in January "at least 100 to 150 pages definitively revised" (1:348). Reporting on her progress in a December 29 letter, Beauvoir writes, "That makes 60 pages of the novel that are definitively rewritten (awaiting your judgment). [. . .] I hope by the end of February to have rewritten all of last year's work. And there are still 200 pages of rough draft that only have to be revised" (1:393).[3] As Sartre's leave approaches, Beauvoir brags to him about how much he'll have to read: "There's the first 160 pages done and I drew up a grand plan [. . .] for the 50 pages that follow; you will have some reading to do" (2:36). Then on January 17, 1940: "I really believe that you are going to heap praises on me when you read my 250 pages (because there are going to be at least 250 [. . .]). At this rate, if I work during summer break, everything will be done in October; that would make me really happy" (2:49). This to a soldier waiting for the German invasion expected in the spring.

Bair, relying on her interviews, characterizes Beauvoir as pathetically sacrificing her life and her work to Sartre. But the correspondence and Beauvoir's wartime diary paint a very different picture of Beauvoir: joyfully absorbed in her writing and even calling on Sartre for help with some background information; torn by jealousy over having to share Bost with Olga and keep their own affair a secret; and involved in sexual relationships with various young women—none of which is in Bair's account. Beauvoir, for example, asks Sartre to write a summary of the events leading up to the war since she has decided to resituate her novel in the prewar period. Sartre helpfully responds with a lengthy treatise on the political situation and advice that she study it herself, which Beauvoir rejects, in a November 22, 1939, letter: "despite your reprimands I'm going to confine myself to your synopsis for the moment [. . .]; I do not want to stop my élan" (Beauvoir 1990, 1:290).

The evidence from the wartime diaries and correspondence suggests that Beauvoir may have lied to Bair about her philosophical work in general and *She Came to Stay* in particular in order to hide the evidence in Sartre's war diary (published posthumously in 1983) that he drew upon Beauvoir's philosophy in writing *Being and Nothingness*. Sartre's war diary shows a dramatic shift following his February 1940 leave, a time when, according to Beauvoir's diary and her letters to Bost, Sartre spent several days reading the draft of *She Came to Stay*. After returning to military duty, Sartre writes to Beauvoir commending her for writing a "beautiful novel" (Sartre 1993, 55), and he begins working in his diary on ideas drawn from her novel, as Edward Fullbrook has observed (see Fullbrook 1999; Fullbrook and Fullbrook 1993, 97–111, and 1998, 82–92).

Before his leave, for example, Sartre writes in a February 1, 1940, diary entry of the "impasse" in Husserl's philosophy over the problem of solipsism (Sartre 1984, 184) and describes his own unsatisfactory efforts to ground knowledge of the external world in Heidegger's concepts of historicity and "assuming" one's situation (concepts upon which Beauvoir will herself draw in the coming months). Not until Sartre's return from his Paris leave does he write of the idea—from Beauvoir's novel—that a proof of the other's consciousness comes in the shameful recognition of oneself as an object in the other's gaze. "[T]here's a certain in-itself not of the for-me but of the for-others," Sartre writes in his February 18 diary entry. "Here, for example, is Pieter coming in: he sees me, he speaks to me, at once he cuts into my very existence and I thrust myself like a knife into his" (205).

As Kate and Edward Fullbrook note (1993, 120–21), Sartre's diary draws extensively from Beauvoir's philosophical account of relations with the other, including, for example, her descriptions of love and sadism, which appear in Sartre's diary entry dated February 27, 1940 (Sartre 1984, 255–57). Sartre acknowledges in his diary and letters that he drew other concepts from Beauvoir's novel and later incorporated them into *Being and Nothingness*, including the concept of "unrealizable situations" and a theory of temporality (Fullbrook and Fullbrook 1993, 117–20; Sartre 1984, 197–99, 208).[4] Why Sartre never publicly acknowledged his appropriation of Beauvoir's philosophy from *She Came to Stay* may be suggested, ironically enough, in his February 28, 1940, diary entry on friendship. In reflecting on his experience "as part of a couple," first with Paul Nizan and then with Beauvoir, Sartre writes, "I had the impression, at every instant, that my friends were *reading my innermost self;* that they could see *my thoughts* forming, even when they were still only bubbles in the dough; and that what was becoming clear to me was already clear to them"—a convenient recourse to solipsism (1984, 271, my emphasis).

But why, in later years, did Beauvoir erase evidence of her own work in philosophy and her philosophical accomplishments in *She Came to Stay*? Did she find her early work in philosophy embarrassing in some way? Or was she trying to protect Sartre's reputation as an original philosopher at a time when he was under attack for his leftist politics? Madeleine Chapsal's 1960 interview with Beauvoir about her autobiographies suggests the possibility that Beauvoir was trying to protect the reputation of her most important work, *The Second Sex*. When asked by Chapsal why she was writing her memoirs, Beauvoir replied that she wanted to show her readers who she was, in order to counter the dismissive reading of *The Second Sex* as a work of "feminine resentment." "I would like it to be known that the woman who wrote *The Second Sex* did not do it at forty years of age in order to avenge a life that had been totally unhappy and that had embittered her. If one interprets the book in that way, one might as well say that one repudiates it" (Chapsal [1960] 1979, 396; my translation).

Had Beauvoir told the full story of how her philosophical achievements in *She Came to Stay* failed to win public recognition while Sartre used them, without acknowledgment, in *Being and Nothingness*, at a time when she was ridiculed as "La Grande Sartreuse" and "Notre Dame de Sartre," it would have fueled the repudiation of *The Second Sex* that she dreaded. In choosing in later years to represent herself as Sartre's devoted philosophical follower, sacrificing her life and her work for the man she loved, Beauvoir may have confused and angered feminists, but, as the author of *The Second Sex*, she would have known that such a self-representation can be a woman's most powerful defense in a sexist society.

If Beauvoir misrepresented her philosophical work, as now seems apparent, we are presented with the problem of how to understand the wartime transformation in her philosophy from the prewar solipsism of *She Came to Stay* to a postwar social philosophy of moral and political engagement in essays such as *The Ethics of Ambiguity* (1946) and *The Second Sex* (1949). In the traditional account of Beauvoir as Sartre's follower, this philosophical transformation can be seen as her emergence from the shadow of Sartrean solipsism (see, for example, Bergoffen's account of Beauvoir's "muted" philosophical voice of generosity and the gift [1997, 3, 110]). But the evidence of the diary and letters indicates that Beauvoir was herself a solipsist before the war. Indeed, in a January 9, 1941, diary entry, she refers to having been a "solipsist." A detailed analysis of her wartime diary reveals the roots of Beauvoir's philosophical transformation in her own experiences of the war, experiences that transformed her philosophy in dramatic ways.

The diary opens on September 1, 1939, as France is mobilizing to meet the German invasion. It has been ten years since Beauvoir completed her graduate *diplôme* on Leibniz and her *agrégation* degree in philosophy.[5] Since then she has been teaching philosophy in various lycées for girls, first in Marseilles in 1931, then in Rouen from 1932 to 1936, and finally, in 1936 at the lycée Molière in Paris. According to her former students, Beauvoir's philosophy lectures in 1937–38 focused on a phenomenology of consciousness, informed by a reading of Descartes, Bergson, Husserl, and, later, of Heidegger as well.[6] She gave such scant attention to moral philosophy that students in her 1937–38 classes were left unprepared for questions on moral philosophy in the national examinations in philosophy.[7] That Beauvoir, who was uninterested in ethics before the war, should become famous after the war for her existentialist ethics highlights the significance of her philosophical transformation (see Beauvoir 1960, 625).

In understanding Beauvoir's wartime philosophical transformation, a useful theoretical framework is provided by Sonia Kruks's analysis of the concept of "situated subjectivity" in postwar French existentialism (Kruks 1990). According to Kruks, situated subjectivity, "a relation of mutual permeability between subjectivity and its surrounding world," has four aspects: it is embodied, intersubjective, shaped by society, and engaged in practical action in the world (11). In *Prime* Beauvoir attributes the originality of *The Second Sex* to the concept of situation: "What distinguishes my thesis from the traditional thesis is that, according to me, femininity is neither an essence nor a nature: it is a situation created by civilizations from certain physiological givens" (Beauvoir 1960, 417). Indeed the working manuscript of *The Second Sex* is entitled "Essays on Woman's Situation." But Beauvoir also claims in *Prime* that Sartre originated "the idea of 'situation'" in *Being and Nothingness* (626), a misleading claim since the concept of "situation" apparently originates with Heidegger, who writes in *Being and Time* (1927) of "an existential phenomenon that we call a 'Situation' [. . .] ('situation'— 'to be in a situation')" ([1927] 1962, 346). Sartre probably first read excerpts from *Being and Time* in the winter of 1938/39 in a French edition by Henry Corbin (see Delacampagne 2006, 251). This is the same edition that Beauvoir apparently read in July 1939, since both she and Sartre adopt Corbin's problematic rendering of *'Dasein'* (being-there) as *'la réalité humaine'* (human reality).[8] But they may have first encountered Heidegger's concept of situation in Gabriel Marcel's 1936–37 article describing man's essential "being in situation" (Marcel 1936–37, 2). Marcel writes in his autobiography that Sartre told him "that it was I, and not Jaspers, who had revealed to him the importance of this notion *situation*" (Marcel 2002, 102).[9]

In what follows, I propose to discuss Beauvoir's treatment of the four aspects of situated subjectivity in her wartime philosophy, with reference to her 1926–27 student diary; her wartime diary; correspondence with Sartre; her novel *Blood of Others* (written from 1941 to 1943); and her essay in existentialist ethics, *Pyrrhus and Cineas* (written in 1943). Beauvoir's postwar philosophy of political engagement, I will contend, was cast in the crucible of the Occupation. While some of the philosophical changes wrought by the war would last only a few months or for the duration of the war, others would become defining elements of Beauvoir's later philosophy.

Situated Subjectivity Is Embodied

The first aspect of situated subjectivity identified by Kruks is embodiment. In *The Second Sex* Beauvoir describes woman's biology as an important element of woman's situation in patriarchal societies, where it is used to justify her oppression as the Other. In *She Came to Stay*, Beauvoir presents Françoise's realization of her embodiment as her first "avatar." Françoise, Beauvoir writes in *Prime*, initially believes that she is a "pure transcendence" and "absolute subject," but she is forced by her emotions and an illness—mirroring Beauvoir's own experience—to discover herself as a "limited" and "situated" "human creature" (Beauvoir 1960, 386). But in *She Came to Stay*, Françoise discovers herself and her freedom in discovering her embodiment. How are we to account for Beauvoir's postwar understanding of embodiment as an element not only of her freedom but also of oppression? For an answer, it can be helpful to return to Beauvoir's earliest philosophical writings on embodiment, in her 1926–27 student diary.

Beauvoir's student diary recounts her early struggles with a Catholic asceticism that views the body as a threat to the spiritual life. But the diary also recounts the early appreciation of embodiment that Beauvoir learned from two philosophical influences. The first is Henri Bergson, whose *Time and Free Will: An Essay on the Immediate Data of Consciousness* (1889) celebrates the bodily passions and intuition as revelatory of the self and human freedom, a work that Beauvoir read with great enthusiasm in 1926 (see Simons 2003). The second philosophical influence is Jeanne Mercier, Beauvoir's early female mentor in philosophy, who encouraged Beauvoir to see her womanly emotions as essential to a full life. In a diary entry dated July 19, 1927, Beauvoir writes, "I want to remain a woman, still more masculine by her brain, more feminine by her sensibility." In a diary entry dated July 29, 1927, Beauvoir challenges the cold rationality of philosophy and dedicates her life to a philosophical quest combining passion and reason (Beauvoir 2006, 294–97). In another passage she defends a concept of embodied consciousness as a basis for philosophy against a fellow philosophy student, Maurice Merleau-Ponty: "I have a more complicated, more nuanced sensibility than his and a more exhausting power of love. Those problems that he lives in his mind, I live them with my arms and my legs. [. . .] I do not want to lose all that" (293).

Writing twelve years later, in the November 3, 1939, entry in her wartime diary, Beauvoir returns to a defense of embodied, passionate consciousness in reflecting on "how I situate myself in the world." The context is a conversation with Sartre about her experience of jealousy in her clandestine love affair with Jacques Bost—a conversation that highlights a philosophical disagreement with Sartre. Beauvoir rejects Sartre's effort to convince her that she has chosen her feelings, refusing to be like those women who "pretend to have chosen what they are made to endure." Despite Sartre's ridicule (saying "that I was sincerely discovering America"), Beauvoir rejects his voluntarist view that passions are chosen and affirms her interest in her "psychological inner life." "In the past I had primarily a moral attitude; I tried to believe I was what I wanted to be. This year, however, the presence of the contingent, the passionate due to Bost has been glaringly obvious."

Sartre's diary entries from the same period reject the notion of embodied consciousness. In a November 1939 entry, for example, Sartre rejects Heidegger's reliance on the idea of humanity as a species. "This is precisely the basis of humanism: man viewing himself as *species*. It is this abasement of human nature that I condemn" (Sartre 1984, 21). "Through the idea of species, [. . .] the intimacy of [man's] connection with the world is indeed sensed, but in the degraded form of a symbiosis with the earth and the physical universe" (26). Sartre recognizes his philosophical difference with Beauvoir on this point: "The notion of human species has made incredible ravages; even [Beauvoir] noticed in conversation one day that she has two fixed reference-points in the infinite series of time: the appearance of the human species, in the past; and the disappearance of the human species, in the future. [. . .] To me, this is nothing and is *boring*" (22).

In a diary entry dated December 7, 1939, Sartre defends a Cartesian notion of absolute freedom that isolates facticity—our body and the physical world—from consciousness: "What we call [human reality's] freedom is that [. . .] nothing can ever happen to it *from outside*" (Sartre 1984, 109). "[A]ll that happens to [consciousness] must happen to it by its own doing: that is the law of its freedom. [. . .] [F]acticity has no relevance here" (113). "For at the very moment when [. . .] my body 'overcomes me,'" Sartre writes, "when under physical torture I confess what I wanted to keep secret—it is of my own accord, through the free consciousness of my torment, that I decide to confess" (113–14). While Sartre thus describes consciousness as dominating the body, Beauvoir, in her diary as well as in *She Came to Stay,* rejects Sartre's voluntarism and defends the reciprocal permeability of consciousness and body.

Given these disagreements, it may not be surprising that Beauvoir, in moving to a social philosophy in January 1941, would draw on Heidegger's notion of humanity as a species: "the [. . .] idea of Heidegger that the human species and I are the same thing, it's really *I* that am at stake," she writes in her January 9, 1941, wartime diary entry. "To make oneself an ant among ants, or a free consciousness facing other consciousnesses. *Metaphysical* solidarity that I newly discovered, I, who was a solipsist." Beauvoir rejects the fascist celebration of man's animal nature, siding once again with Heidegger in defining human reality by its ability to transcend a given nature: "the existentiel idea that human reality *is* nothing other than what it *makes itself* be, that toward which it transcends itself. This brings about the metaphysical tragedy of a fascism—it is not just a matter of stifling an expression but of absolutely denying a certain being, a matter, really, of confusing the human with its animal, biological aspect."

Beauvoir recognizes that she is breaking with Sartre in adopting a humanist philosophy: "I cannot be consciousness, spirit, among ants. I understand what was wanting in our anti-humanism. To admire man as given (a beautiful intelligent animal etc.) is idiotic—but there is no other reality than human reality—all values are founded on it." Later, in *Pyrrhus and Cineas,* Beauvoir again contrasts ants and humans in condemning oppression: "even if I oppress only one man, all of humanity appears in him as a pure thing to me. If a man is an ant that can be unscrupulously crushed, all men taken together are but an anthill" ([1944] 2004, 138). Thus Beauvoir's wartime philosophy grounds political solidarity in the biological reality of humanity as a species. In her postwar writings, Beauvoir continues her interest in political solidarities formed around a biological difference, arguing for a defiance of social practices confining humanity within a biological "nature." In *America Day by Day,* for example, Beauvoir follows Richard Wright in arguing that black people in America must unite politically as a race, while recognizing that the supposedly biological racial differences are actually constructed by white society, through the denial of education to blacks, for example. In *The Second Sex,* Beauvoir argues that women must engage in a collective struggle, as women, to end their oppression, demanding that society relieve individual women of the burdens of reproduction that "enslave" woman to the species (1949, 1:76). Access to birth control and day care would allow women to engage in the transcendent activities that differentiate humans as a species from other animals.

But while Beauvoir argues, in her wartime diary, that political solidarity is grounded in a notion of humanity as a biological species, she also paradoxically argues, with Sartre, that consciousness, as freedom, is isolated from facticity, and thus, in a sense, disembodied. In the undated diary entry headed "On the Novel," near the end of notebook 7, Beauvoir writes, "[O]ne [. . .] can never reach the other except in his exteriority." In *Blood of Others* Hélène is described as "free and limitless" while dying from wounds received in a Resistance action (1948, 289). The key seems to be that Hélène chose to engage in the action that would lead to her death: "I did what I wanted" (ibid.). In *Pyrrhus and Cineas,* Beauvoir refers to the distinction Descartes drew between "freedom and power" to preserve a notion of absolute freedom while recognizing that situations differ: "We must distinguish here, as Descartes suggests, [man's] freedom from his power. His power is finite, and one can increase it or restrict it from the outside. One can throw a man in prison, get him out, cut off his arm, lend him wings, but his freedom remains infinite in all cases. [. . .] He freely lets himself die or gathers his strength to live." Affirming the message of *Blood of Others,* Beauvoir argues, as Sartre did in December 1939, that violence cannot touch one's freedom: "Violence can act only upon the facticity of man, upon his exterior" (Beauvoir 2004, 124).

Beauvoir's wartime defense of an absolute and disembodied notion of freedom may be a defiance of the German Occupation. By the end of the war Beauvoir moves away from this position, motivated apparently by the Nazis' murder in 1944 of a young Jewish friend, Bourla, only months before the Liberation. Beauvoir writes in *Prime* of being haunted by Bourla's last words as he was taken away by the Germans: "I shall not die because I do not want to die" (1960, 660). Beauvoir rejects Sartre's attempt to console her with the notion of human freedom as absolute and unassailable: "Sartre tried piously to convince me that in a sense life is complete," Beauvoir writes in *Prime,* "that it is no more absurd to die at 19 years of age than at 80: I didn't believe it. What cities and faces he would have loved, that he will not see!" (661). In 1944 Beauvoir thus rejects the position in *Blood,* where Hélène reassures Blomart on her deathbed ("But what is there to regret? Was it really so necessary for me to grow old?" [(1945) 1948, 289]), and in *Pyrrhus and Cineas,* where Beauvoir writes, "One can kill [someone] only because she was carrying her death in her. From what point of view can we say that it is an evil that this death occurred today rather than tomorrow?" (2004, 124). In her postwar essay *Ethics of Ambiguity*, Beauvoir no longer claims that violence cannot touch human freedom, and in *The Second Sex* she describes the ways in which society can use the "biological givens" of woman's situation to deny her freedom.

Situated Subjectivity Is Intersubjective

The second aspect of situated subjectivity is intersubjectivity, the claim that self and other are at once separate and interdependent (see Gothlin 2006 on Beauvoir's concept of intersubjectivity). In *The Second Sex*, Beauvoir's focus on the intersubjectivity of men and women is a dramatic shift from the prewar solipsism of *She Came to Stay* reflected in the novel's Hegelian epigraph: "Each consciousness seeks the death of the other." Beauvoir writes in her wartime diary on July 7, 1940, of finding the quote in a volume of selected passages from Hegel as she was completing her novel and beginning her study of Hegel: "I found a passage that I copied and that would work marvelously as the epigraph for my novel." In *She Came to Stay* Françoise begins as a metaphysical solipsist, denying the existence of others as separate consciousnesses and viewing them as "objects in [her] own world." Forced to abandon her metaphysical solipsism, Françoise ends the novel as a moral solipsist, justifying murder as a way to avoid objectification in the other's gaze (Beauvoir 1943, 17–18). But Françoise begins the novel as an unconventional solipsist, having renounced herself in a merged relationship with her lover, Pierre. "For many years now she had ceased to be someone," Françoise observes later in the novel. "Our past, our future, our ideas, our love . . . never did she say 'I.' And yet Pierre disposed of his own future and his own heart" (216). Françoise's selflessness is so extreme in the opening chapters that she sees knowledge not as originating from her own experience, as one would expect of a solipsist, but instead as emanating from the other: "Nothing that happened was completely real until she told Pierre about it," Françoise remarks. "Every moment of her life that she entrusted to [Pierre] was given back to her clear, polished, completed, and they became moments of their shared life." "We are simply one," she says (30).

Françoise's initial position, reflecting the experience of a merged self, is a break from classic solipsism in affirming the interdependency of self and other while denying their separation. Given the extent of Françoise's denial of the self, her initial position might be described as combining elements of solipsism (only-self) with elements of an analogous position that might be termed solaltrism (only-other).[10] Where solipsism claims that the self is the sole existent and source of knowledge, solaltrism claims the same for the other. As an egoistic disregard for others can be a consequence of a solipsistic focus on individual freedom, so an altruistic disregard for the self can follow from a solaltristic focus on love, as Beauvoir explains in *The Second Sex*. While little discussed in philosophy, the problem of loss of self in intimate relationships is prominent in the lives of many women. *She Came to Stay* thus can be seen as launching Beauvoir's work on the complex problem of reconciling love and freedom, which Karen Vintges (1996) has argued is Beauvoir's most important contribution to ethics, providing practical guidelines to young women in the art of living. It's noteworthy that in *Being and Nothingness* Sartre avoids the complexities of Beauvoir's initial position by beginning with a consistent solipsism. But Beauvoir's initial position in *She Came to Stay*, while problematic, has the advantage of assuming a fundamental interdependency that will provide her with an important resource— unavailable to Sartre—in her later work on an ethics.

Beauvoir's interest in the problem of the relation of self and other began when she was a philosophy student (see Simons 1999a, 213–33, and 2006a, 29–50). In the first entry of her 1926 student diary, Beauvoir writes of her struggle to reconcile her intellectual aspirations and desire for individual freedom with a Catholic ideal of selfless devotion. Returning from a pilgrimage to Lourdes, Beauvoir writes on August 6, 1926, of feeling "ashamed" when faced with the physical suffering of the invalids: "Only a life that was a complete gift of oneself, a total self-abnegation, seemed possible to me." But then, anticipating her later critique in *The Second Sex*, Beauvoir rejects self-abnegation, describing the "absolute gift" as "moral suicide" (Beauvoir 2006, 54–55). She vows instead to achieve an "equilibrium" between the duties to self and to others, or as she writes on November 5, 1926, an equilibrium between the "two parts" of her existence—the part "for myself" and the part "for others," that is "the bonds that unite me with all beings" (163).

Beauvoir reflects on a multidimensional need for others in her student diary, including a need to learn from others in order to overcome the limitations of her own viewpoint (2006, 261), a need for comfort from others in times of despair (268), and a need to serve others in order to escape a sense of the "uselessness of everything" (232). Need for others becomes a moral problem when it entails a selfless devotion, as it seems to for Jeanne Mercier, Beauvoir's mentor, who espouses a romantic "Claudelian" ideal of womanly devotion. Under Mercier's influence Beauvoir describes her cousin, Jacques, as "Everything—my only reason to live. [. . .] I wait so impatiently for the day when you will no longer be 'the other' or 'self,' but it will only and definitively be 'us'" (229). Beauvoir is aware of the dangers of this masochistic ideal: "My *self* does not want to let itself be devoured by his" (248). In an important July 10, 1927, diary entry, Beauvoir rejects Mercier's efforts "to convert" her to the Church, as a temptation to bad faith ("I want my despair to preserve at least its lucidity. I do not want to lie to myself" [279]). Beauvoir vows instead to "go more deeply" into a philosophical problem that interests her: the "opposition of self and other that I felt upon starting to live. Now has come the time to make a synthesis of it," she writes (ibid.).

In the beginning of *She Came to Stay*, Françoise has achieved Beauvoir's adolescent dream of fusion with a beloved other, Pierre, and faces the consequences of selfless devotion. Françoise finds herself attracted to a young woman, Xavière, who lives for spontaneity and sensuality, rejecting the demands of friendship and work (Beauvoir 1943, 66, 69, 125). When Pierre becomes obsessed with Xavière, Françoise tries to merge her consciousness with Xavière's. But, after watching Xavière deliberately burn her own hand with a cigarette, Françoise is forced to recognize Xavière as a separate, "impenetrable" consciousness. Feeling condemned to an "eternal exclusion," Françoise realizes that in trying to merge their consciousnesses she has "succeeded only in destroying herself" (355, 365). Compelled to stand on her own, Françoise gradually rediscovers herself as embodied subjectivity, first in the painful experience of an illness and then in the joys of a sexual relationship with Gerbert, who has become Xavière's lover as well. When Xavière discovers the secret affair and charges Françoise with acting out of jealousy, Françoise kills her in an effort to destroy the shameful image of herself in Xavière's gaze. Françoise has thus progressed from an initial fused dependency of self and other to a relativistic epistemology and egoistic morality, using violence to impose her view of reality on the world.

In writing *She Came to Stay* Beauvoir sought a solution to the solaltristic problem of separating self and other as well as a solution to the solipsistic problem of proving the existence of other minds. "In releasing Françoise, by a crime, from the dependence where her love for Pierre held her," Beauvoir explains in *Prime,* "I rediscovered my own autonomy. [. . .] Pen in hand, with a sort of terror I went through the experience of separation" (1960, 387–88). But in establishing the separation of self and other, Beauvoir has denied their interdependency. Françoise, as Beauvoir writes in *Prime,* has abandoned "the effort to find an ethical solution to the problem of co-existence; she suffers the *Other* as an irreducible outrage" (387). To solve the problem of coexistence, Beauvoir will have to move philosophically beyond *She Came to Stay*—a process that has already begun in autumn 1939.

As war is declared and Sartre is called up in the general mobilization of French troops, Beauvoir rediscovers her dependence on others. Terrified of losing Sartre and Jacques Bost, who is in the infantry on the front lines, Beauvoir writes on September 2, 1939, of a desperate need for "a well-organized society of people around you [to] . . . tell your troubles to." Sartre's letters suggest a mutual dependency. "I received a long letter from Sartre," Beauvoir writes in her diary entry for October 14, 1939, the tenth anniversary of their relationship. "He had not received any letter from me and worried about it. It made me sad to feel him so cut off from me, and I need him so much. I wrote him a long letter, sobbing." In a November 12, 1939, letter to Sartre, Beauvoir refers to her "metaphysical and moral" "need" for him (1990, 1:254).

Months later, in October 1940, desperately concerned for Sartre, who is in a German prison camp, Beauvoir has returned to a position of selfless devotion. "I am absolutely nothing more than waiting for you," she writes in a diary entry for October 1, 1940. "You, my only absolute." Fearing that German authorities have halted all correspondence with prisoners, Beauvoir writes in a January 9, 1941, diary entry of her isolation from Sartre, whom she describes as "absent, gagged." Taking up her own life again while Sartre is prevented from doing so, she describes her action as "almost a betrayal." Her response is to reaffirm a merged self: "I seem to work in his name as much as in mine." Beauvoir's denial of the separation of self and other is also evident in her political philosophy; she argues in the same diary entry for a "*metaphysical* solidarity," based on Heidegger's concept of humanity as a species.

Emphasizing the dependency of self and other, Beauvoir argues in the January 9, 1941, entry for a Hegelian notion of recognition: "One idea that struck me so strongly in Hegel is the exigency of mutual *recognition* of consciousnesses—it can serve as a foundation for a social view of the world—the only absolute being this human consciousness, exigency of *freedom* of each consciousness in order for the recognition to be valid and free: recognition in love, artistic expression, action, etc." In the January 29 diary entry that same year, Beauvoir criticizes the egoist conclusion of *She Came to Stay*: "*To suppress* the other's consciousness is a bit puerile." Writing in an undated entry headed "On my novel," Beauvoir also criticizes Hegel's view of the hostility between consciousnesses that she had quoted in the epigraph for *She Came to Stay*. "Another aspect of the consciousness of the other," Beauvoir writes, "in a sense it is the enemy. But then again, nothing has value except through it (Hegel). The only absolute is the consciousness of the other. [. . .] If the meaning of the value of these consciousnesses disappears, then the value of mine does not exist either."

But if the other is an absolute, Beauvoir is confronted once again with the problem of selflessness. Here we find another justification for aligning herself philosophically with Sartre, and against Heidegger, in claiming that freedom is absolute and isolated from facticity: it is a means of establishing self and other as separate existents. "*Relationships* between people [. . .] one [. . .] can never reach the other except in his exteriority," Beauvoir writes in the diary entry headed "On the Novel." "[T]here are only *separate* lives." In *Pyrrhus and Cineas,* Beauvoir rejects the claim that the other is an absolute, describing "humanity" and "solidarity" as myths and characterizing humanity as "a discontinuous succession of free men who are irretrievably isolated by their subjectivity" (2004, 109). Arguing for an ethic of generosity, Beauvoir relies on the notion of absolute freedom in arguing that there are the limits of devotion: "[N]o connection can be created from me to this pure interiority upon which even God would have no hold, as Descartes has clearly shown" (126).

Situated Subjectivity Is Shaped by Society

"One is not born but becomes a woman," Beauvoir writes in an oft-quoted passage from *The Second Sex,* arguing that society shapes woman's feminine consciousness as the Other (1949, 2:13). Beauvoir's interest in socialization was long standing. In a July 10, 1927, entry in her student diary, for example, Beauvoir reflects on the lingering effects of her religious upbringing: "This morning . . . I passionately desired to be the young girl who receives communion at morning mass and who walks with a serene certainty. Mauriac's and Claudel's Catholicism . . . how it has marked me and what place remains in me for it!" But childhood influences are not definitive; Beauvoir has renounced her religious faith: "I do not desire to believe. An act of faith is the greatest act of despair that could be and I want my despair to preserve at least its lucidity. I do not want to lie to myself" (Beauvoir 2006, 279). Beauvoir affirms the freedom to reject childhood influences, seeing her life in Bergsonian terms as a product of her *élan vital:* "My life is . . . an unmarked trail that my walking alone will create," she writes in a May 6, 1927, student diary entry. "It is Bergson's *élan vital* that I am rediscovering here" (246). For Beauvoir, following Bergson, freedom requires that one find the courage to face reality and to act on one's deepest impulses and intuitions. Only then is it possible to overcome societal pressures such as those on Beauvoir to assume woman's traditional feminine role.

Beauvoir's experiences in the 1930s, when she had an open and illicit relationship with Sartre while supporting herself teaching philosophy, encouraged her belief in absolute freedom, as she observes, ironically, in *Prime*. "It struck me as miraculous that I had broken free from my past, and was self-sufficient and self-determining; I had established my autonomy once and forever, and nothing could now deprive me of it" (Beauvoir 1960, 22). In *When Things of the Spirit Come First* (written from 1935 to 1937), Beauvoir tells the story of how a girl found the courage to see through the bad faith of bourgeois society and claim her freedom. Beauvoir thus entered the war years focused on her individual existence and confident of her ability to keep societal pressures at bay—attitudes that the war would change dramatically. When war is declared on September 3, 1939, Beauvoir writes in her diary of "the impression of being connected to everyone. [. . .] I felt no personal life, only the community, which lives in itself as in primitive societies." In a September 16, 1939, diary entry, Beauvoir describes herself as "just a piece of tragic humanity." But she takes an interest in describing the collective experience.

In an October 10, 1939, diary entry, Beauvoir describes in Heideggerian terms a "strange impression" of an experience "typical" of a woman in wartime. She has received a letter from Sartre indicating that he is being moved closer to the front lines. "I started to write to Sartre. I was overcome with terrible sobbing. [. . .] After I washed my tear-stained face to go down and have dinner [. . .] I had a vivid representation of myself, as 'entering the Dôme with eyes still full of tears.' [. . . I]t was the typical image of a woman in wartime. And it was *me*. From the depth of time and space I thought 'it's happening to me,' and something inside me escaped historicity." Beauvoir's ability to use reflection to rise above her situation and "escape historicity" will become increasingly limited as the war engulfs the country.

Beauvoir continues to reflect on how society shapes her experiences. In a February 15, 1940, diary entry on Sartre's departure at the end of his February leave, she writes, "A crowd of soldiers with their women streamed down the passage leading to the lower levels of the station. That moment [. . .] looking at it as a collective event, brought tears to my eyes. [. . .] It was also moving and primitive[,] this elementary separation of the sexes with the men being carried off and the women returning toward the city." Such experiences may have encouraged Beauvoir to reflect more generally on how society shapes her identity. In the November 3, 1939, diary entry on her passion for Bost quoted above, written on a clandestine visit to Sartre in Alsace, Beauvoir says, "I'm going to be thirty-two years old; I feel I'm a mature woman, though I would love to know what kind. Last night I spoke with Sartre for a long time about a point that truly interests me about myself: my 'femininity,' and how I'm of my sex and in what way I'm not. This remains to be defined, as well as [. . .] how I situate myself in the world."

The ambiguity of Beauvoir's experience of gender is striking, anticipating her phenomenological descriptions in *The Second Sex* and reflecting her experience of having escaped defining features of woman's "nature," such as marriage and motherhood. By December 1939, Beauvoir's interest in her situation has extended to her economic class and what would then have been called her "race": "Suddenly I'm conscious of my physical appearance, my relationship with my parents, my milieu," Beauvoir writes on December 9. "I'm only too aware that I'm of French stock, provincial, middle-class, and déclassé; . . . a civil servant, an intellectual, and have contacts with Montparnasse. All that is reflected in the way I dress and wear my hair. I also should look into the fact that I feel an increasing desire to do a study of myself." This passage, which suggests that Beauvoir is beginning to question her Bergsonian concept of the body as an unconditioned source of individual freedom, anticipates her description in *The Second Sex* of the body as part of one's situation.

A month later, in a January 2, 1940, diary entry, Beauvoir broadens her focus to discuss the "situation" of a nineteenth-century Jewish writer, Heinrich Heine: "I read the end of the life of Heine—it interested me because it is impossible to be more 'in situation' than this man, a Jew and German refugee, living in solidarity with other exiles in France, etc.—and it's strange, the German immigration of a hundred years ago, analogous to the one of today." In a letter dated January 2, 1940, Beauvoir initiates a dialogue with Sartre on Heine: "I read a biography of Heinrich Heine. [. . .] A funny individualist life but penetrated as much as possible by the social; rarely has a guy been more 'in situation' than this one—through him one follows the history of German Jewish immigration of one hundred years ago. [. . .] And it's a funny destiny, quite impressive. I was struck by it" (1990, 2:11). Beauvoir admires the biography for showing a life "in situation" and "penetrated [. . .] by the social."

In contrast, Sartre writes to Beauvoir the following day criticizing another book for the same reason: "the book by Rauschning [. . .] allowed me to better understand these guys [. . .] who think only of the social all the time. That has its grandeur but the flip side of the coin is that one is always below the thoughts that one has. [. . .] I know well that they are the product of my freedom" (Sartre 1983, 2:13). Beauvoir sends the Heine biography to Sartre, who replies to Beauvoir in a letter dated January 8, 1940: "The book is truly gripping, you're right, although perhaps one sacrifices a bit too much of the person of Heine to his *situation*" (2:25). Thus Sartre criticizes the biography for precisely that which Beauvoir admires in it, the attention to Heine's situation, highlighting their philosophical differences.

Beauvoir's early experiences of the war thus encouraged her to reflect on the ways in which society constructs consciousness. But those reflections in her diary break off in June 1940 with an account of her bitter experience as a refugee confronted with the German army in a defeated and occupied France: "I could feel what a terrific adventure it must be for a young German to find himself victorious in France," Beauvoir writes on June 28, 1940, "and to feel himself part of a chosen race. [. . .] It was hell with the sun, the hunger and the fatigue of a day that had begun early. But it was also passionately interesting. Nowhere did I get a better feel for what victory must have meant for the Germans; you could touch it with your finger, each look, each smile expressed victory, and there was not a French face that wasn't a living defeat." Not until after the end of the war will Beauvoir return to work, in *America Day by Day* and *The Second Sex*, on the ways in which consciousness is shaped by society.

After the war—in her discussion of American anti-black racism in *America Day by Day* (1947)—Beauvoir will take up the discussion of racism begun in her 1939 discussion of Heine's situation (see Simons 2002). But in 1940, Beauvoir had yet to develop an understanding of racist oppression; nor did she confront her own racism, as is evident from the disturbing anti-Semitic remarks in her wartime diary. In an entry dated December 10, 1939, for example, Beauvoir, who had jealously orchestrated the end of Sartre's affair with their young Jewish lover, Bianca Bienenfeld,[11] described Bienenfeld as crying "in front of a wailing wall that she builds with her own busy hands. [. . .] Something of the old Jewish usurer in her, who cries out of pity for the client he is driving to suicide." Later, in the diary entry from June 10, 1940, recounting her escape from Paris—in the Bienenfeld family car—ahead of the advancing German army, Beauvoir writes that she joined friends "in drinking some bad champagne left behind by an Austrian woman who had been sent to a concentration camp. That made me feel a little better," she reports. Beauvoir's diary entries from the beginning of the Occupation show little appreciation of the danger facing Bienenfeld. In her July 16, 1940, diary entry, after recounting Bienenfeld's story of spending "ten days with a peasant woman gathering green peas covered with fleas (in order to get out of Quimper and avoid the Germans)," Beauvoir comments only on her own disappointment: "I was disappointed seeing her again as I always am when I have expected from people I don't know what completeness that only Sartre or Bost could give me."

In her memoir Beauvoir describes Bienenfeld during this period as "devoured by anguish," which opened a gulf between them, since Beauvoir felt she herself had "nothing precise to fear." "Our affinity, our friendship failed to fill the abyss between us," Beauvoir writes in *Prime*, "neither she nor I measured it and perhaps, out of generosity, she, more than I, avoided probing it; but if she refused bitterness, I could not evade a malaise that resembled remorse" (1960, 528). In a letter to Sartre dated July 16, 1940, Beauvoir refers to "the very excess of her [Bienenfeld's] despair" while admitting that "it is true that her situation is not the same as mine" (1990, 2:179). But Beauvoir's diary recounts only her annoyance at Bienenfeld's attitude toward the war. Following a long conversation, Beauvoir writes on July 17, 1940, "in which I expounded to her a lot of ideas inspired by Hegel that helped me to accept without distress the present situation—she annoyed me a little as she always does with her bias for despair and her sensitivity to purely social appearances (that she was capable of crying because the British fired at the fleet at Oran, etc.)."

In her own memoir, Bianca Bienenfeld, now Bianca Lamblin, describes her shock at reading the anti-Semitic remarks in Beauvoir's diary. She recalls that neither Sartre nor Beauvoir ever expressed any concern for her safety during the Occupation, breaking off their intimate relations with her just as the Nazi threat was drawing near, a sign, for Lamblin, of their egoism and political ignorance (Lamblin 1993, 71–72; translations from this work are my own). But Lamblin denies that Beauvoir was a "conscious" anti-Semite, recalling that "during the three years of our initial friendship, I never felt on the part of [Beauvoir] the least manifestation of a repugnance which could have been due to the fact that I was Jewish" (83). Lamblin attributes Beauvoir's use of anti-Semitic terms, spoken in jealous anger, to a tradition of anti-Semitism in Beauvoir's family background "that she was supposed to have totally condemned" (85–86).

Lamblin's view is supported by other entries in Beauvoir's diary. In an entry dated June 30, 1940, recounting her return to German-occupied Paris, Beauvoir writes: "On the boulevard de Grenelle I passed in front of the former women's concentration camp—the armistice terms stipulated that all German refugees must be handed over to Germany—few clauses seemed more ominous and implacable." In an entry on July 9, 1940, Beauvoir describes a pleasurable radio show as "cut off by alarming German chatter (against foreigners, Jews, in favor of work, etc.)." The concern for the fate of Jews in occupied France expressed in these diary entries lends support to Lamblin's view that Beauvoir was not a "conscious" anti-Semite.

Situated Subjectivity Is Engaged in Practical Action in the World

Action is already a central element of Beauvoir's prewar philosophy, as we have seen in her December 2, 1939, letter to Sartre, where she writes of *She Came to Stay*, "a real act is necessary in order for everything to be realized" (1990, 1:318). But Françoise's action in murdering Xavière, while reflective of embodied subjectivity, is antisocial and apolitical, the expression of a deeply felt bodily impulse with no concern with others or the future. This conclusion, ironically, marks the triumph of Xavière's philosophy of living for the moment. Françoise's practical concerns with work and the future have been discarded as symptoms of bad faith. By 1949, in *The Second Sex*, Beauvoir's philosophy of action has become political. Women can achieve freedom, Beauvoir argues, only through their collective action. How are we to account for this dramatic political transformation?

In *Prime*, Beauvoir writes that Sartre originated the ethics of "political engagement" and presented it to her during his February 1940 military leave. "His new ethics, based on the notion of authenticity [. . . ,] required that man 'assume' his situation; and the sole manner of doing so was to surpass it by engaging in an action. Any other attitude was a flight, an empty pretension, a masquerade founded on bad faith. One saw that a serious change had been produced in him, and also in me, who rallied immediately to his idea" (1960, 492). But Beauvoir's wartime diary and letters to Sartre present a more complex picture. Beauvoir's work on an ethics of political engagement began well before February 1940 and found its first formulation in her wartime diary in January 1941, when she was cut off from Sartre, who was in a German prison camp.

The roots of Beauvoir's political engagement may be found in her 1925 involvement in the idealistic Équipes Sociales (Social Teams) movement, led by her charismatic literature professor, Robert Garric, a devout Catholic and veteran of the World War I trenches. Beauvoir taught literature to girls in the working-class suburb of Belleville as part of Équipes Sociales' effort to overcome class divisions by bringing together young people from different social classes (see Simons 2006a, 32). Beauvoir continued to work with the Équipes Sociales in 1927 although she had become disillusioned with the movement and apparently with politics in general. "[W]hat value could I put on the search for humanity's happiness," she writes in a May 24, 1927, diary entry after a friend tells her that he is a communist, "when the much more serious problem of its reason for being haunts me? I will not make one move for this earthly kingdom; only the inner world counts" (Beauvoir 2006, 264).

The first evidence of Beauvoir's wartime political transformation comes in September 1939, as Genevieve Idt has pointed out.[12] Beauvoir, unlike Sartre, writes of her shameful realization that the next generation will have to pay for her generation's failure to resist the rise of fascism. In a September 15, 1939, entry in the wartime diary, Beauvoir writes of "a kind of remorse, and a desperate compassion" for Jacques Bost, who is on the front lines. In a letter dated October 8, 1939, Beauvoir appeals to Sartre to write to Bost, explaining:

> I have a kind of remorse in regards to him, when I think that we will [. . .] be happy while he'll die in some hole. I know well that we could do nothing about it, but we are, nevertheless, members of the generation that will have let it happen. Our attitude [. . .] to refuse to budge in politics, with the condition that we also accept everything without moaning [, . . .] is correct and satisfactory when one thinks of oneself, but for these young guys who didn't have time to lift a finger it is so very unjust. [. . .] I do have remorse in thinking that another will have to pay for our impotence. (1990, 1:169–70)

Beauvoir also writes in *Prime* of her shame regarding Bost: "There is no way to elude political engagement. In abstaining, one is taking a position. Remorse stabbed me like a knife" (1960, 409).

Beauvoir's realization of political responsibility comes ironically just as the war makes political action impossible. "Suddenly, History swept over me," Beauvoir writes in a famous passage from *Prime,* highlighting the disruption of her sense of time, which had formerly been defined by her personal plans for the future and memories of the past (1960, 424). Now she experiences history not as her personal story but as an external force, out of her control. The result is a loss of agency, replaced by a sense of passively awaiting events. "We are going through a strange moment in history," she writes in her October 3, 1939, diary entry. "I am [. . .] waiting for I don't know what. It seems that everyone is waiting, as if pure time had any efficacy."

24

When Beauvoir takes up her diary on June 30, 1940, the collective experience of waiting marks her account as a refugee fleeing the advancing German army—waiting for a ride out of Paris; waiting for the German troops to appear; then waiting in a crowd of exhausted refugees returning to Paris; and finally, once back in Paris, waiting anxiously for word from Sartre. Beauvoir writes of using her diary to regain a sense of herself as an active participant in History rather than a passive victim. "Suddenly, with all the strength I could muster I believed in an 'afterward,'" Beauvoir writes. "The proof of this is the fact that I purchased this notebook and a bottle of ink with the intention of untangling the history, the story of these last three weeks, and writing everything down for Sartre and Bost and, for the future. It was the first day that I came out of my shell and stopped living like a 'crushed bug' and tried to become a person again." Beauvoir's loss of self is evident as the passage continues: "Those last three weeks I was nowhere—there were big collective events or a particular physiological anguish and neither past, nor future, nor anybody. I would like to find myself again as in September [1939] and think that all of that forms part of my history, my story."

Unable to sustain the effort to reclaim her individuality, Beauvoir seeks refuge in a "spiritual" position akin to those she had condemned in *When Things of the Spirit Come First:* Hegel's account of History as Spirit unfolding. "I worked for two hours on Hegel [. . .] and the *Phenomenology of Spirit,*" she writes in a diary entry dated July 6, 1940. "I decided to go to the Bibliothèque Nationale every day [. . .] and work on Hegel. It's the most soothing activity I could find. [. . .] [T]here's the [. . .] ideas [. . .] about human history of which this is only a moment—I felt more assured in the world than I had for a long time." With her philosophical turn to Hegel's Universal—drawing on his *Logic* as well as the *Phenomenology* (see Beauvoir 1990, 2:173)—Beauvoir abandons her efforts to reclaim her self and assert her individual desires. "[H]ow absurd it is from the point of view of the spirit to speak of an époque as more comfortable, more agreeable to live than another" (2:181), she writes to Sartre a few days later, after finally receiving a note from him in a prison camp.

"Everything depends on what it is one awaits from the spirit," she writes to Sartre, "what one wants and hopes of from it" (Beauvoir 1990, 2:181). The individual is reduced to awaiting passively the results of actions originating elsewhere. As the letter continues, Beauvoir reflects on the struggle to come to terms with life as an intellectual under a repressive regime, and the loss of freedom of expression. "[B]ut after all," she writes, "expression for the sake of expression is not an end in itself. In expressing oneself, it's very much a question, for me at least, of particularizing the universal, of giving my singular mark to a thought that wants to rejoin the universal—but if the universal is realized in a moment such that it excludes individual expression? Isn't there a contradiction in enduring that?" (ibid.). A lasting effect of this dramatic shift may be Beauvoir's new understanding of the historical context of her work: "I was also struck [. . .] by the correctness of this Hegelian idea of enveloping the totality within our individual becoming—because when one is concerned with creating a work, it is certain that one regards the work as itself a moment of the total becoming in which the entire past is achieved and which is the effective liaison with the entire future" (181–82). Beauvoir concludes by explaining her philosophical shift: "the influence of Hegel combined with recent events have led me to adopt from within for the first time in my life this attitude, rather close to Spinozism, that has always been so foreign to me. [. . .] Thus I'm living [. . .] on a philosophical plane where optimism is possible" (182). Thus Beauvoir has turned to a Hegelian Universal in an effort to reconcile herself to the collective events that have swept away her individual existence.

After the July 18, 1940, entry, Beauvoir's diary breaks off for several months, reflecting her experience of being overwhelmed and silenced by History, as Beauvoir explains in *Prime*: "Hegel calmed me a little. . . . Around me embalmed in thousands of volumes, the past slept; and the present appeared to me as a past to come. As for me, I was abolished" (Beauvoir 1960, 526). Beauvoir highlights this theme in her novel set in the Occupation and French Resistance, *Blood of Others,* in which Hélène, the female protagonist, experiences her personal history, or story (*histoire*), as swept away by world History (*Histoire*) (a distinction lost in the English translation of the novel, which does not preserve Beauvoir's capitalization): "'History unfolds, and as for me, I no longer have a history'" (Beauvoir 1945, 255; see also Beauvoir 1948, 235). "With dry eyes she watched the men, the horses, the tanks, the strange guns pass by; she was watching the march of History, which was not her own history, which belonged to no one" (1945, 260; see also 1948, 240). "[S]he no longer had either body or soul; only this voice that said 'I am no longer myself'" (1945, 268; see also 1948, 248).

Over the first six months of the Occupation, Beauvoir's diary and letters to Sartre reveal her becoming increasingly uncomfortable with her accommodation to History and the Occupation. Although her letters to Sartre were written to clear the censors, they reveal her anger at French intellectual collaboration. In a letter from the end of July 1940, for example, Beauvoir writes that she finds rather "disgusting" an actress friend who "is planning future projects with enthusiasm because she thinks that the moment of her glory [. . .] has finally come. [. . .] I was bored to death and thought of you with a pang of anguish" (1990, 2:186, 185). The sense of political and intellectual isolation that follows news of French intellectual collaboration (including censorship of books and news that the prestigious French review *Nouvelle Revue Française* would be published under German control) contributes to Beauvoir's anguish (see Beauvoir, 1960, 534). Her initial response is to attempt to find pleasure in the moment, for example, listening to music with friends, an effort that is only partially successful, with full days followed by restless nights and nightmares.

Beauvoir's greatest anguish concerns Sartre. After learning in mid-September that Sartre's close friend Paul Nizan had been killed and that Sartre has been moved to a prison camp inside Germany (an episode that appears as an emotional turning point in *Blood*), she writes, in a diary entry dated September 20, 1940, that her life is "nothing but a series of insomnia, nightmares, tears and headaches. [. . .] I vaguely see a map of Germany with a heavy barbed-wire border, and then somewhere there is the word Silesia, and then phrases I have heard, such as 'they are starving to death.'" In a diary entry dated October 1, 1940, Beauvoir writes that she lacks "the courage" to continue her diary, explaining her sense of disengagement with reference to the Husserlian method of *époché*, or bracketing of existential claims: "I did not continue this little notebook—I haven't the courage for it[. . . .] As if my entire life were between parentheses, it flows by like this, and it doesn't affirm itself as existent, it is suspended outside of time and the world. The result is that I feel nothing, think nothing, and nothing inside me goes anywhere." The November 1940 diary entries reflect the same sense of disengagement and discouragement. "November 19: Gloom—days of dark depression because after much hope I'm again aware that I won't see you for a long time. [. . .] The best time was in July–August when I tried *to think* the situation. Now I flee[. . . .] I should no longer flee but try to think. Now would be the time to write real memoirs or do philosophy again with Hegel, who brought me so much. But that requires such courage!"

A low point seems to come in December, when the first issue of *NRF* appears under German control. "Overall it's not good," she writes to Sartre on December 14, 1940 (Beauvoir 1990, 2:204). Beauvoir may have found particularly disheartening the reference to "History" in the "Letter to an American," by Alfred Fabre-Luce, who describes the grandeur of Paris as enhanced by the "surging forth of History" of the German Occupation (Fabre-Luce 1940, 68). Beauvoir's response is a philosophical turn from Hegel to Søren

Kierkegaard, whom she had first read in March 1940.[13] An opponent of Hegel, Kierkegaard celebrates the anguish and courage required of Abraham, as an individual tested by God. Ordered by God to sacrifice his son, Isaac, Abraham dares to assert an unmediated relation with the absolute and stand as an individual above the universal (society). "I've gotten a stack of books by Kierkegaard," she writes to Sartre on December 21, 1940 (Beauvoir 1990, 2:212). Increasing her distress, however, as Beauvoir points out in *Prime*, on December 28 there appeared the first announcement that a French civilian had been shot for "an act of aggression against the occupation force," an event also noted in *Blood* (Beauvoir 1960, 541–42; see also 1945, 279).

In a January 9, 1941, letter to Sartre, Beauvoir describes herself as "overwhelmed" by the latest *NRF* issue: "it's so stupid and low that it overwhelmed me. Yesterday I told you that the intellectual solitude didn't weigh on me too much. But when it takes on cosmic proportions, it overwhelms me[,] and Hegel who was helpful to me in August no longer consoles me." Referring, in Kierkegaardian language, to the Occupation as an "ordeal," Beauvoir describes her philosophical turn away from Hegel: "this year that has just passed has indeed delivered me from a bad rationalist optimism. I think that I have been interiorized and rendered more authentic than in the past" (Beauvoir 1990, 2:226). In the diary entry for the same date, Beauvoir outlines her philosophy of political engagement with reference to both Kierkegaard and the *NRF*, but beginning with a reference to Hegel's idea quoted above that the necessity of "mutual *recognition*" of free "consciousnesses" "can serve as a foundation for a social view of the world."

After criticizing fascism in Heideggerian terms, as a denial of the transcendence that defines human reality, Beauvoir presents in the same diary entry her new understanding of solidarity as grounded in the reality of humans as a species, discussed above. French collaboration, then, is a denial not only of the humanity of others, but also her own: "After reading a ridiculous and despicable issue of the *NRF*, I experienced this to the extent of feeling anguished. I am far from the Hegelian point of view that was so helpful to me in August," she writes, before explaining her new position in Kierkegaardian language: "I have become conscious again of my individuality and of the metaphysical being that is opposed to this historical infinity where Hegel optimistically dilutes all things. Anguish."

In the diary entry dated January 21, 1941, Beauvoir defines this confrontation between the universal and the individual as the theme of her next novel, *Blood of Others:* "Hegel or Heidegger? Why would my individual destiny be so precious if consciousness can transcend itself? [. . .] But how could the universal have meaning if the individual has none? That could be the subject of my next novel; it has preoccupied me constantly for a year." Beauvoir has moved definitively beyond her prewar ethical egoism, writing, "The idea of happiness that I used to entertain, how much it seems wanting! It dominated ten years of my life, but I believe that I have almost entirely left it behind." Although she is still revising *She Came to Stay,* she is no longer interested in the problem of solipsism: "My novel. I'm eager to finish it. It rests on a philosophical attitude that is already no longer mine." Her new philosophical project, which will attempt to reconcile insights of Hegel, Kierkegaard, and Heidegger, will, she explains, "be about *the individual situation,* its moral significance and its relation to the social." In *Prime,* Beauvoir disparages this problem of the confrontation between the individual and the universal as "nothing but banality," continuing her practice of belittling her philosophical work in her autobiographies. But an analysis of her philosophical work suggests that this confrontation, which she also describes as "an experience as original, as concrete as the revelation of the consciousness of the other," is a key to understanding her political engagement (Beauvoir 1960, 537–38).

In *Blood of Others* and *Pyrrhus and Cineas,* Beauvoir develops the philosophy of political action first laid out in the January 1941 diary entries. Interestingly, Beauvoir's two main protagonists in *Blood* discover a sense of political responsibility through an experience of shame. Jean Blomart is moved to become a Resistance leader by the shameful realization that he had contributed to the war by refusing to bring French trade union support for the prewar antifascist struggles in Spain and Austria. Hélène is moved to join him by the shameful realization that in collaborating with the Germans she had a shared responsibility for the suffering of French Jews. Thus the experience of shame that provides Françoise with an immediate, embodied experience of the existence of separate consciousnesses in *She Came to Stay* plays an expanded role in *Blood,* where it reveals one's situation and lays the ground for political engagement. But Beauvoir does not discuss shame in *Pyrrhus and Cineas* or *Ethics of Ambiguity.* Not until *America Day by Day* (1948) and her description of her shameful experience as a "white" person traveling through the segregated South does Beauvoir return to the role of shame in political consciousness.

Beauvoir provides two alternative grounds for social-political action in both *Blood of Others* and *Pyrrhus and Cineas.* Beauvoir first describes social-political action as grounded in a spontaneous élan toward others in the world: "my subjectivity is [. . .] movement toward the other," Beauvoir writes in *Pyrrhus.* "Only I can create the tie that unites me to the other" (2004, 93).

In both texts, Beauvoir tells the story of a child, weeping at the death of the concierge's son, who is told by his parents to dry his tears. "But that was a dangerous thing to teach," Beauvoir, writes in *Pyrrhus*. "Useless to cry over a little boy who is a stranger: so be it. But why cry over one's brother?" (92). Thus the spontaneous élan toward others can be suppressed by society. It can also be denied during times of hardship when man "looks for a way to flee from it," Beauvoir explains in *Pyrrhus*, describing her own initial reaction to the Occupation (ibid.).

The second ground for political action in *Blood* and *Pyrrhus* is the need for mutual recognition. Here Beauvoir draws on Hegel's philosophy as she did in the January 9, 1941, diary entry, although arguing in *Pyrrhus* that recognition is necessary not for the "self" but for one's project: "It is not a matter of making recognized in us the pure abstract form of the self, as Hegel believes. I intend to save my being in the world, such as it is realized in my actions, my work, my life" (Beauvoir 2004, 129). Also in *Pyrrhus* she writes, "'Self' exists only through the very project that throws it into the world. [. . . A]s soon as we are thrown into the world, we immediately wish to escape from the contingence and the gratuitousness of pure presence. We need others in order for our existence to become founded and necessary" (ibid.). In *Pyrrhus*, Beauvoir draws on her experience of the Occupation in criticizing Hegel's concept of History: "what is conserved of a man in the Hegelian dialectic is precisely his facticity. [. . .] As long as he falls into the world as a thing passed by and surpassed, man cannot find himself there. On the contrary, he is alienated there" (111). She rejects Hegel's optimistic view of human progress, as she does her earlier ideas of humanism and solidarity, for ignoring the fact that men are separated and isolated by their freedom. "Solidarities are created, but a man cannot enter into solidarity with all the others [. . .] since their choices are free" (108).

In *Pyrrhus*, Beauvoir also develops her critique of Heidegger, while continuing to draw extensively on his philosophy. She rejects Heidegger's claim that human reality is a being toward death, arguing instead for the primacy of the project: "Every moment [man] is seeking to make himself be, and that is the project [. . .] not projects toward death but projects toward singular ends" (2004, 115). "My goal is to achieve being" (136). Beauvoir also reinterprets Heidegger's concept of the "appeal," describing it not as an inner appeal of conscience, but as an appeal from the other "which wells up toward me" (121) and as our "appeal to the other's freedom" (133). But in *Pyrrhus*, Beauvoir criticizes an ethic of absolute devotion. We must recognize the limitations of our actions on others; we are only the facticity of their situation. "And that is exactly what makes for the touching character of maternal love," Beauvoir argues. "We must know that we never create anything for the other except points of departure, and yet we must want them for ourselves as ends" (123). "A lucid generosity is what should guide our actions" (124).

In *Prime,* Beauvoir reviews the dramatic philosophical transformation begun in January 1941:

> I already knew that I was linked to my contemporaries to the very marrow of my bones. Now I was discovering the inverse of this dependence, my responsibility. [. . .] My salvation was bound up with that of the country as a whole. But my remorse revealed to me that I had contributed to creating this situation that had been imposed on me. The individual is not reduced to the universe that envelops him; even in putting up with it he acts upon it, simply by his immobility. These truths took deep root in me. Unfortunately I saw no means of drawing any practical consequences from them. Blaming my old inertia, I found nothing to do, other than to live, survive, and wait for better days. (Beauvoir 1960, 538)[14]

Given Beauvoir's condemnation of collaboration during the war, it's ironic that critics in recent years have charged her with "a sort of intellectual collaboration," describing Beauvoir and Sartre as "opportunists who saw passive collaboration as the way to become rich and famous" (Bair 1990, 242, 280). The charge of passive collaboration, according to Bair, refers to Beauvoir's signing an oath required of all teachers that she was neither a Jew nor a Freemason, and to her continuing to write and publish under German censorship, often working in a Paris café frequented by German officers. Beauvoir defended her signing of the oath, telling Bair,

> "I signed it because I had to. My only income came from my teaching; my ration cards depended on it, my identity papers—everything. There simply was no other choice available to me. I hated it, but I did it for purely practical reasons. Who was I? A nobody, that's who. What good would it have done if some unknown teacher refused to sign a statement that had no meaning, no value, and certainly no influence or impact on anything? Refusing to sign such a statement would have had only one significance: that I no longer had a profession or an income. Who, in wartime, in my circumstances, would have been so foolish as to risk such a thing?" (Bair 1990, 242–43)

A more serious charge of active collaboration was leveled against her by Bair and taken up by Susan Rubin Suleiman (1992). It was alleged that after Beauvoir was fired from her teaching job in 1943 by the German-controlled Ministry of Education for "corrupting a minor"—an affair with a female student—she actively collaborated with the Nazis by producing a radio show for Radio-Paris and tried to suppress the evidence of her collaboration by having the archives closed to the public (Bair 1990, 640n). According to Ingrid Galster, however, this charge includes serious factual errors. Galster made a meticulous study of six of Beauvoir's radio scripts on "The Origins of the Music-Hall." She explains that the programs were produced for the French National Radio, popularly known as Radio-Vichy, and not for Radio-Paris, "the microphone of the occupation force aided by a French woman of the ultra-right who shared the Nazi ideology and considered the Vichy government to be a reactionary and clerical gerontocracy" (Galster 1996b, 113). While other critics disagree, including Gilbert Joseph, a veteran of the Resistance who describes Radio-Vichy as "a formidable propaganda organization" (quoted, ibid.), Beauvoir herself maintained a careful distinction between Radio-Vichy and Radio-Paris: "Writers on our side had tacitly adopted certain rules. One could not write in the newspapers and magazines of the occupied zone, nor speak on Radio-Paris; one could work in the press of the Free Zone and for Radio-Vichy: everything depended on the sense of the articles and broadcasts" (Beauvoir 1960, 588).

Galster agrees with Joseph that entertainment shows such as Beauvoir's were broadcast in an effort "to ensure the passivity of the French" (Galster 1996a, 108). Furthermore, while "by and large the National Radio retained its cultural character," Vichy propaganda increased in late 1943, and "Philippe Henriot—the Goebbels of France—spoke on the radio twice a day" from January to June 1944, "in an attempt to cut the Resistance off from the rest of the nation" (109). "Did Beauvoir's name, which was just beginning to become known in literary circles," Galster asks, "not lend credibility to the names of Henriot and other defenders of the National Revolution?" (ibid.). Galster arrives at an ambiguous conclusion. Beauvoir's choice of texts emphasizes "marginal individuals and rebels against the established order." She satirizes power and defies the "virtuism" of the Vichy ideology, defining thieves' robbery as "work," for example. According to Galster, Beauvoir's scripts thus "do not favor the goals of Vichy"—indeed, "the opposite is the case" (110). Galster concludes that "it would be difficult to group Beauvoir among the pure Resistants, or among the collaborationists, or even among the opportunists" (ibid.).

Galster thus supports those scholars who argue for an understanding of the complex, ambiguous nature of the reaction of the French under the Occupation: "Beauvoir shared the ambiguity of her situation with the great majority of her compatriots, a fact she herself was well aware of . . . writing in her memoirs: 'in Paris . . . the very fact of breathing implied a compromise'" (Galster 1996a, 110, quoting Beauvoir 1960, 549). Suleiman concludes that Beauvoir's wartime writings "contain no revelations nearly as troubling as those that have recently come to light about certain other intellectual heroes like Martin Heidegger or Paul de Man," and that we should be grateful to her for "authorizing the publication, even posthumously, of writings that she surely knew would cast her in a less than heroic light" (Suleiman 1992, 18–19). Beauvoir herself writes of continuing to live "cut off from the world" throughout the war (Beauvoir 1960, 604). Not until the end of the war would Beauvoir's new philosophy of political engagement find concrete expression, inspired perhaps, as I have suggested above, by the Nazis' murder of Beauvoir's young friend, Bourla, in 1944. "Because of his very death and all that it signified," Beauvoir writes in her autobiography, "the moments when I gave myself over to indignation, to despair took on an intensity that I had never known: truly infernal" (661–62). Having survived this young man, Beauvoir is left with a sense of betrayal. "What separation! What betrayal!" she writes. "With each beat of our hearts, we renounce his life and his death" (691–92). Thus the shameful sense of having failed the younger generation may have inspired Beauvoir's postwar activism, as it initiated her philosophical transformation in the autumn of 1939.

NOTES

1. For an account of the pattern of lying about sexual affairs, see Rowley 2005. See Frasier 1999, 102–23, for a discussion of the reaction of the British press to the publication of Beauvoir's *Letters to Sartre*. For a discussion of Beauvoir's sexual relationships with women in the context of American feminism, see my "Lesbian Connections" (Simons 1999a, 115–43). For a memoir by one of the young women whose sexual relationship with Beauvoir is recounted in the *Wartime Diary* and *Letters to Sartre,* see Lamblin 1993.

2. In this introduction I give page references to the original French edition of *La Force de l'âge* but I present my own translations from this work. In the run of text I refer to the title in English.

3. Beauvoir's reference to the "200 pages" of her novel that require polishing (1990, 1:393) appears in the English edition of the *Letters to Sartre* as "300 pages" (1992, 234).

4. In a February 17 letter to Beauvoir, Sartre writes, "[T]oday I worked on my notebook, I spoke about your 'unrealizable situation'—you know, what Elisabeth [a character in Beauvoir's novel] feels all around her" (Sartre 1993, 59). In a February 18 letter to Beauvoir, he writes, "I'm beginning to see glimmers of a theory of time. This evening I began to write it. It's thanks to you, do you realize that? Thanks to Françoise's obsession [referring again, as the translator notes, to *She Came to Stay*]" (61).

5. For a detailed analysis of Beauvoir's early philosophy in her student diary from 1926–27, see Simons 1999a, 185–243, and 2006a.

6. Bianca Lamblin, who was Beauvoir's student at lycée Molière in 1937–38, writes: "In class the course on consciousness was inspired in the first place by Descartes, then by Husserl (Lamblin 1993, 27). Jacqueline Gheerbrant, a student in the same class, recalls assignments on Bergson (Gheerbrant and Galster, 42; my translation). Beauvoir refers to her course on Consciousness in an October 20, 1939, wartime diary entry on a conversation with a former student assigned to a different class: "She told me that she found my courses fascinating, that the plunge from 'Consciousness' to the history of philosophy was too abrupt, and that I had made students unhappy at having to leave my classes" Geneviève Sevel, who was Beauvoir's student in 1942–43 at lycée Camille Sée, describes Beauvoir's courses as "united by the perspective of phenomenology," noting that "phenomenology was not yet at that date taught in the French universities. I was thus very grateful to her for having introduced me so early and with such an intellectual talent to the thought of Husserl and Heidegger" (Sevel 1999, 48; my translation).

7. Jacqueline Gheerbrant remembers the disastrous consequences for Beauvoir's students competing on the philosophy exam: "we had logic, history of philosophy and psychology—psychology was her forté—but never moral philosophy! Moral philosophy was dashed off during the last month of the school year, thus in June we covered it, if I may say so, at top speed. But we, the students she had chosen to compete in the national philosophy examination, were very annoyed, because the national competition was held in May, I believe, and the subject was a subject in moral philosophy!" (Gheerbrant and Galster 1999, 39; my translation). Bianca Lamblin agrees, noting that the class fell behind because of the "extensive development" that Beauvoir gave to the philosophy of science. "This caused her to pass very quickly over several ethical notions. She explained the philosophy of the Epicureans, that of the Stoics, and Kant's 'ethics'" (Lamblin 1993, 27).

8. Bair's biography also misrepresents the date when Beauvoir first read Heidegger. Bair writes that it was in April 1940, shortly after Sartre's second leave, that Beauvoir "decided to put her novel aside and go each day to the Bibliothèque Nationale to read Heidegger and Hegel." "'I wanted to understand their theories for my own satisfaction,'" Bair quotes Beauvoir as telling her, "'but most of all because I needed to become expert in order to help Sartre with his new philosophical system'" (Bair 1990, 233–34). But the letters and diaries indicate that Beauvoir began reading Heidegger ten months earlier, in July 1939, before her work on *She Came to Stay* had begun in earnest. In a letter dated July 7, 1939, Beauvoir writes to Sartre that she is reading Heidegger, and Sartre replies, congratulating her (Beauvoir 1990, 1:77; Sartre 1983, 1:235).

9. The reference to Marcel was helpfully brought to my attention by Judy Miles.

10. Solaltrism would be a position holding that the other, rather than the self, is the sole existent and source of knowledge and moral worth (Simons 1999a, 233). Emmanuel Levinas and Catherine Keller might be considered solaltrists (Keller 1986).

11. Bienenfeld was called Louise Védrine in Beauvoir's wartime diary and letters to Sartre.

12. Genevieve Idt's insightful remark, contrasting Beauvoir from Sartre on this point, came in the discussion following the presentation of my paper "L'indépendance de la pensée philosophique de Simone de Beauvoir lors d'un dialogue avec Jean-Paul Sartre" at the June 24, 2000, meeting of the Groupe d'Études Sartriennes in Paris.

13. In a letter to Sartre dated, March 20, 1940, Beauvoir writes of beginning to read Kierkegaard's *Fear and Trembling,* which Colette Audry lent her (Beauvoir 1990, 2:143). She refers to Kierkegaard's analysis of the Abraham story in a letter to Sartre, March 21, 1940,

where she commends Kierkegaard as someone "who has seen what an existential ethics is" (144, 146).

14. In the published English translation of the fifth sentence in this quotation, the meaning is reversed: "No individual can lose himself in the circumambient universe; though it supports him, it also influences his behavior—if only by its very immutability" (Beauvoir 1973, 566).

NOTEBOOK 1

September 1 – October 4, 1939

September 1*

I had breakfast at ten o'clock at Rey's.† For the first time in many days I was in a really good mood as I felt my entire life around me all settled and happy. The newspapers printed Hitler's demands without commentary or emphasis on the disquieting nature of the news. There was no talk of hope either. I didn't know what to think. I went toward the Dôme with nothing to do, in a quandary. There were few customers. I had barely ordered my coffee when a waiter announced: "They've declared war on Poland." One customer was reading *Paris-Midi*. Others rushed over to him and also to the newspaper stands, where *Paris-Midi* had not yet come in. I got up and ran back to the hotel‡ to wait for Sartre. People hadn't heard the news yet; they walked around just as cheerful as a moment ago before the news. No one at the hotel, I went upstairs, read *Marianne Magazine* to while away the time.[1]

---

* From this date through November 5, the entries in this diary are in part quoted in *The Prime of Life*.

† Brasserie Aux Trois Mousquetaires, avenue du Maine.

‡ Hotel Mistral, 24 rue Cels, where they had been staying since October 1937.

There were moments when it struck me: That's it, we are at war! I went out again, a few people were carrying *Paris-Midi;* others stopped them, asking to read the headlines. I returned to the hotel with the single idea of waiting and seeing Sartre again, immediately. He arrived at noon. We went to get his musette bags and shoes in the cellar. I noticed our skis in a corner; it broke my heart. José* was looking very drawn. Sartre asked me to meet him at half past two and I went by taxi to meet Sorokine.† We went to the Murat, where we ate pastries. The place was deserted and somber. Mobilization had not yet been ordered. Why? We would prefer to know once and for all. I made conversation with Sorokine without too much trouble; my mind was almost blank, from time to time I fell into a daze. We went out to check on the news. There wasn't any. I left Sorokine and went to the Viaduc Café, below the Passy metro station. Passy was completely deserted. All the homes were closed up and not a single soul in the street, but an unending line of cars passing on the quay, crammed with suitcases and sometimes with kids. I even saw some sidecars. Sartre arrived with his musette bag—mobilization had been ordered. The newspapers announced it would begin tomorrow. That left us a little time. We went to our hotel. But Sartre was afraid he would be late reporting to his assembly point. So we left without his bag and went by taxi to the place Hébert; it's toward the Porte de la Chapelle, a little square rather difficult to find. It was empty. In its center was a post with a notice "Assembly Point No. 4" and standing below the sign two policemen. We walked around them a while. Someone had just pasted notices on the wall; we went over to read: an official appeal to the people of Paris, marked with blue-white-red stripes across it, and more modest, the mobilization order in force beginning at zero hour, September 2. Sartre was playing "Mr. Plume‡ mobilized." He walked up to the policemen, showed his draft papers, and modestly requested to be sent to Nancy. "Come at midnight if you like," said the policeman, "but we can't send a train just for you." We agreed to report back at five o'clock in the morning. We left on foot and headed toward the boulevards of Montmartre. We bought a knife from an awful-looking bearded woman and I ate a little at the Dupont; I didn't feel emotional but had difficulty eating. We went by metro to the Café Rey, then continued on foot to the Café Flore. Sonia looked smashing with a red kerchief in her

---

* A hotel employee.

† Nathalie Sorokine (Lise Oblanoff in *The Prime of Life*), one of Simone de Beauvoir's students at the lycée Molière during the previous year. [She was the daughter of Russian émigrés and over time grew quite attached to Beauvoir.—Trans.]

‡ A character in a work by Michaux.

hair, and Agnes Capri[2] like a breath of spring with her shepherdess hat that flaunted a big white ribbon; a rather hard-faced woman had tears in her eyes. Optimism was giving way somewhat. "This time it looks more serious," observed a waiter. But people were still cheerful. We were tired. My mind was still blank, but I had a headache. We walked up rue de Rennes. The church tower of St. Germain-des-Prés was bathed in beautiful moonlight and could be mistaken for that of a country church. And underlying everything, and before me, an incomprehensible horror. It is impossible to foresee anything, imagine anything, or touch anything. In any case, it's better not to try. I felt frozen and strained inside, strained in order to preserve a void—and an impression of fragility. Just one false move and it could turn suddenly into intolerable suffering. On rue de Rennes, for a moment, I felt I was dissolving into little pieces.

Nighttime—I was afraid of the night even though I was so tired; I didn't sleep right away, but didn't think anything, a kind of obsessive horror— we set the alarm for three o'clock in the morning. Moonlight was flooding the room. Suddenly, a loud scream—I went to the window, a woman cried; people gathering, sound of feet running, an electric light in the night. I fell asleep.

September 2

We got up at three o'clock in the morning—suitcases, musette bags in disarray—we quickly dressed. Sartre was obstinately chewing on one of his fingernails. We walked to the Dôme. Silence, it was a very balmy night. Both the Dôme and the Rotonde were dimly lit. The Dôme was quite noisy, many uniforms. On the terrace, two officers flanked by two whores, one of them humming a tune to herself without thinking; the officers paid no attention to them—laughter and shouts inside. We had coffee. A taxi took us to the place Hébert through the mild and empty night. The square, bathed in moonlight, was empty except for the two policemen. It was like something out of a Kafka novel. We felt that Sartre was making a totally individual move, free and gratuitous, which nevertheless implied profound inevitability [*fatalité*,][3] coming from inside, from way beyond men. In fact, the policemen treated this little man with his musette bags, who wanted to leave, in a friendly yet indifferent way. "Go to the Gare de l'Est," they told him, almost as though they were addressing a maniac. We went toward the Gare de l'Est by walking along the tall iron bridges spanning the railroad tracks. It was dawn, the sky turned red. It was amazingly beautiful. The station was almost deserted; one train was scheduled to leave at 6:24, but it seemed that Sartre would be the only one on it. In the end he took the 7:50 train. We spent a while on a terrace on this early mild and almost cheerful morning—if only I could keep from thinking of Bost,* it would be tolerable, but I couldn't. Sartre repeated that he, Sartre, was not in danger, that it would be just a separation. We talked some more at the station, separated by a chain; then he was gone, first his back, then his neck disappearing. I left quickly and walked. It seemed to me that as long as I was walking I would be all right, but that I should never stop. Such a beautiful autumn morning, almost like the happy beginning of a new school year, the boulevard Réaumur, Les Halles, the smell of carrots and cabbages—I stopped at the Dupont St. Michel and started to write. When one is writing, one doesn't think either. The Luxembourg Gardens, Montparnasse; I stopped at the hotel again. A letter from Kos.,† while providing a welcome distraction, irritated me. I thought long about how to answer it. I got obstinate about this little incident; it preoccupied me. I started to write, then noticed Gérassi;‡ I was happy to be able to talk to someone. I was half-asleep. We had lunch together at the Coupole. Sorokine had left Paris. She sent only a brief letter by pneumatic dispatch. I ate, went to the Dôme and wrote letters, then took the metro to go to a movie house on boulevard Rochechouart where I saw *Trafic d'armes* [Arms Traffic]; not particularly good and too short. It was five o'clock when I got out, glad to have an appointment at half past seven; it sets a boundary. I feel the need to keep some directions in time and space. *L'Intransigeant*[4] talked about vague diplomatic maneuvers: Poland is resisting, the Reich is intimidated. For a second I felt hope, without joy, harder to bear than stupor. When I got out of the movie, the air over Paris felt heavy. On the streets people talked little. I stopped by to see Toulouse§—in a café, on one of the boulevards, I wrote to her, then made this diary entry. Tomorrow I need to wake up and think things out, but for today I am saved by my deep stupor—sleep.

---

* As Bost was on active duty, he would be at the front line. [Jacques-Laurent Bost, a former student of Sartre's, became Beauvoir's lover and part of her life. He came from a prominent Protestant family. In the *Wartime Diary* his father is referred to as "the pastor."—Trans.]

† Her friend Olga Kosakievitch. [Olga was first a student of Beauvoir's at the lycée in Rouen and later part of an intimate relationship, referred to in the diary as a trio, with Beauvoir and Sartre. At the time of the *Wartime Diary* Olga was studying to be an actress. Later she acted in plays by both Beauvoir and Sartre. She eventually married Jacques-Laurent Bost.—Trans.]

‡ Painter and husband of Stépha whom she knew when Stépha was governess in Zaza's family. The author told about this in her *Memoirs of a Dutiful Daughter*. [The Ukrainian-born Stépha was a friend of both Beauvoir and Sartre.—Trans.]

§ Nickname of Simone Jollivet, companion of Charles Dullin. An old friend of Sartre. Later she became a friend of Castor. She lived at the time at No. 11, rue de Navarin. [Jollivet once had a passionate love affair with Sartre.—Trans.]

On boulevard Montparnasse, the bookstore Tschann had put a small handwritten sign in the window: "French Family—one son served in 1914, etc.—will be mobilized on the ninth day."

Gérassi thought it was useless to fight as a soldier; he would agree to five months' instruction if they would make him a commandant. I made him angry by telling him that he certainly wouldn't be a commandant.

I walked back to Montparnasse. On the avenue de l'Opéra people were lined up waiting for gas masks. I went up to Gérassi's and dozed off, completely exhausted. Like a maniac I thought of my disagreement with Kos. because that was the only point that I could hold on to and act on in the present. When Gérassi got home, he said with much pathos, "Let's see if you are a woman with heart . . . Ehrenbourg* is finished"; Ehrenbourg no longer eats, sleeps, and all because of the Soviet treachery†; he may even commit suicide—I wasn't really concerned by it. We went to dinner at the Breton crêperie on rue Montparnasse. We chose a little table at the window; it was pitch dark outside. Large posters with SHELTER written on them were posted on the wall across the street, whores walking the streets, and one or two blue-tinted lights could be seen—the air was sultry. The crêperie was short of supplies. It had run out of bread, flour, etc. I ate little. Tonight the cafés closed at eleven o'clock; no more nightclubs. We went for a quick walk. The idea of staying in my room was intolerable. I'll sleep at Gérassi's. I checked my mail. There was a letter from little Bost, who was bored to death—I think he is going to get killed, and it's so absurd and unjust, I broke down. I went back to the Gérassis'. We put a sheet on the couch downstairs. It took me a long time to fall asleep, but I finally did.

Sunday, September 3

I woke up at half past eight; it was raining. This time I was wide awake, I could not count on the dazed sleep that yesterday sustained me all day long; my first thought was: "It's true then"; immediately I felt the need for activity, I could not bear being idle even for a minute. Getting ready took a long time. I think that I'm not exactly sad or unhappy, I don't feel that the sorrow is *within* me; it's the outside world that's horrible. We turned on the radio. No response yet to the last communications from France and England; they are still fighting in Poland, there is no hope left. I went up to my place—no

---

* The Soviet writer, veteran of the Spanish war, like Gérassi.
† The German-Soviet Pact.

mail yet. Mail delivery is very irregular. I had my coffee at Rey's. It's unthinkable: after today there will be another day just like it and another and another, and even worse ones, because there will be fighting. Everything is frozen in me: remembrances, future, and even perception. Every time the body stops moving, looking or thinking, tears well up. What stops me from crying is the thought that afterward, I would have exactly as many tears to shed, while at other times one would like to deplete one's tears so that afterward one feels that something good has been done and a decision reached. I thought of Sartre and Bost, but in words and fixed images without expression. I didn't reread Bost's letter—I couldn't make up my mind whether to do some tidying up, or to go to the hairdresser where I would have to remain immobile for two hours. I thought I would be able to work, but not in my room, in a café. In any case, the problem is not the same as yesterday. Yesterday was just a matter of getting through the day, no matter how. Today and in the future it's a matter of trying to live appropriately. I am anxious to pick up my novel at Védrine's and I'll try to do so.

I read in Gide's *Journal*—time passed slowly. Eleven o'clock: last attempt made in Berlin, the response will be known today. No hope—impossible to concretely realize any hope. I couldn't even imagine being happy if I were told "There won't be any war," and perhaps I wouldn't be.

At noon I stopped by my room; a telegram from Védrine* and a telephone call from Gégé.† I called her back right away. I was extremely happy to hear her voice; it doesn't matter whom you see, what counts is the impression of having a well-organized society of people around you with whom you can meet, talk, and tell your troubles to. I walked over to Gégé's place. Distances have become so much shorter; half a mile walking means ten minutes being busy. Paris seems gathered in on itself and individualized. The city police have superb new helmets and carry their gas masks in little orange-brown pouches slung across their shoulders—some civilians also carry them. Many metro stations are chained off and huge placards indicate the nearest station that's open. The cars with their blue-tinted headlights seem to be decked out in enormous precious stones.

I went to see Gégé. She looked so cute in her pretty white blouse; Pardo‡ was there and another fellow who had striking blue eyes; we chatted a while,

---

* Louise Védrine, a former student, who became a friend of both the author and Sartre. [Louise Védrine was a fictitious name for Bianca Bienenfeld, with whom the author had an intimate relationship.—Trans.]

† A friend of Castor's sister who became her friend and Sartre's.

‡ A friend of Gégé's and her future second husband. Sartre would become the godfather of their son Frédéric, born in 1944.

about Poupette,* about vacation—relaxation. We went to the Dôme, where Gérassi was eating chicken with rice. All four of us had lunch together. Pardo was betting against Gégé and me that there would be no war; my neighbor, an Englishman, said the same thing. In the meantime, the rumor was spreading that England had already declared war. Our discussion took place in a state of vague hopefulness or at least uncertainty. Gégé is leaving Paris to go to the Limousin region on Tuesday. She has only 2,000 francs to support her family. She told of her vacation in Porquerolles,[5] her visit to La Grillère, and the difficult return from Limoges to Paris. It had been an unending series of trains and cars loaded down with mattresses. Near Paris there had been few cars and only men traveling alone who had been called up. The blue-eyed fellow arrived and Ella Pardo;† he vaguely tried to defend the USSR. The Dôme put up heavy blue drapes for the blackout. Suddenly, at half past three, *Paris-Soir* announced, "England has declared war at eleven o'clock. France will follow suit at five o'clock in the afternoon." A tremendous shock despite everything—again, like a flash, the idea "Bost is going to get killed." I returned to my place in tears and like a maniac busied myself tidying up my room; Sartre's pipe, his clothes. I know for sure that I would not live if he were to die, which almost gives me a sense of peace, while in Bost's case the idea is unbearable and mixed with a sort of remorse to survive him.

I calmed down and went out. The streets had a serious air about them. On the place Montparnasse, a scuffle. A woman, I think, had called some fellow a foreigner, and he yelled at her. The people protested; the municipal guard intervened and grabbed the fellow by the hair—protests from the crowd— the guards got confused and told the people to move along. In general, the crowd seemed hostile to this hostility against "the foreigner." I went to the Café Flore and wrote to Bost.

Gégé arrived at six o'clock in the evening. She was upset and had tears in her eyes. Ella Pardo also joined us. She talked to me about her separation from her friend whom she had left suddenly in the middle of the street, unable to go to the station with him. Pardo joked and laughed; some people at the Café Flore were still saying that they didn't believe in the war; but they said it with somber faces. I made Gégé talk about the people at the Flore; impression of being connected to everyone. Amidst the moving and milling about I felt no personal life, only the community, which lives in itself as in primitive societies.[6] We went to the restaurant St. Pères, where we saw So-

---

* The author's sister. [Poupette was the nickname for Hélène de Beauvoir, two years younger than Simone; she later became a painter.—Trans.]

† Pardo's sister.

nia and a great many fellows from the Flore. We sat in a back room where I experienced a terrible moment while ordering pâté and Beaujolais; at that instant, my individual life returned; I thought I was going to scream. There we met a fellow from Hachette, Philippe Aberi (?), a Greek, very sure of himself. They were talking rubbish about politics. Pardo tried to support the USSR, saying that it was a Machiavellian plan intended to incite a revolution and bring about the victory of the party. We left. Aberi told about his work at the press service Hachette with the mobilized fellows, requisitioned trucks, and women who cry. All the bookstores in the different metro stations have been closed down. He got maudlin while looking at a couple: "These simple people, it must be so difficult for them to leave their women"; the imbecile! We went up a dark rue de Rennes with Gégé and sat down at the Dôme; the night was pitch dark. A policeman was arguing with the manager, who was adding still more thick blue drapes so that no light at all could penetrate to the outside. Beautiful sky over Paris and in the darkness the marvel of colored lights and the purple and blue headlights of the cars. Pardo came back, along with Pozner, a young and likable soldier. Bustle, fever, and disorientation at feeling so strongly linked to all these strangers. And constant horror of gasoline set aflame, poisonous gas, mustard gas, and Bost in all of this. We noticed Pierre Bost,* who knew nothing we didn't know already. In the morning we had noticed Téssaide at the Dôme, and the Hungarian.†

At eleven o'clock at night the cafés close. I went to spend the night at Gégé's. Pardo gave me a pill and I slept like a baby, dreaming tenderly of Merleau-Ponty.[7]

September 4

When I woke up at eight o'clock in the blue room, I felt rested; for a minute I had an emotional flashback of normal awakenings: feeling happy about the coming day and at ease. It almost seemed "a chore" to have to reorient myself in yesterday's world. I said good morning to Gégé, who was terribly worried about her family and annoyed at having to go to the Limousin. We had tea and jam with Pardo, and I got ready.

Days have a certain rhythm. There is a tremendous difference between morning and evening. Evening means fever, a breaking down; one thinks of getting drunk, of crying and doing just anything, and one gets lost in the

---

* Pierre Bost, the older brother of Jacques Bost, writer and journalist, chief editor of *Marianne*. [Pierre Bost was also an editorial reader at Gallimard.—Trans.]

† Former lover of Stépha. The author knew him from La [Bibliothèque] Nationale in 1929.

crowd. Morning is lucidity. I was much calmer than yesterday morning. I walked to the boulevard St. Michel to buy *L'Adolescent* [The Adolescent] for Bost. There were soldiers in the Luxembourg Gardens. Magnificent autumn morning, golden chestnut trees, the smell of falling leaves. I was thinking of small pleasures, such as reading *L'Adolescent* or Gide. I told myself Sartre is not going to die, perhaps Bost won't die either, and I felt indifferent to everything, to everyone. Not unhappy, yesterday either. The horrible world is on the outside, and this morning for an hour or two, I withdrew from the world. On the balconies of the Guilles* I noticed red flowers and a woman, probably the concierge. I bought *L'Adolescent* and I read at the Capoulade. War was nowhere.

I am not unhappy because I am not reflecting on my life. The objects "happiness" and "unhappiness" no longer exist, nor does this object called "life." At the same time, and that goes along with it, no "clinging" to will, regret or hope; I don't desire or expect anything, and am well beyond regrets. A kind of peace.

I stopped by the hotel. No letters. I felt a pang of anguish and cut off from the world. Even so, Sartre and I are not separated. I absolutely refuse to think "I will see him again"; I just simply continue to be in the same world as he, with him. I read with interest in Gide's *Journal* for a while and had lunch at the Dôme. Gérassi stopped by for a moment. *Paris-Midi* announced that military operations had begun on land and sea, nothing more. How neat they make it look!—The pale face of little Bost always haunts me like an obsession.

I sent him *L'Adolescent* and called Mme Mancy† from the post office. I had to show my I.D. papers. Mme Mancy asked me very kindly to visit with her. It was difficult finding a taxi; you need to be on the lookout and be there when people get out of one. I got one at the Montparnasse station. What a boring visit! The poor woman couldn't help telling me in her lively manner, "That'll be good for him. It'll teach him that he just can't live as he pleases." She gave me much detailed advice and showed me her sophisticated electric lamp. I stopped by at Védrine's to pick up our manuscripts. But the concierge wasn't in. Many strange-looking tramps were hanging out in the dead-end street of Passy. I went to the lycée;‡ the principal personally measured my face. She gave me a small gas mask and explained how to use it. I

---

* Pierre Guille, one of Sartre's friends at the École Normale Supérieure, who is called Pagniez in the *Memoirs*.

† Sartre's mother, remarried to M. Mancy. [A year after Sartre's birth, his father died. His mother remarried ten years later.—Trans.]

‡ Lycée Molière.

left with the cylinder slung across my shoulder. Seeing the lycée courtyard with its flowers I felt emotional for just a moment; it was the first time that *my* life and my past happiness flashed before my eyes. It was gone in the blink of an eye. I took a taxi again in Passy, which was completely deserted. When I arrived at Gégé's place, she and Pardo were having an argument. She was terribly upset about not having seen off Denonain,* who left this morning. She was going to see Nogues† at six o'clock, which infuriated Pardo, and it annoyed her very much having to leave for Corrèze. She went to her room sobbing. I consoled her, mechanically using affectionate entrapping‡ words, such as "my little girl, my sweet," I almost said "my love"; she was engaging with her attractive dress, her graceful waist and mussed hair, crying tears like a little girl, which were dissolving her mascara. "I'm afraid, I'm afraid for them." She is still fond of Bost and showed me a small photo of him where he looks like a young prisoner—I gave her a good shake. I was hard as a rod today, unfeeling like dead wood. I accompanied her on foot to the St. Lazare train station; beautiful flowerbeds at the Carrousel, people strolling on the boulevards. Gégé talked about Nogues and Pardo; she was stubborn, tense, and terribly nervous.

I returned by metro. A huge line at the St. Lazare station. The metro ran through several stations without stopping, how strange. I got off at Solferino and went to the Café Flore where I wrote to Poupette and Védrine. Pardo came and complained; he was feverish and had tears in his eyes. He was off his rocker. His friend Philippe Aberi (?) said hello; he told us the story of the volunteers who were ready and willing to die. Péricard, the fellow of "Up with the dead!" invented this appeal to all the lame and crippled, those who have nothing to lose by losing their life and who therefore should offer it as a sacrifice to their country. He read from an awe-inspiring letter from a guy: "I am thirty-two years old, have one arm, one eye. I believed my life had no more meaning, but you gave me back my existence by restoring all its glory to the word 'Serve'"; the guy ended his letter by requesting that the half-demented also be drafted. Mme Patisson, countess Montinori (?), often mentioned by Poupette, announced that she joined the Garibaldian volunteers. Conversations. The manager of Café Flore announced that the café

---

* Her first husband.

† Her boss and friend.

‡ An expression that "That Lady," Mme Morel (in *The Prime of Life*, Mme Lemaire), used. She was a good friend of Guille, and of Sartre and the Castor as well. [She often hosted them in Paris as well as at her country home.—Trans.] She used to call homosexuals of either sex "wolf traps." [Both Sartre and Simone de Beauvoir referred to her as "cette dame." The author dedicated her essay in existential ethics, *Pyrrhus and Cineas*, to her.]

would close tomorrow. It made me sad, it was a good little "*quérencia.*"* It's funny to see people in uniform, Breton as an officer at the Flore, and at the Dôme little Mané-Katz† as a soldier of the other war.

Then the Hungarian arrived. He sat down across from me to announce, a little pompous and stammering, that he was going to enlist. When I asked him why he only gestured vaguely. Next to me, an aviator, half-drunk and half-crazy, said to him in a noble tone, "Sir, allow me to offer you a drink." They drank brandy and discussed the foreign legion, the Hungarian saying that he wouldn't want to be with the riff-raff. They were discussing air raids. The aviator didn't think they would use gas but possibly liquid air bombs, and advised that people go to the shelters. Everyone talked about an air raid for tonight; never had Paris been so dark. Gégé and Pardo returned. They were terribly tense and depressed; we went up to the Dôme in their little car; the night was pitch black. We took a table on the terrace. I told them stories even though I had a terrific headache. At half past ten we returned to their place. I was going to sleep there again because of the announced air raid and I fell asleep like a baby.

Nighttime—Gégé came into my room; I thought she was going to pack her suitcases, but the sirens had gone off. How awful to be suddenly faced with the war again! I thought briefly about their lives over there, it's awful. We watched from the window, people walked or ran toward the shelters; a beautiful starry sky and moonlight. We went down to the concierge's booth. She had already put on her gas mask. Then we went back upstairs convinced it was a false alarm. Gégé and Pardo were very tense. Gégé couldn't find her robe; Pardo whined that they should quickly leave Paris. It was four o'clock in the morning. I went back to bed, sleeping soundly until seven o'clock when we heard the all clear. People came out of the shelters. There were two crazy women in flowered bathrobes with towels around their heads, probably intended as gas masks. A fellow riding a bicycle, gas mask slung over his shoulder, cried, "Ah, the bastards!"

September 5

As I awoke, I was still caught up in the events of the night. If only there were more going on and more danger, I thought, then I would be more concerned about myself and the thought of others would be more tolerable. The morn-

---

* A word borrowed from the vocabulary of bullfights and which means a place where one feels well protected, a haven of sorts.

† The painter.

ing hour was almost pleasant. We were having tea. "Contacts with the enemy at the front are increasing," we read in the newspapers. How proper and polite! They use the same word when speaking about diplomats. A young script girl from the Café Flore arrived; Gégé and Pardo were going to take her along; she looked haggard from sheer sadness and fright. They thought of nothing else but getting the hell out. She told about a terrible railroad accident in Aubrais, which happened the night before last: one hundred twenty dead. And many other accidents on the roads. The girl had a frightful hairdo; she claimed that women no longer wear makeup or groom themselves. That's true enough. While they were busy finishing their packing, I read a little in Gide's *Journal*. I watched them leave with no regrets. Right now I feel like living alone, working and using my head. Personally, I think it's fun to make do with such modest resources. I have always liked imagining situations where life had to be lived almost without material means, such as living in extreme poverty, with sickness, or living in a village or province. I consider myself rather well off and the smallest possessions seem immense riches, such as having a few books, Gégé's records, and the movies. However, I can see already that in two or three days and as the fever will go down, I'll get more and more disgusted with this game and I'll need something stronger.

They left, Gégé making fun of her kerchief tied around her head. I read in bed and went to pick up my mail—a letter from Sartre. It made me cry reading, "I feel absurd and so small." This little person of flesh and blood, thinking of him made me cry, but for the rest, I don't miss it, I have not lost him. The letter is old; it was written in the evening of September 2. I went to the Dôme and wrote these notes. J. Barré was at the Dôme saying to Kisling,* in uniform, "So, here you are again for the second time around, my poor friend!" Boubou† stopped by. He told me how last night the whores were walking the streets with gas masks slung across their shoulders. Tabouis in *L'Œuvre*[8] continues to be optimistic; there are still people who don't believe in the war. I listen to all that without the slightest emotion or joy. I tell myself "they'll come back" and try to imagine their return without jumping for joy. This indifference is precisely the absence of belief, I think.

I had lunch with Boubou at the Coupole—I ate Toulouse-Esau‡ without a memory jolt. I am beginning to be sufficiently tough to no longer fear ideas or memories. Boubou acted serious and self-important. He repeated, "It's tragic," as if the true tragedy of the situation would be disclosed in its authen-

---

* The painter.
† Gérassi's nickname.
‡ Sausage with lentils, one of Sartre's favorite dishes.

ticity to him alone. He was talking about organizing for himself a pleasant life by giving the impression of being heroic and repeating that it would be less difficult to be on the front line than behind the lines. He is so profoundly egotistical that when something touches his sensitivity, he is overwhelmed by it, not by the thing itself, but by the fact that he is touched by it—and he makes sure to let you know. He left early. I went to the post office to call Mme Mancy, then to the *Nouvelle Revue Française*[9] trying to get paid, but they were moving. I sat at the terrace of the Deux Magots; the Flore was closed. Capri was at the Deux Magots as were Sonia and her brunette friend. Capri mentioned she might go to New York. A little spasm when I sat down because of Bost's window,* Bost crossing the square (that was before our love), I could still see him. I felt like leaving, but stayed. I can't chase away all memories; I just must not feel them anymore. Indifference to everything—I'm still not unhappy. It still doesn't feel as though there is a real war going on; so we wait. Wait for what? That there is an end, that Bost will be wounded, or for the horror of the first great attack—but at the moment it's almost a farce, these people with their gas masks, looking so serious, their self-importance when they talk about the night alert, the closed cafés. It's only one side of the picture and once the fever has abated, everything will seem empty, naked and dull. Boredom hasn't set in yet but is looming on the horizon. It's the same as with an illness. During the first days of a fever, the sound of rain or a ray of light suffices to fill them; and then it becomes drawn out indefinitely. I am beginning to feel that I want to live and not just float. Write, think . . . but I would need a solid basis. This way I am uncertain, not knowing how things will turn out, neither on the outside nor within myself.

A decree concerning Germans living in France; they will be thrown into concentration camps. Uniprix stores display signs: French Company—French Capital.

Sonia, who before the war had said so gallantly that she would stay in Paris, now is scared to death—she is leaving—they are all planning to leave. It's funny to what extent people can be spineless and cowardly. Everywhere I heard anguished talk about the night alert. (They were German reconnaissance planes that had crossed the border into France, they said.) How can they pay so much attention to them? In the final analysis, it's of so little interest, here, nothing more than picturesque; it becomes nauseating in the end.

How slowly the days slide from morning to night toward disaster—slowly, so slowly. There's something worth describing: the place St. Germain-des-

---

* Rue de l'Abbaye, where he was living with his brother.

Prés looking so dead in the sunshine, somber-faced men dressed in overalls were moving sandbags; the peanut vendor was there; a man playing on a little flute. And silently, time passed.

I read Gide's *Journal* of 1914—many things similar to the situation now.

At times I have unbearable attacks of fear, one of the most horrible feelings to endure. The memories are disarmed by my hard-heartedness, but the idea that I could say or even write "little Bost is dead" makes me want to run away screaming. "Sartre is dead," I would not say to anyone, that I know.

The press releases say nothing. "Military operations are proceeding normally." Are there people already dead?

And all this is going to go on for days.

I couldn't stand it anymore and threw myself into a taxi to get my mail. A very nice letter from Kos. I would like to have her here with me because I feel terribly alone. I wrote her a note and one to Bost, but I heard someone at Rey's talk about an advance toward the Siegfried Line. I imagined an attack, dead bodies; I had a wild panic attack. I finished my letter in a great hurry and left to meet the Hungarian at the Dôme, but I was beside myself. We dined on the terrace of a small restaurant on boulevard Montparnasse. He explained that he enlisted because he could neither return to Hungary nor have an acceptable situation in France; the beginning of the evening was dreadful; he talked about some ideas in general, which didn't interest me for one second. I felt like running away screaming. Finally, when he told me he had seen me at the Dupont with a charming young man, I broke down in tears. It relaxed me. I drank some red wine and tried to make him talk, make myself talk without thinking anything while night fell around us. We went to the Vikings bar* to drink aquavit. The place looked like a tomb. I was completely drunk without having had much to drink. I said anything that came to my mind and he kissed my hands, saying how delightful I was and that he had never seen me like this—I was so thankful to him for helping to make the evening pass that I was holding on to him like a drowning person. If he had wanted to, I believe I would have slept with him even though I loathe him. That's the extent of how little I cared about anything and of how much I would have liked to drown myself in the present moment. He told me amusing things about his sexuality. He's a masochist—it fits him perfectly—he can only sleep with women who are physically stronger than he, in whose arms he feels like a little child; that must be difficult considering he is enormous. He found such a woman in a bordello who could lift

---

* On rue Bréa.

him up with one arm; he made her leave the bordello. In love with a rather fragile girl, he had to persuade himself that she dominated him intellectually and to make love to her he knew some tricks. He used to repeat the words "infinite," "a big sea," "to lose oneself in the sea," and then it would work. He took me to his place to translate some passages of his novel about Stépha. He talked gibberish and got on my nerves. I won't see him again. It was very dark and midnight when I returned. Everything was closed. I had never been alone in such darkness. I got home and went to sleep.

Nighttime—I was awakened by big explosions. I didn't understand right away; how sinister, a moment of confusion while I was looking for my clothes without being able to find them. Why didn't the sirens sound the alarm? I wrapped a blanket around me and looked down the staircase. I heard quiet voices: "They are machine guns." "But the sirens?" "They sounded one hour ago." I dressed quickly and went downstairs. People were calm—I heard no more shots and after ten minutes went upstairs and to bed in my clothes. Then when I heard the all clear, I undressed and slept until almost ten o'clock. I dreamed of a bus, which was driving straight toward Sartre to run him over, and I fainted with fright.

Wednesday, September 6

I got up and went to pick up my mail: nothing. I went to Rey's and read *L'Œuvre* and *L'Ordre*, then *Marianne*.[10] No more crosswords; all these games are forbidden for fear that they may contain coded information. I was reading Gide when suddenly the iron curtain of the bar was rolled down noisily and I saw people running. I returned to my hotel, sirens; some edginess: "Is it going to be like this all the time?" People remained on the street standing about in small groups, really calm. The owner kept on doing her dishes. I read in my room. Soon the all clear sounded. I continued my reading and then went to lunch on the terrace of the Dôme. There, I read *Le Canard enchaîné*,[11] rather funny; I read it for its foolish quotations. Boubou came by; I kept him company for lunch. According to *Paris-Midi*, there weren't any real battles yet on our front; what a relief!—I was calm. If I had done some stupid thing last night, I would bitterly regret it now; therefore, I should be on my guard in the evenings. In the mornings, despite everything, I find *myself* once again in *my* life and I believe once more that I shall see them again and my relationship with them will continue as in peacetime. Boubou said that this war looks to him like a "fake war," something one finds in joke and novelty shops, or like a *trompe l'œil* war, just like a real one, but nothing behind it. That may be the impression of the war at the moment; if only it could last! We went to play a game of chess at his place, insipid, we were playing too poorly. Then I went to the Dupont, wrote to Kos., sending her fifty francs so she could come, and I also wrote to Védrine. I read Gide. Fire trucks and ambulances with their strident sirens were constantly speeding by. All day long I hardly thought of anything at all.

At my hotel I had a brief letter from Sorokine—at the Dôme I wrote to Bost and continued reading until nine o'clock. An almost calm evening at the Gérassis'. We drank brandy and listened to the radio, some Mozart, some Bach. It was a great pleasure for me to listen to music again. I slept there, in the little room upstairs. No air raid.

Thursday, September 7

Gérassi reassured me somewhat by telling me that the young recruits were not the ones being sent to the front and there had been very little fighting until now. I fear from one day to the next; I'm not thinking of next month, but only telling myself that at this moment he is alive. I slept well and the day began as a normal day, a day without boredom despite the emptiness, as if one were alone in a foreign city with nothing to do. The new existence of the object and its riches justify each hour so that there is no room for boredom.

I am extremely fond of this Montparnasse intersection, its half-empty sidewalk cafés and the switchboard operator's face at the Dôme. I feel they are my family, so to speak, and find a certain human stability, which for me represents the stability of the world itself. It's the kind of familiarity that prevents an "anguished disclosure." I had not been sitting long at the terrace of the Dôme reading Gide and drinking coffee when someone called me. We had often seen this horrible-looking, toothless, scarred, and almost hunchbacked individual at the Dôme. "Seeing someone read André Gide could make me think that the great stupidity didn't exist," he said to me. Then he talked to me about Sartre and Wanda* and acted surprised because some time ago he saw all three of us with the older sister while now Sartre could be seen alone with the young one. He is stupid. He told me that Breton's wife made a scene yesterday on the terrace of the Deux Magots, shouting as loud as she could, "General Gamelin is a whore." The fellow's name is Adamov[12] and he is vaguely acquainted with the Surrealists. I killed one

---

* The younger sister of Olga Kosakievitch. [Sartre was having a passionate affair with Wanda at the time.—Trans.]

hour talking to him, then went home. A second letter from Sartre; he was still hanging around in Nancy. I had lunch in the little restaurant Pagès,* where for ten francs I ate very well, then had coffee with Boubou—I bought *Marie-Claire*, the word "war" was not mentioned once. Yet, the issue was perfectly fitting. A whore was fixing her face in the restroom of the Dôme. She explained mysteriously, "I don't put on mascara because of the gas." I went to the hairdresser. He gave me a beautiful hairdo and I felt sad not to have anyone I love for whom I could show off. I went to read at the Dôme. Gide turns definitely senile toward the end. He's not very profound, splits hairs, and on politics and economy he could not be any more boring, and what a life of courtesy. Adamov came back. He talked poetically about Ireland and showed me a horrendous manuscript: empty platitudes and grandiloquence. Is the world populated with nothing but masochists? He talked about high heels and muddy sandals lacerating his face. I would have liked something more precise—boring as hell, even in wartime.

I feel comfortable now in my life and went to get my clothes from the empty apartment.† I put away clothes and books and got settled. A letter from Sartre that gave me an address. He seemed out of harm's way—a moment of true happiness reading this letter. I went to eat crèpes on rue Montparnasse, then settled at the Dôme, near the little German fellow and the pseudo-Hitler, who patted my head in passing. I wrote Sartre an immense letter and went home to sleep.

Friday, September 8

The day started out rather well. The Hungarian called me at nine o'clock and I met him for breakfast at the Dôme. The weather had never been more radiant. He confessed that he was not Hungarian but Slovakian and Jewish. He told me stories about his mother, which held no interest for me, and also about his hallucinations caused by his drinking. Went with him by taxi to Védrine's to pick up the manuscripts. I felt emotional, but ever so slightly, when I saw the empty apartment and the notes neatly stacked in her drawer. I returned home, wrote to Sartre, and had lunch. Boubou met me at the restaurant on rue Vavin and had coffee with me. He saw Ehrenbourg yesterday and Malraux, about whom he had nothing interesting to report. Malraux was trying to help those foreigners who are forced to serve in the Foreign Legion. They have already

---

* Rue Delambre.
† Her parents' apartment, 71, rue de Rennes.

formed a Slovak regiment and 150,000 American Jews suggested forming a regiment, but it seems that the neutrality pact will be strictly enforced, so they can't come over. The newspapers announced "our improved positions" and talked about "fierce fighting between Rhine and Mosel"; Gérassi claimed that a few fortresses of the Siegfried Line had already been taken—it tugged at my heartstrings. I managed nevertheless to remain calm while writing letters to Sartre and Bost and to finish reading Gide. But after sending Sartre Gide's *Journal,* I stopped by the hotel, where the chambermaid told me about a young man who had just finished his military service, like Monsieur Bost, and who was at the front line. He was being bombed. Did he serve one or two years, I don't know, but I am horrified. The Hungarian came by to give me a huge glass clock, spherical, weighing at least two pounds, and books. He also entrusted me with some manuscripts. We had a drink together, but I had a lump in my throat; I needed to be alone. Anyway, he was half-drunk on Pernods. We said good-bye. I took the metro to the Gare du Nord, then walked along the boulevards of Montmartre, rue de Clichy, the large boulevards. In this state of intolerable fear only walking could keep me going. I had told myself that by taking this walk, I was trying not to flee anymore, but to think of Bost with his helmet, his greatcoat, his survival kit, his dear little face. I also wanted to recall some memories, but that was impossible, I couldn't face that. Right away my stomach was in knots, my lips so dry that once more I could only worry about myself, not to cry or scream, and I walked while running away again from the pictures in my mind. Terrible state, almost every evening like this, Bost is dead; in the mornings he is sometimes alive, but tonight was especially painful. A while ago, as I was eating dinner, I skipped a page in the book that described life in the trenches. I can't very well make myself imagine these scenes; that's needless torture.

One week of struggle, why? It was as if I was expecting a miracle, but in a week I haven't advanced by even one step; it has barely begun. That's what I should end up thinking that I cannot think. I don't know how to get a hold on the war, nothing critical, as de Roulet* used to say referring to his illness, but a constant threat. There are moments when I consider the state of fear, a crisis, that one has to make allowances for, that one should, however, try to minimize, and there are others when it seems to me the moment of truth, and the rest only a cowardly flight. Besides, no, it isn't even truth, it's having no hold on any object, but solely a flight pursued to the point of panic.

---

* A former student of Sartre suffering from bone tuberculosis. A friend and the future husband of the author's sister. [They were married in Portugal during the war.—Trans.]

I had no emotional reaction seeing the rubble of the Maison Rouge,* felt no emotion about anything; however, it would be different if it were a rift, a total break. A break, as Sartre used to say, means giving up a world while the world is still there and you have to wrench yourself away from it everywhere and the heartbreak is terrible. But in this case, the world is destroyed once and for all. Only a shapeless universe remains. Any melancholy, even heartbreak, is forbidden. There should be at least some hope.

I stopped by my hotel. On the place Edgard Quinet people were looking up to watch some big gray observation balloons float upward into the pink-gray sky like big gray sausages. No letter. I ate two crêpes and went to the Dôme, where I wrote this entry. They make you pay your fare right away now in the cafés, so you can leave in case of an alert.

Gérassi talked about painting. "If I did that," he said, "I could have respect for my vitality. Ehrenbourg already thought that everything I did had so much vitality." He infuriates me; he dawdles, that's all. He makes me want to work and be hard. However, tonight I hardly felt able to work. Depressing. Everything would be tolerable, solitude and absences, if it weren't for this terrible fear. Impossible to bear it for long. After an hour or two it gives way and only a dull headache remains.

And despite that, the same impression as Sartre had during his liver attack.† The real pain, the true horror, must be more intense than that.

Boubou came by and suggested a game of poker. I hesitated, but then I went. We had some drinks, we played, I managed to get somewhat interested in the game, but deep down I remained terribly morose. I got home at midnight and found a message: "I am here, I am in Room 20 at the end of the hallway. Kos."—mixed feelings of pleasure and some fear to find a part of my life. I knocked at No. 20, where a man's deep voice answered—then with my candle—I've had no electricity for the last two days—I was wandering in the hallway listening to the voices; the Russian across from me came out of his room and looked at me suspiciously. I finally knocked at the door of No. 17, where I found Kos. half-asleep. We went on chatting until three o'clock in the morning.

Saturday, September 9

A day almost as though there were no war. A long moment of respite that surprised me, just like seasickness that stops suddenly upon landing while

---

*A charming Montmartre restaurant where the author used to come often with Bost or Sartre.
† It was in fact a renal colic.

one thought that the rocking of the boat would never end. The mail brought me a letter from Sartre, who seemed to be very calm—and finally a letter from Bost, who for the time being was out of harm's way. It seems I have been freed from shackles; it's a physical relief, a whole day of living without fear. All at once I found myself if not with memories, at least with a future. We all will be together again, we will love each other and work, and life will still have meaning.

Kos. and I went to the Dôme. Next to us were two little lesbians; one was yelling at the waiter. She seemed very edgy. "I don't talk to waiters," she said. The mustached waiter, mild-mannered but threatening, yelled back, "But waiters have ears to hear with and can repeat what they hear, and the Vincennes prison isn't far." Kos. was telling me how the war had changed L'Aigle:* trains with refugees passing through and the boy scouts fiercely snatching the children from them to gorge them with condensed milk; society ladies going for walks in the city streets; military trains crammed with moaning horses and men passing through all night long; and the incessant traffic of freight trains in the station. Only the Negroes among the soldiers were singing. We went to stay at Gégé's apartment, ate lunch on rue Vavin, then came back here and I wrote to Sartre and Bost. We finished the afternoon at the Deux Magots; familiar faces, among them was Sylvia Bataille. The weather was very sultry. We walked back to the Dôme, where we stayed a moment in complete darkness; people were milling about; we dined at the dairy shop on rue Delambre and met Boubou, who was saying that things were going badly in Poland; Warsaw was said to have fallen.

We got back at ten o'clock, played some music, and went to bed. Amazing, this day, almost like a day in the past. A brief glimpse of what this year's life would be like: go to the lycée, see Kos., that's all, and for the first time the impression of lost happiness, because I feel I am in *my* life again and then I feel that this life has become so diminished. But that is a deceptive feeling; it will not only be a calm and boring year, fear will make its comeback. One of these days there will be real fighting. At the present my life continues to be terribly confined.

Sunday, September 10

Second day of respite. I think I am settled for a while in this kind of vacation. I got up at half past nine in the morning; we had tea while chatting

---

* Her parents' place of residence.

and the morning was spent very leisurely. I passed by my grandmother's*
around eleven o'clock. I found her with a woman of the civil defense service
who wanted to persuade the old lady to leave. "Our priority goes to evacuating children and old people first," she said. My grandmother put her hands
on her little round stomach and said in a rebellious and stubborn tone, "But
I'm not a child"; really senile. "Wonderful" letter about the war from my
mother, who claimed that in St. Germain-les-Belles a spy was arrested who
wanted to derail the Paris–Toulouse train. I stopped by my hotel and found
that I had missed the boxers,† who were passing through Paris. Letters from
Sorokine, who wipes kids' behinds in Salies-de-Béarn, sounded depressing.
A letter from Sartre and an old letter from Bost. Also a notice of a telegram,
surely from Védrine, but in order to obtain the telegram you have to have
the notice stamped at the police station, which requires a certificate of do-
micile and then you can go and collect the telegram at the post office. I
didn't go. I met Kos. and we lunched at Pagès; at the Café Deux Magots we
saw Sonia, who hadn't left; Agnès Capri was wearing a gorgeous blue-green
print dress. We chatted, then went to Montmartre and climbed up to the
place du Tertre—crowds, but it didn't really feel like a Sunday. We stopped
at Wepler's, then returned by metro to Montparnasse. We had dinner on
rue Vavin and sat at Boubou's table. He scared me half to death; some of it
was intentional. Then we strolled along boulevard St. Michel, which looked
superb in the darkness. In the restaurant, a man whispered to Kos., "Do
you dance?" People seem to take us for women of easy virtue, or at least for
women who are looking for men—there are very few carefree women in
Paris wearing makeup. It's amazing the way people look at us wherever we
go. The Seine is beautiful at night. It seems that airplanes can orient themselves by the Seine alone to find Paris. We had a drink at the Capoulade
and went home. Long explanation of the Wanda affair; Kos. harbors much
bitterness against her sister as a result. We finished the evening idyllically. I
went to bed and while I was reading some pages in Pearl Buck's *The Mother*,
an insipid book, I heard loud voices coming from the street "Lights! Lights!"
I tried to argue with them, but heard "Fire a few shots into their shutters . . .
If you want to spy, go elsewhere!" I decided to turn the light off.

At four in the morning, a brief alert. We went down to the shelter because
Kos. did not feel very safe—boards on the floor, chairs on which we sat
down—several residents came with little folding stools and the concierge

---

* Rue Denfert-Rochereau, 91.
† Bonafé, a former colleague of Sartre at the lycée François 1er of Le Havre, and his wife, Lili. He
had done a lot of boxing.

told us that the chairs we were occupying belonged to the gentlemen across the street. We went back upstairs under the pretext of getting seats and we stayed on my bed until the all clear. In the morning, a soldier in the restaurant told us in a loud and emotional voice that in the barracks two soldiers had hanged themselves so they wouldn't have to leave for the front; one of them didn't want to leave his four children behind.

Monday, September 11

At half past nine we had tea and talked a long time, until noon, Kos. telling me about a book by Lawrence, *The Death of Sigmund*. Feeling of leisure, time no longer means anything. I really feel like working now, but I have to wait. At noon I stopped by my hotel. I had a touching letter from Bost. He was not too bored and wondered whether he would be afraid when shot at. I went to collect Védrine's telegram; she wanted me to visit her and I'll go. I wrote to Bost from the Closerie des Lilas. It was raining heavily but I felt in a good mood. I can't believe that I'll have those moments of horror again as I did the other evening.

At two o'clock I met up with Kos. and we went to lunch at the dairy shop, then had coffee at the Dôme. The mustached waiter, who had been yelling at the little lesbian last Friday, was saying, "My first Kraut, he was so big that when they picked him up, they put him in a wheelbarrow, but he didn't fit, so they had to hold on to his feet. I was so impressed that when I was wounded, my blood didn't clot."[13]

We spent the afternoon very much like "women on the home front." We bought some blue powder, which Kos. diluted in water and oil and even mixed in Gégé's suntan lotion. She smeared it on the windowpanes[14] while I played *Petrouchka* on the record player and wrote a stack of letters: to Sorokine, Védrine, and Sartre, and while she was writing to Bost, I wrote to Bost also, officially. We stayed cooped up like that from three to nine o'clock, interrupting our work with a cup of tea, cookies, and conversation. We even talked about clothes and hairdos as if it were a regular start of the school year and life would begin again. I even felt a touch of ennui coming over me at the idea of being separated from Sartre and Bost, as though they had left for one year of military service.

At nine o'clock we went out. Our windows are now marvelously blue. We went to the Dôme through total darkness, stumbling against the curbs of the sidewalks. We were in a happy mood. We had dinner in the little empty dairy shop; then on to the Dôme, where we found Gérassi surrounded by a crowd of people, and we sat down. Among the people at the table were the following: a very handsome Greek, but of a spurious beauty, who seemed bored stiff; a Spaniard who had escaped from a concentration camp and seemed severely retarded; a very handsome tanned Spaniard; another Spaniard who underlined his talk by a lot of gesturing; little Flores, who said he was depressed because of all the sadness in the world; a charming young Spanish woman; and finally a woman whom I had often seen there, a vaguely surrealist poetess, reminding me a little of both Toulouse and the Moon Woman,* round as a barrel, but with beautiful skin, eyes, and teeth. She was raving mad, because a friend had introduced her to two guys whom he didn't even know and this friend then asked her about her husband (who is not her husband, as she explained). She had made some vague reply and one of the guys had said, "I don't like the way Madame's line of conversation is going." It seems that they were *agents provocateurs*. She told her story twenty times over and was scared to death. All these foreigners feel hounded. Many are getting the hell out of here. Gérassi was thinking of inviting these people up to his place for a drink and some singing, but he was afraid that it might create a scandal. Just the two of us went with him; we listened to an elegy by Fauré, *The Firebird*, and some beautiful variations by Beethoven on a theme by Mozart. Then we went home and to bed almost immediately.

Tuesday, September 12

Kos. woke up tired with the face of a sullen little girl. She had a toothache during the night. It was a gray morning. I went out to buy some milk and eggs. The Sita trucks† pass only at ten o'clock in the morning and a plaster statuette was lying in the middle of the street—everything looked rather depressing. We had tea in a pleasant mood; always the same news, local advances on our front, Warsaw is resisting. I went to pick up my mail. Some short and depressing letters from Védrine, who wanted me to come, a lousy letter from Bost. He was leaving with ten days' supplies; he didn't know where. A lousy letter from Sartre. He hadn't been assigned to aviation but to artillery; and besides, he was getting upset for not having received any mail from me. How cut off we are, how far from each other. But most of all, I am afraid; once more I plunged into the war, yesterday's serenity seems folly; they are going to kill Bost, and Sartre will be in harm's way. I walked

---

* [Called "Moon Woman" because of her dreaminess.—Trans.] Sartre had an affair with her while a student in Berlin in 1934. (Marie Girard in *The Prime of Life*.)
† Municipal service trucks.

down the boulevard Arago unable to give these words a real meaning or to hold back my tears. I was overcome by a kind of resignation expecting the worst, thinking that when the worst happens I'd see whether I'd kill myself or lose my mind. The concierge at Poupette's wasn't in and I had a coffee at the Italian's place while writing this; writing calms me a little, but everything is poisoned, horrible.

Had lunch at the dairy shop with Kos.; afterward we took a walk on the Champs-Élysées, gloomy. Saw a bad detective movie. We went to my parents' place and rummaged through everything, but none of those souvenirs moved me except the smell of Victor Hugo's *Orientales*. We had dinner on rue Vavin and came back exhausted. Kos. went to bed—the lamp looked funereal with its blue veil—I wrote several letters.

Wait—what am I waiting for—so we wait for months and months. I'm tired of constantly running away, but as soon as I try to sort out my sadness, it immediately brims over and becomes unbearable. I need to think of Bost as of a dead person—my God! To put so many things into a presence and an eternal absence will never be anything that is full and can be grasped, but will always be an indefinite nothingness; how easy it is to throw something into nothingness![15] Impossible to grasp for him as it is for me. Thinking is frustrating. There is nothing one can realize, even if one has decided to gorge oneself with sadness.

Gérassi assured me that Sartre would not be in danger, but what does he know?

Those young Englishmen who were at the Dôme last night, how romantic they seemed—youth, adventure, evening in Paris after having been in the trenches. They made me think of a page out of John Dos Passos.

In bed at night, I looked at photos of Sartre and reread his letters for the first time.

Wednesday, September 13

Though gloomy, the day was much calmer—one gets used to anything, even to this uncertainty. Tea in the morning; we listened to the Fifth and Seventh Symphonies. I went to get my mail: a letter from Sartre, whose work was going well and who was "interested" in the war. He still hadn't received anything from me. A short note from Toulouse inviting me to Férolles*— I'd like to go. Nothing from Bost. I went to wait for Kos. at the Dôme and

---

* Dullin's country home near Paris.

waited for her a long time while reading *The Portrait of a Lady* by Henry James. Saw Boubou briefly; Stépha would be coming home,* he said, and assured me again that Sartre was not in danger. We ate lunch at the dairy shop, then had a drink at the Deux Magots; saw Sonia and Fernandez there. We went to the dentist at the Trinity, then on foot to the Gare du Nord, came back by metro to Montparnasse, where we tried to get records and books at Zuorro's† place, but in vain, the concierge refused. We went back to our place where Kos. cooked macaroni. We put on *Petrouchka,* ate dinner, and worked on some cultural projects for Kos. until eleven o'clock. A pleasant evening; she was very nice. I read a little in bed and fell asleep.

Thursday, September 14

I just love this moment after the morning tea when I go to get my mail, alone, do some errands, and write a little, all alone. We talked about Bost at breakfast. Kos. told me that if he died, it would be a great tragedy for her, but considering their relationship, it would not affect her deep down. That confirmed my resolution never to give up Bost because of her. She also surprised me by not having had her mail forwarded and being able to remain a whole week without news. She is often sensitive and touching, but there's also something profoundly frivolous about her.

The news of the war remains unchanged. The Poles are resisting; they took back Lodz and the rain is holding up the German advance. There are severe restrictions inside Germany and, it is said, discontent. Little movement on the French front; reserve troops are being massed there in view of coming events. All in all, the war hasn't really started for us. When there is real fighting and Bost will actually be under fire, when Paris is being bombed, everything will look different. One cannot really *believe* that this will happen, which explains the strangely neutral state in which we find ourselves these days.

Paris is reopening its movie houses, and even the bars and dance halls are open until eleven o'clock at night. Everything is returning to normal.

I went to the Mahieu and wrote to Bost and Védrine and started writing this entry. At the Bobino, where I wanted to rent records, everything was closed. I returned by rue d'Assas, walking through the Luxembourg Gardens, which were deadly quiet. The ornamental lake had been emptied and

---

* She had stayed in Nice.

† A friend of Sartre who had met him at the university residence in 1929. Professor of literature, gifted with a remarkable voice, he had hoped to make a career as an opera singer. He had taught in Rouen, then in Paris. Called Marco in Beauvoir's *Mémoires.*

the little remaining water was all stagnant; sandbags were piled around the Senate. Fragile barriers of chairs were separating the adjoining area of the small Luxembourg. There was a whole pile of cut-off branches, and soldiers were kind of digging up the ground. I wondered what the hell they were doing there.

Went up to see Kosakievitch, who had prepared marvelous milk rice for me. I went out to buy honey and some delicious raspberry jam. Then we went for a stroll down boulevard St. Michel. We entered a news cinema, where we saw a very pleasant *Mickey chasseur d'élans* [Mickey the Elk Hunter], and a stupid American short, *Jack le satyre* [Jack the Satyr]. Afterward we went to the Dupont, on the exact square where I used to go for breakfast with Bost, and we discussed Kos.'s short-story project.

We went to Pagès for dinner and then went home; she went to bed very early and I read *The Portrait of a Lady*.

Friday, September 15

Sartre finally received my first long letter; I was very happy about it. Always the same routine existence: tea and conversation. I stopped by my place, had a letter from Bost posted on Tuesday. He seemed rather disheartened; he traveled for two days, yet was asking for books. He must still be somewhat behind the front lines. I wrote him a note and one to Védrine at the Rallye café, met up with Kos. at the Dôme, and bought some tobacco. The waiters were teasing us: "I would like a little of all this tobacco," they said.[16] We really acted like pen pals of soldiers on the front lines. In the restrooms of the Dôme we made up huge parcels. We had lunch at the Milk Bar. For a while Kos. spoke childishly about politics, but not for long. We sent off our parcels. In front of the post office we met Levillain,* a cavalry officer, acting casual and smacking his beautiful boots with his riding crop while talking with us. A perfect officer, and Bost and Sartre must respect guys like that, that's funny. There was a long line at the post office and Mme French was in that line. She was having a shouting match with a gentleman. The least argument these days turns immediately into a national issue and the volunteer mediators consciously embody the sacred union. We walked to the Dupont on St. Michel. I wrote to Sartre and several other short letters, and Kos. wrote to Bost. Then we went to see *Snow-White*. It was insipid and rather dreadful. During the movie, I was again overcome by anguish and a kind of remorse,

---

* A former student in Rouen of the "Action française." [Action francaise was a right-wing movement active until World War II.—Trans.]

and a desperate compassion for Bost—I feel that he is alone, totally alone in the face of death and suffering, and it tears me apart. We went back up to our place a little glum; we made milk rice again and talked about macabre things—but in a pleasant manner—wondering whether we would kill a guy who was too incapacitated. Kos. went to bed at half past ten, but I couldn't sleep. I finished reading *The Portrait of a Lady* and started *Jane Eyre*, which is less boring than I remembered.

Saturday, September 16

I awoke at eight o'clock after sleeping badly and not enough. I was out of sorts—but somewhat cheered by the idea of changing my lifestyle, seeing other faces. This last week was as pleasant as possible, but I would like to be without Kos. again and do something. I remembered the little card I received yesterday from Védrine, who reproached me for not having gone to visit her yet. How unpleasant. Tea with Kos., she was so nice; conversation about people's complexes. I have been more open and sincere with her than ever before. She looked lovely all wrapped up in Pardo's large beige robe, with her pale face and curlers in her hair. We talked. I stopped by the hotel. A long letter from Sartre, which made me extremely happy. He was stationed in a quiet Alsatian village and was working. Contact with him has been completely restored; he talked to me about my letter and that I had really come alive for him, and I felt the same about what he was telling me. Nothing from Bost. I met up with Kos. for lunch. We rummaged through Gégé's letters and cleaned our little living space. It was pleasant; our relationship had been very harmonious all week. I wrote a few letters; then—our suitcases ready—we stayed a whole hour smoking and chatting. I promised to do everything for her so she can come back. We sent off a parcel to Sartre with books and paper. Then we had one more drink at the Versailles and said an emotional goodbye in front of the metro Montparnasse. A whole way of life just ended.

In the metro and even more so at the Gare de l'Est, where I had accompanied Sartre two weeks ago, I felt immersed again in the world and the war, once more alone, just a piece of tragic humanity. Before, during these last few days, in fact until that very minute, I still had my life around me. With Kos. leaving, this life has come to an end, and Sartre and Bost have gone away from me. Alone. From the door of the train I looked for a long time at the Marne appearing so poetic and gentle in the evening, and I was certain that I would never see Bost again.

It was heartbreaking in the café in Esbly, where I was waiting for the train to Crécy. I was sitting outside on the terrace and the people were inside near the lighted windows. They were talking about a woman who had received a telegram: "Husband killed in action," and they were outraged. Usually it's the mayor, they said, who goes to the home and says, "Listen, my poor woman, your husband has been seriously wounded," but the way it was done in this case was cold-hearted. They said that the mayor of I don't know what little village had fifteen telegrams like that, which he didn't dare deliver. They also said "15,000 Germans dead, and how many Frenchmen does that make then?" They were talking about telegrams, the mailman's rounds, and the women who constantly run to the post office. It's really horrible. Without thinking of my own case, this horror affects everything in this little village as well as all the people in it. They were drinking port wine and Pernod and discussing the wearing of mourning. "You're not allowed to wear mourning," said a man indignantly, "or else they put you in a concentration camp." The women agreed on the vanity of wearing mourning. Night was falling and cars were passing . . . A woman said, "and those we love, we can't send them anything." Trains passed; one of them was loaded with soldiers. They were nearly silent while passing through. Night had now completely fallen, and I was sitting on the terrace of another café. Soldiers and war were the only topic of conversation. The war was everywhere, here and again in the very depths of myself.

I was counting on arriving in Crécy in one hour. But the trains were not running on schedule. I arrived there only at seven fifteen after reading some of *Jane Eyre* in the train and dreaming for a long time at the coach door. Bost: How can I write to or think of someone I will probably never see again? A consciousness that bears witness to the world, but is withdrawn from the world, and that can conceive the idea of being able to completely annihilate itself without fear—I remained like this for a long while. I recalled so many other trips: the one to Amiens,* for example. For the first time I remembered clearly what happiness was, and sadness overcame me—simply sadness, as though I was still very much alive and disappointed. Then I withdrew into a kind of indifference.

At Esbly I was told that I had to wait an hour. One café made me leave; I wrote all this in the second and third cafés. I loved this stop, this night and the clatter of trains. It's not a stop. This is what is true: to be without a house, without a friend, without a purpose, or anything around me. Kos. or

---

* In July 1939. Bost was assigned there for his military service.

the home of Toulouse are brief getaways from this truth, mere soporifics. At present, what is true are these moments when I am detached from my life, when I am no longer exactly anyone, nothing but suffering at the ready in the morning following a tragic night.

I took another little black train with dull blue nightlights on the ceiling and which gave off no light at all. I stayed near the door. The train projected a patch of light onto the embankment. In the smaller stations, an employee called out the name of the station, swinging his lantern. I thought I had to go up to Dullin's place on foot, but at the exit I found Dullin, all wrapped up in shawls. He put his arms around me and had me climb into his old cariole, where a black dog was taking up entirely too much room. The cariole was not equipped with lights conforming to regulations and Dullin rode through Crécy looking conspiratorial. It wasn't cold, so we had the blanket folded back on our knees. It was pleasant hearing the horse trot in the night. It was too dark to see anything. At the entrance to the village some men asked for our papers. In his most tragic actor's tone of voice Dullin repeated, "It's dreadful, just dreadful." He is disgusted with the men who are staying safely behind, in particular with Giraudoux and his clique of censors and shirkers, and with Jouvet, whom Giraudoux made into a big movie tycoon and who, with his monocle, acts like a general. As he had started on several films, he declared, "We have to finish first the movies we started, then encourage film production . . . For the radio we need things that boost the morale, happy things and easy to understand, such as Claudel's *Le Soulier de satin* [The Satin Slipper] or Péguy's *Joan of Arc*. No foreign authors." He refuses to do anything for the theater. Baty conferred with Dullin* for a long time; they considered touring America and neutral countries, but Dullin doesn't like America and besides he thinks that it would be like running away. He would prefer to create a kind of touring theater company in France but is quite concerned because it seems difficult to make a go of it. As soon as I spoke with Dullin, I was caught up in this new kind of life and gladly let myself be immersed in it. When we entered Férolles, I saw a shadowy figure holding a small blue light. It was Toulouse. She escorted the cart; two soldiers, who were making fun of the old rattle trap, joined us. Soldiers were everywhere. Mme Jollivet's house served simultaneously as an infirmary; she didn't have a room of her own and even shared the bathroom with the sergeant. On the street corners were small signs marked "Section X, Section Y." They took the

---

* Dullin, Baty, Jouvet, and George Pitoëff had formed a theater cartel, which lasted from 1927 to 1940. They wanted to defend jointly their professional and moral interests.

horse to the stable and unharnessed it while taking great care not to let any light filter through. They are as careful here as in Paris. We then went into the dining room, where Mme Jollivet looked at us sternly, ready to blame Dullin for whatever; she kissed me nevertheless on both cheeks. She looks a little scary, with her red hair showing white roots, protruding eyes, a drooping mouth, bags under her eyes, and a harsh and cutting voice. We sat down at the table and Dullin and Mme Jollivet got into a bitter argument about a slice of sausage. Yet, she called him Lolo and kissed him before she retired. Afterward I remained alone with Toulouse, who told me how her mother had become addicted to ether and what a scandal it caused in the village. It became especially shocking when her father contracted lethargic encephalitis and was cared for by this drug addict who used to go sprawling on the floor, splitting her head open on the andirons. In the end her father had to be taken to a clinic at Lagny, where Toulouse had watched his agony for an entire week. She wasn't particularly moved by it, only touched by the external event itself.

She lent me the prologue and first act of her play on des Ursins, which I read in bed; it's rather clever, just a little dull. It could be successful. I fell asleep and did not wake up until eleven o'clock the next morning.

Sunday, September 17

Sadness when I woke up—a pleasant light filtered through my little window screened by green color and I felt dreadfully sad. But while in the past the worst part in my sadness was the astonishment it caused and my outraged rebelling against it, here I accepted it willingly like a familiar face.

Toulouse was telling me through the door that they were going grocery shopping. I got ready and went downstairs. I love this house. It's so inviting, profoundly inviting, and so cozy that at this moment I found it really touching. The corsair room even had acquired some additional embellishments. I noticed a beautiful antique trunk and a red bedspread embroidered with magnificent ships. I had coffee out in the garden, served by Mariette on a little wooden table. I finished reading Toulouse's play and wrote to Sartre. How charming this garden is! Flowers, sunshine. From the kitchen came the clatter of pots and pans and the sound of boiling water. Everything looked so happy. I felt quite mellow and wished desperately, almost to the point of tears, that Sartre were there in the next room with a newspaper and his pipe. Across from the garden were soldiers; soldiers everywhere, the village is transformed by them. Toulouse and Dullin returned; groceries were unpacked and we lunched on the covered patio, a succulent meal accompanied by a good wine and brandy. Dullin's relationship with his mother-in-law is always fascinating to watch. We were quite merry when Dullin's niece, a young, somewhat misshapen girl, arrived. She kissed her uncle, greeted everyone, and then announced that the Russians had crossed into Poland. In no way would this put an end to their neutrality in regard to other nations, they claimed, but it was an appalling piece of news. It appears that they are negotiating a treaty with Japan and with Turkey too. That could mean a war that may last three or five years, a *long* war. I had never even considered a long war. Dullin talked about the war again. The night before, he had already described in detail life in the trenches where he spent three years without being wounded; he had enlisted. He stressed in particular the physical hardships and the cold; he described the changing of the guard during the night. It seems that despite the horror and fear something human remained in their lives, a possibility of freedom and morals. He talked about it again this morning, and I was disgusted to hear that he also admires what Céline called "the heroic and indolent soul" of certain military leaders. He has the idea of the classic example of a commander, the very impressive type with a certain gallantry. The only stories that move me are those where the individual shows positive and lucid thinking and self-control instead of courage. He also described artfully the fate of the light infantryman, poisonous gas, flamethrowers, bombings, and soldiers mounting an attack with bayonets and grenades. I was thinking Bost, Bost, Bost, it's terrible to put his face on those stories; he is going to experience all that, perhaps he is already living through it or has finished living through it. I had tears in my eyes; they noticed it, but I didn't care. Nevertheless, I managed to calm myself.

Walk with Toulouse. We went across the fields, the sky was partly cloudy and very beautiful; the orchards were heavy with apples, peaceful villages with dark red roofs and bunches of beans drying against the walls of the houses. We discussed Toulouse's work and travels. We stopped at the side of a road, near a little railroad station, and drank lemonade at the café terrace of a hotel. Two soldiers were guarding the tracks, one with a heavy beard, a painter from Crécy; the other was holding a policeman's nightstick; cars passed, often with officers, a continuous line of cars; one could definitely taste the war. For a while we followed the road and then went back through the fields and villages. It was a powerful moment and I remembered what Sartre had told me in Avignon, and which is so true, that one can live through moments surrounded on all sides by dangers and still experience great sweetness. I'm not forgetting anything about the war, separation, death, and our future thwarted, and yet, nothing could kill the sweetness and light of the countryside. It is as if we were imbued with a meaning, which is sufficient in itself, which doesn't enter into any history, but is torn from its own history and entirely disinterested. It's this kind of disinterestedness that makes it look a little distressing. These are the best moments, better than pure horror or complete diversion. And I feel strong, able to endure just about anything.

We went home and listened to the news. Dullin was unhappy with his plans; his projects were not developing favorably. Muddled news. The importance of the Russian intervention is being obfuscated. Faced with so changed and uncertain a horizon, we remained despondent for a long moment.

Dinner. Dullin came to life and told amusing stories about Gide and Ghéon.[17] We chatted until ten o'clock. I went upstairs and wrote to Sartre, made the entry in this diary, and finished reading *Jane Eyre,* which is insipid. I fell asleep at about one o'clock in the morning.

Monday, September 18

The maid brought me my coffee at nine o'clock as I had asked her to. The weather was not very good. I got up feeling neither happy nor sad, assigning myself the task of writing letters. I got ready, wrote a long letter to Kos., and clarified and corrected entries in this diary. I went downstairs at about eleven o'clock and sat near the stove. Looking busy, Dullin was carefully writing pages and pages. I think he was working on his projects. I read the first part of Shakespeare's *Henry IV,* which I had started in English some time ago and never finished—it's rather poorly translated, but it enchants me. Toward noon Toulouse appeared in her negligee. We listened to a short piece by Couperin "C," . . .* quite nice. Then the news: calm night on the entire front. But Poland is caught in enemy crossfire; there is not much left of it, almost nothing. Toulouse reappeared, this time elegantly dressed, wearing a black blouse with blue polka dots and pretty black jewelry. We ate lunch and talked once more about the war. All morning long we had heard the loud voices of the soldiers coming from across the street, as though already the flesh and the voice were required to build an armor-clad universe. Each command, each whistle blow, and each soldier seemed sinister to me; I cannot imagine Bost caught in such a machine, and always with an under-

---

* Illegible.

current of something contingent, familiar, human or intimate, wounds and death. A beautiful precise war machine at the beginning of the war, and the presence of blood makes it all the more unnerving. After lunch I went up to the corsair room to chat with Toulouse. I read her some of Sartre's letters. Afterward we walked down toward Crécy; she had the dog on a leash and looked young and elegant today. In Crécy we had some fine bottled cider. Soldiers and requisitioned cars were everywhere. Then I took the little train. It was five o'clock.

It took two and a half hours to get to Paris, with another half an hour stopover in Esbly—long, empty trains passed going east and their leaving had a depressing effect; another train passed with troops and cannons. There is another world, far away from here, an unimaginable world. I read *The Hound of the Baskervilles*,[18] which I found rather amusing. The Gare de l'Est was in a total blackout as were the hallways of the metro except for their blue lightbulbs. I found a whole stack of mail at the hotel. I had three brief letters from Bost, who was quite embarrassed that we worry about him. He is so modest and touching that it brought tears to my eyes. There were two letters from Sartre, who still didn't receive my letters—which annoys me— and a long letter from Sorokine, whose life is depressing and impossible because of all those children that needed to be wiped clean. I also had some touching letters from Védrine in which she told me that she desired me very much, but I should come only when I really feel that I want to; I felt a great desire to see her. I quickly went to the Dôme to write Bost a long letter; it seemed like being out on a date with him. I wrote to Sartre also, until half past ten. C. Chonez* asked me news about Sartre while explaining to me that she would gladly give ten ordinary lives in order to save Sartre's life. At ten forty-five the restaurant suddenly began throwing people out. They tried to hold on; even though the interior of the Dôme is depressing, people don't like to be booted out. Nevertheless, it was time to go home. I was happy tonight because Bost was not in immediate danger and his letter was so kind. I like those dark streets and the small bars with their somber blue lights in the rue de la Gaîté, and the voices that can be heard: "No, the dromedary has one hump, it's the camel that has two." I went to bed—my room looks funereal in this light. I read my letters over again, finished *Grand Cap,* and read *Taras Bulba.*† It took me a long time to fall asleep.

---

* A writer and journalist who had interviewed Sartre.
† By Gogol.

Tuesday, September 19

I awoke at eight o'clock and without weariness, as though it were a normal day. I got busy putting my room in order because I was going to leave tonight. I packed my suitcases and then had breakfast on the terrace of the Dôme. I was waiting for Colette Audry.* The weather was nice and I was happy to visit Védrine, happy about this autumn day in Paris, to have found my solitude again, and about the letters I received last night. It was almost an uplifting feeling of joy, although an awkward kind of joy, because it couldn't have a future. But how I love to live, despite everything.

I read a little in *Taras Bulba* and at half past ten Audry arrived on a beautiful bicycle with shiny nickel fittings. The first thing she did when war was declared was to buy a bicycle for nine hundred francs, which left her broke— it's funny to observe people's reactions. She had left for Seine-et-Oise and got very bored. When she learned that the situation was calm, she returned. She is worried about discomfort and boredom and tries to lend a little consistency to her war. She gives the impression of being unable to get a handle on it. She is married to Minder,† about whom she can't talk to me at all; he has been declared unfit to serve in the military and complains about his colds, which annoys Audry. I think she would prefer more pathos. Her sister,‡ married to a general, is now very important. It seems that one can do many things when one has connections, for example, have Bénichou called back from the front to serve as interpreter, or secure a pass so a woman can visit her husband. But how does one get connections? She told me about Katia Landau, whose husband has been taken away and not heard from since, and who, as a German Jewess, is in deep trouble herself. For five minutes we saw Rabo, the brother of Rabinovitch. He claimed that the soldiers' morale is appalling and that they talk about nothing but poking one of their eyes out so they won't be sent to the front. While I was with Audry, I noticed Alfred,§ who told me in a low voice that Fernand had been arrested. I went up to see Stépha and found her in tears. Yesterday some individuals came for Fernand and he has not been seen again since. While she was telling me that, M. Billinger arrived and said with much pathos, "I spent the night with Fernand." As he was leaving the Rotonde yesterday, he was asked for his pa-

---

* Colette Audry, whom she had met in 1932 at the lycée Jeanne-d'Arc in Rouen, where Colette was a professor of literature. She remained her friend all her life.
† A specialist in German.
‡ Jacqueline, the moviemaker.
§ The brother of Gérassi (Fernand).

pers. He has a pass as an Austrian subject; twice already he spent time in the concentration camp at Colombes and was given a document that allowed him to leave the camp. The policeman, nevertheless, took him to the station, where the police chief furiously tore up his pass. He was then taken to police headquarters, where, to his surprise, he saw Fernand in the company of many other Spaniards. They were thrown a piece of bread for dinner and locked up for the night in a kind of coal storage room. All Spaniards had been arrested, even merchants who had been living in France for months. Billinger was released in the morning, but the unfortunate fellow must return to Colombes, and Stépha was preparing a lunch kit for him. As for Fernand, they kept him there. Stépha wants her neighbor, a delectable young whore and friend of a Socialist delegate, to intercede on his behalf. I said that in all likelihood Audry would also do something. Alfred stopped by while I was having lunch with Stépha at the Breton crêperie. She was afraid for her mother, who was in Lvov. She calmed down a little during lunch and told me how she spent a night in Nice with a guy she had met on the bus, how she was afraid afterward of catching syphilis and she had dropped him. I went up to her place for a while, then stopped by the hotel, wrote letters, and called Raoul Lévy* on the phone—he had left me a note—asking him to meet me at the Dôme. In a way he is charming, but boring. He applies the probability theory to everything, especially to his odds of being killed in the war, which seems very likely, without him being bothered too much by the idea; neither is Kanapa, while Ramblin is more affected by it. He told me about the German propaganda in France, how the troops stationed at the Siegfried Line planted huge billboards in the ground, which read, "We have nothing against the French. We will not shoot first." And how a German mother was addressing French mothers saying that everything was England's fault and that we should not let young Frenchmen be killed for England. He also told me about an article by Massis that argued that German philosophy is a philosophy of *becoming* and that's why the Germans surpass their promises and don't keep them. He mentioned furthermore an article, "The Kraut is not intelligent." He is funny; for weeks he has made up some sure ideas and spills them out avidly; he doesn't know how to listen, he says, "yes, yes," in a way that makes you want to stop. He maintains that five million men or one are the same thing since there is no one who could think the totality. But when talking like this he confuses consciousness and the "das-man."† I left, went

---

* Raoul Lévy, with Kanapa and Ramblin former students of Sartre at the lycée Pasteur. [Lévy was a historian.—Trans.]

† The "one" according to Heidegger.

back up to see Stépha, who didn't know anything new, stopped by rue de Rennes to get a coat and at Gégé's to finish up a pot of honey and return the key. Then, at the hotel I had letters from both Bost and Sartre that I read in haste in the funereal light of my lamp; a touching letter from Bost, I would have loved to read it more attentively, but I had to leave for the railroad station. The suitcase was heavy. A very long train stood out in the open on the terrace overlooking avenue du Maine. What struck me was not so much the number of travelers as the piles of suitcases stacked in the overhead nets. I found a seat and went to write Kos. a note from the bistro across the street; I dated it Wednesday from Paris—I am expected to arrive in Quimper on Friday morning—and reclaimed my seat in the compartment, where some well-meaning women were already worried about me.

Nighttime—at a quarter past nine the train moved off. The light was so dim that I couldn't reread my letters. I deciphered *Taras Bulba,* wrote a few lines, then dozed. I reflected on my life, with which I am deeply satisfied. I reflected on happiness and how I had always considered it mainly a privileged way of apprehending [*saisir*] the world, and how, if the world changed to the extent that it could no longer be apprehended in this way, happiness would no longer have any importance. I had some vague memories and reveries. With me in the compartment were seven women and one man. The man and two women had suitcases with them that were stuffed full with silverware. A nasty kid prattled about spy stories and watched disapprovingly for the faintest gleam of light. In this atmosphere of panic you would have thought the train was crawling with conspirators on its roof and under its belly, armed with bombs ready to blow up. The people were watching for "signs": "I saw a flash of light," said one shuddering; "I smelled an odor," said another, "I heard a noise." The noise in fact was the toilet-seat cover in the restroom being slammed down; they mistook it for explosions. The train made some frightfully sudden stops; old train engineers, called out of retirement, are now in charge. At one stop, a woman felt faint and made a show of her fear; she was trembling and people gorged her with cold tea. Everybody thought it was a derailment. It's true, in one of the compartments a suitcase fell on some fellow's head. It knocked him out cold; he was carried off on a stretcher. It was a long and drawn-out night, without boredom. We passed Nantes, where I read on a boutique "Au Vrai Castor."[19] Dawn came up slowly. I recognized the ugly Breton countryside and those gray and squat church steeples. Lorient. Quimperlé. All that is ugly, but I found it amusing to arrive in the country to a completely new lifestyle.

Wednesday, September 20

Védrine in her blue suit, looking slender, graceful, and shy, was waiting on the platform. At first she didn't recognize me; she had tears in her eyes. She invited me for coffee across from the station, telling me that her mother had made a terrible scene because of my coming here; she claimed having filched a letter, which she would send to the minister of education. But I didn't believe any of it and didn't get worked up about it. Védrine was terribly nervous. She is leading an impossible life with people who forbid any diversion and talk rubbish from morning to night. She herself is prone to be a bit overly dramatic. She also talked to me about the Germans' anti-British propaganda and the fact that many people here were influenced by it. She told me about their terror-stricken travels across France. This idea of hiding out in Quimper is incredibly stupid. People don't know what's good for them; and what is she going to do? She took me to my hotel, the Relais St. Corentin, which used to be very elegant, and where I have a room for twelve francs. True, it's a minuscule room, of the kind we had at the Petit Mouton;* I am the only client besides an officer. The old Breton woman owner closes the door at almost any hour and one enters through the back, a kind of coal storage room and a stinking backyard. It's extremely pleasant and I'm enchanted to be here.

I freshened up and went with Védrine to a pretty crêperie where we had crêpes, then while she was having lunch with her family I had a coffee out on the wharf and wrote to Sartre and Bost. Quimper is pleasant; I very well remember our† stay here in the rain.

At two o'clock Védrine came back. The weather was beautiful. We left for a long walk; first along a road, then through heath and moors; we walked down toward the Odet and had a beautiful view from above: charming farmhouses, gray under the white roses, but inside, idiots with empty stares, sick people and frightened children. The banks of the Odet are pretty; we went back up and again had an unobstructed and pleasant view. Walking along little paths we found a road. The entrance to Quimper is a little drawn out. We were tired; it was almost seven o'clock and we had to part quickly. The whole day was a day of peace, pleasure, and total oblivion. I even felt a strong desire to go and see the Pointe du Raz[20] and St. Guénole. I found my-

---

*An old hotel in Rouen where Castor and her friends lived in 1935.
† With Sartre, at Easter in 1932.

self alone and felt a little out of sorts while the sky turned pink behind the spires of the cathedral. I looked for an inexpensive restaurant for I was very poor; I landed in a disgusting bistro, filthy like anything, where I was served bread-soup while the radio told about a terrible German–Polish battle. I ate in a quarter of an hour and I went to write this at the Brasserie de l'Épée. It was eight o'clock when I entered. At half past eight they pulled heavy blue curtains, moved me close to the cash register, and turned off nearly all the lights. Something so lugubrious shouldn't be allowed. My table and the one of a man with two whores were the only tables occupied. But the depressing aspect was rather mixed in with my sleepiness and therefore remained confused. I was going to write to Sorokine and then go to sleep.

Thursday, September 21

I had a heavy sleep. I dreamt that I had a terrible scene with Védrine because of Sartre, whom she had wanted to see these last ten days and whom I had also wanted to see. The alarm clock rang at half past seven, but I went back to sleep until a quarter past eight; then I got dressed in a hurry, but there was no need to, Védrine did not arrive at the café before nine o'clock; her mother had made some terrible scenes. There was no way we could go out to Pointe du Raz today. We climbed Mount Frugy, a small hill overlooking Quimper. We sat in the sun for a while and toward half past eleven I accompanied her home. In the empty dining room of my hotel I wrote to Bost, then had lunch in a rather pleasant bistro and drank lots of cider. I ate cold veal, hot veal, too much veal, and had a coffee. I continued reading *Tête d'Or* [Golden Head],[21] which I find beautiful, especially the death of Cébès. But it's a fascist and I would almost call it a Nazi play. Védrine returned in her little red dress, country style, so lovely. We followed the Odet along the towpath and then took small paths. The river is already an estuary in these parts. It smells of silt and algae. Lovely autumn landscape. We returned through the interior and the suburbs of Quimper. At half past seven Védrine left and I wrote to Sartre in this café. It's a little less somber than the other one even though the iron curtain was rolled down. The lights stayed on; there were leather instead of plush seats and customers at two tables.

This was a lovely day; I hardly thought of the war. But I am beginning to miss Sartre terribly, and I would like something solid to eat.

Friday, September 22

Life continues, one day at a time. This morning I got up at half past seven. I washed myself thoroughly and met Védrine at the café at a quarter past eight. Beautiful sunshine. She had a pile of sandwiches, but tears had disfigured her poor little face. Her mother had been hysterical because of me and had practically thrown her out and forbidden her to see me again. We walked around a little sad, then sat down on a kind of deserted low rampart in the public garden, and talked gently. I tried to calm her down and gradually she did quiet down. At eleven o'clock we took a bus to Concarneau. The old walled part of the city is charming. It is surrounded by ramparts and juts out into the sea like a miniature St. Malo; the old gray houses with their slate roofs are really beautiful. We climbed onto the ramparts and I gorged myself on bread and *rillettes* while watching the boats that had blue fishing nets hung out to dry. For a while we were happy, as during this stop, the walk in town, our walk along the seashore and the stop under a blue veranda, in a deserted hotel where we drank some bottled cider. We walked for quite a long time; I told Védrine about my travels on foot. We went through moors and saw some charming places, such as the gentle inlet where cows where drinking. In the end we were afraid of missing the bus, but a friendly driver took us straight to it. We returned and went up to my room. Embraces. But I did not feel sensual at all; nor did I have reveries or desires. That's also a kind of blockage. I went to the Café de Bretagne; a visit from Védrine; her friends had worried her by asking her to return home quickly, but she didn't find anyone at home; then a second visit. Her mother had cried all day believing her daughter had disappeared, an idea that mollified her. We went for a walk in the moonlight; the cathedral looked beautiful under the stars. I returned to my room and read a little in *La Jeunesse de Théophile* [Théophile's Boyhood].*

Saturday, September 23

From half past eight to half past ten I read *Tête d'Or* in the café at the quay and the second part of Shakespeare's *Henry IV*, which is not as good as the first part. Védrine arrived, still looking a little haggard, irritated by the nuisance of the lost key and ID card. At the post office I had a card from "That Lady" inviting me to La Pouèze;[22] I was pleased about it. Zuorro was in Con-

---

* By Jouhandeau. [Born in 1888, Marcel Jouhandeau was an essayist and fiction writer.—Trans.]

stantine, Guille in Dijon; they were all right for the moment. We went to the train station, the police station, and a locksmith. On the market square Canadian soldiers on huge khaki motorcycles were driving by. Everyone was watching. A very young soldier among them resembled Bost. I lunched in a pleasant bistro–tobacco shop, drinking a liter of cider and reading *Mars, ou la guerre jugée* [Mars: or the Truth about War];* it's excellent, but while it seems tranquil on the surface, it's horrifying underneath. That upset me. The radio broadcast news on Poland. How strange, these Breton women under their white headdresses turning their heads toward the radio and letting the Polish disasters reverently glide down their stubborn faces. A speech addressed to the French farmers followed, which put me to flight.

At half past one I took the bus with Védrine and her sister to Beg Meil. The beach was deserted and magnificent with its white sand and cows. The sea was alive and tinged with many colors, and the horizon immense. The ice-cold water was like fire, but this fire felt voluptuous and I experienced a deep joy of feeling my body skim so lightly and almost naturally through the water. We returned—then took a walk in Locmaria, which has such a beautiful Romanesque church. Védrine was getting increasingly sad. At the post office I had two letters from Sartre, which made me happy but stirred me up. My letters were finally reaching him now. I took Védrine back to my room and tried to console her a little, but she remained depressed. She left me at the crêperie, and then I became morose. I wrote to Sartre and Bost, then made entries into my diary. I went back to my room to read a little and then sleep.

Sunday, September 24

I awoke at half past seven, then for an hour read in bed *Mars, ou la guerre jugée,* which is excellent down to the last page. I wrote to my sister and mother in the café and met Védrine. We went to Kenfennten, which has a charming squat church with a tall bell tower. The situation doesn't change: Germany and Russia have divided Poland between themselves; on our front there have been "contacts," but one still doesn't have the impression that a war is going on; and yet, some people have already been killed. We walked around the village and sat down in a meadow, then returned. I had lunch in a really good little restaurant. Sartre thinks of himself as a despicable character for being so tranquil. It scares me a bit too having such joy in living, simply enjoying life, eating, sleeping, breathing, and feeling indifferent

---

* By Alain. [Alain was a pseudonym of Emile-August Chartier (1868–1951), an influential philosopher and educator.—Trans.]

to everyone as I did during this lunch. Am I really so shallow or frivolous? These last few days were spent without clashes and almost without feelings. I met Védrine at two o'clock and we went for a walk through the moors along the Odet; those pines are beautiful, as are the sad-looking furze shrubs and the gray waters. We sat down a while and returned by the road and bus. Afterward I had some milk and crêpes at the crêperie. The place was packed with squawking people, well-to-do refugees who come by car and complain about the lack of entertainment.

I am glad for a change of scenery tomorrow. I want to change all the time and am glad to visit That Lady. The person I am going to see always seems more desirable than the one who is with me; and each time I am disappointed because it's really Sartre I am looking for in vain. I read *Rimbaud in Abbyssinia*. It was not very exciting. No letter today.

Monday, September 25

I got up at seven o'clock. I was happy to be alone and curious to know how the next three days of travel in Brittany would turn out. I wrote some urgent letters, ate a brioche, stopped by the post office where a very nice letter from Kos. was waiting for me, and took the bus. The weather was beautiful. I did my accounts in my head, because I'm almost out of money. I didn't dare bring my backpack but put my alarm clock and two books in my swimsuit. It was a ridiculous package constantly becoming undone. The bus took me to Morgat in two hours. The little port charmed me. I was already hungry, but ate nothing so as to save money, and walked along the coast through a pine forest and moors. In the scattered villages people looked at me as if I were a spy. The old women mumbled something in Breton when I passed; nobody spoke French. I went to the Cape Chèvre, but access to the last five hundred meters was prohibited on orders of military authorities; from there I reached Cape Dinan by a small path. I stopped at a bakery where I ate a piece of bread, some chocolate, and very bad cookies. I deeply love this countryside characterized by a white background made up of sky, air, water, and stone, and set off from this dull whiteness, dreary colors. The presence of the sea is everywhere, in the moors, among the windmills and the houses. It gives them their meaning. Because of it and because of its unsociable people and its jagged coastline, which lets you see inside the high plateau where the houses are, I thought of Santorini,* as a Western and Nor-

---

* The author visited Santorini in the summer of 1937.

dic Santorini; there is an analogy. The paths also reminded me of Santorini, especially the relationship of the sea to the land. I returned to Morgat on the five o'clock bus, which let me off at Locronan. The day had been exhilarating and radiant, radiant with sun, beauty, and wind. I had a headache, no doubt because I hadn't eaten anything, and I was getting emotional. All day long I had thought of Sartre, our travels in Brittany and other travels as well, and I started to miss him desperately. I recognized Locronan and our hotel, and I remembered our conversations to the last detail. I wanted to return to this hotel to stay, but they had turned it into a crêperie, which was closed. The hotel had moved across the street and now occupies a beautiful Renaissance building. They served me milk and eggs; the dining room is magnificent with its ceramic ware, its heavy beams and view of the bay, but it was empty and the owner had just finished tidying up. She is leaving tomorrow; it's no longer profitable to stay open. She also had a small crêperie in Megève on which she can no longer count. I took another bus, this time for Douarnenez, where I took a room at the Hotel de Bretagne, which was ghastly. I went for a walk at the port. I recognized it very well with its fishermen in their red trousers, the small boats and blue nets. The moon was shining as the sun was setting; the moon won out. It looked like a night scene, illuminated by a magic device. I walked along the coast and returned to the port. It was completely dark now; girls were laughing and boys singing while walking out on the jetty, cigarettes stuck between their lips. You would think a peacetime evening; I felt a violent desire to have Sartre by my side and I started to sob. It seemed to me that I had never been nice enough to him and told him often enough how I loved him. I returned to the hotel and wrote to him in the café of the hotel. There were some sinister-looking bearded fellows at a table. One with a twisted jaw uttered some inarticulate sounds. I went to bed; the lightbulb was so blue that I couldn't read. I fell asleep.

Tuesday, September 26

It was still dark at half past six—which surprised me—I was still thinking of July mornings. I got up and walked through Douarnenez, equipped with my package and two pâté sandwiches. It was cold. I took a small road, which ran along the coast within a 3-km distance from it and with beautiful vistas of the sea. From time to time I cut through the moors, and the cold of the dew-covered chestnut groves and the fallow land made me think of the Limousin. The villages had no cafés, only stands in grocery stores with counters but no tables; it's primitive, not like the nonhuman wilderness of the mountains, but a human primitiveness that gives you chills all the more. A great number of airplanes over the coast and warships on the sea made me think of the war, as did the sight of the population: only women, kids, and the sickly. The absence of men could be felt very keenly. I walked 24 km on the road and arrived at the Pointe Brézellec with its jagged cliffs and the blue and raging sea. I went swimming in a cove; I still can be so blissfully happy. I took up the path again and walked along the Bay of Trépassés, where I went for another swim, and then followed the path to the Pointe du Raz. It was as beautiful as everything I had heard about it, one of the most spectacular sights I had ever seen in the world. At the tip of the point I read *La Comédie de Charleroi* [The Comedy of Charleroi] by Drieu de la Rochelle,[23] all the while enjoying the sunshine; I managed somewhat to imagine that war.[24] However, I felt great joy; my life has been so full and I feel an immense joy at present whatever my future may hold.

I returned at sunset. Near the signal tower are four hotels: a large one, which was closed, and two small ones, also closed. The fourth one is barely alive; they removed some papers from a little room to let me stay there. They fed me dinner, which I devoured with physical joy while drinking a liter of cider. A sailor and his teacher wife were dining next to me and discussing practical things, such as warm pajamas, etc. To light the rooms we had petroleum lamps; it was pleasant and I read *Les Mémoires de Gramont* [Gramont's Memoirs], which I found somewhat entertaining. I went out for a walk in the moonlight; I had drunk a little too much and was amazed at the starry sky and the vastness of the sea. Why is human consciousness driven to constructions of distance, mass, etc., which are not on a human scale? That's like asking why the *hylè** is what it is, the "why" is absurd, but like everything, it could be quite different. I still felt the same joy, but also some excitement because of the drink. Two fellows in sailor uniforms approached me. They were most likely from the signal tower: "Are you from here?" "No." "You're taking a walk?" "Yes." "At this hour of the night? You can't see anything." "I can see the moonlight." "You could see the moonlight just as well in Quimper or Landerneau." Their voices rose gradually until they were downright insulting. I suggested I'd show my papers, which they examined with a flashlight, then they apologized half-heartedly. I returned to my room; it was almost at ground level and looked out over the moors and the sea and almost made me feel I was sleeping out in the open. I went to bed and continued reading *Les Mémoires de Gramont* by the light of my

---

* A phenomenological term used by Husserl. Here it is analogous to "consciousness" in general.

petroleum lamp and fell asleep. I will never forget this evening and the profound joy, which, I am sure, was not frivolous. Nevertheless, it's always embarrassing, for the misfortunes that I deny in my present joy are the misfortunes of others before they become mine.

Wednesday, September 27

I got up at six o'clock and got dressed, feeling my way in the dark. A candle was lit downstairs and I continued reading *Les Mémoires de Gramont;* I then got on the bus. It was cold, I had slept poorly and felt out of sorts; a little mournful. While we were heading toward Audierne, the sun rose over the moors. I went for a walk at the port of Audierne, which was rather pleasant, but that's all one can say about it. I had a cassis[25] at the food and tobacco-store-plus-drink-stand while waiting for the bus. Until Pont-l'Abbé we followed a flat coastline from a distance. I went on foot to St. Jean-Trolimon, which has a magnificent church, then to the calvaries of Tronoën, then through the dunes as far as St. Guénolé; the whole countryside was flat and desolate. The red rocks of St. Guénolé did not impress me. I drank a glass of beer and continued reading my book while waiting for the bus. The bus was crowded. It looks funny when those Breton women wear makeup under their sugar loaf–shaped headdresses. We drove through the flat, yellow and depressing country of Penmarch before arriving in Quimper.

I had a great letter from Bost; a short one from Sartre, dated from the eighteenth; a long letter from Kos., a very nice one; and a word from the boxers. I went to eat crêpes and drink milk, my only meal for the day, and wrote letters to Sartre and Bost from the crêperie, and a letter to Védrine from the train.

Nighttime—I had a corner seat on the train, which pulled out of the station at seven o'clock in the evening.* It was full, but the people were not too unpleasant. For an hour I could still read, then night fell and I could only listen to the people and look. The countryside was flat, but the moonlight made it look more attractive; "It looks like a movie set," said a woman ecstatically. People were discussing the Breton butter and from time to time I dozed off. I felt infinite patience; it was like a state of grace with which the war had endowed me. I thought vaguely how we were separated Sartre, Bost, and I, and how I had the better part and I was somewhat ashamed of it. If I had to choose, without anybody knowing about it, what would I choose? Would I be able to choose their lot and exchange it for mine? I am afraid not.

---

* She was on her way to La Pouèze, near Angers, the country home of That Lady.

We arrived at two o'clock in the morning. At the exit a serviceman addressed me, "Mlle de Beauvoir?" I was a little surprised and thought that That Lady had sent him, but he stammered something about Mlle de Stoecklin,* who had telephoned. He took my suitcase and my arm saying, "I'm old enough to be your father," and took me to a room he had reserved for me; he brought some beer, bananas, and sandwiches. I was delighted at this reception and very amused to find myself at three in the morning in an unknown town, in a hotel room with an unknown serviceman. It felt quite unreal and like a chapter out of a war novel. Incidentally, he had a shifty attitude. At first he asked to stay with a bizarre look on his face, then, as I was bothered by his stare, and remained standing, he said, "Sit down." I pulled up a chair: "Sit down on the bed." I took the chair and invited him to drink. "I would have to drink out of the same glass as you. It doesn't bother you? Are you sure?" We talked casually. He was a former Rome Prize winner for painting and used to live in Nizan's apartment on rue Vavin. It seems that he didn't know the Stoecklins very well and we got a little mixed up. Of course, we talked about the war. He finally left, saying that he would have my breakfast sent up. And I went to bed, amused and delighted at the idea of entering once more another kind of life.

Thursday, September 28

I awoke early and happy. My breakfast was brought up to me and I went downstairs to write a few letters in the café. I wrote to the boxers, Sorokine, and Kosakievitch. I continued writing in a big café at the place du Ralliement. I was a little worried as I had hardly a penny left in my pocket, but I was sure that That Lady would come. She arrived by car around noon with Mops;† they were both all decked out. I was awfully glad to see That Lady; the feeling seemed *real* to me. With the exception of Bost and Sartre, she is the only one with whom I have a close and true relationship. And I was happy to get away from sentimentality. Near That Lady I feel so close to Sartre; she is also the only one who has shared everything in our lives for ten years. They left me one hour to visit Angers, which I liked in the cold but beautiful sunshine. I visited the castle, the quays, and the little streets. They picked me up and drove me through an ugly countryside. I was happy to be taken into a structured way of life [*forme*]—that's what I have been looking

---

* A friend of the Morels.
† The nickname of Jacqueline.

for this entire past month—structures that grab me and within which one only has to let oneself go.

We arrived in La Pouèze around half past one. The village is ugly too, but the house is charming. Everything reflects the unaffected graciousness of That Lady, who is as attractive in her way as are the contrived charms of anything that has to do with Toulouse. The first thing I saw was the huge dog, then the dining room where a sumptuous meal was being prepared, then the bedrooms of That Lady and of Mops with their red tiles, so comfortable in their rustic simplicity. The many books in this house dazzled me: three armoires on the second floor were filled with them. The house is also filled with jams, fruits, and canned goods; that impressed me less but looked generous and rich. I first stocked up on books and went to the post office. Three letters from Sartre were waiting for me. They were dated from the twentieth, twenty-first, and twenty-second—the one from the nineteenth was missing, it is probably floating around somewhere in Quimper—and three letters from Bost, dated from the twenty-first, twenty-second, and twenty-third. Seated in the large easy chair of the dining room, I read Sartre's letters first. I couldn't get over it, because he was finally *responding*, we were communicating, and he was so close; we were remaining very united even in the slightest details through our letters. Bost's letters were so pleasant and nice; if only there could be a war without killings and nothing bad would happen to him. After reading these letters I had a day of profound happiness. They were so close to me, we loved each other, and we were not separated. And I felt so good here in this dining room, where a big fire was roaring in the wood-burning fireplace. That was also my room; there was a washstand in the closet. Mops gave me charming photos of Sartre and myself.* I wrote a huge letter to Sartre; we had tea with That Lady and chatted. Guille is a telephone operator at Headquarters; Zuorro is in Constantine. I read *Bessie Cutter*, which I found very amusing. We had dinner and afterward at bedtime, I was treated royally; That Lady and Mops busied themselves preparing a snack for me and supplying me with robes, pillows, and lamps. The fire in the fireplace was still roaring. I felt so at ease that I read *Bessie Cutter*, *La Marie du port* [Marie of the Port] by Simenon, and *Mademoiselle Bécut* by Véry† until one o'clock in the morning; they were all entertaining. I fell asleep with a mad desire to see Sartre opening this door and entering in his little white sweater, sitting down next to me and talking endlessly.

---

* Probably the photos taken in Juan-les-Pins in August.
† Pierre Véry (1900–1960), author of numerous detective novels.

Friday, September 29

Charming day. In a sense, war makes each instant of my life so precious. Never before have I felt things so fully and so intensely as I do at present. Everything here enchants me, especially this intoxication with reading, which I no longer can afford except during periods of illness. I got up at eight o'clock. I wrote to Bost and reread his letters while eating delicious apricot preserves with my breakfast. Afterward I went for a walk on the roads, but the biting cold and the ugliness of the countryside discouraged me. I returned to read; I read *Les Généraux meurent dans leur lit* [Generals Die in Their Beds];* it's horrible, unbearable at times, but the fact is that people still don't believe in it. In the meantime, Warsaw has capitulated, the treaty between Russia and Germany has been signed, and Germany announced that it would make a peace offer to the democracies. And we will refuse the offer and then it will start for good. I am telling myself these things, I read these books, and yet I still don't truly believe it. It's a nightmare; we are going to wake up.

Around noon I went up to the attic and fleeced an entire armoire of books; I took them down by the armfuls. How pleasant it is to have all that at one's disposal! That Lady took me to the cellar to choose a wine and I chose a Chambolle-Musigny, which we drank with the roast, and it was indeed delectable. I read *Campagne* out in the sun until four o'clock; then we left with a totally deaf Russian princess to pick up Aunt Suzanne in Angers. I abandoned them to walk in the botanical gardens. Hundreds of gypsy refugees with their trailers were camped on a large field near the Loire. I wrote Védrine from the café, and we drove back home. Reading in the dining room, then dinner; in bed I read *La Tradition de Minuit* [Midnight Tradition] by Mac Orlan.[26]

Saturday, September 30

Another charming solitary morning! I got up at eight o'clock and wrote to Sartre. That Gentleman† had sent for a collection of *Crapouillot* for me. It's about war and I started reading it while taking notes. Letters from Sartre dated from the nineteenth and twenty-third—one letter from Bost. I read until noon and went once more rummaging through the attic. This time I gathered a vast collection of books, many of which were about war. That

---

* The book is by Charles Harrison, an American author.
† Husband of That Lady. Since his return from the war, where he had served as a physician, he had not left his room and hardly received anyone.

Lady took me to the wine cellar where I chose a marvelous Meursault—what a shameful life in the lap of luxury. I telephoned my principal: I could stay until the sixth or seventh. The afternoon was spent on the couch with the light on, reading the *Crapouillot* series on war until I got a headache, then a small volume by Rathenau, one by Kautsky; the fire was roaring in the fireplace; in the next room, Mops was typing; it was raining. I hadn't had such leisure in a long time. A short drive in the car with That Lady, then some more reading, dinner, and reading of *Le Clavier universel* [The Universal Keyboard] by P. Véry.

Sunday, October 1

I awoke past eight o'clock feeling a little weak. I read in bed *Guerre* [War] by L. Renn, which is really bad. Breakfast. I finished P. Véry and plunged into Kautsky. I answered Sorokine's questions on Kant.

Stalin and Hitler are pursuing a peace offensive. Of course we won't accept, but we know nothing of what's going on, or of what's going to happen.

Lunch accompanied by some Pouilly that I brought up from the cellar—all day reading of *Crapouillot* on war and *Plutarque a menti* [Plutarch Lied]. I knew roughly about the incompetence of the General-Staff in 1914, but to read about it in detail, it's amazing. At night, in bed I read one of the *Aventures du Saint* [The Saint's Adventures];* it's really bad.

Monday, October 2

A letter from Sartre—two letters from Bost—I answered them. The importance of mail is extraordinary, that's what I was thinking with respect to the war; how the day turns out depends on it entirely. All morning long, reading on the war of 1914. After lunch I read outside *Les Aventures de Jack London* [The Adventures of Jack London].† I had a moment of profound bliss, stretched out and reading in the sun under the poplars. It reminded me of the Limousin. How beautiful everything is: the meadows, the white fence, the apple trees, the big plums; abundance of a happy autumn.

We went to Angers, where I stayed in a café writing to Kos., Védrine, and Sorokine. In the evening, again reading, as well as later in bed until midnight. I read *The Secret Agent* by Somerset Maugham and *The People of the Abyss* by Jack London.

---

* By Leslie Charteris, born in 1907.
† A book written by London's wife.

Tuesday, October 3

I slept poorly. I was thinking of Sartre and Bost and my desire to see them was overwhelming. We are going through a strange moment in history. Hitler proposes peace, but it's a kind of peace that no one could want. Then what sort of war are we going to wage against them? What does the word "war" mean exactly? A month ago, when it was written in bold letters in the newspapers, it meant an undefined horror, a tension affecting the entire person without knowing where it was heading. It was confusing, yet replete. Now, there is a vague scattering of nuisances and minor fears; it's no longer anywhere or anything. I am relaxed and vague, waiting for I don't know what. It seems that everyone is waiting, as if pure time had any efficacy. Incidentally, what is so striking at first in the history of the 1914–18 war is the fact that it was a four-year-long wait punctuated by completely useless slaughter. It seems as if the massacres served only to fill out a little of this pure passing of time, which suddenly in the end was condensed into victory. It's as absurd as it could possibly be and more contingent than I would have ever thought. In the afternoon we went to Angers—in the evening I read a good Curwood, *Au Bout du fleuve* [At the River's End], and an atrocious Stevenson, *Adventures of John N.*

Wednesday, October 4

I woke up in a very gloomy mood. Again I'd like a change of existence. I am happy to leave for Paris the day after tomorrow. What is my life going to be like? Until now I have been on vacation, an unsure beginning. Paris, the lycée, I am going to get settled in this wartime existence and from a distance it seems rather depressing to me. Almost five weeks have gone by now. There are several distinct phases:

a) From September 1 to 8, inclusive: A great horror, a useless and constant flight—solitude, reading Gide—beautiful autumn in Paris. And insane fears.

b) From September 9 to 16, inclusive: Life with Kos. in Gégé's apartment. Life in slow motion, empty and sweet; newness of this rediscovered sweetness.

c) 17–18–19: With Toulouse—amused to be there, mixed with the horror of the first week.

d) From 20 to 25: Quimper and Védrine—state of peace—pleasant holiday.

e) 25–26–27: travels on foot; spending some beautiful hours.

f) From 28 to the present: a week of retreat, entirely spent reading. No inner life, only comfort and study.

I remember that during the first week I was content with practically anything. I have become more demanding as the interest in this object called war has paled.

The desire to flee this tranquility, to get hold of something again, came over me like a panic this morning. There was the vague hope after reading Sartre's letter that I would be able to go see him in Marmoutier. At the same time, fear came back, impatience and agitation. I decided to leave and they took me to Angers at seven o'clock in the evening. I'm writing in a café near the station. What a depressing place! I had wanted to go to the movies; there were army barracks located in this section of town. Whores were soliciting soldiers and bistros were packed with army personnel. I hesitated a long time before entering the café, where I read *Marianne*. The movie house was closed. I walked back through these streets that terrified me. War is again in me and around me, and an anguish that doesn't know where to alight.

NOTES

1. Beauvoir's descriptions of Sartre's departure and the beginning of the war in the September 1 and 2 diary entries are taken up in chapter 9 of her novel *She Came to Stay* and in *Prime of Life*.

2. Capri ran a cabaret in Paris. The author would frequently go there with her friends.

3. The French term will be inserted within brackets in the text when necessary for philosophical clarity.

4. *L'Intransigeant* was the paper associated with the Munich-oriented (read: appeasement politics) Chautemps (cf. Sartre's Letters). Camille Chautemps, French politician (1885–1963).

5. Islands in the Mediterranean near the city of Hyères.

6. One is strongly reminded here of Jules Romains and his ideas on "unanimisme," popularized in his literature. The emphasis on the absence of any individual life here makes one think of a society where people live as one body and act like "une âme"—one soul.

7. Maurice Merleau-Ponty (1908–1961), a friend and fellow philosophy student with Beauvoir in 1927, later was coeditor with Beauvoir and Sartre of *Les Temps Modernes* and one of France's leading phenomenologists.

8. An influential newspaper at the time.

9. A distinguished journal that published many of the contemporary writers, including many of Sartre's books and reviews.

10. These are titles of newspapers

11. A weekly magazine famous for its acerbic satire of politics and culture.

12. Arthur Adamov, who later became known as a playwright of the Theater of the Absurd.

13. He was telling his customers about his experiences in World War I.

14. The concluding chapter of Beauvoir's novel *She Came to Stay* opens with a scene of a young woman applying blue paint to a window.

15. The author uses the word *anéantissement* here, not in the sense of annihilation or destruction, but consigning something or someone to nothingness.

16. Likely a pun on one of the various meanings of "tabac."

17. Henri Ghéon, pseudonym of Henri Vauglon (1876–1944), French dramatist and poet.

18. A tale of Sherlock Holmes by Sir Arthur Conan Doyle (1901).

19. "The Real Castor." Beauvoir was given the nickname "Castor" (Beaver) by René Maheu, a fellow philosophy student and a friend of Beauvoir and Sartre.

20. France's westernmost point.

21. A play by Paul Claudel (1868–1955).

22. La Pouèze, located near Angers in the Loire Valley, was the family home of Mme Morel's invalid husband. In the *War Diary* Mme Morel is called "That Lady." The author dedicated her essay *Pyrrhus and Cineas* to her—*cette dame.*

23. Pierre Drieu la Rochelle (1893–1945).

24. Beauvoir must be referring to World War I, the war she had just read about.

25. A black currant liqueur.

26. Pierre Mac Orlan (1882–1970), French writer.

NOTEBOOK 2

October 5 – November 14, 1939

Thursday, October 5

I did not sleep well at all. Hope is a feeling difficult to sustain when it's founded on such shaky ground—steps in the hallway and the light coming in through the transom kept me awake, but mostly my inner unrest. I was anxious to get back to Paris, though I really didn't know why.

I got up at six o'clock. I had something to eat and drink at the station and took the train at seven in the company of three plump nuns. The weather was nice. The countryside flew past, flat and golden. We passed Chartres—I could see the cathedral, and St. Cyr, filled with memories, and Versailles. I finished *Le Cabaret de la dernière chance* [The Last Chance Saloon], which I find entertaining, and I read *Moll Flanders,** which is excellent.

I passed by the Hotel Mistral, where I had a pile of letters. I took my belongings to get settled at rue d'Assas. I saw Gégé, all haggard looking. I barely said hello to her and threw myself on my letters. One, a very nice one, from Kos., who was feeling miserable in L'Aigle; two letters from Sorokine, feeling utterly wretched; short messages and a letter from Védrine, getting

---

* The first, a novel by Jack London; the second, a novel by Defoe.

settled in Rennes; a stack of letters from Bost and Sartre. I read through all that and impatiently hurried to the police station. There I said foolishly that I wanted to go and visit "my fiancé, who had been drafted." I was told that such requests were systematically denied and that *he* would be punished if I managed to meet him anyway. I decided to go to another police station and be less stupid. But it was not that easy. I went to the Bon Marché[1] to have my picture taken and next to the photo booth, at the lunch counter, I ate some pork with lentils. My photos turned out horrible. A new residence certificate so I could change police stations was the hardest to get. Mme Parrier refused to give me one; "But you don't live here; that would be under false pretenses," she said dryly. It was obvious that war was here too with the firing squad on the horizon for those with the heart of a concierge. I went to Camille Sée,* a superb building. I waited a while and went to see the principal. She is a rather young, slender, elegant, and powdered woman with a bluish chin under the powder. She pretended to be energetic, whimsical, and dauntless. "I'm very plucky," she said shamelessly herself. She talked to me about my duties. It seems that I won't have much to do; the school has two hundred students and I'll have only twenty. They have a surplus of women teachers and don't know what to do with them.

I returned to rue d'Assas by taxi. The concierge was sitting at her sewing machine and said that she couldn't give me the certificate in view of the fact that I was subletting. I just remained standing there in front of her; she continued sewing for a long time without either of us barely saying a word and then suddenly she got up and wrote me a certificate as of September 14. I gave her fifty francs, which at first she refused indignantly. Then she gave in, saying, "Only half of it"; but then she took all. Everything went well at the police station. I was telling them about my sister suffering from a bone disease and that I wanted to pick her up in Marmoutier. The employee, very fatherly, wrote me a paper in his best handwriting. On the other hand, a blonde who wanted to visit her husband in Seine and Marne was dissuaded from going: "Not for that purpose." "Then for other reasons I can go?" "You still need a valid excuse," said the paper pusher who was writing my paper. I was promised safe conduct for Monday or Tuesday and left there all excited and extremely nervous. I went to the Dôme to write to Sartre and then at six o'clock went to say hello to the Gérassis. We had a drink first at their place, then at the Café Rond-Point. Fernand was held in prison for four days. He said that someone had informed against him for "propaganda

* The author had a teaching assignment there. She was also teaching at the lycée Fénelon, the lycée Molière having been relocated to the provinces at the outbreak of the war.

against enlisting foreigners into the legion"; a fellow had told him that he was a White Russian and asked him whether he thought that he could go to Spain. Gérassi had said that he certainly could. "But I don't have a passport." "You go to the border and you walk." Well, the guy was an *agent provocateur;* Gérassi was sent to the prefecture and then to a camp where the soldiers and sergeants were extremely nice to them. One of them had even slipped him some tobacco when he said that he had fought for Spain and upon mentioning that he had been a general, the soldier had given him one more pack of tobacco. His friends were surprised that he was released so quickly, he said, and were even a little suspicious. He had the impression of being watched by the police and didn't dare go visit Ehrenbourg. It seems that Malraux wanted to enlist in the tank corps, but they didn't want him there because of his nervous tics. Two days before the arrest of the communists, Nizan[2] sent Duclos a very curt resignation from the Communist Party stating "my situation as a serviceman makes it unnecessary to add anything further." Stépha stayed alone with me for a whole hour, nice of her. I had dinner at the Coupole; it was crowded. Montparnasse is overrun both by military personnel and a whole new clientele, and the few old regulars seem somewhat prehistoric in the midst of that crowd. They seem like witnesses of a world that is dead. Thoughtlessly I asked for "un demi Munich"; the waiter laughed, saying, "We've got to cross the Siegfried Line first." I went to the Dôme and wrote to Bost—I was dead tired. I had forgotten what a powerful effect nighttime in Paris has on me: the Big Dipper with its reddish glow over the intersection Vavin; it's so eerie and so beautiful. Hardly anyone left outside on the café terraces; the weather is beginning to be too cool. Everything was even more deserted than last month. I returned home through streets as dark as tunnels. A short letter from Bost, slipped under the door, filled me with tenderness for him.

Friday, October 6

I slept poorly. At ten o'clock my book dropped from my hands, but when Gégé came home at midnight she woke me up and we talked: She just returned from Castel Novel, where she saw a whole throng of women and Spanish refugees. But nothing she said was entertaining. I couldn't go back to sleep. I wore myself out in useless and feverish schemes of how I would hide from Kos. Sartre's coming to Paris and that of Bost. At night it seems extremely urgent to me and brings on nervous exhaustion. Toward half past six in the morning the sound of a siren, but weak and odd. People were standing at the windows, wondering whether it was an air raid warning. It turned out to be only a mechanical fluke. I went back to sleep for a little while, then got up, said hello to Gégé, and went to the lycée Pasteur.* The hope of seeing Sartre put me in a good mood. I dressed smartly: I put on Sartre's sweatshirt with a green scarf and turban. It looked pretty and I was moved, wearing a piece of his clothing on my body. I took the bus to Neuilly, then with bulging pockets I went to the lycée Molière, where I spoke briefly to the superintendent; the lycée is being transferred to Meulan. Finally I stopped again by Camille Sée to sign some papers and then went to wait for Baba† at the Lutétia because she wanted me to meet her there to go swimming.‡ During all this time I read *Les Ames mortes* [Dead Souls] by Gogol, which I bought for Bost and which I find somewhat entertaining. Boubou arrived on a bicycle to tell me that Stépha could not go swimming. I picked up my clothes at the concierge and took them to Gégé's place, where I had several letters: one from Bost, one from Védrine, and two from Sartre, one of which had been opened by the censor. It was the first time it happened. Alas! on October 3 he had left for an unknown destination. All my plans had come to naught. For a moment I felt utterly distressed. And to make things worse, I read in Bost's letter that they had been instructed on how to behave under fire. I went to have lunch at Pagès. I was completely choked up. The last three weeks were a respite whose sweetness I could no longer understand; it was like sleep without truth, and now I find distress again. It was already present yesterday; it was everywhere in Paris. But today it has become a part of me also and forms the substance I'm made of: distress and fear. I had a moment of revolt when faced again with all that bitterness and mawkishness, and to think it will go on. It no longer interests me. At present I keep this diary only because I feel that I must do so, while in the beginning I felt curious about all my reactions. Since Saturday I have been rereading all of Bost's letters and have now an impression of his life that chills my blood. It's the enumeration of his small pleasures that is depressing; he also feels them as such, the roasted goose, for example, the flannel belts, or "the louse and the spider." I felt a terrible need to cry.

I went to the Dôme, wrote to Kos., Védrine, and Poupette, and read *Les Ames mortes,* then wrote to Sartre. Hirsckovic, looking great in a purplish-blue tie, remained next to me for more than two hours without budging.

---

* Sartre's lycée in Neuilly where the author had to go and get his salary. Neither had a bank account. [As a government employee Sartre was entitled to his salary while mobilized.—Trans.]

† The nickname for Stépha, who was Polish.

‡ The Hotel Lutétia in Sèvres-Babylone had a swimming pool.

I kept my mind occupied with budget matters, schedules, and organizing concrete things. I bought *L'Idiot* [The Idiot] and Green's *Journal* for Sartre, but the *NRF* is no longer published, or rather, is sold only by subscription. I stopped again at rue d'Assas. Gégé told me that she could no longer put me up; just as well, but then I have to find a place to stay, the Hotel Mistral being too far. I checked out some hotels; those in rue Vavin I rather liked. I bought a beautiful pipe for Bost and the merchant made me some great packages wrapped in purple paper. Two women, kind of female scouts, entered the boutique and asked for a pipe G.D.B. *"gueule de bois renversée,"*[3] they said, joking all the while, giving us to understand that the pipe was intended for a soldier. Too late to take my packages to the post office. I went back to the Dôme to write to Bost and make some entries in my diary. Then I went to see the Gérassis. The couple had been fighting because Stépha had spent a whole hour with me yesterday. And when I told Boubou that that wasn't very serious, he answered, "It's serious to spoil someone's good mood, and it's difficult enough these days to stay in a good mood." That really takes the cake: the right to a good mood. We had chicken with rice; the dinner was rather gloomy. Then we played dominoes, which was very entertaining. At eleven o'clock I went home to go to bed, and I slept, kind of.

Saturday, October 7

I read Green's *Journal* last night in bed. This fellow is disgustingly mediocre. He feels nothing and what he thinks he should say on a subject are depressing platitudes. I remember, on the contrary, Gide's happiness at each of his choices. In Green's case it's pitiful.

I must not have fallen asleep until after midnight and this morning I was already dressed at half past seven. I have a great need to be active; I must get back to my novel,* but I'm waiting to be settled again in my existence and above all to have given up any hope of seeing Sartre. I chatted a while with Gégé, who told me about her inferiority complex, and I brought this diary up to date.

A letter from Sartre, written Monday, warmed my heart. The idea of leaving the Hotel Mistral had saddened me last night. It seemed to me that I was giving up on my existence with him, that it was a definitive leave-taking. And here he was writing me all I wanted him to tell me and then some. When I don't see him, or even when he doesn't expressly make me feel it, I

---

* *L'Invitée* [She Came to Stay].

don't think of his love for me as something alive for him. It almost seems to be a condition for life, which he no longer discusses, which he even likes, but almost a condition for life more than a personal relationship. And this often lends a harsh quality to my love for him. Partly to blame for this is the distaste I feel for the sentimental illusions of the kind that someone like Poupette or Védrine harbors on the subject. The idea that I too could be deluded disgusts me. It's mostly this: the delusion based on the idea that one has a privileged situation. I'm well aware of how behaviors and words addressed to "others" are interpreted in psychological terms as conscious and cunning, while the same word, the same behavior with respect to *oneself* is considered a meaningful [*significant*] object. It's not the difference between true and false; I don't think: he lies to her, but he tells me the truth—because then the idea would occur to me that he could also lie to me. It's the difference between an object "put between parentheses" and an object posited absolutely.[4] I think, "He writes her that he loves her—and he loves me." The first sentence does not mean that he does not love her the moment he is writing it; it's yes and no and not very important. This explains the extraordinary power of Poupette's illusion concerning the woman from Oran, and Védrine's illusion with respect to Wanda. But it's annoying, this attitude of not even supposing the parentheses possible for oneself. And yet, the moment it is introduced we give up "being just one," because then we are confronting each other [*on s'oppose*]. I need to explain this well in my novel with respect to Françoise and Pierre* and Elisabeth too. But moreover, I feel so very strongly how between Sartre and myself these parentheses are absurd—I don't believe I will feel it for a long time to come.

A letter arrived from Bost that made me very happy. When he tells me sweet things, in his case, on the contrary, I put them as it were in well-meaning parentheses. Not only do I think that they are true, but as soon as they get a little creative, I think that telling them to me was important for him, and this intention, considering his character, is an act of tenderness in itself that moves me more than anything else.

I read the letters, then went to mail my packages and money orders and moved out of my room at the Hotel Mistral. I went to have my hair washed, bought some toiletries, and made myself beautiful, a little because I wanted to convey the image of "a woman who doesn't let herself go" in war times. Then I had lunch at Pagès and went to the Champs-Élysées to meet the Audrys.

---

* Françoise and Pierre, the two principal characters in *She Came to Stay*, as well as Elisabeth.

We had made a date for the Marignan, but military authorities closed it down on account of staying open after eleven at night. I went across the street to the Colisée and read *Meurtre en Mésopotamie* [Murder in Mesopotamia] by Agatha Christie. A disreputable clientele of expensive call girls and officers "who will die in their beds" and draft dodgers; the public of 1916 as seen through John Dos Passos and the *Crapouillot* magazine.

I met up with the Audrys and we went to the Pam Pam. The Audry sister, younger looking than ever with her hair cut at the neck, declared that the war "is too great a public misfortune for anyone to have the right to think of personal misfortunes." Her husband, as a general and an influential member of the air force general staff, earns more then twenty thousand francs a month—she is prosperous. Colette Audry told me in all seriousness that she appreciated her sister's distaste for the propaganda movies that are being made now. "She will perhaps work in them anyway," she said, "but for the moment she feels that they are distasteful." Incidentally, the Audry sister is charming, knows lots of addresses of good restaurants and volumes of obscene stories that she tells with much charm. Colette Audry collects war anecdotes and pastes newspaper scraps into notebooks. She bought great fur-lined gloves and will take me to Bon Marché to try a culotte-skirt for bicycling.

I left her to go to the Ursulines. They were playing *Saint Louis Blues* and I began to cry at the sight of a nightclub. I wept over Bost and my evenings with him—and during *Cavalcade* I also cried the whole time having reached a total and shameful emotional low and feeling horribly certain that I'll never see him again. I left the movie theater still sobbing. The night was a little foggy with a hint of winter already in the air, but so beautiful and tragic that I melted and became once again impersonal consciousness of a cataclysm. That's what is so marvelous about Paris, the cataclysm is present everywhere, and it is almost a sufficient occupation to become aware of it.

I stopped by my place and feverishly read Sartre's letter. He left for a place about twenty kilometers from Marmoutier; but they were moving him farther away; I have no hope left. Again I cried very hard, then fixed my face to the extent possible, and went out to eat fries and crêpes at the crêperie while finishing Agatha Christie. A merry gang there was exchanging kepies. I went to a quiet corner of the Dôme and wrote a voluminous letter to Bost; I was just starting one to Sartre when they threw me out. I crossed a completely deserted Dôme; the tables were upside down and three waiters at the cash register were tallying up the day's account. Outside, on the sidewalk, groups of people reluctant to disperse. I returned home, wrote some long pages to Sartre, and once in bed, read a little in *Le Singe d'argile* [The Clay Ape], then fell asleep.

Sunday, October 8

I awoke at about eight o'clock. I stayed in bed and only had to reach for my book. I read *Le Singe d'argile*, then Green's *Journal;* I was waiting for the mail. At ten o'clock it brought me a little letter from Bost, nothing from Sartre. I went for a coffee at the Closerie des Lilas while finishing Julien Green's book. The place was completely deserted. Then I went to mail Sartre a package, ate something at the Milk Bar, went to see Stépha for five minutes at her place, and from the Dôme wrote to Védrine, Sorokine, and That Lady. Then I went on foot to the Atlantic, rue Boulard, to watch *Anges aux figures sales* [Angels with Dirty Faces]. No seats available before the five o'clock showing. I went to avenue d'Orléans to read in the Oriental, decorated all in green, where one morning Sartre straightened out things between Bost and me. I read *Colonel Jack* by Defoe and the second part of *Les Ames mortes* [Dead Souls]. It being Sunday, many people out for a walk passed by the café terrace. The weather was mild.

I returned to the movie house at five o'clock—a huge line, mostly very young people. There was a stampede toward the entrance. Everyone had a ticket, the ushers were shoved about, and the doors just about beaten down—a hugely popular movie house. The movie was entertaining and James Cagney funnier than ever. After the movie I went to eat at Pagès and then wrote to Bost and Sartre from the Dôme. I went home to go to sleep early. I read for one hour in bed *Les Enfants du limon* [Children of Clay] by Queneau, which is a funny book.

Monday, October 9

Horses trotting under my windows for a long while. I woke up. It was eight o'clock and raining, a dreary day. I stayed in bed and read Shakespeare, *The Merchant of Venice,* which I did not remember well, and *The Merry Wives of Windsor.* Then I got dressed; mail: nothing, except for a message from Sorokine, who was returning to Paris, and a charming letter from Kos., which I answered immediately. I want to see her, but at the same time I realize that I will be settled in my life for the next year and perhaps for years to come with her as my only resource, without Sartre and without Bost. It's a dark and gloomy feeling that started to come over me. No letters from either

Sartre or Bost—perhaps this afternoon. I read, had lunch with Stépha at the Coupole, and passed by rue Amélie. *Europe** is no longer published and I went to Gégé's place to wait for the mail. While she worked on her designs I waited, scarcely able to read. Nothing, except a message from Védrine. Sorokine came by around five o'clock. We walked toward the Odéon. They gave me a pass for Sarrebourg, no farther; there's hardly a ray of hope left. We had a drink in a little café and walked down to the Duroc metro station. With an awkward and pleasant gesture she took my arm, but I remained at a loss, not knowing what to say to her. I left her, ate a little, wrote my letters, and played dominoes with the Gérassis.

Tuesday, October 10

Pardo returned home; it was my last night in Gégé's apartment. We chatted a while. I had two letters from Sartre; in one he spoke of our anniversary, our tenth anniversary,† which we were to celebrate with great pomp. I am too sad for words. There's barely a chance to meet him; he is on the move all the time. I began moving into my room; I like it. Then I had a grilled ham sandwich at the Milk Bar and went to see Sorokine. We stayed a while at her place. She showed me some poetry she had written in ninth grade. There were some rather nice verses among them. She was squirming nervously. I just can't find the right tone with her. We went to a café, where she bemoaned her unhappy situation. She cannot register at the Sorbonne if she has no identification card, nor can she have a card if she is not registered. It's always the same song and dance. Her father is left without an income and her mother has no work permit. Crying, she said, "Why does Norry‡ have all the rights and I don't have any?" It's terrible to have one's future obstructed, and to have always to resort to makeshift solutions. I ran into Mme Mancy at the pastry shop Mangin, rue du Havre; she is a good woman. I stopped by Gégé's again. Sartre is going to be sent to a village that has been evacuated; that's the end of any chance I had to see him. It was a blow for me, and then I almost felt relieved because there is no hope anymore. I've got to settle into my wartime life, and that's all. I went up to my room and put my things away. I really like this room; I'll buy some firewood and it will be warm and staying there will be a pleasure. Thanks to heavy red drapes I can have plenty of light in the evening, which is also very nice. I made a

---

* The review.
† "Wedding" anniversary.
‡ One of her classmates, who was practically retarded.

list as to what clothes I may need, a coat, for example. I decided that from tomorrow on I would get back to my novel. And feeling so full of courage I started to write to Sartre. I was overcome with terrible sobbing; I realized that there will be war for a long time to come and that I won't see him for ages—I felt utterly unhappy.

I cried very hard. After I washed my tear-stained face to go down and have dinner and while away some time at the Dôme, I had a strange impression: I had a vivid representation of myself, as "entering the Dôme with eyes still full of tears." It seemed to me absolutely necessary; it was the typical image of a woman in wartime. And it was *me*. From the depth of time and space I thought, "It's happening to me," and something inside me escaped historicity. It was *existentiel*,[5] but it was also the split image of a crazy woman. In fact, I did go to dinner, then to the Dôme to write to Bost. Adamov, looking haggard, sat down next to me. He looked crazed. As the waiter returned a thousand francs change to me, he said, "This goes completely against the rules, but may I ask you for fifteen francs?" I gave him twenty. He no longer has any income. He has his draft papers and is waiting to be called up. That's the way it is at the Dôme, full of human wrecks.

Poker at the Gérassis', where I recovered my twenty francs. Rumor has it that a thousand soldiers at the front took over a train by force and went on leave illegally without anyone daring to arrest them.

I returned home at about eleven o'clock. I enjoyed going to bed in this room, turning on the light over my bed and reading *East Wind, West Wind* by Pearl Buck, although it's not very interesting.

Wednesday, 11

I slept until nine o'clock thanks to those heavy drapes. It's like the beginning of a new form of life for me, the definitive form: staying home and working instead of distracting myself and looking for help on the outside. I don't even feel like going to Provins anymore to see the boxers, who were so kind as to invite me, nor do I want to go to Crécy to visit Toulouse. I shall wait for these people to come to Paris. I am eager to begin again something of my own.

I got up in a good mood. I found it charming to eat breakfast at the counter of the Dôme. Stopped by at Gégé's for my mail. Had a sweet little letter from Bost. Then I went home, read *Le Canard enchaîné*, wrote to Védrine, and made entries into this diary. I am going to get back to work. I need to re-read my novel from start to finish. First I had lunch. At the idea of rereading my novel I felt a little apprehensive because I was afraid that I would find it no good and also that it would make me sad. I read a hundred pages and did so with real pleasure. On the whole I find it lively, entertaining, and interesting; I felt encouraged. After that I wrote to Bost; then Sorokine came by. She made a funny scene because I refused to show her my diary, I don't know why she was making a fuss over it—and then she collapsed in my arms as she did in July and we exchanged passionate kisses. It seemed to me that she was looking for precise caresses, and I complied. In the end she became sad. She told me lots of things in Russian, I'm sure they were passionate, then in French: "I love you so much! I really do!" She is charming, often too eager and high-strung, but pleasant in her tenderness. But I don't know what to do and it really makes me feel ill at ease.

I left her and stopped by rue d'Assas, where I had only letters from my mother and sister, then at half past six I went to the Milk Bar, where I ate some ham while writing in this diary.

I wrote to Sartre—then stopped by the Gérassis—and at eight o'clock I was back in my room rereading my novel. I finished it by ten; I'm rather happy with it despite some big mistakes. I really like the general tone and the individual dialogues, the episodes and moods as well. But Pierre's character does not exist, Xavière's does not stand out enough, and their relationship is too vague. It's lacking at least one important transition between chapters 5 and 8. Françoise's drama is not really center stage. The whole plot structure is good; it's teeming with people, and their stories interact well. But the essential subject has so far been treated only allusively.

A good day. I am happy to have found my work and the taste for solitude again, and a goal in life, something that depends on me.

Thursday, October 12

Another good day. I got up around nine o'clock, had my coffee at the counter of the Dôme, and bought the NRF.[6] It has a short article on Le Mur [The Wall],[7] neither good nor bad. The rest is hardly interesting. Two letters from Sartre, who still was not sure whether he was going to stay where he is. I worked well for two hours. I devised an extensive plan for the correction of the first chapters and another big plan for the entire ending. I established a list of books to read; I felt busy and full of enthusiasm. I wrote to Sartre also for the purpose of consulting with him about the following idea: What if I situated my novel between 1938 and 39 so that Bost and Sartre would be leaving because they are going to war, which would make everything more definitive and lend more purity to the final crime?[8] I am rather fond of this idea. Lunch at Pagès, then more work. I started writing and was quickly back inside the subject matter and involved in the storyline. Sorokine came by at half past two. She was mad with anger because yesterday, after she had swiped my diary and then thought better and given it back to me, I told her, "If you had taken it with you, I would have never wanted to see you again in my life." She criticized me, saying, "Your feelings for me don't go very deep, do they?" I sat down on the bed next to her, comforted her, and right away, embraces and passionate kisses. She was still quite obstinate: "I occupy the fifth place in your life." I tried to persuade her not to be jealous of my life and told her that I loved her tenderly. With a sure instinct she hates "my red-haired friend." I really feel much affection for her and talked to her with all the sincerity and tenderness I could muster. She relaxed and left, feeling—for the first time perhaps—reassured, confident, and affectionate. She has these beautiful moving and tender facial expressions. But now I'm committed regardless of how I may feel about it. After she left I stopped at Gégé's; I had a long letter from Védrine, who got settled in Rennes. I found the Moon Woman, who was looking for me. We went to the Dôme together; next to us sat a weird old man in blue overalls reading *Science and Health* in what looked like a black missal. A drunk came up to him to explain a phrase he had said in front of him the night before. The other didn't want to listen and it almost came to blows between them. The drunk turned to us, saying, "I may have narrow shoulders, but I have a heavy forehead." "I don't give a damn about your shoulders," said the Moon Woman. Two guys had to come over in order to pull the drunk away from our table. I find the Moon Woman funny, so I took her to the Breton crêperie, then we went to the basement of the Schubert, boulevard Montparnasse, which was depressing and expensive; but they did have a piano that played jazz tunes and that represented a change. "Now I wonder where everyone may have gone," said the Moon Woman in a loud voice, which provoked a grumbling on the part of the waiter. It gave me the feeling of a wartime party, which seemed utterly fantastic. They booted us out at eleven o'clock and we went to the boulevard St. Michel, then to the Châtelet and for a stroll along the Seine. Police patrols in the night, the policemen wearing wide capes and shiny helmets. Whether on foot or bicycle, they shine electric lights on passersby and stop all men, asking them for their papers. They even search the public urinals. I finally accompanied the Moon Woman to her place and went home at about one o'clock in the morning. It had been a long time since I had gone to sleep that late and I found it pleasant. The Moon Woman told me lots of stories; if one is patient enough to disregard the inanities with which she embroiders them, her stories are sometimes funny. There is first of all her passion for a young, twenty-one-year-old Spanish refugee, handsome as a god, whom she was meeting secretly in the mountains where he lives half naked and as a fugitive. The village people loathe these refugees. She claims that they have even beaten some to death because they didn't want to enlist. She therefore had to act very prudently. One night she got lost and lost her shoes. She walked barefoot through some brush for three miles, falling into gullies. She was being watched keenly. The guy knows only about twenty words of French. I could just imagine their conversation. Her only thought is to go and find him again. She told me about her stay at the Pointe du Raz with the Moon Man, how they had tried to instruct the inhabitants of a fishing village on matters of morals, history, and politics. She gave a good description of the life of these people, and of the women who used to say, "In bad weather we worry about them, but when they have been on land for two weeks, we can't wait for them to leave again." She was not very clear in her stories about their travels to Corsica, which sounded like a crazy escapade and remained obscure to me. They were stories involving sex, of course: how, at the age of twenty, out in an open field, she fought off two guys for an hour by saying "Our Fathers," crossing herself and uttering curses. In the end, when she was cursing them through their daughters, saying, "I wish that all your daughters be raped," the guy who was watching suddenly changed and became nice. He stopped the other guy and said, "A girl was born to me yesterday. Light a candle for her," and then accompanied her back to Paris. She also told me how Leduc, a New Age fellow, heard knocks at his door the other night: Police! Open up! He screamed, "You lousy bastards!" believing they were his buddies. This went on for quite a while; then he opened the door and five policemen entered, guns drawn. They had mistaken him for a communist. They found a package at his place with women's shoes and an I.D. card that he had picked up in a train. It looked suspicious. In the end no charge could be leveled against him. So he was put in prison for a week for theft because of the package.

The Moon Woman is convinced that Daladier asked Hitler to declare war so as to crush the Popular Front.[9] And she holds forth like a defeatist. She told about a funny train trip where she was pawed ever so much and then tried to make the soldiers feel sorry for Giono.* "Don't say such things to young soldiers," one of them told her in a stern voice. She does not mind going to prison because she'll have forty thousand francs saved at her re-

---

* Giono was a known pacifist. [He was a twentieth-century regionalist author.—Trans.]

lease. She explained to me, "For women of our generation the war is tough! Are we going to have to start walking the streets again after already going through so much trouble just to earn our keep!" She claimed that Giraudoux[10] would soon be fired because he was not forceful enough. She talked for six hours nonstop, often expressing herself felicitously with much charm in her gestures and facial expressions.

Wednesday [sic], October 13

I frittered my time away today. I could have worked better, but I'm no longer in the habit of sitting for hours facing blank paper; it seems strange to me. I got up at half past nine, stopped by for nothing at rue d'Assas, then went to the Dôme, where I met Stépha. I sat down next to her and she questioned me to find out whether I was really a lesbian. We read the newspaper, looked at *Marie-Claire,* which suggests model letters intended for soldiers. They were too funny for words. We ran some errands; then I ate a brandade of cod at the Dôme and wrote to Bost and Sartre. The Hungarian came over. I shook hands with him and ran over to Stépha's place to borrow a lipstick. At three o'clock I was at work; it was late and I didn't get much done. I started to write on sickness but was not yet into the subject. I made my diary entry, stopped by Gégé's, where I had a long and charming letter from Bost. Then I went to the Capoulade. I wrote to Toulouse, Poupette, and the boxer. My life is getting organized; I only need to work more. At noon the Dôme looked perfectly normal with familiar faces and well-groomed women. The same was true for the Capoulade tonight. Is that what war is like, I wondered? Amazement at not suffering more and especially at not having our lives more unsettled. Suffering is perhaps still to come, but no upheaval; I don't think so. At the moment, it's not really war yet. The worst is yet to come.

The Moon Woman arrived at seven o'clock and we went immediately to the movies at the Panthéon. We arrived in the middle of a documentary on oil. But afterward they showed a charming English cartoon, *La Chasse au renard* [The Fox Hunt], much different in style from American cartoons, more artistic refinement, at times shades reminding one of Chirico and mostly very graceful. *Pilote d'essai* [Test Pilot] with Clark Gable and Myrna Loy was entertaining. Then we went to the bar of the Capoulade and ate steaks with French fries accompanied by a bottle of Beaujolais. Our conversation became animated and we began declaring our friendship for each other. As we were thrown out at eleven o'clock we went to buy two bottles at the pastry shop on boulevard St. Michel. We bought a small one for ourselves and a large one for Youki,* whom the Moon Woman wanted to visit. I found this amusing. We arrived at rue Mazarin and went up two floors in total darkness. We rang; the dining room was filled with smoke, people, and glasses of red wine. On the walls, paintings by Foujita, one of which represented a nude Youki with a lion. The paintings were in color because she asked him to prove that he could paint something other than in black and white. Incidentally, I didn't find the painting very attractive. Youki was presiding, wrapped in a Japanese kimono that left her beautiful arms and throat bare. She is blonde, rather beautiful, and entirely fake. Among the guests was Claire, the sports instructor with the large forehead, former friend of Kiki of Montparnasse, of Pascin,† and of Sonia Krog, and who is beginning to flounder in mysticism; she too was speaking with teary eyes about her suffering at the hands of men. Her husband, Manuel, the exhibitionist with the long calamitous face, was drawing cards in the adjoining room; he drew them on behalf of "humanity" and predicted nothing good in store for it. Other guests included Blanche Picard in a red kimono with the face of an intellectual and a victim. She didn't stir all evening. Other guests included a little lesbian smoking a pipe, and a rather beautiful brunette, and yet another woman. There were furthermore Michel and very young silent men, and a rather handsome blond guy wearing a blue turtleneck, and a soldier on leave who looked like Buster Keaton and whom I had seen before at the Flore. All these people were discussing a letter from Desnos in which he was calmly describing his life at the front. They became most indignant because they wanted him to rebel. The Moon Woman became indignant too; she was calling for a rebellion. Those people were drunk and dreadful, but the soldier who was right in their faces with his pathos about tanks and barbed wire was just as disgusting. It was a well-performed comedy: they playing the role of belated surrealists, cynical and rebellious, and he the role of the combatant disgusted with civilian mentality. I couldn't get over seeing their studied refinement of an attitude, their complete disregard of reality. For them only words exist and the meaning they had assigned to them based on their past and a few recognized authorities. They no longer kept up appearances. The soldier was covering his dick with his hands and people laughed hysterically. Youki was smiling voluptuously and looking for a gutsy paradox. What monotonous vocabulary: "Shit, you're a pain in the ass," she said, while deliberately spacing her words and pronouncing them with much artifice. All these people acted as though they were in heat. The

---

* Ex-wife of Foujita, married to Desnos.
† The painter, who killed himself in 1930.

Moon Woman had herself kissed endlessly by the blond guy. Youki pointed to Blanche, saying, "Blanche is hysterical, she hasn't had sex for a month." The soldier said, "We don't give a damn about women, be sure to tell your female friends; we're not waiting for them, we jerk off." "Tell your buddies that we're not waiting for them either," said Youki, "only we don't jerk off." It made a strong impression on me, the alcohol helping along. I felt so little like a woman, so little sexed, I really didn't know what was going on. But I imagined how the Kos. [sisters], given their awareness of their bodies and their femininity, must feel "compromised" by all these women—this world exists for them, and yet they are disgusted by it, which explains the aggressive nature of their scorn. They feel threatened all the same. That inspired me with a strong feeling of friendship for them. They want to live decently, but in a world full of shady and dirty things. It's not easy. The matter of our universe, on the contrary, Sartre's, Bost's and my own, is very clean.

The Moon Woman and I declared our friendship again, and she told me that since Berlin she felt a great friendship for me and in a sense "against somebody," against Sartre. She said that because of him she had gotten into big trouble, without her wanting to go into detail. She harbors a serious grudge against him.

We sang songs. They sang an excellent one by Prévert and some patriotic chants of the last war, and a few beautiful antimilitaristic songs; one of them moved me, the tune was beautiful:

> He who kills me
> shall be my comrade.

All night I was seeing little Bost's face superimposed on the scene amidst the discussions and songs, and I felt like screaming; everything was depressingly tragic.

We left at four o'clock in the morning and I took the Moon Woman and the blond guy back with me. We drank the small bottle and the Moon Woman, stretched out on the bed, talked nonstop for three hours. She talked at length about her life; I was familiar with almost all of it. She talked about her husband, whom she deemed, all things considered, a little superior to Sartre, and about Wanda, who she thinks is very nice but who has too high an opinion of herself. Sartre overestimates Wanda, as well as the Moon Woman and himself. Only I was above the esteem he has for me but which she considered too cold. I found this a little annoying as I always do when I see a foreign consciousness judge my relationship with Sartre. It was obvious that the blond guy was aching to have an affair with the Moon Woman.

They left at seven o'clock in the morning. I find the Moon Woman charming and feel some friendship for her despite the intense vulgarity of her vision of the world and of people. I went to bed and slept like a log.

Saturday, October 14

What a sad anniversary of our morganatic wedding.* I received a long letter from Sartre answering the question I had at the Pointe du Raz about the infinity of the world. He had not received any letter from me and worried about it. It made me sad to feel him so cut off from me, and I need him so much. I wrote him a long letter, sobbing. I got up at noon and saw the Hungarian for one hour at the Dôme. He bored me to tears. Then I wrote to Sartre. I felt mournful and empty with a slight hangover. Hairdresser, purchase of material for a turban. I stopped by Camille Sée and Fénelon,[11] where I did not find anyone, then ate a little at the Capoulade while writing to Bost. Then at seven o'clock I went to see Sorokine at her place.

Her friend was there. Timid and insignificant—she was sitting in a chair knitting. Sorokine had put a plaid ribbon in her hair; she looked charming and looked at me passionately. We chatted, then accompanied her friend home and went for a walk under the archways of the metro, boulevard Exelmans, and along the banks of the Seine. It was beautiful to see the trees all covered with dead leaves and big yellow lanterns lighting up the dark. I took her arm and talked to her affectionately. She answered by timidly rubbing her forehead against mine. We talked again about the school year and her efforts to see me. We returned to her place. She snuggled up in the chair, a teddy bear on her lap, and we talked gently. For the first time she accepted an affectionate complicity with me; her eagerness and nervousness were gone; she was soft and pliable, you would think a tamed animal. The awkward girl had the most charming grace this evening, which showed in her smiles, her looks, and the little wrinkling of her nose. She moved me; she is exactly the "nymph with the faithful heart," as Sartre would say.

I left and went home on the metro. I wrote Védrine a long letter and went to sleep.

---

* That is the term they had given their relationship in September 1929.

Sunday, October 15

Kos. was supposed to arrive today. In the morning I dressed up and did my nails. I had a very short letter from Sartre at Gégé's. It was dated from the tenth. At the post office I had two long letters from Bost and a short anonymous message giving me his address. It seemed so close on the map. It irritated me to be able to locate him, to be aware of the railroad connecting us and knowing the precise number of kilometers, without being able to join him.

Hitler is raving mad about the Franco-British "no." Some say that he wants a quick war. Others say that there will be no fighting before spring. But there will be fighting—deaths, deaths—and it will last a long time.

Sent Sartre a package—a letter—and no Kos. at the station at one o'clock. I ate at the Dôme, worked a little at my place, and returned to the station at five o'clock. Still no Kos. So I went to Montmartre to spend a while at the movies. The weather was balmy, it was Sunday; people were out for a walk and the sky was blue. I did not mind waiting for Kos., just to wait for something. But then I gave up waiting for her; her absence chilled me. I remembered the Moon Woman's song, it was going around and around in my head: "Oh! Cursed be the war!" But who would rebel, how and against whom? I had a drink at the Café de la Poste; how peace seemed remote.

I saw *Pieter Ibbetson*—it was really bad although Gary Cooper was as entertaining as he could be. The balcony at the movie theater was dark; my neighbor tried to play footsy with me; I moved two seats further down letting the seats snap back. Then I returned to the Montparnasse station. In the metro I scarcely focused on my reading of *Les Illuminés* by Gérard de Nerval. Throngs of people were arriving on the trains. And there in the crowd was Kos., smiling, wearing her blue coat and a little red blouse and carrying a suitcase in each hand. We went on foot to the hotel, where we were shown many rooms. They gave her a temporary room. Then we tried to go to the Dôme, which was crowded, and we wound up at the Rotonde. We chatted. I told her lots of stories, in particular about the Moon Woman. We chatted some more in my room until one o'clock in the morning. It seemed strange that she was telling me about Bost, and it did not feel exactly pleasant, but just like desire; jealousy has become dormant. I did have an unpleasant dream in which she asked me to show her a letter I was writing to Bost, which made me break out in an agonizing cold sweat.

Monday, October 16

Classes started again, not a pleasant occasion. Now the days will no longer have anything exceptional. Finished, the poetry of leisure, which used to save them. My life has become serious and without recourse.

The alarm clock brutally woke me when it rang at half past seven. I got up. At eight o'clock I was outside; the weather was nice. I walked down boulevard Montparnasse and had coffee at the Dupont. Then the metro for ten minutes, another ten minutes' walk to the lycée. How empty this big building is; a lavish teachers lounge with club chairs, bay windows, etc. I taught two class periods to nine very well behaved little girls in blue uniforms. It did not bother me; I taught a good class—had a slight impression of the unreal and absurd. The staff and the principal are friendly, as are the study-hall teachers.

Sorokine was waiting for me at the door, but I hardly paid attention to her, poor girl. I went by taxi to Fénelon where I was given my teaching schedule: another class in philosophy. That makes seventeen hours of work and that's a lot. The lycée Fénelon is dismal; now it's located at Henry IV, which is a charming lycée, but it's being demolished. The classes were moved to a modern and very ugly wing. The hallways are narrow with signs posted: Shelter 1, Shelter 5—and women in black with their putty-colored gas mask containers slung across their shoulders. The woman principal is the worst of these shrews. She is quite haughty because I am not enthusiastic about working with her. I stopped at the Sorbonne to see Mr. Monod* since I had been vaguely threatened to be transferred to Bordeaux. I met Audry and some woman from Marseilles, Mme Chazotte. At rue d'Assas I had a letter from Sartre, dated from the thirteenth. He seemed to have received my letters the previous day, but I did not receive his letter from the twelfth. We feel uneasy as if conversing in the dark; it's unpleasant. Lunch at the Milk Bar with Kos. Taught two class periods at Fénelon. There are twenty-four students, no school uniforms, well groomed, wearing makeup, very much the Latin Quarter type. They bring their gas masks to class and place them beside them.

At four o'clock I met Kos. at the Capoulade. Her face was slightly purplish and we got worried. She assumed that her coloring stemmed from a bar of bad soap, and I had to admire the delicacy of her skin. But it was the coloring of a powder puff that had come off on her skin. We went home, I wrote to Sartre—we ate at the dairy shop. Then we went to the Dôme and were

---

* The superintendent of schools.

back home at half past nine. I had a letter from Védrine, very charming. I wrote to Bost, then made the entry into this diary and went to sleep.

News of some German activity on the Western Front and a new peace offensive by Hitler.

Tuesday, 17

It would seem that fighting is beginning in earnest. A German attack followed by a counterattack of the French troops. Bombing of the Scottish coast by the Germans. We are waiting to know Stalin's decisions, but it seems to be going rather poorly. I read all that in the newspaper, but without reacting to it. I am indifferent, inert. It's not that I am bored, but I don't feel anything, neither love nor fear nor sadness.

Second day of classes, heavy teaching load. This morning I went to Henri IV; it's not at all unpleasant. I have only a ten-minute walk. After crossing the Luxembourg Gardens, golden, hazy, and quite sumptuous, I had a coffee at the counter of the Capoulade and arrived on time at the lycée. I had two class periods interrupted by an air raid exercise. The principal was running through the hallways with her hat on and blowing hard into her whistle. We went single file down to a shelter, which was beautifully appointed. We sat on something like garden chairs. The principal had us practice putting on our gas masks; all of a sudden she took off her hat and shouted from under her mask "professors too!" But I didn't have mine. She left the students for a while with their gas masks on. They laughed seeing themselves this way and she muttered, "That's not funny!" She was having a field day. She explained that in a shelter one should neither speak nor move so as to save oxygen. We finished the class. I'm rather having fun being back in the Latin Quarter. It was eleven o'clock. At Gibert I bought Les Deux Dianes [The Two Dianas] for Bost and ate at the Source while writing to Védrine. Then on to the lycée Camille Sée. The principal there is very affable. It seemed quite natural to me teaching my courses and not any more futile than before. I went to the Montparnasse station on the metro. I had a letter from Bost and sent him the package [with the book] and wrote both to him and Sartre from the Versailles.* Then I went on foot to the Deux Magots[12] to wait for Kos. while I finished reading Les Illuminés by Gérard de Nerval. My life will be full, I have no fear, but how austere it will be!

Spent a rather dreary moment at the Deux Magots; Kos. was in a bad

---

* Café–restaurant–dance hall, on the place de Rennes, No. 3.

mood. We went to buy a beautiful red muslin turban for me, then on foot to the dairy shop to eat dinner. I stopped at Gégé's, where I had a letter from Sartre. Afterward we spent the evening at the Café Flore. The Flore had heavy blue drapes and new red seats; it looked beautiful. Since September the cafés have changed. Now that they know how to comply with the blackout, they light all their lights inside. When coming in from the outside, this flood of light is dazzling. We saw Sonia, looking great, and several other familiar faces. The bistro was filled with men; in fact, they were almost all men toward closing time, and heavy tobacco smoke and political discussions filled the air. We chatted, went home on foot, and then to sleep.

Wednesday, October 18

It was a day of freedom. I spent a pleasant moment in the morning when I had my coffee at the Dôme and returned home to read the paper *Le Canard enchaîné*. Afterward I worked contentedly; I ate at Pagès and at half past twelve Sorokine came by. I was embarrassed because Kos. was in the adjoining room. She cried a little when I told her I would see her only twice a week. She made me promise to see her one additional time to work on philosophy with her. She left at half past two. I wrote to Sartre and Bost, then went to the Dôme with Kos., who was sullen like anything. Then I went to the Austerlitz station to pick up my sister. The station was depressing; hordes of soldiers, a cop blocking their way and asking for their leave papers. I took Poupette to the Milk Bar, we chatted about St. Germain-les-Belles; it was rather sad. She told me that for six weeks they had been waiting for the refugees from Hagueneau and that the town crier had been going through the streets reminding people: "Don't forget that the Alsatians are French, after all!" We went to the Gérassis', where we chatted for two hours. I went home to sleep. I had a short letter from Sartre in coded language informing me that he was stationed in Brumath.

Thursday, October 19

I got up and went to the post office on rue Littré, where I had a long and tender letter from Bost written Sunday-Monday. I went to the Versailles for breakfast and to answer Bost. The café was very dark; the waiters were still cleaning the tables. It made me think of the cafés in the provinces where one arrives by train in the morning—like Bordeaux or Carcassonne—I remembered one particular morning in Carcassonne* and I was very moved. On the whole, however, my memories have dried up. I can't even have regrets any more; it seems that everything has always been as dreary as now. I went to the lycée, then found a place in my beautiful little armoire for a small suitcase full of precious papers.† Afterward, classes until half past noon. I ate a very good lunch in a small Hungarian restaurant, then metro, then to a café on the place Jussieu, then lycée Henri IV, where I had only six students left. I like to have my lycée in the Latin Quarter. At four o'clock I met Lévy and Kanapa‡ in the Balzar. Kanapa no longer seemed at all crazy, no longer had any tics, was without affectation and rather nice. Then Kosakievitch at the Capoulade. Afterward Poupette at the Dôme. We ate dinner at the Milk Bar and I took her back to my place. She talked to me for a long time about her relationship with Lionel and how he wanted to make her into his slave, but she was unwilling.

Friday, October 20

Had the morning free. Kos. prepared a good breakfast for me with hot milk and an egg. I wrote to Bost, Sartre, and Védrine, made my diary entry, and even worked a little. It'll never go anywhere unless I can get back to it. I had lunch on rue Vavin with Poupette, then walked to the Capoulade and the lycée. At present I have only five students left. I passed by the post office and sent a money order to Védrine. A little girl came up to me; speaking with a foreign accent she told me in a graceful way, "I'm going to give you this letter since I meet you here. You don't know me, but I know you well." It was one of the students who was taken out of my class. She told me that she found my courses fascinating, that the plunge from "Consciousness" to the history of philosophy was too abrupt, and that I had made students unhappy at having to leave my classes. I was flattered. I met up with Kos. at the Capoulade and spent two hours with her. Then on to the Mahieu, where I met Poupette. I took her to the small Alsatian restaurant and to Jean de la Lune. The moonlight was absolutely gorgeous when we returned. It was the first time that I really *saw* moonlight in Paris. At the hotel I found Koestler's *Testament espagnol* [Spanish Testament], which Gérassi had probably dropped off for me. I read for quite a while in bed getting passionately interested in the book.

---

* In August 1939 with Sartre.
† Especially her correspondence with Sartre and Bost.
‡ Former students of Sartre.

Saturday, 21

Two class periods at Camille Sée. I then met Sorokine, and we went to Montparnasse by metro. I picked up Bost's letters at *poste restante* and put them in my bag. It has been two and a half days that I have not heard from Sartre and it made me sad. They are mostly the contingent moments that are dark, in the metro or on the streets. We went to the Versailles, which is always somber and empty. We chatted pleasantly while holding hands. She was content with me and seemed rather happy. I chased her away at noon to read Bost's letters, then I went to see Kosakievitch. We ate at the Coupole and met a very sad Bel Eute.* She said that Guille was in Alsace, where he was playing bridge and driving around the countryside with his lieutenant. But he was terribly bored. She was leaving for Monceaux and intended to open a nursery school. That sounded just like her. After twenty minutes we had entirely run out of things to say to one another. We left for the Café Flore with Kos. The Luxembourg Gardens are no doubt in need of gardeners because the pathways were heaped with dry leaves; it was really pretty. We sat down at the Flore, then I wrote from the Dôme. Poupette was there with Gégé, who gave me a letter from Sartre dated from the seventeenth. The letter of the sixteenth was missing, which annoyed me. I wrote to Sartre from the back of the Dôme; he seemed so far and I so alone . . . I did some errands with Poupette, boulevard de Tourville, boulevard Exelmans. She talked, talked nonstop; she exasperated me. I would like to be alone, I am so excited by the new possibility of seeing Sartre; hope is born anew. We went to buy sewing material: some blue and yellow material for turbans, and we looked at materials for a coat. We returned home and spent an hour trying on those turbans. I dressed up; I like the feeling of dressing up for an evening out. I put on a black pleated skirt, the yellow suit jacket, and the yellow blouse with matching turban. Then we left for the Jockey Bar, Kos., Poupette, and I. At half past eight the Jockey was empty. The clubroom is very pretty, only larger than before with the bar to the right on a kind of platform. The same movie posters decorate the walls, but they are clean and there's a beautiful dance floor in the center. It's really great—but it's empty. A redheaded and plump *chanteuse* was working through her program at the piano, very poor quality jazz. The boss walked up to us to give us good news: As of Monday guests can have dinner and the musical performance for twenty-five francs. Dinner is served in all of the nightclubs now. It's the new system. He ex-

---

* Nickname for Guille's wife.

plained to us that he had the room modeled after the dance halls in Seville. It made me think of the Alameda; what a change for us and for Spain. So far removed in time, it seems irretrievably lost and historical. Never before had the passing of time given me a feeling of history. The place was gradually filling up with Annamites,[13] middle-aged couples, military personnel in navy-blue uniforms without serial numbers, and two rather sad whores. The plump redhead was funny singing sad songs; another *chanteuse,* she too a redhead, was singing bad songs badly. I was afraid that thinking of Bost would bring back memories too painful, but no, the evening felt like war, mainly because there was no dancing. Hardly anything reminded us of peacetime—except for the bottle of Vat 69. I felt depressed, paralyzed. Poupette is terrible with her constant sense for the comical. She pretended to laugh by herself standing in front of the obelisk and the statue of Marshal Ney; but Kos. carried the weight of the entire evening. She likes to play this role. At eleven o'clock a bell rang and the orchestra played "Lights Out." On the sidewalk, groups of people were standing around undecided. It was the end of the evening, an end that had the neat finality of artificial things. And yet, we all knew that it was only eleven o'clock; it was a strange moment. We returned home; I was tired as I usually am at night and yet I read *The Spanish Testament* until half past one in the morning. I like what Koestler says about soldiers, that they are afraid of dying, not of death, because they are soldiers of life, not of death; and always this idea of the contingent, the everyday aspect of the most extreme situations: the horror lies always beyond that. Around half past one, screams; there was a commotion on the staircase. A woman screamed. We went out into the hallway, Kos. and I, like two old gossips, but the woman—it must have been the beautiful blonde Norwegian—had such a heavy accent that it was hard to understand her. She wanted to pack her bags and the guy perhaps wanted to hold her back by force, because it was obvious that they had a fight and she was shouting, "Let go of me! Let go!" She seemed to be quite a woman. The owner of the building came up and scolded her in a hushed voice. We will never know the real story behind it.

Sunday, 22

Wrote a long letter to Bost this morning in bed. Breakfast with Kos. I did my nails, we chatted a little, then entry in this diary. At Gégé's I had a letter from Sartre from the nineteenth; the one from the eighteenth was missing. I felt cut off. I went to write him at the Closerie des Lilas, then lunch with

Poupette at the Coupole. We went to the movies. I went to see *Les Trois Lanciers du Bengale* [Lives of a Bengal Lancer] while she watched *Gunga Din;* I waited for her in a little tobacco café, where I finished writing my letter to Sartre. On foot to Gégé's. The sunset over the Carrousel was gorgeous. Yesterday too, how beautiful the Tuileries were in their autumn colors and the light sky. Said hello to Kos. and went to the Dôme to meet Poupette and the Moon Woman. Also with them was Wanda, all blotchy and fat, looking just awful. With the Moon Woman and Poupette we went to eat crêpes and drink fine bottled cider. Then to the O.K.,* which was warm, crowded with people, and not unpleasant at all. Again a group of Annamites. The Moon Woman talked nonstop; her stories no longer amused me, nor did her remarks about married people. She had three hundred francs stolen from her by an air raid warden. I listened and wondered, "What am I doing here with these women?" and I felt pathetic. I had a headache, went home, and slept like a log.

Monday, October 23

The anguish I feel each morning upon awakening is almost pathological— having to face everything all over again: war, separation, boredom. I went to Camille Sée, then took steps to secure a safe-conduct pass. I had my picture taken at Uniprix and filled out the request at the police station in the fifteenth district. This way, I am covering my previous tracks. The weather was nice and balmy; I dared hope again. I went to Montparnasse by metro. A letter from Bost was waiting for me. I answered it right away from the Versailles. Then I picked up Kos. to have lunch at the Milk Bar. She had also received a letter from Bost, longer than mine. He called her "my dear love." It gave me a slight shock; I know it's foolish; he loves me too and that should be enough for me. I don't give him my all either. But, that doesn't matter, it will remain a small open wound inside of me. It reminded me, however faintly, of the time last year when I was terribly vulnerable, when one word by Kos. could hurt me to the quick and make me suffer, sometimes unfairly, and then I had to keep the hurt carefully to myself until a moment of solitude. Just like the other day when she said to me, "He may come home on leave," I felt my passions come back to me. Horror is worse than desire, but sadness and gloom are benign compared to this tension, this denial and persistence of passion. Rather than looking forward to Bost's leave I am almost

---

* At the Vavin intersection.

afraid of it. It would be the same with Sartre had he not promised me all of his leave time—or almost all. I feel this rebellion rising up in me that is so hard to endure, and this struggle and deceit to deny my frustrations, to keep myself in check and not to desire any longer.

Anyway, all that has paled now; it only comes keenly back to me in the unreal, while I fall asleep, for example, and then, that's different altogether.

Kos. and I ran some errands—we ordered a coat pattern and bought my beautiful material; in the well-to-do parts of the city the stores are still rather luxuriously stocked. We went to the Marignan; she left me there and I wrote to Sartre. Then Poupette arrived and we went to the Flore, where we met Gégé, slouched in an armchair; pretty women including Jacqueline Laurent, looking ravishing, a doll's face, gorgeous clothes. Gégé hates these women and suffers. We spent an hour in a kind of Cintra that looked like a ski resort bar; it's near the Palais Royal. It has deep armchairs, small barrels, deer heads mounted on the walls, cozy corners, and a fireplace. A group of young boys and girls, dressed in sports clothes and flirting with each other, were eager to dance. Someone got a record player. They ordered green beans and ate them in a corner of the room. Then we witnessed a strange pimping scene: a young girl was introduced to a man with whom she started drinking. Gégé and Poupette chatted; I felt tense and unsociable.

At nine o'clock we went to Capri's.* Establishments are all getting very casual. They no longer care about their appearance, just like a theater without lights on rehearsal night, or a picture gallery seen through the eyes of the secretary's sister. They no longer care about attracting the general public but try to hold on to some regulars; individuality is disappearing—it's pleasant, this change. Seated at a table in the center were Capri herself, wrapped in a white fur cape; Sonia in black fur; Marie-Helene; and Montero wearing a funny little hat with a red veil. Deniaud, one of those former "beards," dressed up in a tuxedo, was having dinner. Leduc, also in a beautiful tuxedo, was serving; he was the maître d'. At another table, the Dutch painter Tony with a beautiful Viennese woman, at still another table two couples, two very pretty women with their husbands. We watched the people. Deniaud sang "La marchande de violettes." That was just too inane and got on my nerves; a funny monologue about a peddler of necktie devices. Then Capri sang; she looked charming: black and gold dress, black and gold platform shoes, three feet high. Many of her songs are censored, but she still has quite a few beautiful ones in her repertoire that I enjoy listening to.

---

* Rue Sainte-Anne.

We went home in a taxi. I had letters from Sartre, from the sixteenth and eighteenth; in the end only the letter of the twelfth got lost. The connection with him has been restored; he is present again for me and we are chatting just as we used to.

Hitler still doesn't want war with France. He wants to do battle with England only by air and sea. Nothing at the Western Front until spring.

Tuesday, October 24

I got up at nine o'clock, got ready, then had breakfast with Kos. She wore her beautiful blue dressing gown trimmed with orange and a big "K" on one pocket, while I wore my black and yellow robe I bought at the flea market. She prepared two eggs and some tea for me. Wanda also appeared in a beautiful dressing gown, blue also, with her initials in yellow and green on one pocket; she looked ugly but was rather pleasant. We chatted and I kept the conversation going, because I want to be friends with Wanda; I find it amusing; besides, I like her and I spent a fun hour with the two of them. I left at half past eleven to get my daily letter from Bost. I had lunch at the Dupont; ate a big plate of calf sweetbreads while writing to Sartre. Then off to Camille Sée; gave a three-hour lecture on psychoanalysis. My students just loved it. Sorokine was there, tender and charming. I took her to the Select; we chatted a while. Then we went to the Dôme, meeting up with Poupette. Aliza, who had an appointment with Sorokine, was there too. Those Russians have a terribly hard time making a living; Ilrine* is washing floors in an American hospital.

Poupette announced that she would stay until Sunday, which annoyed me terribly; it really grieved me to the point of not being able to talk anymore. I took her to the Champs-Élysées to see *Comme tu me veux* [As You Like Me] and afterward we went back to the Select, from where I wrote to Bost and Sartre. I was very curt with her. She made discreet attempts at being affectionate, but I couldn't bring myself to respond to them. She costs me dearly. I can't spare anything this month for M. Védrine. I need to come up with:

> 1,000 francs . . . That Lady
> 1,000 francs . . . Poupette
> 1,500 francs . . . Kos.
> 500 francs　 . . . clothes

---

* A good student from the previous year.

500 francs . . . Sartre
4,500 francs

From October 1 to 30 inclusive, I will have spent 2,500 francs: 300 francs rent, 1,500 francs (50 francs per day) daily expenses, and 700 francs for book shipments, ready cash, evenings out, invitations, and other personal expenses. That's correct.

Wednesday, October 25

A good day—how life has changed since I have been working. I got up at half past eight. At nine o'clock I was downstairs to go to the Dôme and have coffee while reading the papers, *Le Canard* and *Marie-Claire*. Then three hours of work. I wrote without interruption a large part of chapter 9, on sickness—everything is so present in my mind and I would like to write everything all at once. It was dark here in my corner, but outside I caught a glimpse of a beautiful autumn day. I was calm.

I went back to the hotel to say hello to Kos. and while she was getting dressed I wrote to my mother, Sartre and Bost. There is talk about ten days' leaves every four months. I got annoyed thinking that I'll have so much trouble seeing Bost a little, so much trouble seeing Sartre the entire time or almost, knowing that I am going to worry and suffer greatly, given this dark and hopeless situation, if my passionate feelings return. I have this in common with Védrine, the panic-stricken fierceness when our future is at stake. That's probably why it irritates me so much in her. We ate at the Milk Bar with Kos.—then shopping. She wanted to buy a coat on boulevard St. Germain, but it turned out that the coat she had wanted was a military cape and the sales girl laughed at us. We went home and I sent her away so I could work, or rather, she went on her own, but showing an ever so slightly unhappy face. Wanda brought her belongings over and I changed rooms* with her; the move was quickly done. This new room is less attractive, but not at all unpleasant and I am not as glued to Kos. Work. Then Poupette arrived; she brought me a letter from Sartre. These letters are so tender and intimate. They give me back my life.

We went down to the Milk Bar, where I treated the Gérassis. The evening was quite cheerful, and I went to great expense. Then by taxi to the movie house of the Pantheon where we watched *Knock*,[14] which really made us

---

* Wanda preferred Castor's room.

laugh, and a not so bad documentary, *Nanouk,* about the life of the Eskimos. We had a drink at the Capoulade and I went home. Said hello to Kos., who was not very gracious to me. She was pleased because the classes at the Atelier may resume. She showed me a rather pleasant letter from Delarue and Lexia.*

I'm quite content with my day. Got much work done and an evening out; that would make a possible existence. At the moment the movies are almost a necessity for me and I feel in the mood to see practically anything. Incidentally, many old but good movies have been shown again lately. Gérassi said that the newspapers print a bunch of lies and that the war would last long. I no longer react when I hear all these predictions. I live in a kind of stupor with a strange system of beliefs where my future is no longer part of the real. And what an abyss between my past and me!

Thursday, October 26

In the morning Kos. greeted me stone-faced. I had it out with her, and it even came to shouts. She was complaining about not seeing me and especially about my working last night instead of spending the entire time with her. I left angry and curt. I stopped at the post office and answered Bost from the Versailles. Camille Sée. At half past twelve Poupette was waiting for me at the exit and we went by metro to Jussieu. We lunched in a rather good little restaurant, A l'Escalope, on rue Monge. Then to the lycée Henri IV. I got out at four o'clock and stopped by Gégé's, where I had a letter from Sartre. I wrote and worked at the Closerie des Lilas. Then I went to get the Kos. sisters. Kos., the real one, looked somber and tired; she sat huddled in her bathrobe and said she didn't want to go out. I talked to her very amicably. I carried away a mixed impression of disgust and tenderness. She looked so familiar to me and yet she often seems transfigured by Sartre's former love for her, by Bost's love—it seemed funny to leave her in her room, alone, dulled by sadness, and this solitude somehow took on the magic character she had in Rouen. We took Wanda along, nice looking in her little black sweater, which showed off a charming neck. Her hair is flat and pale, very short in a page-boy haircut, and her complexion is fresh; her face looks young and heavy. I was fascinated all evening by this moving and often childish face and understood what Sartre could love in her with so much tenderness. I find her touching. The Jockey Club was crowded

---

* Fellow students in Dullin's courses.

because of this new arrangement of dinner accompanied by a musical performance, which makes money for the club. Some young couples, among them the beautiful Mauritanian woman from the Dôme with a guy and one of the Negro women. We were seated on the platform, near the bar, at a strategic table overlooking the room. There were the two *chanteuses* of the other day, the little pleasant one wearing a long black dress, which suited her well, with a bodice like a bag of candies. The redhead was wearing a print dress, drinking champagne and having fun. There was also a brunette with a beautiful voice and big legs, wearing a sad-looking deep purple dress and looking like a maid. Strange evening. I got a letter from Védrine telling me that she wanted to go and see Sartre. That provoked passionate jealousy on my part. It irritates me that she appropriates him like this and that in her heart she believes that he is hers. Wanda does not bother me, on the contrary, I feel almost tenderness for her, but it also makes me sad knowing that in a certain way she also thinks of Sartre as belonging to her. I drank a big glass of calvados while the others drank whiskies, and I felt a great desire to be alone in the world with Sartre, with no one else, no one around us. We chatted; I wanted to chat with Wanda, but as soon as I said something Poupette interrupted to go one better; it was annoying. Wanda was so beside herself with politeness that all she could say in a lively and spurious way was, "Oh, that's funny," to anything we said. At eleven o'clock the proprietor politely threw us out. We went home. I went up to Kos., who was already in bed asleep. I said good night to her affectionately and even kissed her and she seemed affectionate too. I wrote Sartre a long, long, somewhat troubled letter.

Friday, 27

Very amicable breakfast with Kos. and Wanda. A slight hint of last night's animosity was still in the air. I wore Sartre's beautiful white sweater with a purplish scarf and the purplish turban; it really looked stunning. I ate and worked a little at the Capoulade; then three class periods at the lycée. Each day the principal circulates some memoranda and twice a day a list with the volunteers and monitors in charge of closing the windows in case of an air raid warning, etc.—she's a maniac. Sorokine, who was supposed to meet me after class, wasn't there. I waited for ten minutes; it was cold; I wanted to work and cowardly took off for the Mahieu, where I worked. Then I went to get Bost's letters and wrote to him from the Versailles—afterward I met Poupette at the Dôme.

Stépha happened to be there too; she had fled her apartment because it was too cold. But when we got there at eight o'clock, we found the small room upstairs well heated by two electric radiators. We dined on slices of dark bread covered with tomato paste, herring, and red caviar, washed down with vodka. Then we played a game of dominoes. At that point the Pardos arrived with Jean Ossola* in tow. We had Gégé play with us. She looked pretty in her gray-green dress with a mauve scarf—and Pardo and Ossola, sitting on the couch, were bored. "I don't like parlor games," said Pardo haughtily. He took advantage of a pause to question Gérassi [and me] about the end of the war, but we sent him packing. He thinks the war will never end, it's easier that way. They all talked about going to Santo Domingo. It seems that the dictator there has opened the doors to a hundred thousand refugees and is requesting intellectuals.

Pardo left in a huff with his soldier, and we played poker until half past eleven.

Saturday, October 28

Slept very badly. I woke up with a headache. Two classes at the lycée. At the exit I found Sorokine out of sorts because of yesterday, but she quickly got over it. I was very nice, but on the whole, I don't treat her too well, the poor puppy. This morning I took her along on errands with me: going to the police station, nothing yet—buying a roll of film, pomade, and batteries for little Bost. At the post office was a long letter from him sent Tuesday night—it filled me with affection for him. Some very long letters from Sartre, so intimate, so tender. But I am nervous because of everything concerning their coming home on leave. I'm getting used to the idea that I will scarcely see Bost, but I am like Sorokine often is, I'm afraid of suffering, I think ahead of time that I'll suffer and I'll be without resources, Sartre far away, that will be extremely difficult. As for Sartre, I'll see him, I'm sure of it, even see much of him, but I'm annoyed because of his parents and Wanda. If I could only believe that I shall see him, then everything else will fade away to make room for passionate joy.

I saw Kos.; we lunched together at Pagès and chatted until three o'clock. Letters, work—a telegram from Védrine suggesting she'd come today, but I did not respond because I didn't want her to come. At half past six Poupette came by. We had dinner at the crêperie on rue Pauline, then we settled at

---

* The nephew of Guy de Maupassant.

the Dôme and I finished reading Sartre's letters. I remembered many incidents that I had forgotten and gained an overall view of his existence—I felt full of happiness and love for him. We went home—washing, beauty care. I fell asleep toward midnight after having brought this diary somewhat up to date.

Sunday, October 29

I slept very poorly. I got up exhausted with my head aching. It was raining. I put on my old red jacket with a yellow scarf and a yellow turban; it looked very pretty. I took a taxi to Bonne Maman, where I picked up Poupette and took her to the station. She was loaded down with canvasses and stretchers. I left her, feeling greatly relieved. Number 11 took me to Montparnasse from where I sent a package to Bost and where I had a very nice letter from him. I went back to work for an hour. Had a friendly letter from Toulouse and an annoying one from Védrine: "Send all these people packing," her sense of empty self-importance must have made her write that. Meanwhile I had an hour of profound happiness writing my novel, feeling liberated from Poupette and facing a life where I shall be able to work.

I knocked at Kos.'s room. She was all mournful and touchy with a terrible toothache. (I returned a wallet stuffed with money to Wanda. She had lost it in the ladies room.) Wanda was in my room—so pleasant with its full-length mirror, and the table full of her things—in the company of her friend Arlette Ménard, whom she met again at the hotel and who is quite a tart. Kos. told me how for a while this girl earned three hundred francs a night as *chanteuse;* she also worked in the movies. Kos. told me other entertaining hotel gossip. The Swedish woman of the other day is a hysterical alcoholic who gets drunk all the time and her guy beats her when she has had one too many to keep her quiet. In No. 7 lives a hermaphrodite, a Viennese woman, legally male with a female constitution, but the sexual organs of a man, a beard, and hair on her chest. Besides many problems with her love life—because she appeals only to homosexuals—she has other, more serious problems. Germany claimed her for military service and in France she was put in a concentration camp. When she took her clothes off, people realized with horror that she was a woman. She cries all the time. Kos. left me alone for five minutes. I had the bad idea of looking at a letter from Bost: "I remember very well when I told you: I am your lover. That was in Arles, not in Avignon . . ."—suffering. I recognized in a faint, less intensive form this unpleasant feeling to which I could not give in—I must smile at Kos., who was returning to the room—the extent of which I was even unable to fathom right there; so I must keep it to myself. I'll see to it later, but already during the silent pauses in the conversation, I tried to defend myself: That was before this year, he really wasn't that much in love with her, etc.—weak excuses. He loves her and I know it. As an abstract idea I accept it, but I will cease being jealous only when I cease loving him. I tried to take into consideration our relationship as a whole, so that it may be possible again for him to love her and for me to love him though I feel too depressed to make this effort. I left for the Coupole wallowing in this unpleasantness and rehashing it until it lost all its flavor; it's such an old trick—what is essential is that when I see him I'll be happy with him, why want more? But I'm a stickler. I have seldom been in such low spirits as I was during that hour. What a strange situation, being jealous of a person who lives in such proximity; jealousy feeds on it. No fever of passions, only total despondency. If only Sartre was there to put some sense into me as he did in Juan-les-Pins. The idea alone made tears come to my eyes. (That's a clever switch, there's an obvious and clear sadness to which one can willingly give in—the other was suspect and so undesirable.)—there you have it. I wrote it all down, and I have calmed myself a little. Everything has become dull—Bost's love for Kos.—for me—Kos. and Bost and myself, no more reason to suffer anywhere. And the knowledge that Sartre exists was suddenly brought fully back to me.

I went back up to see Kos.—we went to the Rotonde, which was gradually getting crowded. We stayed chatting until half past four. Afterward we took a taxi to go to a concert. The conservatory hall had a sad-looking courtyard and a sad-looking entrance hall; but the concert hall is not too unpleasant with its Empire-style décor. They played *Les Indes galantes* by Rameau, a Concerto in D by Haydn, Beethoven's First Symphony, and Ravel's *Le Tombeau de Couperin,* which we found charming. Then dinner at the Milk Bar; we chatted a while in my room and I wrote to Védrine and Bost and a long letter to Sartre. I was writing with tears in my eyes, because the desire to see him was choking me.

Monday, October 30

After spending a short but good night, two class periods at Camille Sée. Sorokine was waiting for me in the hallway. We went to the police station, waited for a while, and when I gave my name, the man looked at me with a knowing and promising expression. I got my permit! I could have jumped for joy. The permit is valid until next Monday. I can go as far as Nancy, but that'll give me five full days if the doctor gives me my certificate in time.

Sorokine was very happy to see me happy and quite charming, and I was nice to her, as nice as I could be. I took her with me running errands, the poor girl: collecting Sartre's money, going to the Jardin des Mots [bookstore], buying books for Sartre and Bost and sending them off, etc. We had lunch at the small Alsatian restaurant. I gave her a hundred francs and some presents, including photos of me. I had coffee in a pleasant bistro at the corner of the rue de la Montagne and Ste. Geneviève. Then two hours teaching at the lycée Henri IV, afterward to the post office; I had long letters from both Bost and Sartre. I went home to go to bed and call a doctor. Kos. lent me beautiful blue pajamas and I spent a voluptuous moment writing letters and this entry while lying in bed, full of energy, happy and warm. I was tense waiting for the doctor. The realization that I was going to see Sartre had not struck me yet. But once I have my certificate, my joy will know no bounds.

I waited until half past eight reading *Les Mutinés de l'Elseneur** [The Mutineers of Elsenor] and chatting once in a while with Kos., who paid me brief visits. I was really resting so that I had almost the impression of being truly ill, a benign illness. At half past eight Kos. went downstairs to look for the doctor. He was coming up the stairs and she came back up with him, announcing, "The doctor is here." I slipped a little further under the blankets and prepared myself to complain. Kos. left to go up to the next floor and the doctor entered. He had graying hair that was combed back, wore tortoise-shell glasses, and looked the part, dynamic, young, and stupid. He palpated me and immediately arrived at an idea that I docilely followed: Alas, he believed in a simple muscle ache and asked me in true Knock style:[15] "You didn't climb up a rope? You didn't lift heavy suitcases? Very strange." He also asked me very pointedly, "Don't you sometimes have the impression of sitting on a pebble?" He believed I had indigestion due to cold feet, but went nevertheless to get some small instruments to make sure I didn't have appendicitis. Kos. came downstairs again; I told her what went on; when the doctor returned, she escaped once more. "My friend can't stand the idea of a needle," I said, because he was a little disappointed. He was having a fine time going slumming in this little hotel with such funny women. He pricked my finger and drew my blood with a small pipette, then diluted it in a green liquid. We were exchanging lighthearted banter and I was forgetting that I

---

* By Jack London.

was in terrible pain—he took his booty with him, Kos. came back, the doctor came back, Kos. took off again. He found that I had a blood count of seventeen thousand white blood corpuscles, which was too high, but not sufficient for acute appendicitis. He sounded my chest and began to lecture me on the dangers of cold feet, lifting his pant leg to show me his long underwear. He also told me about the circulatory loop in Negroes and Eskimos. "When a Negro steps out of his hut and puts his bare feet on wet grass, he experiences right away an intestinal reflex," he said. He ended his lecture with general considerations and in the end gave me my certificate, prescribing sick leave until next Monday. After he left I cried, "Boo-hoo!" and Kos. came running from her room, afraid I was being tortured. She came down and we chatted until half past midnight. Between the two doctor visits she had secretly fed me three eggs and two big pieces of cake, but I still felt a little starved. I packed my suitcase and washed up; I felt as happy as possible and slept very badly.

Tuesday, October 31

I got up at half past six, got dressed, and went down boulevard Montparnasse, still engulfed in the darkness of night. The Dôme and the Rotonde were just beginning to stir. I took a taxi to the Gare de l'Est. I would leave on the exact same train and from the same platform as Sartre had two months ago. With a ticket in my pocket I went to a bistro for a cup of coffee and a croissant while writing a few lines and addressing envelopes, a whole stack of envelopes, which I stuffed with letters already written. My Paris life now well organized behind me, I slipped the stack into the mailbox and boarded my train.

It was packed with troops. But still, I found a seat. The man next to me had one hand with fingers like a horse's hoof and a ruddy and stupid face. The others were reasonably bright peasants returning from an agricultural leave. They played *belote*,[16] said little, and were not unpleasant. I soaked up their way of speaking, their smell, their clothing, and began to immerse myself into Sartre's and Bost's world—an ambiguous impression: some horror at the thought that these fellows might get into harm's way. And yet, I couldn't quite believe it; the war still looked like maneuvers, a fake war. I went to the dining car for a cup of tea, read *Barnaby Rudge* by Dickens, which is good, and watched magnificent fall landscapes. For a moment I realized that I was going to see Sartre and had a moment of perfect happiness. The countryside was flooded. Those trees and hedges emerging from giant ponds looked both poetic and cataclysmic. We passed Bar-le-Duc surrounded by low hills in fall colors. I thought it would be easy to go and see Bost. I returned to my coach and spent the rest of the trip quietly reading *Barnaby Rudge.*

Nancy, one o'clock in the afternoon. They didn't even ask me for my permit. I went down a broad street carrying my little suitcase. Dead silence; the boutiques were open alright, the confectionery shops filled with candy, huge caramels, looking freshly made, but not a soul in sight. The city looked as though it had been evacuated; it had quite an impact on me. I reached the place Stanislas, which, with its mysterious gilded grillwork, had always struck me as poetic when reading about it in Barrès's novel *Les Déracinés.* The square was indeed beautiful, in this deep stillness under a blue sky, and behind its golden gates the russet of the park's autumn foliage. I went to the military general headquarters at the place de la Carrière; from there I was directed to the gendarmerie, which was still closed. I decided to have a bite to eat first and crossed the park, a magnificent vast park, it too in autumn colors. Suddenly, the strident sounds of sirens. People, however, did not seem to panic; on the contrary, they were more numerous than a while ago. I thought it was an exercise that the people of Nancy were familiar with, but still, I was surprised. And finally, I understood: I had arrived in the midst of an alert, and this was the all clear. That's why the city had looked so dead. Now there was life; I discovered the main street lined with numerous Uniprix stores, movie houses, and restaurants. It reminded me of Strasbourg but less pretty and picturesque. Nearly all the houses were barricaded with wooden planks, which gave the town the appearance of an encampment. A fellow called out to me, "When I look at you, lady, I think I'm back on the Paris boulevards." It's because of my yellow turban. I entered a restaurant crowded with local customers. I was blissfully happy. I ate as much pâté as I could and an enormous piece of blood pudding cooked with apples and had white wine to accompany the meal. But I didn't linger, I returned to the military police headquarters. A dense crowd had lined up. People were stepping on each other's feet; a woman was complaining about her phlebitis. Another one was in tears; she had just learned about her son's death. Any permit for Mulhouse was refused by order of the general. Everyone spoke German, even the soldiers. After about half an hour I reached the head of the line; they took my paper. The fellow shook his head when he read "Brumath" and went to see the lieutenant. I hurried after him. The lieutenant looked at me through his glasses: "You're not going to see a boyfriend of yours, are you?" I protested and he granted me twenty-four hours. I left bewildered and disappointed. Only twenty-four hours; would it be possible to get an extension? If not, it meant that I wouldn't be able to spend my Christmas vacation there. It was more complicated than it seemed. The weather was still gorgeous. I crossed the park and went strolling along the canals in a melancholy mood. I remembered vacations in Bruges, the canals in Amiens. My heart felt a chill and everything seemed unreal. I went back to the station and in a vast, sad-looking restaurant decorated with huge sad paintings, I wrote to Bost. I don't really know why it made me think of Cologne, of the square in front of the station and the restaurant from where I wrote to Guille. At that time, I was also going to see Sartre and felt vulnerable. That's what both situations had in common, I thought, and a certain similarity of the vicinity of the train stations.

At six o'clock I was on the station platform. It was cold and my feet hurt from having walked so much in high heels. We were waiting for the train. Our crowd was made up of civilians and military personnel. The night was very dark. Blue, red, and whites lights were flickering on the tracks, but they were never the lights of the train, only lanterns. Sometimes a train stopped, but it was never the one we were waiting for. Seven o'clock, then half past seven. Fatigue, cold, and unreality. At last the train arrived; lots of pushing and shoving. The train was packed, but somehow I found a corner seat in the first compartment. Many Alsatians; a big woman was snoring so loud that it made everyone in the compartment laugh. No one spoke French. The people were calm; hard to believe that the train was headed toward the front. I remembered the flight of the Parisians toward Quimper, how different this was. Here one felt that the world was still solid and whole. I dozed a while. Outside, a bright moon over a flat and frozen landscape. The train stopped at every station and I was on the lookout because I didn't know where Brumath was. We passed through Sarrebourg and Saverne, and then the train emptied out completely. I remained alone with a soldier. I started to get the feeling of a real adventure. Only five stations left to go. The story was becoming true. Two stations, then one and I was in Brumath.

I got off on a dark platform and followed the people; no one asked me anything at the exit. There were soldiers, but they didn't stop me. An inn had its lights on near the station, then a long deserted road in the moonlight. I thought with amazement and disbelief, "Sartre is here somewhere." And yet, I believed in what I was doing. I deciphered Taverne de la Rose and was touched. That's where he goes for breakfast. I was looking for a hotel and knocked at the door of the Hotel Lion d'Or; no one answered, but a light was flashed on me. It was a patrol; a curfew was in force after midnight. I showed my papers and two friendly soldiers suggested that they escort me. They were from Paris themselves and we chatted mundanely. With their rifle butts they banged against the shutters of the Écrevisse, but no one answered. For half an hour we walked about. Finally, at the Ville de Paris I entered a shed, then a backyard, and then a door leading into the house. Over a door a sign "Proprietor." I knocked and a big blond Alsatian opened up. He gave me an icy cold room with two beds. Shivering I got ready for bed and slipped between the cold sheets. I was nervous and tense—but I fell asleep nevertheless having first set my alarm clock for seven o'clock.

Wednesday, November 1

The alarm clock rang stridently. I jumped out of bed into the cold, slipped into my coat, and walked over to the window. A gray dawn. All the houses were shut closed. Nobody on the streets except a few soldiers. Bugle calls. I wasn't happy, but rather worried and wondering how I could get in touch with Sartre, whether I would be turned back, how to obtain an extension. All these questions felt like vague threats surrounding me, depending on the whim of one of the fellows, on the contingency of a chance meeting or a mood. The impression of an adventure stayed and despite the worries it was deeply romantic to wake up in this little village. Trucks stopped below my windows; sound of footsteps, voices, and people being loaded onto the trucks. I was desperately afraid that Sartre would be among them today of all times; afraid of being upset, and of the emotional breakdown it would cause me. I quickly dressed and went down to the Taverne du Cerf; it was strange to confront the real places with the way I had imagined them when I made my conspiratorial plans. Long wooden tables, chairs with rush seats, a large tile stove. The place was still half-asleep and the windows were open. It was cold and I didn't feel safe. The two women looked good-natured enough, but when I asked them for the address of the school and they told me "headquarters," I stammered that I wanted to see someone there. I wrote a brief note to Sartre: "You forgot your pipe on the terrace of the Cerf; it is waiting there for you" and I went out into the muddy street. I passed a porch, crossed a kind of empty lot, and noticed a big modern red brick building with all its windows painted blue, like stained glass. In front, a group of soldiers. I felt intimidated, but approached them anyway and asked if someone could deliver my message. "That must be some fellow in the office," said a soldier, perplexed, and promised to deliver the message in a moment. I went back to the hotel and on my way from there to the Cerf I caught sight of

Sartre's silhouette at the end of the street. I recognized his gait immediately, his figure and his pipe. But he had a horribly scruffy beard that disfigured him; he had not received my telegram and was not expecting me. I took him up to my room because the cafés were off-limits for us. We sat on the edge of the bed and talked for an hour. Seeing him did not have a very strong emotional impact on me; it was quite natural for me as though I had left him only a few days ago. I was less emotional than I was in Marseilles* after two weeks of separation and much less bewildered than at that time in Germany,† probably because of the letters. We were together for only one hour and I went back to La Taverne du Cerf, where I read Dickens. I was happy but not yet completely, the problem of the gendarmerie still tormenting me. Sartre and I put our heads together, but he seemed to say that the military police was quite strict. I am unflinching in my decision to stay be it at the risk of imprisonment, but the uncertainty made me tense.

At eleven o'clock Sartre returned, clean shaven, looking neat, his usual self. He and his associates are the only ones in blue air force uniforms; they don't look bad at all. No regiment number, like all the guys at the front. The tavern was packed, probably because of its being November 1[17]—soldiers in khaki uniforms with a beret or a policeman's cap with pompoms. They are the light infantry—some civilians, but very few. At a table in the back we ate a delicious pork roast accompanied by white wine and we also drank some plum brandy (which, incidentally was bad Cusenier). We decided to replace my sick sister with a cousin that Sartre would find for me. The women running the place were looking at us in a friendly way and I was beginning to feel less harassed.

Sartre was made to leave the Cerf at one o'clock and we went up to my icy cold room. He went to roll call and I to bed; I was completely exhausted and slept like a log for three hours. My alarm clock got me out of bed and while I was getting ready, the proprietress came up to tell me in Alsatian dialect that she had promised my room for the night to a lady who came from the interior of the country to see her husband. The local residents find this quite natural and turn into accomplices. One need fear only the gendarmerie. I didn't even protest, but just as a precaution, she yelled at me in Alsatian. I packed my bag and went to look for a room at the Lion d'Or and the Écrevisse, but in vain. I ran into Sartre; he had the address of an obliging laundress and while he attended to finding me a room I went to the police station. I was nervous; having been ill-informed I was looking for the offices

---

* Her first teaching appointment in 1932.
† When Sartre was in Berlin in 1933–34.

at first on the main street; then I went up to the second floor of city hall from where the police redirected me to the ground floor of city hall. The mayor was in the middle of an endless discussion—in Alsatian—with a sergeant and two husky civilians. He finally looked at my paper, understood nothing of my request for an extension, and stamped it without having a clue about it. A gendarme was called in to help out and he, impressed by the seals affixed to it in Paris, also declared that it was valid until Sunday night. I was deeply relieved and ran to the Cerf. The restaurant was packed with military personnel. The woman told me, "Monsieur has just left." I went outside and walked around in the dark, but it was impossible to distinguish anything from afar. I felt lost and went back inside, leaning on the bar. An infantryman came up to me; he was tall, rather handsome, with a little moustache and reeking of alcohol. "What, you're still here? We were waiting for you at the Écrevisse just now!" he said. I then remembered, as I was going into the police station, two fellows called out, "See you in a while at the Écrevisse!" I thought that they were the friendly soldiers from last night and that they were joking about our efforts of having the Écrevisse open up for us. I had smiled politely. But it turned out that he had a date in mind. I told him, "I'm waiting for someone," but I was embarrassed because I didn't want the whole world to know that I was here to see a soldier. "Why couldn't that be me?" he was holding me tight, got annoyed, and thought that I was a professional whore. "I know very well that you didn't come here with bellicose intentions"; if there happened to ensue only the slightest brawl I would really be in deep trouble since I didn't feel that I was there legally. A large buddy of his came to the rescue: "Well, are you coming with us or aren't you?" he said impatiently. A third fellow said to me on the sly, "Just drop them." "I would like nothing better than for them to drop me," I said despairingly. The drunken infantryman then added promises of protection to his threats. Looking me in the eye he asked me, "Well, are you with us or against us?" and as I said, "Neither one nor the other," he continued, "Are you Alsatian or French?" "I'm French," I said. "That's all I wanted to know," he said happily and mysteriously. He offered me his walking stick, a funny kind of big club, which I turned down.

Finally Sartre arrived looking for me; I motioned to him. "Someone down there is waiting for you impatiently," a soldier told him. We left and went to the Lion d'Or. I would stay at Sartre's landlady, but without him because when he had said, "My wife is coming," she had said with a shocked expression, "But you don't have a wife," and he had to correct himself, saying, "my fiancée." That made me sad, but in any case we were sure now that I would be able to stay several days. The Lion d'Or was packed: several civilians, even a woman who had obviously come to visit her husband, but on the whole they were military personnel that had come to eat and drink. We dined too, on sauerkraut and white wine. It was amazing, this mixture of worrisome adventure in cold and darkness and great Alsatian comfort. There were the full, deep voices, tobacco smoke, the smell of sauerkraut, and warmth. It brought to mind Munich and Strasbourg. Sartre pointed out that he was being addressed with "vous," that people spoke to him as a civilian because he was with a woman, which bestowed a civilian individuality and a privilege on him. We ate and talked and went to pick up my suitcase and get settled at Mme Vogel's place. We passed in front of the school, whose blue-tinted and lighted windows did in fact look just like stained glass windows. Mme Vogel received me amiably. She is an Alsatian brunette, rather young, and not at all bad looking and who speaks only German. Sartre talked to her a while. The room was barely heated, but it had a big soft bed, a tiled stove that was cold, and on the walls inscriptions embroidered on cloth in German: "Sleep without care!" Sartre could only stay for a very short while since the curfew for military personnel was at nine o'clock. Once more I slipped between ice-cold sheets. But I warmed up quickly and slept soundly.

Thursday, November 2

I got up at six o'clock to have breakfast with Sartre. I washed and got ready very quickly in the cold. This early departure on an icy and dark morning gave me a familiar impression that I couldn't identify. Every now and then a light was visible in the darkness. I would have liked to be in bed still and yet, the dark, the cold, and waking up so early were accepted and desired as conditions for happiness. It wasn't a reminiscence of some travel and yet it was the reminiscence of some happiness, which couldn't be defined. With this kind of vague poetic feeling I arrived at the Taverne de la Rose. The impression grew stronger without losing its vagueness. The tavern was very dark, the lights being covered with blue paper, and only one of them was lit. They were lighting the stove, the place was almost empty, and the women working there were barely awake. The dawn was full of promise, uncomfortable and still dark but headed toward joy. Sartre arrived almost at the same time. "He's laughing and talking today," said the woman good-heartedly as though she was referring to a kind of automaton. "Usually he is here reading." She pushed my books aside and in a conspiratorial tone she said, "There will be no reading today." They served us horrible Alsatian coffee, worse than the ordinary coffee served in hostels; it too had that poetic quality like the coffee at the railroad stations or the coffee served on our hikes. We talked for an hour in this semi-darkness. Sartre had to leave on some kind of survey and I stayed alone in this large empty room, which gradually became brighter. Outside, soldiers were passing by, shovels over their shoulders. One of the girls in the house, a redhead, put a cup of coffee with a glass of rum on the windowsill for the military policeman, who drank it while controlling the traffic in the intersection. He was wearing heavy woolen gloves and his breath rose like steam in the cold air. I stayed there feeling immersed in the world of war, it permeated me—I felt sublime and happy. I read Sartre's novel:* one hundred pages. For the first time I was reading such a large part at one time, and found it excellent. I made some critical comments—in particular about Marcelle's character, that it needed to be redone. Then I went to the Cerf, where I had a coffee while I continued reading Dickens. Sartre returned. We again ate sauerkraut with white wine, followed by plum brandy. As a result I felt a little dizzy from the alcohol when he left me. At half past noon two of his associates came by, the corporal Pierre, a shy intellectual, and the big Jew, Pieter, the resourceful one. Muller wasn't there because they had had a falling out with him. It was funny seeing them, as they were precisely as Sartre had described them to me, showing me much useless attentiveness. They left with Sartre to look for a room for us. I returned to the Taverne de la Rose where I chose a place near the window. Soldiers came and went. In the morning there was one who was holding the brunette very close. I wrote a long letter to Bost, a short one to Kos. and Sorokine. I mailed them and met Sartre's associates, who insisted on having Sartre come over right away. I went to Mme Vogel's, but it was closed and I had to wait in the rain for a long while. Sartre finally came. He found us a room at the Bœuf Noir saying it was for him and his wife. The local people oblige the military as they sustain their economy; they are much friendlier to a soldier than to anyone else. We went to the Bœuf Noir with me walking about ten steps behind Sartre to throw the police off our tracks. We spent one hour in the ice-cold room and then came down here. Everything had been arranged. I finally felt at ease and completely happy. We discussed Sartre's novel for a long time, and we talked about the war. He was convinced that there would be no fighting and that it would be a modern and crucial war without massacres, just as modern painting is without a subject, music without melody, and physics without matter; it brought se-

---

* *L'Age de raison* [The Age of Reason].

renity back to my heart. We also discussed our historicity. It felt great to talk to someone, to find my intellectual life again.

We had dinner—it was only mediocre. There were fewer soldiers than last night. Around eight o'clock I went to pick up my suitcase at Mme Vogel's and Sartre got a flashlight at the school; I waited in the damp darkness; soldiers returned to the school, their flashlights lighting the way. We went to our room too. I had thought that we would spend the night talking, but we had to go to bed because of the cold, and once in bed, sleep came fast. We were shivering in bed and it took a most skillful balancing act to keep the featherbed on and get warm.

A day of profound happiness.

Friday, November 3

This morning at half past six while I was pushing the door open to the toilet I suddenly understood why I had this poetic impression that I had not been able to identify yesterday morning: It was an emotional memory of winter sports. The same darkness, the same cold, the same effort made gladly in view of pleasures to come, when you have to plunge into the cold and dark of an early morning; the same smell of damp wood in the hallways. And in the morning in the greatroom the analogy continued. Just like the skiing instructors having a drink before the first run of the morning, the soldiers in uniform were standing at the bar; the cold and their professional work were waiting for them outside; it's a moment of fleeting comfort in a very wintry dawn. The impression finally faded toward midmorning, but in the early morning hours it was very strong. Here, I was also in a vacation-like situation, just as if I were on a winter sports holiday; no more lycée, no more friends and acquaintances weighing me down; solitude with Sartre in a village. This stay is a time for comfort and leisure. We went downstairs for breakfast in the restaurant of the Bœuf Noir. It was empty but already heated. The restaurant is rather pleasant, decorated with mounted butterflies, stag heads, and stuffed birds. However, after Sartre had left me, I changed over to the Cerf where I wrote in this diary and read Sartre's notebook*—I felt immersed in his life and the war and found it immensely interesting and gripping. I was wondering what impression it would make on someone who didn't know him and then would get to meet him. Great intellectual emulation; I too would like to have time to think more about myself. When Sartre

---

* He wrote down everything about his life from day to day and arrived at a kind of assessment of his past.

returned we talked about his notebook. We also talked about Védrine and Wanda—and were a little surprised that Védrine had lost some of our esteem and affection; I often see a caricature of myself in her I told him, but he assured me that this wasn't the case.

In the afternoon I came back here, wrote to Védrine and Bost. The stay here, my being emotionally drained and the serenity that Sartre gave me, only strengthened my desire to see Bost but cleansing it of any passion and situating it much more on the plane of friendship than of love—I'm thinking of conversations with no possible deception—rather than a desire for possession, for passion that is proscribed in advance. It seemed to me that reading Sartre's notebooks and just watching the soldiers passing by in the streets, coming in droves to the tavern or leaving at one o'clock sharp, and then trying to get back in on the sly during the day, helped me to understand a soldier's life much, much better now than before—indeed, a deep gulf separates it from civilian life. In Sartre's case, however, there has been no problem; we did not lose ourselves at all because of the social milieu in which we live, both at a distance and nearby. I needed only these few days to feel that I have lived these last two months entirely with him and erase the impression I had of being separated from him.

I mailed my letters at the post office and took a walk through the streets . . . but cautiously. At a grocery store I noticed two soldiers in front of an enormous jar of mustard. Never had I seen so much mustard in such a huge jar. They wanted to take the jar along, but the saleswoman didn't let them. "But I can't very well carry it in my hands," muttered the soldier and he added spitefully, "These Alsatians just have no business sense." There, again, is an example of the deep hostility between the so-called French and the Alsatians. The local population does not want to be evacuated because the rest of the country would consider them to be *Boches*.[18] Besides, they are calm and peaceful, even though they live only about six or seven miles from the front. What a difference compared to the panicky Parisians fleeing to Quimper and all those people in Brittany! Returning here to the tavern I read some letters from Védrine and Wanda addressed to Sartre. Wanda's letters were quite charming. A policeman was eying me, and I felt uneasy and suspect. I went up to my icy-cold room where Sartre joined me; then we went downstairs to eat and drink. We had a long and happy conversation. Sartre read this notebook and said I should develop it more—I'd like very much to do so if I had the time.[19]

We talked about Bost. Sartre explained to me again how in a way I preferred my relations with him just as they were and how Kos. was necessary to balance them out. He explained further that Bost did not *belong* to me because I did not *belong* to him. I gained an overall view of the situation that satisfied me. While I'm on the subject, I acknowledged that I omitted in this journal, and did not mention to Sartre either, one of the things that was most annoying to me: that his letters to Kos. were longer than his letters to me. I hadn't mentioned it although I had never been able to blot out the consciousness that I had of it, and also because magically I thought that Sartre would not know what to answer and then it would exist out in the open in a definitive and crushing way. Nevertheless, I told him afterward and my line of reasoning behind it. I also told him how irritating it was to know in advance that I would suffer during Bost's home leave—he is supposed to spend it with Kos. Theoretically this arrangement spares me from even worrying about having to face a choice. The fact that it has to be like this doesn't make me suffer, but I'm aware that hour by hour during his leave I will know him to be free within these parameters and freely in love with her. For me it'll be hell. And knowing about it can't change anything. That's what's so irritating.

Sartre told me he didn't feel that all my jealousies, my little heartaches and behavior concerning Bost, were so terribly bad. I, however, am embarrassed and never really honest about them. In a sense I home in on them because I like to plumb the depths of this affair as it concerns myself, live the situation to the fullest, even overdoing it—and then, regardless, I look at it from different angles, and when it gets too sticky I get out of the affair in order to free myself. I don't like that. The image of Jahan, Lumière,* and the heroine of *Intempéries*† haunts me, as do a thousand others—passionate and intellectual women who pretend to have chosen what they are made to endure and who believe themselves to be superior only when they get to the end of their resources. These reactions of healthy pride are not for me; "after all, this is happening to me, it's in my life," etc.; I prefer to humbly tell myself "it's nauseating" so as not to resemble these women. And this voluntary humility affords me some superiority, which isn't really sincere either. I explained this to Sartre, who said that I was sincerely discovering America. But the truth is that this psychological inner life is new to me. In the past I had primarily a moral attitude; I tried to believe I was what I wanted to be. This year, however, the presence of the contingent, the passionate due to Bost has been glaringly obvious. Now I enjoy it like a new field. I wouldn't enjoy writing about it, for it's too frivolous and mundane, but it's always interesting to discover and find out about myself. It's a step toward knowing myself, which is

---

* Colleagues from Rouen.
† By Rosamond Lehman.

beginning to interest me. I think that I'm becoming something well defined. In this respect I feel my age . . . I'm going to be thirty-two years old; I feel I'm a mature woman, though I would like to know what kind. Last night I spoke with Sartre for a long time about a point that specifically interests me about myself: my "femininity," and how I'm of my sex and in what way I'm not. This remains to be defined, as well as, in general, what I expect from my life, my thought, and how I situate myself in the world. If I have the time I shall address these matters in this notebook.

We went to bed, falling asleep toward half past ten. The weather was less cold. Another profoundly happy day.

Saturday, November 4

Once more we got up at half past six—breakfast. At half past seven I went back up to my room and shamefully went back to sleep until ten o'clock. This visit turned out to be one of blissful idleness, eating and sleeping. I no longer—or almost—felt that I was in a town at war. Outside nothing but uniforms, all the cars camouflaged, a constant stream of horses and trucks; all this seemed natural to me. I went to the Cerf and started to write down the history of these last days. I should write this journal from day to day, exactly as things happened, and in moments of intellectual leisure, not when I am tired. That would definitely be more productive. Had lunch with Sartre; again a succulent steak like yesterday. I wrote to Bost and then went to the station to find out that I am not leaving before eight o'clock tomorrow evening. Afterward I took a walk in the village. The weather was mild; Alsatian houses, without looking particularly picturesque, seem pleasant; soldiers playing ball at an intersection, others enjoying a breath of fresh air on a garden bench. Relaxed military life and entirely integrated into village life. Incidentally, this relationship puts its particular stamp on everything here: taverns for the soldiers, the local kid with his helmet, merchants who sell only to the military, the streets they march through, the houses and yards where soldiers are encamped; they represent the life and death of this place.

I read *The Idiot* at the Bœuf Noir, where Sartre joined me at five o'clock. We stayed a while and then went to dinner at the Cerf. As always it was packed with soldiers. We went to get some books at the school, and at night I had to wait a long time for Sartre. Old impressions of Tours and St. Cyr* came to mind, only simpler and more complete. As a young person, I think

---

* Where Sartre had finished his military service.

it is difficult to defend oneself against the impression of the marvelous. A little like Védrine, it goes along with importance: "It's happening to me, etc." I should think about what it consists in, this fact of getting older that I've felt so strongly in myself these last few years—because I've had a well-defined youth with lots of youthful faults—and that remains present in my mind. I can very well see the difference. There is something inauthentic in youth, as Nizan has said so well, and that's what Védrine illustrates perfectly. But nothing has grown stale about my feelings.

Sunday, November 5

The weather was mild today. When we came downstairs at half past six, I said to Sartre, "It's the thaw. De Roulet would say it's the *Foehn*."[20] We went to the Taverne de la Rose, where I read *The Idiot* for much of the morning until my eyes hurt. I sent books to Bost, and then returned to the Cerf to write to him, Poupette, and to Védrine as well. Afterward I continued reading *The Idiot*. Some fellow who works in an office struck up a conversation with me. He talked about Strasbourg's being deserted, except for some officials and a few civilians who had come to get their personal belongings but were not allowed to spend the night—and tobacco shops that were selling out quickly; otherwise, the city was basically dead. He said that people there expect peace around Christmas; he also said it was a diplomatic war, which would see no battles. The closer one gets to the front in this war, the more it loses its horror while also losing its poetry, just like impassioned jealousy. If it were a full-scale war, it would become more and more horrible, but apparently, it's the contrary. Paris reassures arrivals from L'Aigle and Quimper, and Brumath reassures those arriving from Paris.

We ate lunch and as it was Sunday, Sartre could stay until half past two. Then I went for a walk. What a lovely Sunday this was! Because it was warm and the sky blue and because I was leaving and no longer felt harassed and began to step back, I saw the village in an entirely new light. Until then it had simply been a village in France, a "somewhere in France" where I had come secretly to see a soldier. Defiantly I went from the Cerf to the Bœuf Noir; the roads didn't lead very far: military blockades were at half a mile in front and in back. It created a strange impression of closed-in individuality, but closed-in differently from the isolation that I like during my hikes. I love that natural isolation created by mountains, lakes, and distances, which presents a challenge waiting to be conquered by human endeavor. It draws its poetry from this possible endeavor and endows it with poetry as well. Here the land is flat, miles to hike are easy; but there is an artificial barrier that denies value to any undertaking on a human scale. The social world here engulfs nature and nowhere else do the body, the muscles, and in cor-relation, the sky, air, waters, and the hills, seem so useless.

Today, however, on the side streets near the tranquil canal, peace stirred below the surface of war. Blue road signs still exist indicating that the roads lead somewhere; they did not say that these roads were blocked. The roof tiles were covered by useless moss, the trees stood out against the sky, and the clouds seemed to exist indolently for themselves. At each step one's im-pressions are checked by reality. There was an old country bus, but it was really a camouflaged vehicle with a military driver and on the window, in place of an unfamiliar but distinctive village or proprietor's name, one could read "Military Mail"; dirt roads border on military encampments that are off-limits. All the same, the village is eaten up by these khaki uniforms, these impersonal divisions, and this wartime socialism. However, a timid personality makes itself felt in this magma: the village, closed in on itself, with its own means of communication and its resources of its own and for itself, instead of this administrative and nationalized reality.

Walking through these streets gave me a strong sense of joy. For the first time I didn't feel lost in the war with the idea that the more I felt lost, the more the war became a reality inside me. The war is an event of the world, which I grasp through my life—and just like once in Megève, I felt joy at the riches of the world and of my life. I also felt that I was a witness, a witness to this village in wartime as if I were beyond time and space.

For the first time also, after talking with Sartre about it, I came face to face with my life as it had been unfolding during this war. For the last two months I had lived my life simultaneously in the infinite and in the moment. I had to fill the time minute by minute or long hours at a time, but entirely without a tomorrow. It had reached the point that even the news of military leaves, which gave me hope by defining a future-with-hope, had no effect on me and was even painful to me, or almost. To be happy about the leaves I would have had to place myself within a limited future where absence and war would become accepted realities. Now, however, I am looking ahead to a year or eighteen months of wartime existence, filled with work, inter-spersed with leaves. This appears not as a moment outside of life to be got-ten through no matter how, but rather like a part of life that needs to be put to good use and lived fully. I am curious to know how things will turn out once back in Paris. But I feel so strongly about this that, when looking back, I almost consider these last two months as time lost in relation to a totality of work and thought.

I don't think that I shall engage in this kind of study and definition of myself. I would need to feel more like "being retired." Perhaps during my vacation—right now I feel the desire to work on my novel, to continue to live actively rather than take stock of myself. I have a great curiosity about the coming year—which begins only today. And I almost feel a desire to live life as it presents itself, without miracles from the outside.

Sartre met me at the Bœuf Noir at four o'clock. We were seated in a back-room, as the café was not yet open to the military. It was a nice spot to chat, at the corner of a long table covered with a blue-and-white oilcloth. Every so often someone opened the door and quickly retreated with an air of apol-ogy. Sartre was a little annoyed by a letter from Wanda, who was getting serious about him and wanted to visit him; she said that she has had enough of being a light and a fragrance; it seems that she now wanted to become a companion. Védrine in her letter boasted that she did not hate us; "if I were a bitch," she said, "I would hate you." We talked about this. Védrine seemed superficial to us with her outbursts of passion and excessive activity; with the way she feels, her world has not changed; except that from time to time, against this intact background, great waves of despair well up. On the con-trary, when Kos. feels depressed, or whenever it happens to me, the world changes calmly, but definitely; it is much more profound. Sartre told me that he understood very well that in times of war and absence I desired a hierar-chy and that he felt the same for me. In fact, when I am with him like this, there are no doubts.

At about five o'clock we went into the other dining room and ate blood pudding with apples amidst the crowd, the noise, and the smoke. I wasn't sad. It was dark already when we left; the night was mild with an immense starry sky. We passed by the school to pick up some books and Sartre ac-companied me to the square near the train station. In a small, dark street I kissed him for the last time. He disappeared into the night, walking very quickly. And I went in the direction of the train station. I could think only of the trip ahead of me and of getting some sleep; my head and heart were filled with some vague, tender feelings. The waiting room was dark and crowded with soldiers; I read *The Idiot* for a while; then we had to wait on the plat-form where it was warm; no one asked me for papers; civilians loaded with packages, many with backpacks; a strong odor of kirsch on the platform. The train was a little late and so crowded that we couldn't open the doors. I ran up to the first coach and got in after a bunch of soldiers; and yet, I found a seat immediately, right in the first compartment, in a corner. I sat down. The train moved slowly, stopping at every station until Saverne.

Saverne. Nine o'clock at night. A huge dark and busy station. When I asked an employee for the exit and the station restaurant, an aviator followed me. We went outside onto a completely blackened-out square. The aviator accompanied me to a hotel and argued through the glass door with the maid, whom he seemed to know well. They let us in; in a sad-looking dining room, with tablecloths, nevertheless, I drank lemonade, sitting across from the aviator, who was fooling around with the maid. Almost immediately we were chased out and had to return to the station. The express train was not to leave before midnight; I felt a little harassed. The station had only one restaurant—waiting room, where no drinks were served. The place reeked of war. The tables were pushed together and covered with sad-looking belongings: mattresses, blankets, the baggage of evacuees; the evacuees were huddled together on chairs in a thick cloud of smoke: smell of bad cigars, and the unhealthy heat of a stove emitting carbon monoxide. I remained standing in a corner while reading *Les Mutinés de l'Elseneur,* then I continued reading sitting down and finally went outside. In the underground passage they had piled up some bags; soldiers were sitting on them, eating, while others were resting on the stairs. The platform was so crowded with troops that you couldn't move. I remained standing, indifferent and like a Stylite, so absorbed in my thoughts that the one-hour wait went by without my noticing it. I felt a great desire to work, to think—I saw my relationship with Sartre and Bost, and the existence of Wanda, Védrine, and Kos. well in place, and was deeply satisfied. At the same time I had a very powerful impression of war. As Sartre had explained to me that this war "couldn't be found," I understood that, just like the God of *Les Nourritures terrestres,*[21] one could not find it at any particular place, but everywhere. And this crowded platform, *it* was war, just as much as Brumath and even Forbach.

The first train that pulled in picked up all the soldiers within three minutes. Only a few of us were left waiting for the express that arrived a little later. I got on and entered a comfortable compartment with green leather seats. "Are you alone" asked a husky Alsatian soldier, "then you may come in," and I settled down into a corner. A big civilian who had already changed his bowler hat for a cap and two soldiers, peasants from Deux-Sèvres, were the other travelers in the compartment; the soldiers were on a special mission. The Alsatian was a middle-aged soldier who was returning to his wife, leaving a son at the Rhine. He ordered a soldier to block the door, which he did by keeping it firmly closed even though people on the outside were yelling for him to open up. The Alsatian was clumsily bantering about the pleasure of traveling with a lady and climbed on the seat to scrape the blue paint off the light with a knife. It shone on my nose, my eyes, and my chin so I could read *Les Mutinés de l'Elseneur,* which I didn't find at all entertaining. They suggested that I lie down and sleep. The Alsatian put his greatcoat around me, and the civilian, wanting to go one better, gave me a beautiful soft pillow. I stretched out full length and felt blissfully content. My feet were pushing against the Alsatian; I drew them back, but he said, "Please, go ahead, it's the first contact I've had with a woman for twelve weeks." We passed around Alsatian marc and I drank half of the cup. It was excellent. It was all I needed to relax voluptuously and listen to their stories in my half-sleep. They told some more stories about the peace offensive: how Germans and French were fishing on each side of the Rhine, and how once, when a German machine gun was fired unexpectedly, a sign appeared right away with the following: "French soldiers, excuse us, it was a clumsy fellow who fired the shots. They were not meant for you." They talked about Strasbourg and the sad drama of evacuating the population. One fellow had cried when he returned to his home, which had been completely trashed. The soldiers were indignant and told about a house occupied by the military where a rabbit had been skinned by nailing it to a mirrored wardrobe. It upset them that a beautiful piece of furniture with its mirrors had been sacrificed in the process. They spoke kindly about their officers, mentioning that one captain had gone at night to a bistro, buying liquor for his troops. All the same, the peasants from Deux-Sèvres didn't understand much about the war. The Alsatian was holding forth a little and was bantering: "The two *chèvres* and the two billy goats. You're the two billy goats."[22] Then he laughed. He grabbed my feet, took off my shoes, and put my feet on his knees, asking me if that was all right. I answered carelessly, "You can do what you want with my feet." During the night I woke up with the sensation of my ankles being tenderly squeezed. But I drew my feet back and he didn't persist. I slept very well.*

Monday, November 6

The train was late, arriving at a quarter past eight. It was one of those beautiful golden, warm days, part of what is called the St. Martin summer.[23] In the washroom of the train I fixed myself up as best I could and jumped into a

---

* At this point the author discontinues the use of the *Wartime Diary* in *The Prime of Life.*

taxi as soon as I arrived. I got to the lycée at half past eight sharp. Two hours of teaching. Then the principal called a meeting to discuss the matter of aiding evacuees. The discussion turned around sweaters, sewing materials, and how to collect the necessary money from the students. I went to sleep. Again a taxi; I went to the post office on rue Littré. With a friendly smile the employee handed me my letters: six from Bost and five from Sartre. With this huge package I went to the Versailles. I read Bost's letters one after the other. I feel great love for him; no more passion, but full of feelings aroused by everything I read in these charming letters. They contained many tender hints and I feel that he loves me and think he's just wonderful. With an élan of joy I was anticipating the moment when I'll see him arrive at the railroad station. I read Sartre's letters. I didn't expect much from them, but I was wrong. They impressed me with their liveliness and strength. He echoed everything he had told me in person and when he writes that he'll be very happy to see me, my happiness and peace are twice as great. When I left the café I felt happier than I had been in a long time. That's how happiness used to be in peacetime. My entire life and my feelings are all around me, strong and vivid. I was happy to see Kos. again. It's amusing to think that the two Kos. are at the hotel. It feels like home to me.

I had my hair washed before going up to see Kos. She was very charming when she opened the door, charming with me and charming in herself. I was moved and felt great tenderness for her. She told me about her life during the past week. Then I went to wash up, dress, and pick up my mail downstairs. A pile of letters: from Sorokine, who seemed to feel good about me, a pleasant little note; letters from my sister, Védrine, and the Hungarian—which didn't interest me. Kos. and I went to eat at the bar of the Capoulade. I was quite moved to cross the Luxembourg Gardens and found it delightful to be back in Paris. Afterward two more hours of teaching—then on to Mangin's, rue du Havre, where I told Mme Mancy about my trip. Since it was Kos.'s birthday I bought her a beautiful briefcase of kid leather. I was retained in my room by Boubou for five minutes before I could join the Kos. sisters at the Vikings. Wanda got there first, fresh and pleasant-looking in her black pullover. Then Kos. arrived, delighted with the present I had left at her door. I told about my trip; then Wanda joined the Moon Woman, whom we noticed at the Milk Bar where I went with Kos. She seemed a little cool toward me, seeing that I had dropped her. Kos. was an angel. We spent a very good evening, which ended early because both of us were falling asleep on our feet. I had just enough strength left to write to Sartre.

Tuesday, November 7

A tiring and wasted day. I wrote to Bost from the Mahieu between eight and half past eight; it was a rather pleasant moment. Then lycée. Upon leaving I saw Sorokine, with whom I had an appointment; she was sitting on the steps, bare legs in heavy shoes and a red ribbon in her beautiful blonde hair. She looked like a little girl that had grown too fast; she was most pleasant. But there is something tragic in her life and her poor eyes were red from crying. I took her to a little café where she finally told me that her parents make her life unbearable. As she had broken two teeth in her father's comb, he had thrown himself on her, yelling and his fists drawn. Her mother also yelled. They called her a parasite and took two lousy francs from her that she had saved, calling her an old miser. I took her along to send books to Sartre. I met Jolibois,* who told me that Merleau-Ponty was near Longwy and that he felt bored. After some hesitation we each confessed that we just returned from a visit to the front. She had a pass only until Longwy, but no one asked her for any other papers. We ate at the Source with Sorokine, who accompanied me to the lycée. Three hours of teaching. A collection box for soldiers was placed right next to where you go and collect your salary at the bursar's office. I pretended not to notice. Goetschel and Liamley† were waiting for me at the gate. I took them to the Vikings but didn't find them at all entertaining. Their parents had succumbed to the bourgeois panic in September, taking them all across France. They said that crowds of students were attending the Sorbonne and even many foreign students. I went up to my place to work, but was bothered by some hysterical sobbing. A woman was wringing her hands, moaning, "It can't be true, it just can't be true." I had the impression that it was coming from upstairs, that Kos. had discovered everything and I was upset. I understood Bost's anguish. Anything would be better than that. It would be awful. At that very moment Jolibois arrived on the scene, simpering. She asked me for Sartre's address, but I nearly threw her out. It turned out that the crying came from below. It was probably a foreigner who was being deported, or the hermaphrodite. I was really too tired to work. I worked just a bit on my novel, then wrote to Sartre. Kos. came by at eight o'clock. We ate at the crêperie, then went to Hoggar on this beautiful evening, passing by the Luxembourg Gardens. We could hear owls hooting and the voices of soldiers behind the gates. In the distance, the noise of

---

* Merleau-Ponty's future wife.
† Two former students from the lycée Molière.

heavy gunfire. It was an impressive moment filled with poetry, under a sky brightly lit by the Milky Way. The Hoggar had been given a facelift. A strong whiff of peace came over me—how far away it was. The owner welcomed us. The place was crowded, and the clientele seemed somewhat shady. We chatted pleasantly and returned home around eleven o'clock at night.

Wednesday, November 8

A day of work. At eight o'clock I was already up and at half past eight I was sitting in semi-darkness at the back of the Dôme with my coffee and some newspapers. I read until nine o'clock and worked until half past twelve. Wanda arrived as I was leaving and I made friendly conversation with her for a quarter of an hour. Then I did some errands. At the Versailles I reread all of Bost's letters and wrote him a long letter. At my place I worked from half past two until five o'clock. Wrote a letter to Sartre. Then went to see the Gérassis, who are staying with some Germans in a beautiful apartment at the Porte d'Orléans. From the balcony you can see the blue sheds where the machines and equipment are kept, the suburbs, Mt. Valérien, and all of Paris. It's really beautiful. I told them about my trip and gave Fanny* a kind of certificate stating that she was very fond of France. I met Kos. at half past seven and we went to the Hoggar. We felt very much in harmony. We ordered a complete dinner: an oriental salad and couscous for me, and for Kos. a funny dish with eggs and little sausages flavored with aniseed, mint, and sugar.

Like the previous night, the clientele seemed somewhat shady. A fat little brunette was doing a belly dance in front of a tall Tunisian. Speaking about some fellow, she told the owner, "If he ever comes back, I'm out of here." At that moment a kind of yellow and nasty-looking Arab arrived on the scene. The owner refused him entry. They were yelling at each other: "You're not the one to tell me what to do!" yelled the owner; "neither am I going to let you tell me what to do," shot back the other. The fellow entered nevertheless and the following remark was overheard: "The establishment is now separate from the bordello." There must have been a moral straightening up at the Hoggar and the fellow hadn't probably been put straight and was now undesirable. The evening was beautiful and dry when we returned home. I went to bed extremely satisfied with my day. Five hours of work (chapter 9)—one hour of diary entries. And some long letters. It should be like this every day.

---

* A German friend, close to Alfred Gérassi.

Thursday, November 9, to Sunday, 12

Védrine's stay in Paris.

Thursday morning I got up early. The memory of the previous evening had left me full of zeal. At half past eight I was sitting at the rear of the Dôme and working until ten o'clock. Then classes at the lycée. When I finished at half past twelve I saw Sorokine in her new blue coat in one corner, her face turned toward a pillar, and in another corner, in her long beige coat, Védrine, who affectionately threw herself on me. I hesitated, saying that I had an appointment. She said to go ahead, we would meet at four o'clock. I wasn't very happy to see her because of the frenzied nature of her last letters and what Sartre and I had said about her.

I took Sorokine to the Latin Quarter by metro and since I told her about the Hoggar, she wanted to go there. I ate spiced fried eggs and she a couscous that she didn't think was good and didn't finish. She took out a little notebook where she had marked everything she had to tell and discuss with me, and she told me her whole life's story. But in the end we quarreled a little, as always, because she demands more time from me than I can give her. She hates my red-haired friend and would like to strangle her. When I left the lycée at four o'clock, she was still there. She came to make up; she was touching. Together we went down rue Soufflot and I went to the Mahieu. I said hello to Lévy, Kanapa, and Ramblin* and someone with big glasses I didn't know. I would have liked to stay with them—from time to time I enjoy disinterested, superficial, and easy relationships, but already I cringed at the thought that, instead, I would have to give myself over to Védrine's frenzied hands. Her cheeks were trembling with emotion and her hands were feverish. We crossed the Luxembourg Gardens and somehow she turned the conversation to my budget and the money I owe her father. She was calculating my expenditures and began to sort out my spending. It was absurd. I realized that her behavior stemmed from her very helplessness and confusion, but this combination of passion and practical consideration irritated me. I mentioned that I must go and let Kos. know that I wasn't going out with her at night and she got mad, and when I gave her to understand that perhaps I could see Kos. for an hour each day, she almost had a fit of hysterics right there on rue d'Assas. She was all keyed up with empty demands—I went to tell Kos., who accepted it good-naturedly, and I made a date with her for the following day, something Védrine held against me. We stayed in my room

---

* Védrine's friends, all students in philosophy.

for a while and she calmed down. She told me about her life in Rennes, which consisted of sitting for hours in a chair picking at her nails while conjuring up images, and added that this undefined inactivity was exhausting. I told her that this was mental masturbation; "but I also do the other kind," she answered. I explained to her that she must live our absence in its authenticity, that is to say, live in a world focused on us, on the place where we are, and not realize false presences. It's a self-destructive effort, which would leave her alone with her own substance feeding all her dreams, and which in reality would cut her off from us. The reason why she is so anxious and demanding is precisely because she is completely out of touch with our reality. She only writes short letters. Instead of spending more time creating a true connection through letters, she prefers to meditate in a void and cry and tremble. We went to the Dôme and wrote Sartre a very short note, but it was not pleasant to write like this. Then we took the bus to visit Agnès Capri.

We dressed with much care. Védrine wore her beautiful red dress and I a mauve blouse with a mauve turban. We were seated at a small table near the stage. We ordered a *salade provençale* and some cake, rather expensive. Gradually the club filled up. It had again the look of a show, which the last time had been lacking. There was a chic clientele paying big money. As usual, Sonia and her entourage were present, of course, and also the beautiful Mayarakis and women with pearls. We had a friendly chat; Védrine was relaxed and I felt at ease with her. As usual, Yves Deniaud was the *chanteur.* For his performance he wore a tuxedo, but afterward he returned dressed in a khaki uniform with his gas mask pouch slung across his shoulder. It had a funny effect. Agnès Capri sang new songs but the stories she told were especially charming. However, in the middle of a story about hares that had been placed in a mirrored wardrobe in order to refresh their hare-brained memory, she stopped with a confused smile. "I can't tell my stories when people are talking," she said. The talkative customers paid no heed and kept on talking while she sang. Others pointed their fingers at them whereupon they left in a dignified fashion. People applauded their leaving. "But they were my friends," said Capri when she came back into the room, pretending to be confused. At eleven o'clock we were thrown out and walked back home. I felt emotionally cold. Védrine talked to me about Sartre. All this time I felt the lie of their relationship and the danger that this lie implied because it had to be made to have the appearance of truth, nevertheless. We went to my room. In bed Védrine threw herself passionately into my arms. Her sensual swoons seemed terribly physical to me. But in a perverted kind of way I found the relationship more pleasurable than I normally do. By taking advantage at least of her body and being somewhat amused at feeling my sensuality deprived of any tenderness, I had the impression of being very boorish. It had never happened to me, or almost never (with Gérassi I had felt the vague tenderness of a drunk and then it was true physical turmoil, while in this case it was turmoil I consented to perversely).

Friday, 10—We stayed in bed late. Around ten o'clock we picked up my mail and had coffee at the Versailles. Some tender letters from Sartre, the first ones since my return. I don't feel that I have left him, now I'm "with him in the world" for a long time, I think. I met Kos. at half past eleven at the Capoulade. She feigned confusion at my arrival; she was supposed to attend classes but didn't go. We had lunch at the bar and I told her about the night before. She was very reserved when I spoke of Védrine, but extremely nice and told me lots of funny stories about Tyssen* that she heard from Lexia.† She also had stories to tell about Arlette Ménard and her guy, and about the hotel where we are staying, which, as it seems, is under strict police surveillance. She accompanied me to the lycée, where we noticed Sorokine, who was waiting for me but then went away with an awkward and contrite smile. It brought a laugh from Kos., who pretends to find Sorokine quite pleasant, partly in contrast to Védrine, I think. Three hours of teaching, which was too long. I escaped to a little café, Au Vieux Paris, on the place du Panthéon, which was terribly poetic, and wrote a short letter to Bost. I hate to write him in such a truncated fashion. Afterward I met Védrine at the Mahieu. We went to rue Vauquelin and picked up Guastalla's dossier, then to rue d'Assas for my letters. We then returned to the hotel, where we talked for a long while. Védrine continued making demands: She told me that she had reproached me for having incurred expenses because of Poupette, etc., thinking that I could have had her come to Paris more often—that she had wanted me to give up teaching, etc. I answered that she was smothering me a bit and I made an objective assessment of her character which included: Pathos—Seriousness—Importance,[24] and at the same time belief in a kind of platonic paradise to which she feels entitled, which leads her to feel constantly wronged. What I did not tell her was how deep her notion of entitlement goes. She listened seriously and was again interesting and nice while reflecting on what I had said and telling me her little fantasies, such as thinking of offering herself to her three young friends so they won't be leaving for war as virgins. Still that does not make her fantasies any less vulgar. This rational and organic sensuality shocked me. She is truly abstract and

---

* Berthe Tyssen, actress, and one of Dullin's students at the Atelier Studio, like Olga.
† Lexia, a friend of Olga and Wanda.

her feelings do not run too deep. She told me nothing, absolutely nothing interesting about her life in Rennes, the people she associates with, etc. She reads Spinoza, which is the extent of her intellectual pursuits, and otherwise gets along so-so with incoherent behavior and childish ideas.

We went to the Vikings and wrote to Sartre—then we went home and to bed. Embraces. A Negro was sleeping with the big blonde woman next door. During the night we had an air raid warning, which was a nuisance because I didn't want anyone to know that Védrine was with me. We hesitated a while, then decided to stay in bed. No one came knocking at the door. Above us we heard laughter: it was Wanda, Kos., and Arlette Ménard. I thought it poetic and pleasant to imagine their night during the air raid warning. I had seen Kos. in the evening, looking fresh and beautiful. She looks more and more like the forbidden fruit while Védrine seems to me like an old mistress with her demands, her claims to entitlements, and implacable presence.

Saturday, November 11—I woke up at half past seven, tired after a night of passion and air raid warning. Two more days to go with Védrine; it's weighing me down. She accompanied me to the Dupont for breakfast, then to the lycée in pouring rain. Sorokine was waiting for me when I got out—and Védrine was waiting for me in a café to take me to Kos., who was waiting at the Dupont. I felt terribly put upon. Sorokine, by the way, was very nice; she came to tell me that she had left her parents' home after calling her father "a piece of shit" since he had called her horrible vermin. She took refuge at her friend's house but didn't really know what to do next. I couldn't give her any advice. I met up with Védrine, who was reading Sartre's novel and talked to me a little about it. She accompanied me to the Dupont—no Kos. For half an hour I remained alone reading the Ellery Queen novel. It seemed too good to be true, this little scrap of freedom and leisure. Kos. didn't arrive until half past eleven; she hadn't gone to her classes because she didn't wake up. She told me about their night and lots of other stories and we discussed the classes she had attended the night before. The Sorbonne disappointed her deeply. Fortunately for her, Dullin's classes are resuming Monday. I enjoyed her company and would have gladly stayed with her a while longer, but I had to meet Védrine. I said hello to Kanapa and Lévy, and Védrine and I went to lunch at Mirov; it was not unpleasant at all. We were seated in the back at a quiet table with a little lamp and ate rather good Russian food. But the afternoon before us, how long it seemed! It was raining a little and we were tired from last night, our nerves on edge. We passed by the post office. One letter from Sartre and two from Bost. I couldn't read them leisurely, so I took them home with me and read them hastily while Védrine finished reading

Sartre's novel. Sartre's letters were so funny and tender—Bost's were full of impassioned friendship. But he told me that he felt sad and tense from Saturday to Tuesday, that it seemed to him that he just became reconciled with me; it's hard for me to think that he was holding a grudge against me. It's probably because I had said I would go and see him this Sunday and then didn't go. That must have been very annoying for him, I understand, but it upset me a little, physically. When I have a disagreement with Sartre I am all tense and ready to fly into a rage—like the time in July when he scolded me about Védrine. With Bost, however, I become physically sick. I think I have an idea why, but I'll have to look into it another time. We went down to the Dôme to study Spinoza. Our nerves were on edge for another reason also: we had a discussion about Sartre's leave. Védrine said that she wanted Sartre for six days and in a threesome to boot, and in addition she wanted him during my hours of teaching the other four days. I was flabbergasted and told her, "Five days, agreed." I also told her to give him a breather and not to throw herself on him as soon as I leave him for two hours and that perhaps he would like a few minutes to himself. "But why would he," she asked naively. She really is like lichen;[25] besides, she said so herself that she views love like a symbiosis. The fact that someone finds pleasure in being alone and breathing freely for a while goes completely beyond her. When I told her in a nice way that it was after all a great sacrifice for me to let her have Sartre for five days, she seemed surprised. "You have lost the sense of the threesome," she pronounced with an air of authority. I was extremely irritated—even though I knew for a fact that we would hide his home leave from her—and she was also very morose. My head felt heavy and I had a difficult time explaining Spinoza. The Germans were threatening to invade Holland. People were selling small artificial flowers for the poor soldiers. Pardo passed by, fat and smooth, with one of those flowers, a poppy, in his buttonhole. We wrote to Sartre. Védrine wanted our letters short, the night before also—she is not connected to the people she loves. But, nevertheless, we wrote for a rather long time. I also wrote to Bost. When we left the café, we went for a walk through the dark streets; both of us felt out of sorts with our nerves on edge. She began to tell me she was angry because I wouldn't leave her six days with Sartre, considering that I had such an outstanding debt toward our threesome. I felt extremely irritated and asked her bluntly if she really envisioned that we make a bipartite division of Sartre in our lives. She said yes and I said that I had never wanted that—that it seemed unfair to me since in the past I had totally shared my life with Sartre, and now she intended to leave me only one-third and compensate for it by letting me have one-third of my life with her. She defended herself fiercely. We went back to my room and she sobbed, saying that I loved Sartre more than her. I never told her the contrary. I hate how easily she creates illusions for herself. She has done this from the beginning of our relationship and not because of me but really in spite of me. I told her frankly that I needed Sartre more than I needed her. For a moment we were confronting each other like two enemies. Then she calmed down and I explained to her that her justice was not fair because I was not in situation in relation to Sartre in the same way as she, etc. I convinced her somewhat. But what really convinced her was an appeal to herself. She recalled that in the past she viewed the threesome quite differently. However, I really dislike her way of attaching an exorbitant price to her love, believing that it can compensate for anything. It's a childish presumption combined with an embarrassing humility as soon as someone takes a jab at it. A little like a madman who pretends to be Napoleon and suddenly agrees modestly, "Yes, I am a barber," if someone affirms it as a fact. We had dinner at the Select, where I painted a lively picture of the difficulties I had with Sartre over the ten years of our life together, stressing the fact that it did not constitute a debt of heavenly bliss, but a situation in the present in relation to him. She seemed convinced. We returned home. The night was pathetic—passionate, sickening like *foie gras* and not of the best quality.

Sunday, November 12—We got up late and had breakfast at the Milk Bar, then went to get some books at the Hotel Mistral. We went by bus to Montmartre and took a walk on the boulevards and on the Butte. We had a drink in the little red café on Montmartre, warm and welcoming as always, and then walked down rue Pigalle all the way to St. Lazare station. Almost all the nightclubs were closed; however, a few open timidly at seven at night and close at eleven. Védrine was wearing her blue suit, her little fur hat, and her muff. She looked very pretty—and she was in a meditative state of mind and well behaved. I felt affection for her because she was going to leave, because last night's conversation freed me from her, and because she was in a reflective mood. I explained to her that she must imagine herself in the center of her life, not us; she must become a person who is in touch with her own self. She said yes, but it seemed difficult to her. As she says, she is an extremely public person, not like Sartre, who readily consents to being in the public eye, but irresistibly and organically. It's rather disgusting—there must be a minimum of distance and detachment in one's relationships with people. When one makes Védrine reflect, when her problems force her to do so, she can make this new start and then it is possible to be conscious of her and love her. All day she was charming, full of wise resolutions and

147

morality. I felt a little mean because I had talked to her out of nastiness, irritation, and harshness and she wasn't mad at me for it; on the contrary, she took my words as a starting point for a moral reform. I tried to tell her that, but it only made my disgraceful behavior worse because she protested passionately and said it seemed generous to her that I was accusing myself. There was nothing I could do but keep quiet. Yet it bothers me about her that sometimes you can deal with her on an objective, factual, and impersonal level and immediately afterward you are back on a subjective level of passion. If one wants to get out of it one stirs up an endless reflection and gets more and more bogged down. Therefore, one must not be carried away by a favorable opinion of her but treat her like a little girl. I accompanied her to the Montparnasse station. She was touching, refusing any emotional pathos, and we experienced a real moment of true affection and trust. For a long time she stood in the door of the train holding my hand, then waved to me as the train started moving. I left her, feeling ill at ease because of my remorse and affection, but nevertheless free and happy to be so.

At the Select I wrote to Sartre and Bost, then met Kos. at the hotel. She gave me a cool reception, somewhat unintentionally hostile, and she was gloomy. We had dinner at the Select, where she told me some gossip: how Wanda, the Moon Woman, and Arlette Ménard spent the night with three guys from the Hoggar. The Moon Woman had suggested that Wanda stay with her and when she left her she said to Wanda's suitor in a severe tone of voice, "As for her, don't touch her, she's a special case." She also told me about a movie with Mae West and then stopped, stating ironically, "I'm not going to tell you the whole movie." She knew from the proprietress that Védrine had slept in my room and talked bluntly about it. I talked to her about Védrine but was embarrassed and she was quite grating. We left and went to the Vikings café. She told me that she was in trouble because she had again stopped writing to Bost and now feared she couldn't get herself to start anew. He was complaining that her letters were dry (I found that amusing for I think he complained about her letters because he compared them to mine) and she said, "But I'm not thinking all the time about Bost." She also asked how meaningful could be a relationship with someone you see only ten days every four months and she concluded that there was nothing left of it. Her voice betrayed a grudge she was harboring against Bost. I knew why this was so because she was angry about his reproach, but I was pleased. I think he is safer with me than with her; I know I can love him better than she can and that is one of the things that is most important to me. Our conversation got friendlier as we were talking. Kos. felt gloomy and worn out, and so I talked affectionately about her. In the end she felt again on good terms with me and we continued our conversation in my room. I didn't go to bed until midnight and even finished reading Ellery Queen in bed.

Air raid warning. We are getting used to it. It hardly wakes me up now. But the loudspeakers and whistles disturb your sleep.

Monday, November 13

I woke up tired but happy, divinely happy first of all about my freedom. The idea of writing my diary, my letters, and breathing freely I found so attractive that I didn't even feel like working. I was ridiculously happy about Bost–Kos. It amused me because it was a peacetime reflection, all those preoccupations. But most of all, I was happy because I truly felt I was in the same life, the same world with Sartre. I am not speaking of memories or expectations; I'm in the same world in the present, and distance is not a separation. To feel happy in the everyday and the contingent gives me immense pleasure. This hadn't happened since the war started. Nevertheless, I felt some remorse thinking of Védrine, alone in Rennes, struggling with all those problems weighing her down.

Breakfast at the Dôme while correcting papers. From half past eight to half past ten teaching. Then to the post office, where two letters from Sartre were waiting. They were so loving that they filled me with poignant happiness—one of those rare feelings of complete and exhilarating happiness, which seems to give us a glimpse of our entire happy life. He had included some delightful photos of him with wind gauge and theodolite. He looked like a Velasquez dwarf, as he himself said. I had tears of joy. Delightful letter from Bost. The thought that I had drawn closer to his life brought him closer to me, I believe. I understand this well. I also understand him being apprehensive about seeing me and yet, I would like to go and see him. I ate a pork chop, wrote Sartre a long letter, and did my diary. I felt happy and content all over. At about half past one I went out. On rue Vavin, in front of a leather goods store, I saw this fellow in rags, unshaven, and haggard looking, and a little deranged. He was looking; looking neither with admiration nor revolt, but with astonishment; it was pure astonishment through which the man-boutique couple revealed itself to me not so much as a social but a metaphysical scandal. He talked to himself, pressing his nose against the window, he talked to the objects and stepped back, then he moved away and returned, fascinated. I too was fascinated. I felt the world of this man as an absolute; the boutique speaks to other absolute consciousnesses, and these absolutes are mutually exclusive. I left, deeply affected by this incident.*

I walked through the Luxembourg Gardens; the trees had lost all their leaves, but a beautiful russet carpet was covering the ground. Paris was wrapped in a blanket of gray mist. Pantheon Square left a strong impression of Paris in wartime; rue St. Jacques, though running straight into the heart of Paris, was almost deserted. People, looking correct and stern, were not out for a stroll. The world seemed impoverished and diminished: only one place left for each thing and one thing for each place as in certain streets in Berlin. And yet, it was poetry, gray poetry of Paris and autumn, but more like a poetic abstraction. It reminded one of Rilke, it was the Paris of Rilke, but it was also war, an atmosphere of mysterious fog, but over a sober glaze. Density but hollowed out, emptied. "A wartime afternoon in Paris in the fall"—as Sartre said in *Nausea*. Saying these words very fast could best sum up this nature. When I finished teaching at four o'clock, the mood was still the same and guns were rumbling. At the bakery, people were discussing the air raid warning during the night. Some had gone downstairs to sit in the bakery but the baker who was busy baking his bread threw them out. Anyway, those air raid warnings no longer upset anyone.

I went to the Mahieu and sat near the window; I could see the Capoulade and the rue Soufflot. Sorokine passed looking like a lost puppy. I wrote to Bost for a long time and while I was writing I noticed Gibert† going downstairs to the restrooms; I ran after her and offered her a drink. Her face looked waxen with red spots on her cheekbones; her eyes looked tired. She had lost some of her beauty, but her face still looked pleasant. She told me that Wagner‡ was scared to death and that he sent her a kind of literary and emotional testament. Then she talked about herself for more than an hour; it was quite boring for she talked only about self-image and appearance. Her gestures and voice were sober, an almost deliberate sobriety in order to stress the pathetic aspect of what she was saying. She teaches literature at a secondary school for boys in Argentan. She explains *Horace* to ninth-grade boys: "When I get home, I cry," she told me, "and ask Corneille for forgiveness!" She has one graduating class, nineteen-year-old boys. Coty's[26] son is

---

* The absolute which represents any individual consciousness forms the guiding theme of *She Came to Stay*.

† A former student of Dullin, also a philosophy student whom the author met at Montparnasse in 1938. In *The Prime of Life* she is called Cecilia Bertin.

‡ A professor of literature, former friend of Sartre and brother-in-law of Merleau-Ponty.

in love with her and often takes her out in his car. "In the first four courses I read the symbolists to them, Verlaine, Baudelaire; they didn't understand a thing, but they felt my pain in my readings, and the truth of my pain has touched them." She is currently on leave to apply for the Conservatory; Jouvet wrote to her and asked her to come, that he would take care of everything for her but that he had done absolutely nothing. She built up her story about Jouvet into a delirium almost as pathological and of the same nature as Renée Ballon's.* She explained to me that Jouvet was a fellow who was afraid of love, because when he is in love, he feels bound hand and foot to the beloved woman. "So he carries it to the point of seeing me only in hallways and staircases. Oh! How we make each other suffer." This way she interprets every sign of indifference as a sign of passion, which becomes more violent the more she is rejected. As it was the case with Renée Ballon and Malraux, she believes Jouvet to be jealous. When, for example, he turns up her coat collar to protect her from the cold, she thinks, "He wants me to wear a mask so men can't look at me." She even imagines that he is stalking her out of jealousy and believes that she saw him at the Mahieu. Saturday she missed some classes, and in the afternoon he told her harshly, "Why did you miss class this morning? Clear out now!" And he had put his arms around a pretty woman. So she imagines him insanely jealous because he may think that she went out with other men the night before. But in her writings, as was the case with Ballon, we get the impression of an indifferent man, barely coquettish, a man who pretends to be gruffly jealous, without any intention of being taken seriously, just to flatter the woman over whom he thinks he has some rights. She told me that when she plays Hermione in front of Jouvet and the role calls for "Oh! Cruel lover, I did not love you! What have I done?" he covers his face to hide his emotions. He never complimented her on her acting and yet, she believes he wants her to continue with her work. She talked about her loneliness and pain and that they feed her genius. When she is acting a part her entire body vibrates and this vibration is the very meaning of the text. It makes it hard to believe that this girl has the least bit of an education, even less so in philosophy. She spent her vacation at the beach because Jouvet had forbidden (?) her to go on tour with her classmates. It was there at the beach, in an "explosion of solitude," where she found extraordinary effects in *Phèdre*: "inner" effects, she specified. Incidentally, she fainted while playing *Phèdre*. She met Géraldy: "It was

---

* Castor's colleague in Rouen in 1933 who developed a frenzied passion for Malraux to the extent of going mad over it. This tragedy is told in *The Prime of Life* where Renée Ballon is called Louise Perron.

just like *Toi et Moi*" [You and I] she said. He was struck by her talents but dropped her regardless. She talked to me about her great love affair with Sartre and said that it had been useful to her since as a virgin she could not have had this relationship with Jouvet. She takes pride in not having offered herself to Jouvet, who, by the way, didn't ask her for anything. Quite a set piece; I'm sure it's not of much comfort in her everyday life. I imagine that she must have flashes of pathetic illumination where she delights in her own stories, and she must tell herself that these instants are worth a life of suffering. But it's too much on the surface to be really interesting.

I went home, finished my letter, and corrected papers until half past eight. Kos. didn't come by earlier because she had been working hard on a letter to Bost, which she finished. We ate at the Milk Bar; I read her a letter from Sartre. She lent a sympathetic ear and seemed to have lots of warm feelings for him. We went back to my room and talked about "rancor," a homework assignment given by Meyerson.* We came up with some funny ideas.

Tuesday, November 14

When I woke up I was still in a good mood. I went through the Luxembourg Gardens and had coffee at the Capoulade. After an hour and a half of teaching I went to the Mahieu to write to Sartre and make my diary entries. Saw Gibert again. Sorokine came by at noon looking sullen. I took her to lunch at Mirov; she hardly opened her mouth. However, she told me that she had gone back to her family, but is no longer on speaking terms with her father. She is insanely jealous I think because of "my red-haired friend." She accompanied me to the Montparnasse station and left me at the metro. Then as I was entering the corridor I heard someone in a mad rush: It was Sorokine; she stopped right in front of me, looking as if she wanted to say something. I was late and annoyed, I said, "What's the matter? I'm in a hurry," and without saying anything she ran off in the other direction. I find her amusing fighting against herself. They are struggles against pride and affection, very childish and funny. Hers is a raw sadness without pathos.

Teaching, then post office—a letter from Sartre, who was bored. It made me sad. A huge, interminable letter from Bost; I recognize him so well in his writings. My letters sent from Brumath drew him closer to me. I think he wrote so much because he had a falling out with Kos. and I was a little disillusioned, although glad that he was on bad terms with her. However,

---

* A professor at the Sorbonne.

at the hotel was a letter from him for Kos. with a little drawing on it. So I thought he wrote to me because it gave him pleasure, but the fact that he was on good terms again with Kos. cast a shadow—but ever so slightly—on my joy. However, it's the pleasure that outweighs it by far. I read his letter at the Versailles, then from four to seven o'clock I worked at my place and wrote briefly to him while doing some light household chores.

Books and other things to find for Sartre

Bidou: *Hte [Histoire] de la grande guerre* [History of the Great War]
Gordon Cast: *Géographie historique de l'Europe* [Historical Geography of Europe]
Jean Français: *L'Affaire Röhm-Hitler* [The Röhm-Hitler Affair]
Rougement: *Journal d'Allemagne* [Journal from Germany]
Aldrovandi Marescotti: *Guerre diplomatique* [A Diplomatic War]
Sforza: *Bâtisseurs de l'Europe moderne* [Builders of Modern Europe]
Dictateurs et dictatures [Dictators and Dictatorships]
Les Frères ennemis [Brothers as Enemies]
Synthèse de l'Europe [Synthesis of Europe]
Pachitch et l'union des Yougoslaves [Pachitch and the Yugoslav Union]
Austen Chamberlain: *Au Fil des années* [As the Years Go By]
Churchill: *Les Grands Contemporains* [Great Contemporaries]
Paul Guérin: *Le Problème français* [The French Problem]
Ancel: *Géographie des frontières* [Geography of National Borders]

Imitation leather notebooks
Verdun by Romains
Pélude à Verdun by Romains
La Séduction du nihilisme [The Seduction of Nihilism] by Rauschning (next to Hermann's)
Le Testament espagnol [The Spanish Testament]
Le Bœuf clandestin [The Clandestine Steer]
Heidegger
Dostoevski—Troyat
The Marquis de Sade—Desborde—Heine

Halva, a big piece
3 boxes of capsules
1 package of tobacco St. Claude
Quarante-huit [Forty-eight], by Cassou
Cervantes (Pleiade edition)
Shakespeare (Pleiade edition)
Retz
Verlaine
Edgard [*sic*] Poe

NOTES

1. A department store.

2. Paul Nizan (1905–1940), a close friend of Sartre from the lycée Henri IV and the École Normale Supérieure. Nizan left the Communist Party after the signing of Nazi-Communist Non-Aggression Pact.

3. "The French phrase *gueule de bois* means "hangover." And *renversée* here refers to the inverted initials: not G.D.B. but G.B.D.

4. "Put between parentheses" is a reference to Edmund Husserl's method of phenomenological reduction, when one brackets, i.e., suspends, one's belief in the everyday world in order to study how the meaning of reality is constituted.

5. "Historicity" and *"existentiel"* allude to Martin Heidegger's philosophy in *Being and Time* where he makes a distinction between the *existenziell* (French *existentiel,* which relates to the ontical, the *ontisch-seiend*) and the *existential* (French *existential,* referring to the *ontologisch-sein*). See Heidegger 1962, 33.

6. *La Nouvelle Revue Française.*

7. One of Sartre's short stories and also the title story of the collection.

8. The letter for October 12, 1939, is missing from *Lettres à Sartre,* but Sartre's letter to Beauvoir dated October 17 responds to her idea about setting the novel in 1938–39 (Sartre 1983, 357).

9. Le Front Populaire, a coalition of French leftist parties that came to power with Leon Blum in 1936.

10. French novelist and playwright of the first half of the twentieth century who at the time was heading the French Propaganda Ministry.

11. Both are girls' schools.

12. A bistro that later became known as an existentialist hangout.

13. People later called Vietnamese. Annam was a part of Indochina (Vietnam), along the coast.

14. From the comedy *Knock ou le triomphe de la médecine* by Jules Romains.

15. Another reference to Jules Romains's *Knock ou le triomphe de la médecine.*

16. A game of cards.

17. November 1 is La Toussaint—All Saints' Day—a holiday in France.

18. *Boches* is a pejorative term for Germans, like "Krauts."

19. There is no paragraph break at this point in the original text.

20. A German word for a warm and dry wind blowing down on the northern side of the Alps.

21. A work by André Gide.

22. This is a pun. The two soldiers were from Deux-Sèvres. The word *Sèvres* rhymes with *chèvres* (nanny goats).

23. Roughly the equivalent of what Americans know as Indian summer. The Feast of St. Martin is celebrated on November 13.

24. The author capitalizes these nouns.

25. The author uses a botanical term here to emphasize the physical and dependent nature of Védrine. According to *Webster's New World Dictionary*, lichen is characterized as a dual plant "growing in an intimate symbiotic association." The simile continues throughout the sentence.

26. René Coty (1882–1962), a French statesman, was president of the French Republic from 1954 to 1959.

NOTEBOOK 3

November 15 – December 25, 1939

Tuesday, November 14   (continued)

I left my room after seven at night to meet Kos. at Montmartre. It was dark on place Pigalle and the boulevards. The upstairs of the Dupont was closed, and Kos. was waiting for me downstairs. She felt quite at ease having just attended Dullin's class, where she found herself in familiar surroundings from last year, her friends—she talked to me about Vallon, for example, whose "friend" had been drafted and who was lamenting her lover's absence like a wife while knitting sweaters. We had dinner in a little Italian restaurant on rue Fontaine; its clientele included blacks, poor whores, and a wretched fellow in a tuxedo with a red flower in its lapel, who was going to sing somewhere. Lots of nightclubs are open now; Paris is slowly coming back to life. We walked down to Montparnasse, place de l'Opéra, and rue de la Paix; we had the impression of being in a German film of the fantastic. Huge black streetlights produced just a tiny little yellow flame, like a candle. We returned home. Kos. went to her room and came back down in an agitated state holding an envelope from Bost in her hand. In fact, she was raving mad because they had removed the carpet from her room. She was talking about leaving the hotel. These fits of anger for such trivial things amaze me; I'm incapable of getting upset about them. Hotel personnel, restaurant waiters, merchants, and the like are for me a body of forces like the weather that one can't fight but must tolerate without getting upset. Besides, I'm not engaged in the world like Kos.; I can detach myself from almost all kinds of situations. She left and I fell into a deep sleep.

Wednesday, November 15

A day of work. I got up at eight o'clock; at half past eight I was reading *Le Canard enchaîné* then *L'Œuvre* at the Dôme. After reading *Le Canard*, I read *L'Œuvre* in the same frame of mind and had the impression that it was really a good imitation of it and really funny. I must say, it fitted perfectly. I worked; I am making progress without finalizing the text because I'm anxious to finish at least the rough draft. I could have it done by Easter. Kos. had lunch with me. She told me some gossip about Vallon and Clarisse. She said her letters to Bost were giving her a nervous breakdown. For some time now he had been annoying her in his letters, which were nothing but monologues—I believe his line of thinking does not relate enough to her. He had annoyed her in his letter on Thursday; she answered curtly and since then she had not written. She was expecting a letter of reproach before she would start writing again. But the whole correspondence aggravates her. She repeated that they lived in two different worlds and it would be better to break it off, that already last year they were living in two different worlds. I honestly defended Bost's interests, and moreover, not because of moral scruples, but in all sincerity, since I would not want him to be in trouble. And besides, since their correspondence and relationship have lost their poetic quality because of Kos.'s distaste for them, the idea that they exist no longer upsets me. Besides, I do sympathize somewhat with Kos.—it's so difficult to live in absentia. She prefers giving up everything instead of clinging to something abstract, out of a kind of sincerity to herself. Yet, as far as I'm concerned, Bost's letters and my relationship with him are alive and present for me. Of course, things are in abeyance, but much more than just memories and promises remain; he stays truly *him;* distant from me and cut off from my life, but very real. I feel like sharing my ideas with him, everything that's happening to me. He is my world as before. I went to my room and worked for two hours, then went to pick up my letters, one from Sartre, so tender that tears came to my eyes right there on blvd. Montparnasse. In this case, on the contrary, absence has made me stand back just enough to allow my love and his to become more tangible. Never have I felt it so strong. Shortly after I got home Sorokine arrived in a pleasant and happy mood, wearing a pretty little new sweater. "Go, hide," she told me. I turned around while she put funny little drawings she had done on the wall. We chatted and kissed. I get more and more attached to her. She has a way of giving herself completely, but keeping control of herself, which charms me. Besides, those moments of giving herself are rare; her face quickly recovers a slightly ironic expression. Even in the fury of passion, I think, one must show some consideration for the *other* to whom this passion is thrown full in the face. Then right away there is a slight detachment and reserve. Védrine cares only about expressing *herself* and does not worry about the other person. That's a gross indiscretion—with Kos. it was the opposite. It was a matter of not expressing herself at all, and her only concern for the other was one of mistrust. Poupette would like to express *herself* like Védrine, but knows theoretically that it is an indiscrete act and so she gets uptight or tries to find means of getting away from the sight of the other. In this matter Sorokine is perfect to my liking. For those who are not passionate, like Sartre or Bost, even though there are many differences, expression is still something else. It is in itself a *gift* freely granted. As for myself, it's difficult to know. I think that most of the time I'm in control, but often, especially with Bost, I express a bit more than might be necessary. Moreover, I sort of do this on purpose.

I wrote letters while Sorokine read. We went together to the Montparnasse metro station, then I went to see the Gérassis. They have a beautiful poodle. On the telephone they had enticed me with a promise of a surprise. It made me think of Sartre's grandfather: "You know, little fellow, I have a nice surprise for you, I'm feeling better." We talked—it wasn't boring—I cashed a check for five thousand francs that I had received this morning and had brightened my day because now I'll have greater financial means at my disposal. I can buy books and go out, for example; everything becomes possible and my debts will be paid.

Thursday, November 16

I woke up at half past seven but didn't find the courage to get up and stayed in bed until after eight o'clock. Then I went to the Dôme and leisurely and with pleasure made entries in this diary. It will always be like this, now that it is up to date. I continue to be profoundly happy. I'll have time for my work, all in all enough distractions, enough company (Kos.) and the support of daily letters. Those daily letters are terrific because they are the foundation of my life and not just a little happiness three times a week. I don't think of Sartre as someone absent. While I was getting dressed, some of our conversation about Bost came back to me, and it overwhelmed me with love for him, just as if I was going to see him again in a few hours. When I see what absence means for other people, I realize that also on this point our relationship is terrific, that it remains a life together, in a world in common despite everything. It is true that the very fact of an intellectual life essential for both of us makes things so much easier.

At ten o'clock I went to the post office. I had a letter from Sartre; he seemed less cheerful than in his last letter, his eyes were getting tired—some letters from Bost. A photo fell out of an envelope; I hadn't expected it and seeing him suddenly alive and smiling had a strange effect on me, an impression of a heartache. I think that with Sartre I react by being stressed, because he belongs to me and I know that one letter suffices to restore things, as I would like them—or else I suffer with him if it's something bad affecting both of us. My emotions with Bost are emotions of helplessness; it's because I am aware of his character of otherness and independence with respect to myself.

Sorokine arrived at half past twelve at the lycée, overexcited and disheveled. We had lunch at a small blue brasserie on rue Lecourbe, then to the metro in the rain. On blvd. St. Michel I bought a beautiful umbrella in cassis-colored silk with a small curved wooden handle. I'm already in love with it and sad at the idea of losing it soon. Sent Bost a package with books by Tchekov. Lycée. Then to the Mahieu. Some of the clients were old people, very much Latin Quarter types, with white hair and makeup on their cheeks. They were discussing Massenet, emphasizing their arguments by humming his tunes. I worked, continuing chapter 9; I'm making progress. Then letters to Bost and Sartre. I had wanted to go to the movies, but when I went to see Kos., she was very tired. I went for some take-out at Dominique's, and we spent the evening in my room. She left at half past ten, which gave me plenty of time to finish my letter to Sartre, write to That Lady, and read a little of Conan Doyle, whom I find entertaining. In the room next to me people were talking very loudly and I had trouble falling asleep.

Friday, 17

I was to accompany Kos. to the Sorbonne and got up early. But she wasn't ready, as usual, and I went to the Dôme to spend the morning working, still feeling deeply satisfied about my well-ordered life. Good work—finished chapter 9. At half past eleven I wrote letters, then met Lévy and Kanapa at the Biarritz and ate an omelet while conversing with them; to be exact, I talked the whole time. I would have liked to talk with Kanapa, but Lévy was always there. Three hours of teaching. When I finished, I was completely exhausted. Worked a little at the Mahieu, where Kos. met up with me—tried to write my letters, but even that was too tiring, and at half past six we walked down blvd. St. Michel, where we took the metro to Barbès. We had dinner on the lower ground floor of the Barbès Dupont, which was comfortable, light, and almost empty. Sitting near us was this gorgeous woman who looked like Merle Oberon. I finished my letters, and we went to the movies. We saw a film with Shirley Temple, who is a little bitch, and heartrending news with Maurice Chevalier, old and shaky, who was singing for an audience of soldiers. It was downright disgusting. A good cowboy movie, *The Return of the Cisco Kid,* with Warner Baxter. I returned to my room and went to bed completely exhausted. The people in the room next to me were talking like last night. I yelled at them to shut up. They quieted down, frightened.

Saturday, November 18

Two hours at Camille Sée, then to the post office; letters from both Sartre and Bost, who seems morose these days. Worked at the Versailles for an hour and a half. I finally closed chapter 9 and started chapter 10, on Elisabeth, which is fun. Then to the Dôme, where, sitting next to Kos., I ate a delicious stew. We went to get our earrings, which are gorgeous, and at two o'clock I was again at work in my room. Letter from Védrine. She was touching in her effort to accept everything I had told her. And I felt a return of affection for her, because at this moment, her relationship with me seemed true. She's not unhappy and I'm very glad about it. Gégé talked to me for half an hour. At five o'clock Sorokine stopped by and told me all about her life, where, in her opinion, chemistry takes up too much space. Gérassi came to say hello; he admired my turban and earrings. I too found myself quite beautiful. I went to see Sorokine and explained Descartes to her for an hour. She understood readily and was delighted. In fact, she was so happy with me that she brought me some chocolates and even told me in so many words that I meant everything to her. At half past seven she accompanied me to blvd. Exelmans, where I was going to have dinner with Colette Audry.

The idea of seeing "people" amused me somewhat, but not for long. Audry lives in a very bourgeois building and has a large room that functions simultaneously as furniture storage room—twelve chairs placed in a round as if set up for a board of directors meeting. The other part of the room, where the table had been set, was arranged in a pleasant way as a studio apartment. Colette Audry was wearing a brown suit with a turquoise-colored blouse of fine wool. Her husband arrived, chilling effect: half-bald, a little stooped, and very thin; lips that never laughed. We ate a carefully prepared dinner, cooked by Audry herself. I told them stories, but got the impression that the guy was judging me unkindly, which made me feel a little uneasy. Colette Audry told me that Alain had been arrested for having signed a pamphlet,* together with Giono and the Almendos, who were grilled for forty-eight hours. She also said that the DCA[1] last Monday had fired on a French pilot. In vain had he performed some acrobatics to show his markings, but they had kept on firing. He was mad as hell after he landed. Toward the end of the meal, we said a few words about philosophy. Minder told an anecdote about Husserl, a childhood memory that he had heard from Husserl himself: one day, wanting to sharpen a knife, he sharpened it so well that there was nothing left of it. "I wonder whether my philosophy is not unlike this knife," he had asked himself. But whether it was shyness or contempt, Minder did not press the conversation. Once or twice he looked affectionately at Colette Audry, but they are so poorly matched that they don't look at all like a couple. The evening lasted until ten o'clock, going as well as can be expected. He spoke of Pascal Copeau, whom he detests and who does such bad work directing propaganda on the radio. He also talked about English propaganda and their pamphlets. They published very risqué ones with saucy illustrations accompanying the gravest captions just to get the soldiers to read them. The French were somewhat scandalized by it and didn't dare go that far. I took a whole armful of detective novels and went home reading Saint-Exupéry. A rather gripping passage of Guillaumet's odyssey where he walked through the snow for five days and five nights.† I saw Kos., who looked a little tense and who invited herself in for a half hour. She had seen Delarue, who had been so panicky about the war that he wanted to go to Spain. That was the reason he had been to Holland last year; but he had been turned back at the border. He was appointed to St. Maixent.‡ She left and I wrote to Sartre and Bost even though I was dead tired. One additional hour of sleep this night because of the time change.

---

* A pacifist pamphlet.

† In *Terre des hommes* [Wind, Sand, and Stars].

‡ St. Maixent is an officers school.

Sunday, November 19

Got up at eight o'clock—a bright blue sky this morning, but humid and cold weather. I went to the Versailles, wrote to Védrine and worked nearly two hours on my novel. Then to the post office, where I had my two letters. I then went to lunch at the Coupole. I also wrote to Toulouse and made entries into this diary. I was going to work all day. That would make a whole week of work without a breather; little sleep, little reading, without a break, work or letters; I'm pushing myself hard, as Sorokine would say. I don't know whether I'll continue at this pace for very long, but for the moment I like it and am happy. I hardly feel the need to go out or read a little.

Worked at the Dôme after lunch, then at my place. Kos. came to tell me that Delarue wanted to go to the concert with us. We found him at the counter of the Dôme, in uniform; it goes well with his face and peasant accent. At the concert hall, no more tickets; we were disappointed. We went to the Cintra. The discussion turned around pacifism, insane talk, for Delarue is confused in his mind. Then we went to the Rotonde. It's funny how a military man belongs to everyone, as Kos. said. The neighbor at the table next to us questioned him on the manufacture of cigarettes and interposed himself for quite a while. This Delarue liked to be in our company and stayed almost until the last minute. Then I went to the Milk Bar with Kos. and in her room read in a 1933 issue of *Europe* some old "Letters to the Dead," full of obscene and horrible stories.

Monday, November 20

Classes at Camille Sée. A letter from Sartre. One hour of work at the Coupole, then I read St. Exupéry at lunch, and it shook me up. I'm easily shaken by something coming to me from the outside because I live so much off my own resources; any encounter becomes precious to me. I liked very much the story "In the Heart of the Desert." There is a description that I found moving, of thirst and the absence of concrete suffering in the midst of something horrible: "I no longer produce saliva, nor do I call up any more sweet images over which I could have cried. The sun has dried the well of my tears," he wrote. Suddenly, instead of being in the heart of this harsh world without regrets, I was looking at it. Something snapped; the dry crust cracked and the sweet images timidly rose to the surface. Perhaps a glass of red wine helped bring it about. It was a powerful moment for me, when I was a little outside of myself contemplating my condition. Image of a night spent with Bost, a room in yellow light, a red carpet and a folding screen. I closed the window; he smiled at me and kissed me. I remember well the violent arousal of those first kisses. The memory suggested itself timidly and remained dead, just enough for me to feel the difference and absence, not enough to make my heart heavy with tears. Troubled peace without a complete heartbreak. I do not regret the troubled peace, but I do regret that full heartbreak has become so totally impossible for me.

Next to me, some fellows were eating coffee-flavored parfaits after a good meal with some red wine. The manager of the Coupole told them that dancing would resume on Sundays and they got indignant: "I find it immoral to dance. The soldiers over there don't dance!"

On foot to Henri IV. I like crossing the Luxembourg Gardens. The sky was gray, refracting a white light; the bare ground and trees conveyed a strong impression of solitude, of the novelty of life in the midst of an uncertain world. I was sensitive today.

Two hours of teaching. Then to the Mahieu for two hours of work and one hour of correcting papers. I felt like going to the movies, but Kos. was exhausted. We had dinner at the Capoulade and returned by taxi. I wrote my letter to Bost. While I was writing, tears came to my eyes. How hard this absence is, absence that threatens our future. Sometimes I feel that I'll never see him again, that he'll be changed and that everything will be changed. Happiness close at hand, and even these images that are already faded will be completely erased. The days I spent with him already seem magical and incredible to me and if I lose them, I won't even know how to desire them, that's how unimaginable they will have become. "Sweet suffering"—not so sweet . . .

Tuesday, November 21

Classes at Henri IV from half past eight until ten o'clock. Two hours of work at the Mahieu. Lunch with Sorokine at Mirov's. Three hours at Camille Sée interrupted by an air raid warning exercise. Austere but without either boredom or sadness. At half past four I was at the post office. "Is there something for me?" "Oh, indeed, I would say there is!" answered the post lady, handing me one letter from Sartre and three from Bost. I went to read them at the Versailles, and they filled me with joy. They were as fulfilling as their presences. Bost's letters were more affectionate than they had ever been. He spoke to me about Kos. in a rather indignant tone. Last night at the Capoulade I thought that there would be some safety in never dirtying one's hands by engaging in minor intrigues. You could always tell yourself, "I didn't want it." How depressing it must be to use political ploys and then realize that they were useless. That really represents a defeat. Besides, I'm actually not that calculating. I answered Bost immediately, I was happy. Then I worked. I returned to my room and worked some more. Three hours and a half of work, that's good after four and a half hours of teaching; and I didn't feel tired.

After Kos. came to pick me up at half past seven, we went to the Dôme for dinner. I had sauerkraut without remembering that I had already had some in the morning, to be exact, that was a Polish dish. We chatted; she explained that the incident with Bost lifted their relationship out of the ordinary and that now things were going very well—what she hated was the ordinary. The idea that their relationship was recovering was ever so slightly unpleasant for me. I recognized the eternal balancing act and laughed about it. As far as the notion of the "ordinary" is concerned, I think it's nonsense. It always stems from the same sentimental idealism à la Proust. If one is alone with one's emotions they quickly become unbearably insipid. They need to be renewed, be it at the price of some cataclysm, as in the case of Toulouse and Kos. But if one has a *real* relationship with someone, the relationship has the inexhaustible richness of this reality that only becomes available to us precisely by means of the ordinary. With a somber look on her face she said that since her early years she had made "concession after concession," but she herself added that she was acting a little when she said that. We returned home and I continued reading *The Idiot*.

Wednesday, November 22

At half past eight I was at the Dôme reading *Le Canard enchaîné*. I worked from nine o'clock to noon. I didn't have a penny left and had to go knocking at Wanda's door. A. Ménard, in her nightgown, as usual, opened. "Always in my gown," she said modestly. A log was burning in the fireplace. It looked frightfully like a woman's place: the bed undone, the perfume and lotion bottles, and the general disorder. Our conversation wasn't very animated. Wanda had gone to get some brioches. She came back upstairs, her arms loaded, and not too happy to see me. She was half-naked under her coat, looking nice and fresh. I borrowed ten francs and complimented her on Lexia's portrait, which is pretty. Then I went to the Gérassis', whose dog bit fiercely into my coat, something they congratulated me on with much feeling. They admired my earrings and lent me two hundred francs. By taxi to the Opéra.* Only half of it was open and prices had been lowered: the second-tier loges cost the same as the formerly fourth tier, and so on. It's the same for all entertainment in Paris. It has lost its glitter and lacks money. For twelve francs each I was able to buy two excellent seats for a ground floor loge. I returned by bus. The weather in Paris was wonderfully cold and dry. At the post office I had a long letter from Sartre that was a huge summary of the year 38–39 and intended for my novel. It was very interesting and I would have liked to study it in more detail, but first I want to push ahead without taking a breather and when I have run out of steam I'll spend a few days reading it.

I read this at the Milk Bar while eating hurriedly. From a quarter past two until a quarter to five I was at the Dôme. Adamov came by and held an icy-cold hand out to me, both in the literal and figurative sense of the word. A while later he sat down across from me with a horrible-looking redhead, I assume out of a kind of bravado. I worked and wrote my letters and worked again. When I left the Dôme shortly after a quarter to five, I saw a little fury coming toward me: it was Sorokine: "You forgot our date, you're disgusting." She came from the hotel, where she had been looking for me in vain. I hate this kind of anger. We went up to my room where I told her curtly, "If you have come just to whine like this, you'd better leave." With an air of offended dignity she left without closing the door. I let her stew. A stupid rage was building up in me, and I understood those rages that Sartre spoke to me about in the past: you're angry with yourself for not being able nor wanting to keep yourself better in check, and this turns into the most unfair and shameful irritation. After a while I thought how sad she would be if she really left, and I was ashamed. I opened the door and told her in a gruff voice to come back up because she was slowly walking down the stairs, slowly, the poor puppy. She came back up, just as slowly, and I made her sit across from me and lectured her for one hour on "substance." She began to fidget, looking at the clock. "Afterward we'll have no more time," she said mysteriously. I stopped and don't remember by what skillful maneuver (ah, yes! I had gone to return the ten francs to Wanda) we quite naturally wound up on the bed. I talked a little while she amused herself by making her legs and feet shake; she was terribly tense. I was so annoyed and my head so tired that I said something extremely rude without noticing it. "Wait a minute," I told her; I was red-faced about it, but she didn't blink, on the contrary,

---

* To make reservations for Gluck's *Alceste*.

she calmed down and five minutes later the embracing and kissing session started. Obviously, it must be terribly cruel for a girl like her, who, after giving herself passionately, is told, "It's seven o'clock." Right away she rolled herself up into a ball on the bed, halfway crying. I tried to comfort her, but only halfheartedly because I wanted to get dressed and not be late. I said to myself that these scenes were annoying, always ending up in an unfair and nasty irritation that is inherent in the situation. I took her by taxi as far as the Opéra and was as sweet as possible to her. Then at the place de l'Opéra I left her with a heavy heart, the poor thing.

I waited ten minutes for Kos. and felt anger beginning to boil up inside me also against her, when she arrived all smiles saying that I looked very beautiful, which flattered me. At the moment my looks appeal to me. It's because of my earrings and the turban. I find them just as beautiful as if somebody else wore them. I was wearing my turquoise blue shantung silk blouse, which looked very pretty. We were seated in our ground floor loge, right next to the balcony. We were alone and felt like royalty. Kos. was enchanted by the mirror, the sofa, and the little table. The audience was sparse, but the performances of *Aïda,* a few days later, were all sold out. Beautiful music*—Lubin's beautiful voice—the tenor was acceptable, but Singher with his quavering voice was dreadful. Kos. was upset about the décor and the movements of the crowds; it was absolutely awful, really, but since it was subdued it didn't bother me much. And toward the end, the scene between Admète and Alceste was even gripping. I felt in heaven to be there. I liked the music very much and also the fact that I was at the Opéra. It was fun thinking of Gluck in his black outfit, his loose greatcoat, seated at a table while carefully aligning his notes, and that this resulted in Lubin's pompous gestures and this bombastic production. What connection was there? And what connection did Gluck himself see between the notes and the performance, I wondered? During the intermission we got sandwiches and cakes at the Pam that we ate in our loge. Before the last scene Kos. had had enough and wanted to leave. I remembered how in the past we would have fled immediately—but this time I forcefully turned a deaf ear—luckily, because the last scene was the most beautiful, with the scene at hell's gate. And there was a rather nice ballet with a charming little fourteen-year-old ballerina who danced like a goddess. We returned home by taxi. Kos. left me right away; she was really going to pieces. I finished reading *The Idiot* in bed; the ending

---

* *Alceste* (1767).

was as beautiful as I remembered. I put in my earplugs, but about half an hour later I nevertheless heard the wailing of the sirens and above my head laughter and the stamping of feet. These women have a party when there is an air raid alert, and they find themselves justified to get together in their nightclothes, drink chamomile tea, and converse loudly at night—but thank god, by pushing my little earplugs in a little deeper I heard nothing more. However, it seemed that there was a lot of noise; the cannons boomed so loud that people went down to the shelters.

Thursday, November 23

I got up at eight o'clock and had breakfast at the Dôme—one hour of work. I like the mornings; they are a cost-free benefit, leisure time at the fringes of my life because I spend the morning just as I would spend a working morning at the lycée and yet I'm free until past ten o'clock. I sent some detective novels to Bost and picked up my letters at General Delivery. I had a short letter from Sartre and a long one from Bost, who had never before written me in such an amiable way as he has of late. Lycée—the metro station Vaugirard has been reopened. It shortens my way from the metro to the lycée. Sorokine was waiting for me at the post office. She was very friendly, bringing me caramels and philosophical problems. She was quite trusting and not at all tense. We went to the little blue brasserie on Lecourbe Street, where the food was good, and then to the metro station Sèvres, from where we went on foot to Henri IV, stopping by my dry cleaner and crossing the Luxembourg Gardens. We even had ten minutes to stop at the Mahieu. Sorokine talked to me about her problems: chemistry, philosophy, her parents, and even myself included, whom she considers somewhat of a problem, even though I'm better than nothing. And I began telling her the story of my life that she was begging to hear. Two hours of teaching. I went back to the Mahieu and worked for about two and a half hours. I started on chapter 11 and had fun doing it. I wrote a long, long letter to Sartre. At half past seven Kos. wasn't there. At first I wasn't worried and wrote a letter to Poupette, then for a long time made entries in this journal—I had much to catch up with. In the end I felt sharp pains in my elbow from all the writing. Some fellow stopped by; he was selling pictures that could be combined in various ways, for example, Hitler's head on a gorilla's body, or on that of a flea, an elephant, etc. He insisted that I'd buy some, however, it seemed to me that this kind of trafficking and stupid gizmo was not very widespread. In the restrooms at the Mahieu a sort of old witch was making a great to-do about my turban. "But you must be young to wear something like that," she said solemnly and with great admiration. I began to get worried about Kos. being late. In cases like this I imagine that she discovered something and a kind of anguish takes hold of me. But no, she arrived at nine o'clock, as tense as she could possibly be because she hadn't been able to recite poetry very well and was delayed because of something having to do with her moving. I took her to dinner to the Mirov. She was completely stressed out and near tears. Yet she was charming with me and explained how much she enjoyed "performing" for people at the Atelier. It reminded me of Kos. as I knew her last year, and I didn't like it too much. Moreover, since the affair of the letter with Bost something has been destroyed that will take a long time to rebuild, to wit, a kind of complicity between the two of us as I know it with Sartre and Bost and often even with Védrine, a way of being with her that lets me take what she says for reality, as authentic and important as any reality. Now it's again "put in parentheses"; it's "she says that . . ." etc., and it's like I am watching a performance, I am no longer given. For me, that's what changes esteem into a lack of esteem. One thing that has been achieved remains: old resentments have been totally erased—if I feel again hostility toward her it will be for new reasons. This as well: a strong and trusting relationship—Trust according to Heidegger's vocabulary consists in that which at each instant it indicates in the future. But with Kos. there has never been this indication, which is so total with Sartre and so solid also with Bost. You think, "at this moment I am on good terms with Kos.," and you know that she doesn't think any further in the future about it either. And this could go on for years so that our relationship would become stale while preserving its ties linked to memory and the fact of growing old. But it will never possess the force that the future lends to it, which precisely prevents relationships from going stale while preserving an indefinite newness like that of the future itself. This brings to mind stories about everyday life and goes with passive idealism à la Proust. Emotionally speaking, the link between future, transcendence, and objectivity is just as essential and justified as it is for the world of perception.

We returned early and Kos. left almost immediately. It's always a godsend when Kos. or Sorokine spends *less* time with me than I had counted on— the hours of solitude are precious to me; there are always a thousand things needing my attention. Tonight I made the most of my time by writing Bost a huge letter between eleven and midnight. Then I slept like a baby.

Friday, November 24

I got up at eight o'clock, well rested. I put on my red dress, which, after having been at the dry cleaner, looked smashing, like a new dress. Then I went to pick up my mail at the post office. A letter from Sartre—I went back to work at the Dôme—reserved two tickets by telephone for the Bach concert on Sunday. The following Sunday we'll visit Toulouse. I enjoy making plans for recreation. I also enjoy looking forward to organizing my budget and making plans for shopping, dressing up, and personal care.

Bitter cold; −4° outside and inside impossible to get warm anywhere. Last night beautiful moonlight was flooding Paris like in the country, and all the railings of the Luxembourg gave the gardens an enchanted air with its white statuettes, its bare and dark trees in the light of the moon; it was very beautiful.

Waking up in the morning is not unpleasant. My mind focuses immediately on my hours of work. It provides a very solid structure and the rest gets organized around it and justified by it.

Worked at the Dôme from half past nine to a quarter to twelve (two and a half hours). Kos. didn't come and I ate a rib steak Bercy while reading a little in *Le Diable boiteux** [The Lame Devil] and writing to Sartre—then on foot to Henri IV, crossing the Luxembourg Gardens in a dry cold that was not unpleasant. Three hours of teaching. I went to the Cujas, a small café, very peaceful, at the corner of rue Cujas. There were no customers and I felt very much at ease. In the future I shall work there. I wrote to Bost and Védrine and worked more than another hour and a half. That made a total of four hours today, excellent. Afterward I met Gégé and Gérassi at the Mahieu. At the Ursulines we saw an excellent film, *A l'angle du monde* [At the Edge of the World], about a lonely island of the Orkneys: cliffs and storms—and a very entertaining movie with Mae West, *Fifi peau de pêche* [Every Day's a Holiday]. I went home accompanied by Gérassi. The moonlight was still more beautiful than the night before; it made me think of a snowy landscape. At home I had a note from Kos.; I went up to see her and found her gloomy and depressed. I stayed a half hour and went to sleep, too late, alas— but I slept well.

---

* By Lesage (1707).

Saturday, November 25

Camille Sée from half past seven to half past ten. Post office. Letters from Sartre and Bost that I read at the Versailles—it gave me a moment of profound joy. Those whited sepulchres and all that have lost their meaning entirely and it seems to me like an extraordinary first bloom of our love.[2] In the past I was living it from the inside, but didn't grasp it in such an obvious and happy way. Bost's letter gave me enormous pleasure. He shows inventiveness in his tenderness now, and I feel that there is something much stronger between us than this passion to which I sometimes foolishly cling. A moment of great, great happiness. For one hour and a half I worked at the Versailles—I then spent an inordinate amount of time putting a package together for Bost with some brandy, cigarettes, a pipe, and a comb and sending it off. I like to have money in my pocket and spend it. Sending alcohol to soldiers is not allowed, so the merchant kindly packed it for me, hiding the bottle under straw and cotton. I also had to send my mother some undergarments; so much ado, it's ridiculous. I couldn't manage wrapping it correctly and it made me fume. I felt grotesque with that huge bundle. I finally got rid of it nevertheless and went to eat a rib steak at the Dôme. I wrote to Bost and worked for another two hours, but I was tired for lack of sleep. I went home, wrote to Sartre, then Sorokine came by. She was tender, all soft, amorous and looking rather happy. Kisses; she asked whether I also kissed my redheaded friend like that—she said no one had ever kissed her like that—she said I must help her discuss everything with me and trust me; she was quite disarming, tender and entertaining. For one hour I explained Descartes to her, then met Kos., who seemed in a good mood and feeling fine. We ate at Dominique's, then went to the lower ground floor at the Hoggar. While passing by the Luxembourg Gardens we noticed a huge red glow caused by a fire that was setting the sky ablaze—but it went out almost immediately. At the Hoggar we had a nice table in a niche. The dancer looked as if she was possessed, like a devil struggling in a cage of muscles. Then another dance, more languid, however, and then these belly dances take on an air of anatomical demonstrations. Kos. was animated and looked charming in her wide country skirt and little blue sweater, but I felt lifeless inside. Two Franco-Annamite couples that had gone there to pet intruded on us and we fled. We went home, talked a while, then I finished my letter to Sartre and went to bed.

A great many images have come back to me lately and impatient desires for many special joys—the mountains with Bost—skiing—dinners in Paris with Sartre—that, and also some days—even my entire life with him. When will I regain it?

Sunday, November 26

I was tired and stayed in bed until nine o'clock. Post office—two letters, both short ones, and inside I also felt tight. The weather was overcast. I worked two hours at the Versailles, which I enjoyed enormously. It seems that this chapter on Gerbert will turn out to be excellent. And the entire novel is getting organized in my head in a very satisfying way. My work has never counted as much as now, and has never been such a pleasure for me, so much so that at night I wait impatiently for the morning to come so I can get back to writing. Went to Santeuil* in vain. Read a little in *Le Diable boiteux,* which is moderately amusing. I went for lunch at the Dôme; C. Chonez came to say hello. I was hoping to hear her tell some anecdotes, but she knew nothing at all and I was the one talking to her about Sartre, Nizan, etc. I had the pleasant impression that, apart from the specialists, I have really grasped as much as any civilian could of what this war is about. She left and I worked another two hours. The Dôme was a familiar and peaceful place this afternoon. Brien was hanging around Chonez, and Adamov was there too, asking me with a scandalized look, "Is that a real novel with a subject? With a beginning and an end?" just like my father, who would have said, "A book without a subject? Without a beginning and an end?" Nearby a woman was knitting, probably a balaclava, while trying to identify the waiter who was waiting on her—the waiter took on the stylized voice of a maître d' suggesting a menu: "Perhaps it was at the Bastille at the Dupont, place Pereire?" She was still shaking her head, looking disappointed. He finally joined in the game and was still searching his memory when she had already lost interest. At four o'clock I went home, did my nails, and read casually. Kos. came to take me to the concert. Taxi. She looked smashing and was as nice as she could be. Incidentally, she doesn't do a thing and won't pass her certificate by a long shot. We picked up our tickets. The concerts are scheduled every Sunday and are sold out. We had a drink in a little bistro where two officers were playing cards while a young Englishman, who must think he's still in his father's cottage, ordered tea and some fruit cake that was scary to look at; some sailors were drinking at the bar. The smoke and the heat tired us out and we settled down in the concert hall. Our seats were in the orchestra

---

* Her sister's studio.

section, good seats—the usual sad audience—two old men behind us were reviewing the entire history of the human mind: Hugo, E. Gallois, but they were unsure about the name of a musician, a certain Duparc. When they played the "Marseillaise" all stood and a young officer stood at attention, his chest out, eyes half closed. He was puffing himself up. They played an overture in B, the fifth Brandenburg Concerto, and the entire *Art of the Fugue*, alas! It's beautiful, but sad. We went back to Monparnasse; it was crowded. We had something to eat at Pagès and went to my room to chat a while. At ten o'clock I wrote my letters and went to bed. I have an ugly pimple on my cheek that hurt all night.

Saturday [sic], November 27

Uneventful day—breakfast at the Dupont while reading *Le Diable boiteux*, which I finally finished. Lycée Camille Sée—letter from Bost—lunch at the Dôme and good work on Gerbert—letter to Védrine and Toulouse. On foot to Henri IV—two hours of teaching—on foot to Poupette to pay her rent, then on the 91 to Montparnasse; letter from Sartre.

Spent a pleasant moment at the Versailles; had some free time ahead of me from half past four to half past seven, and the chapter was almost finished. I completed it without feeling hurried, and used the remaining time to make entries in this diary and take care of my correspondence. I have a clear conscience as far as my work is concerned and feel that I have enough leisure time.

Evening with Kos.—we dined at Pagès and stayed a long while on the terrace of the Dôme—a pleasant terrace, without a brazier this year, almost empty, the floor covered by a large, coarse sisal rug the color of horse manure and the windows all hung with blue drapes. Kos. practiced reciting Baudelaire; she did it quite well. It enchants me reading Baudelaire, it takes on an almost touching historical value. It's like a retrospective for me, as though everything that existed before the war receded in relation to it and placed itself at a definite moment in time, with time itself ending at the declaration of war. At the same time, I have the impression, as I often do, that, as St. Exupéry once said, one can grasp an object only through a craft or a technique. A text has all the resources, pitfalls, and nuances only for someone who recites it. And for each one, it represents a more definitive limitation of his world than not having the money to go to China.

Tuesday, November 28

Uneventful day of work. Lycée Henri IV—two hours of work in a little deserted café on the place du Panthéon—at Mirov's with Sorokine. Camille Sée, where I corrected papers during a written test. Post office—no letters from Bost—work at the Versailles, then at home—correspondence. Met Kos. at the lower ground floor of the Dupont Barbès; we looked at Baudelaire again, then went to the movies to see *Le Gorille* [The Gorilla] with the Ritz Brothers, which was very funny. I have such an ugly pimple on my cheek that I decided to put a plaster on it. It's horrible and gives me sleepless nights.

Wednesday, November 29

Two hours of private tutoring for the new students at Camille Sée—some extra income for me. Then by taxi to Neuilly to collect Sartre's salary and to rue La Fayette in order to pay M. Védrine—and to the Dôme to eat and work for two hours. Then I went to Lutétia to meet Mme Mancy. She brought me a woolen scarf and gloves, not very nice looking—conversation where she described her sad conjugal life—she talked to me about I don't know what cousin who insisted on sending packages to needy soldiers. They begged Sartre to make a list; he signed up noncommissioned and regular officers and after having sent the list the cousin didn't send any more packages and Mme Mancy wound up paying for them. She left at four o'clock and I finished my correspondence. I felt dead tired, had a headache, blood rushing to my head while my heart felt drained. It's really hard.

I returned home and found Sorokine on the steps of the staircase. She looked somber because she had been waiting for me for five minutes. She was nice enough to forget about it and offered me a piece of chocolate. I stretched out on the bed, exhausted. We chatted while kissing each other tenderly whereupon there was a knock at the door. It was Colette Audry, all sprightly, wearing culottes, and carrying a small backpack, and over the whole outfit, a horrible rubberized cyclist cape. You put it on by pulling it over your head from the middle, like a chasuble, and it's hideous. She sat down and began to chat in her lively way while Sorokine, hot with anger, tapped the floor nervously while looking pointedly at the doorway. Audry was making some vague plans with me for going on a skiing vacation and invited me for dinner on Saturday with Wahl,* which I accepted because, all

---

* The philosopher [Jean Wahl], a professor at the Sorbonne.

things considered, I need to see people and have some serious conversation. I will be disappointed. It seems that Minder said nothing about me; he only had asked whether I wasn't an alcoholic. He also said with reference to his being bilingual, "It's sad to be a hermaphrodite"; he asked her to invite me again. By the way, she didn't ask him any questions, for then "he wouldn't have answered," she said. It's funny to take such a modest attitude thinking that one cannot do anything about a guy's character and his relationship with oneself, for then one can truly do nothing. It's a little like Sartre's observation on ambition for which we set limits ourselves and which will then certainly hold us back in what we would have dared to do. But in human relationships we need to be more audacious. That's really too much to accept things passively like this. She left and the conversation resumed. Each time Sorokine offers a little more trust and tenderness—but the poor thing, then it was Wanda who interrupted to tell me that the seamstress was there. The Moon Woman said hello and looked sternly at my plaster. "If it weren't for that you would be very beautiful," she said, "but that's just unfortunate," and she repeated, "that's unfortunate," as if it were some kind of innovative and daring but ill-chosen makeup. The seamstress, one of those horrible gnomes for whom the Kos. sisters make allowances if they deem them to be devoted, also looked sternly at me, especially at my coat; they made me turn around and suggested some touchups. I finally could go back downstairs and stay with Sorokine until half past seven. But then I had to go and pick up my parents, who were arriving at the Austerlitz station, my father having been able to find a job here. I waited for fifteen minutes in the crowd and felt increasingly tired. I was afraid that my sister would also come to Paris, for then I would have to see her. However, that wasn't the case, thank heavens; they arrived alone, more depressed than ever; my father's eyebrows were standing up on end. They were complaining loudly about the route the taxi was taking and the price the porter had asked. Even though I was tired, I was in a good mood because I had two letters from Sartre and a very charming letter from Bost, who had received my package and felt quite overwhelmed. I like to have these ties created by objects; they're different from those formed by letters alone. We went to dinner at the lower ground floor of the Lumina,* not too bad, and our conversation went as well as could be expected. I had some white wine and a little brandy, which was enough to make me stagger. I helped my mother take the luggage upstairs, I like doing things like that, it eases my conscience somewhat, like sending money to my sister. I was

---

* A restaurant, rue de Rennes.

so tired that I fell asleep in the chair in the study. When I finally woke up, I went home by taxi. I spent an hour and a half with Kos. telling her about my day. She told me a bunch of stories that slipped by me somewhat because of my fatigue. She was angry with Vallon for insinuating things about her and Lexia—her worrying about her image at the Atelier got on my nerves. I went downstairs and collapsed on my bed, dead to the world.

Thursday, November 30

Hard to wake up—it was nine o'clock, but I hadn't slept well, I had a hangover, felt achy everywhere, and my head was like a forge. But I went to the lycée all the same because if I had to miss work I'd want it for better reasons. I just drank a quart of Vittel and when I started my class I thought I'd faint, but it went away. At half past noon, Sorokine. We lunched at the small blue brasserie, then on foot to Henri IV—she gave me a little note in which she asked me a thousand things; I talked with her about everything, about her laziness in her work, etc.—she asks all the time, but does so gracefully. She explained in a charming way why she respects and loves me. Math. class— bought books for Sartre at Gibert—by metro to the post office. I had one letter from Sartre and two from Bost, one written Sunday and the other Tuesday. They delight my soul. With reference to Kos., he told me that he always felt like a stranger, at least not like a lover, and that will reassure me for a long time because I had dreaded the idea of a new and deep intimacy between them. I wrote my letters, then went home to be there for the seamstress. The Moon Woman was trying on a very beautiful dress, but her chest was a disaster, worse than I'd thought. I left again to write a bunch of letters (Bost, Sartre, Védrine, and Poupette) and until half past nine corrected a stack of papers. The last few days I have been rereading the beginning of *The Trial* by Kafka and started reading *Fermé la nuit* [Closed at Night] by Paul Morand.

Kos. returned from the Atelier at half past nine, and together with Wanda we had a bite to eat in the back of the Rotonde. I felt lifeless because of my intense fatigue. They were telling me stories that I didn't find very entertaining. We went home at eleven o'clock and I read Morand in bed for a while.

Wednesday, December 1

I got up at eight o'clock to take Kos. to the Sorbonne. She swore that she would go, but at half past eight she appeared on the stairs in her robe looking embarrassed. I went to the Dôme and worked for two and a quarter hours. A woman was sitting there writing without ordering anything, and when the cleaning personnel turned the light on for her she got quite embarrassed. She became desperate, saying it would draw attention to her and indeed she was told that it was not allowed to use the official stationery without ordering. I felt good, no more fatigue, and as far as my boil is concerned I made up my mind—it does look ugly, but it's slowly coming to a head under its plaster. I work and feel good; it is difficult to realize that there is still a war going on, at least the war no longer seems to me like a transcendent and justifying object that must be thought out; it's only a circumstance, a condition of life less fortunate than another. I worked rather well—then went to the post office to send my package and pick up my letter from Sartre—he was leaving, everything seemed uncertain. I don't know whether I'll be able to go and see him and that's beginning to irritate me. I went to the Biarritz to meet with Kanapa and Lévy. I feel a kind of affection for them because for me they're "remnants" from last year. Kanapa talked about coming with me on a skiing vacation—they told me that the little movie house was open; I was delighted to hear it. It also seems that the Atelier is going to reopen with *Richard III*.

Teaching from one to three o'clock. Metzger came to see me at the gate and accompanied me to my hotel—nothing interesting. I went up to work and write my letters. Then spent the evening with Kos.—dinner at Pagès and then to the Rotonde.

Saturday, December 2

Lycée—work and lunch at the Dôme, then at home. I reread the work of the trimester: already over one hundred pages and it's shaping up rather well. For a moment I thought it will definitely be printed and it felt strange; I had the impression of being taken seriously. Sorokine arrived at a quarter past four. As always, kisses, some tender small talk, kisses; afterward we worked a little on philosophy. She accompanied me to the Duroc metro station, which took me to Colette Audry's place.

Her husband and Wahl were there; Wahl had long hair and was even uglier and more pathetic looking than I remembered. Minder looked more youthful than the other day; he has a rather interesting and not unpleasant kind of face. The conversation dragged on at the start, then we sat down at the table; Audry had prepared an excellent dinner. She was dressed in black, looking very much like an officer's wife; and the conversation got livelier. I was amazed that I could hold my end of the conversation with so much ease, just as it amazed me twelve years ago when I began to dare to discuss and speak up at the Sorbonne. I always considered other people more "serious" than myself. However, the slightest observation made by Sartre or myself has the effect of a brilliant flash of intelligence in one of those stagnant conversations. Amazement, each time I'm faced with the dearth hiding under a serious appearance. Yesterday Wahl had been to the *NRF.* There he met Paulhan, who comes to the meeting each month, and Malraux, Petitjean, Chamson, Audiberti, and Benda—in a low voice, giving the impression of being very daring, he whispered little war anecdotes that had been making the rounds everywhere (the matter of the projectors)—Aragon had been present too, but he didn't tell me much about him. It seems that he remained steadfast in his positions; he declared, incidentally, that there wasn't any war, only a civil war. Thierry Maulnier was also present, and the two had to be put in separate rooms; after that they were put face to face and nothing dramatic happened. Aragon was in uniform while the fellow from the Action française[3] was not. Malraux, to no avail, was still trying to enlist in the active combat unit. Before judging Stalin he would wait and see whether he would "sovietize" or "protect" Finland, a strange point of view. He said that in any case a revolution at that price seemed too costly to him. All those fellows have strange and vague attitudes lacking continuity and a sense of their responsibilities and appearances. It seems that Gide is in the South working with refugees once again. There also was some talk about concentration camps and espionage, but very little of it was interesting. Minder showed pamphlets that were distributed to Germans, serious pamphlets, such as Hitler's contradictions, Hitler played by Stalin, etc. He said that morale behind the lines in Germany was bad but still solid on the front. Some Germans sent letters to Denmark with "we are hungry" written on the back of the stamps. However, the facts were ambiguous, he said; were they hungry or did they want to move the Danes to pity? We talked until half past ten and as I was leaving they pushed Wahl on me on the pretext that he was taking the same metro. He explained to me that Sartre should submit *L'Imaginaire* as a thesis.[4] I went home and said hello to Kos., who had received a mysterious note from Bost saying that he won't be able to write for several days; she was dead tired and depressed. I went to sleep reading the *NRF* that they had lent me over at Audry's.

To study: my position with respect to people, my representation of myself in relation to people; why do I not take myself seriously when faced with intellectuals? In part it is because of my political incompetence and the lack of social ties. But there is something else besides. If my novel is published will all this change? I feel that I can adapt when I'm around people. I'm even good at it. With Minder, for example, I watched myself doing it and it was fun because it presented a challenge. I never try to give a total impression of myself, but always look for the particular conduct and answer that suits my interlocutor. But I don't feel situated when I'm facing a group of people and don't know what attitude to adopt in front of a large number, when my attitude is no longer called for by the needs of adaptation, and I don't like to conceive of myself as a function of them.

Sunday, December 3*

A pleasant day with Toulouse.

At half past seven I got up to wake Kos., otherwise she would certainly not be ready. I went back to bed; I was sleepy and remembered vaguely other pleasant mornings when I got up sleepy like today, for example, when I used to see Bost in Amiens—the height of happiness! To think I left Sartre to see Bost, and in the evening, after having visited Bost, I found Sartre again—and these actions seemed so natural. True, despite everything it never ceased to amaze me. Kos. brought me some tea and croissants that I had while reading an *NRF* article by Bachelard on Lautréamont, which I didn't find all that entertaining. I finished getting ready; my boil was almost gone and I removed the plaster. I put on the white sweatshirt with green and coral trim. I knocked at Kos.'s door and in a toneless voice she answered that she wasn't ready and I should go on alone. I felt that she was about to hate me and I was furious inside; I wanted so much to take her there. Thank heavens ten minutes later I went back up and she was ready, no makeup, but ready and proud of it. We could still make the train by taking a taxi. We took the train, an ugly old wooden train with people smelling of garlic. A soldier in a crazed voice told of a shell splinter in his thigh that he had treated himself and could show us. A woman across from us was choking with tears. The train ride lasted an hour; then in Esbly we took a luxurious railcar instead of the little old train, and we arrived in Crécy. But two guards of the militia were stationed at the entrance gate. Since we didn't have a pass, they wanted to send us back to Paris. I pleaded with the one, who seemed inflexible, but he finally relented and being unsure of what to do, sent me to his boss, who started yelling at me. But I showed him my passport, all the while talking nonstop. There was a woman whose mother was ill and they had to let her pass, so they let us go

---

* This day has been transcribed in *The Prime of Life*.

too. They were scrutinizing Kos.'s papers because of her foreign name, but found nothing wrong and we left, our heads held high.

The weather was dry, the sky blue, and the sun quite warm. I took my coat off to climb up the shortcut; it brought back to mind the most beautiful days in Megève. Kos. was grumbling a little because the ground was wet, but I felt in heaven to be in the country—she was intimidated by the idea of meeting Dullin. We arrived at the village and I pointed out Mme Jollivet's house, where a man was busy shoeing a horse. He turned toward us and lo and behold it was Dullin himself, wearing corduroy pants and a large sackcloth apron. He greeted us and said to go on up and see Toulouse, who was waving to us from a second-floor window. I showed Kos. the house; she was delighted by it and by the garden, all dried up by the wintry weather. Inside was a brand new small sofa, covered in a charming blue fabric, and toward the back, a kind of sunroom decorated with artificial flowers and beautiful pictures of birds on the walls. Toulouse came downstairs looking gorgeous in a housecoat of several shades of mauve, which she had dyed herself, a purple bejeweled ribbon in her braided hair, wearing bracelets, a necklace, and a Berber ring on one finger. We chatted a while, her little black dog playing with a kitten, which was quite entertaining. Dullin came in and all four of us drank some delicious Dutch drink, a kind of port flip* to which we added some more port; it tasted delicious. Mme Jollivet came in, looking less terrifying than the other time, her hair in three colors: white in front, red in the middle, and at the neck a gray twist—still the same relationship with Dullin. She's funny when, for example, she gives her opinion on Dickens in her heavy Toulouse accent. We ate very well; there was neither uneasiness nor affectation. Kos. looked charming and conducted herself with perfect ease. In the afternoon Dullin worked on the décor of *Richard III*; he sawed, glued, and built a model of the tower of London. Mme Jollivet watched him with a disapproving eye: "Four o'clock! I didn't think building a décor was all that difficult. I thought you put furniture on the stage and that's all there was to it." Kos. meanwhile was copying a scene from *Richard III* and Toulouse was knitting a purple and white sock. She drew me to the bathroom to tell me that Kos. would perhaps be given the part of a page in the play, and if not, then certainly that of a walk-on. The afternoon went by. We drank a glass of cider before leaving; then Kos. and I went out into the night carrying a small blue flashlight that Toulouse had lent us. Train; exhausting return trip that seemed long. We ate at Pagès. Kos. had a toothache and was depressed because of the note from

---

* It was advokaat.

Bost, who had alerted her the previous night that she wouldn't have a letter tonight—I was annoyed too. We got home at half past nine. I wrote to Sartre, Bost, and Védrine—then I collapsed from exhaustion.

Monday, December 4

Lycée. Received same note from Bost as Kos. had—two long letters from Sartre. Perhaps I'll be unable to see him, but he hoped to be moved from the front toward the interior. That would be great. I stayed at the Dôme for a long while and meditated wide-eyed on this news. I wrote Sartre because I was too excited to work—I lost a large amount of time looking for photographic items for him. Nevertheless, I was able to work a little; the novel continues to come along well. Lycée; I went home and worked a while. Gérassi stopped by and the seamstress came for a fitting for my coat. I wrote my letters and went to eat with my family. Then I met up with Kos. at nine o'clock and we spent the evening at the Rotonde. She was on edge and I was also a bit down because of this problem with Bost. But she was on edge "with" me instead of bristling right away as she usually does. She spoke with respect of Toulouse and Dullin, now that she had seen them in their private surroundings—she told me about Lexia's second suicide attempt—something to do with Kéché-lévitch,* etc. We went home; I finished my letters and read a while in Mac Orlan's *Le Nègre Léonard et maître Jean Mullin* [Black Leonard and Master Jean Mullin], which is pleasant to read. I was annoyed for Bost, but a spineless need for peace and quiet left me almost indifferent.

Tuesday, December 5

Lycée. Work at the Mahieu—lunch at Mirov's with Sorokine—lycée—a short note from Bost that reassured me. He had moved and moved again; it seems that that was all. A sleepy short letter from Sartre. Telegrams from Védrine, who is coming to Paris on Thursday and seems intent on coming each week, which annoys me considerably. Worked a little; letters and updating of this notebook. At the Dupont I found an extremely agitated Kos. Movies: *The Return of Zorro*, rather poor. On our way home we had a bite to eat at the Milk Bar. I then went to bed at eleven o'clock. I finished this notebook and read a while in *Le Quai des Brumes* by Mac Orlan.

---

* Olga Barbezat, her friend, also an actress.

Wednesday, December 6

At eight o'clock in the morning the Dupont was swarming with people. I had hot chocolate while reading *Le Quai des Brumes*. It was a pleasant quarter of an hour. Then two hours of teaching, post office, and a long letter from Sartre, who left me some hope that I might be able to visit him. I went to work at the Dôme and saw poor shy Mouloudji. "I'm waiting for Olga," he said; he had to wait an hour for her, naturally. I worked and went to have lunch with the two at the Rotonde. Mouloudji was really pleasant. I went back to my place, wrote my letters, and worked again, but not too well because I had a slight headache. I decided to rework the novel from the beginning, in the definitive version. It seemed lots of fun to me. Got a charming letter from Védrine saying that she didn't want to be a burden like the last time. Suddenly I felt happy to see her.

Sorokine arrived a six o'clock—straight away she made her funny little sweet faces, which meant that we had to get down to kisses first—and embraces—but we had to leave soon to send Védrine a telegram. We stuffed ourselves with pastries and bought some bananas and dates. The bus took us to the theater. We ate and had something to drink in the Café Biard nearby. I was touched by Sorokine and tried to be as nice as possible. I was telling her anything she wanted to hear, and she was in heaven. They gave us two seats in the back of a loge and during the entire performance she held my hand and rubbed her cheek against mine. Kos. used to have this childlike behavior too but was restrained by her pride and sense of propriety, which resulted in a rather strange attitude. Sorokine is very naive and admittedly tyrannical, which makes it less fearsome.

The Damnation of Faust; I knew almost the entire text but had fun listening to it again from beginning to end. The staging was burlesque, with the devils sporting red goatees and using exactly those disingenuously stylized gestures that Zuorro was making fun of—average voices, without dazzle. After the last intermission, *L'Invitation à la valse* [Invitation to a Dance] suddenly burst onto the stage and the curtain rose on a boudoir all in white. We left in a hurry. I really love the Opéra, the red loges immersed in darkness yet suffused with a light that seems to come from their very color. Tonight's performance was sold out. But people don't dress up anymore. On the tickets the price of thirty-three francs had been crossed out and replaced by twelve francs; the notice "Formal dress required" had been left, but people were wearing suits and hats and plain street clothes. The impression of war was quite strong in this theater with its discounted prices and in the company of the little person holding my hand.

It was cold and dark outside and we had difficulty finding a café because it was close to eleven o'clock. For five minutes we sat down on red velvet-covered seats. Then we went out into the dark. She was very happy telling me how fond she was of me. But we almost got into a quarrel because she was afraid to cross the streets alone and wanted me to accompany her to the metro; a funny little tyrant.

I went home, barely mustering enough strength to go to bed. I don't get enough sleep these nights.

Thursday, December 7

I stayed in bed until half past eight. Had a letter from Sartre that I read at the Versailles. I worked for an hour on chapter 1; had fun doing it. Lycée Camille Sée. Sorokine had lunch with me at the blue brasserie; she brought me some chocolates. She was still in great form, telling me that she was so happy because we had made such great progress in our relationship in three months. But when I said that it had reached its maximum best, she protested; she expects much more still. However, I'm not worried. I would never leave her and even if I make her cry a little for not seeing her often, she is better off having me in her life than not having me at all. She accompanied me to Henri IV—two hours of teaching—I went home waiting for Védrine and the seamstress. I wrote to Sartre and Bost and updated this notebook. At six o'clock there was a knock on the door; it was the Moon Woman. She had an appointment with the seamstress. We were chatting casually when Védrine arrived—stopped in her élan by the Moon Woman's presence, but quickly adapting and acting pleasantly. Nevertheless, the conversation was flagging. I left the Moon Woman at my place and took Védrine to the Coupole, where we dined in comfort, seated next to a guy who scandalized me for treating himself to red caviar and a truffle cooked in embers and served in a large papillote covered with ash. Inside was a beautiful little puff pastry and inside it, a sumptuous truffle.

We chatted and went to the Vikings to drink aquavit. Védrine was neither tense nor demanding; she was quite charming and I felt again much affection for her—but on the dull side bordering a little on boredom. She slept at my place; caresses as clear as spring water and a little insipid. I slept well; her presence did not weigh me down as it did the last time.

Friday, December 8*

Védrine left for the Sorbonne and I went to the post office. Letter from Sartre, who changed his whereabouts. Letter from Bost, sent Sunday, who seemed more interested in his moving from place to place than overwhelmed by it. The absence of letters really makes a difference. I do write, on principle, but without much pleasure; our relationships retreat into the past. I went to the Dôme, where I worked on the first chapter for more than two hours. It's great fun making revisions of what has been done. Kos. came by, she was charming; we had exchanged letters the evening before last. She took me to buy beautiful black shoes, flats, at Willy's. They make my feet look at little mannish, but they are so comfortable. We had lunch at the bar of the Dupont—she told me gossip about Mouloudji, Lexia, etc. Lycée—I went to the Mahieu to finish my letters that I had started while I was giving a written test. There I met Gibert† in the restroom; she was well groomed and wore a rather luxurious red velvet dress. "I think I came here to see you, without realizing it," she said. We then had coffee together and a heart-to-heart talk. She told me mysteriously that she had money and lived in a luxury hotel in the eighteenth arrondissement, and that she managed somehow so as to devote herself entirely to do "research," but didn't know exactly what kind; she has broken off with every one, even with Frances, who, when she had slept at her place the other day, had moved her because she had found her weak spot: "because I do have a weak spot," she said laughingly—but who doesn't. She showed me, feigning distaste, a fan letter from Perrin: "Do you think I care?" She lives alone and writes: poems first of all, in order to desocialize the meaning of words, then with these desocialized words she writes clear and intelligible short stories. Guys disgust her with their offers of sex: "a hundred francs, that's all I'm worth,"—she only does theater now. The evening she flunked the Conservatory she had gone to see Jouvet; she was calm and serene. He had taken her hands and looking into her eyes had asked: "Are you calm and collected?"—she had said "yes" and he had kissed her hands with an extraordinary look on his face, "the look of a being who has finally found what he had been looking for all his life," and "I'm happy to have flunked just to have seen this look." Jouvet needed someone and the only being who could be this someone was Gibert; but he would not want

---

* This day has been transcribed in *The Prime of Life* and condensed with that of Monday, November 13.

† She had left the Atelier in order to work with Jouvet.

to impose himself on her, given his boorish character. And so he would no longer see her and she didn't try to influence him because that would not be worth anything—she talked about nothing but being, soul and passion. "What do you think of me?" she asked me with fiery eyes. But I wriggled out of it. She salvaged all that a bit by her charming facial expressions. She had been seeing Wagner, who was completely disgusted with the war because he cannot be without a feminine presence—he continued to court her, but poorly and timidly, all the while professing that he was still in love with his wife like the first day they met.

At that moment Védrine, looking tired, arrived with Lévy and Kanapa, who left right away. She was amused to see Gibert, who, by the way, also left immediately. We went to a small café and then to the Ursulines to watch *Le Goujat* [The Scoundrel] with Noel Coward—it wasn't good, too narrow-minded and conceptual, but one male character was fascinating on the screen. However, he should have been placed within a complex plot, which is not possible on the screen. We watched again the beginning of *Si j'avais un million* [If I Had a Million], which was somewhat funny. Afterward we had a bite to eat at the Capoulade and then went to the lower floor of the Hoggar to watch belly dancing. We talked about me; it's true, I'm interested in myself these days, in my habit of adapting to conversations by remembering what impressions to make, etc. I found it pleasant to chat with Védrine. Our embraces were a little hurried once we got home because we had to get up early.

Saturday, December 9

Lycée Camille Sée. Suddenly I'm conscious of my physical appearance, my relationship with my parents, my milieu—all because of my earrings; Védrine told me that they did not look vulgar and Kos. has said a thousand times that I looked distinguished to her. And yet, I lack style and have some of Poupette's homeliness. I'm only too aware that I'm of French stock, provincial, middle-class, and déclassé; what's more, I'm a civil servant, an intellectual, and have contacts with Montparnasse. All that is reflected in the way I dress and wear my hair. I also should look into the fact that I feel an increasing desire to do a study of myself. I have the impression that this year will be as productive for me as my year in Marseilles; leisure and attention to myself; solitude. Solitude sustained by Sartre's existence, a privileged condition: to think for him, but without him, with him, yet far away from him. A coming to terms with and taking stock of myself, and a kind of inner stability I had never had before. I wrote Sartre from the Versailles—then lunch with my family. My father told me about the war and that he had never been afraid, not even during the shelling of a village that others had rushed through light-footed, while he, too tired because of his heart, had lain down on the ground too dazed and exhausted to be afraid. By reading the *Carnets de moleskine** and all the rest I'm really becoming aware what the everyday life of war is like.

At the Biarritz I met up with Védrine and Kanapa—we chatted for an hour, then on foot and by taxi Védrine and I went to the Opéra Comique. Concert Thibaud, a sonata by Fauré, one by Debussy, and the Kreutzer Sonata. Debussy rather bewilders me; he follows Gide's motto "not to take advantage of the acquired élan." The comparison is funny because Fauré takes advantage of it ever so much and Debussy in this sonata definitely refuses to do so every time and in a way that could be said to be almost aggressive, which makes the piece difficult to grasp. We went back to Montparnasse and found the seamstress at my place, finally bringing me my new coat; it's very beautiful.

Went out with the Moon Woman. With my beautiful coat, a green scarf and turban, my earrings and the beautiful shoes, I went back to the Dôme. Ten minutes later the Moon Woman arrived looking almost pretty under her large brown felt hat, with her fur-lined coat, purse slung across her shoulder, and a big umbrella a la Chamberlain. There was a moment of indecision; neither one of us knew what to do with each other. In the end we decided to go to the Villa. It's a large dance hall on the cheap side that reminds one exactly of the Royal in Rouen; bad orchestra, flimsy tasteless décor cluttered with pictures, and on the seats against the wall twelve girls in faded pale satin. The Moon Woman ordered some cold cuts. We drank half a bottle of Chablis and as the maître d' made a sour face, we ordered one more. We danced; it was the first night of dancing; it just started up again. The girls put on a few acts. They appeared dressed up like school girls in black pleated skirts, with plaid ribbons in their hair, and plaid collars that left nothing bare but the breasts; thus isolated they seemed like sickly growths, but the Moon Woman was moved by them. Then the girls appeared with a *tricolore* Marianne; they were dressed like English, Polish, etc., soldiers and singing the "Marseillaise." The act looked like a 1917 music hall parody, nothing more. The police arrived; now, that seemed like war, those policemen among the lights and the satin, wearing shiny metal helmets, flash lights right on their bellies, and asking for papers. The Moon Woman was amusing. At first, on

---

* War journal from 1914–18, by Lucien Jacques, preface by Giono.

her way here, she said she didn't want to tell me her stories, but then she did so anyway and very well. She compared herself to Dostoevski's idiot, but preferred to turn this idiocy into a politics, which really doesn't go together. She admired power and specialization, which is a form of power over whatever the specialization is about. She talked to me about Youki: the other day, after a night of drinking, when everyone had left—Blanche Picard was sleeping in the adjoining room—Youki had kept her newest lover and the Moon Woman with her in the dining room. The lover had put on a Japanese robe and Youki in her slip gave some dance exhibitions. At some point she left to vomit up her drinks and came back declaring, "I took off my pants, it will be much more convenient," and she sat down in her lover's lap. The Moon Woman realized that they were making love and kept herself busy putting on a record—incidentally, she was mad at herself for not looking. Then Youki went to get a tiny washbowl: "It was funny," said the Moon Woman, "because all three of us are big and tall and the washbasin was so small," and she proceeded to wash herself in front of the others, who were quite embarrassed. Then, as the Moon Woman had been invited to sleep over, she went to stretch out next to Blanche Picard, who is not very fond of her. They heard that the other two were making love again, and then Youki came into their room, noisily, but delighted. She also lay down with them and wanted to fondle the Moon Woman, who at first defended herself, but finally, without reciprocating, managed "to get Youki to sleep" while Blanche next to them was hopping mad. In the morning the Moon Woman was disgusted at how awful Youki looked without her makeup: "Good god, we were all dreadfully drunk last night," she had said to her. "You were the one who was drunk," Youki had said in a mean tone, "as for me, not at all." "I meant to say, we were just a little tipsy," the Moon Woman had remarked, shamefully and cowardly correcting her statement.

Around ten o'clock we went to the Poisson d'Or, a posh place. The décor was sober; it was done in red with green plants—the entertainment was very decent, a wealthy clientele but neither racy nor elegant, the Champs-Élysées crowd, as bad as they come. It was packed; you need to reserve a table days in advance, and everyone was having dinner. Nevertheless, they found us a small table in the back that we changed for one that was a little better. The Moon Woman, a little drunk, felt Russian and inclined to pull out all the stops. She bargained for a cheap bottle of champagne, but they just gave us "a deal" on our ice cream, which we ate while sipping our champagne. The ice cream was out of this world, delicious. We chatted about me, but she

186

always repeated the same thing, namely that Sartre oppresses me, etc., and that's hardly amusing. I have taken a poll about my looks and the results were as follows: Kanapa found me "good-looking" but not pretty—Lévy, pretty and even "quite beautiful"—the Moon Man, very pretty.

They made us leave at eleven o'clock. The Moon Woman felt like having "Stimmung"* and since I couldn't provide her with any, she went off alone through the streets. I went upstairs to say hello to Kos., who was charming with me, and I went to bed.

Sunday, December 10

I woke up rather late and began a letter to Bost before going to meet Védrine at the Dôme. We chatted, and then went to the Dupont and afterward to lunch at the Coupole. No news from Bost; a letter from Sartre, who leaves me less and less hope. These last few days I noticed that I was beginning to get nervous because of this uncertain departure. I wrote to Bost, then from the Dôme a letter to Sartre that turned out to be huge since I had plenty of time, Kos. not showing up before three o'clock. We left on foot, walking through Paris. The weather was mild and hazy with stunning effects of light; the green dome of the Opéra against a pink sky and a large sign on rue La Fayette attracting the sun like rocks in the Alps or tree trunks in the woods. We arrived at the concert in the Conservatory hall. They were playing the *Requiem* by Guy Ropartz, a premiere—insipid—then a symphony by Franck, conducted by Charles Munch, that was first-rate and that I could follow effortlessly. It really engaged me and even touched me physically, which very rarely happens to me when listening to music. We were on the way home, in the metro, when things turned sour because I told Kos. that I was going out with Védrine. She had not understood that I was spending only the afternoon with her. Perhaps I had been too vague. In any case she had a fit of outraged dignity. I was sincerely sorry and followed her until our hotel, offering my apologies. But it's amazing, this core of spiteful hostility against Bost and me as soon as we wrong her—an annoying trait of hers. She left full of rancor against me and I went to the Flore to meet up with Védrine.

Védrine had drunk too much during the day, but there was no trace left of it; she was completely charming. We ate some chocolate and orange marmalade and went to the College Inn,† which had reopened. The pianist alone

---

* Ambience.
† At rue Vavin.

remained and there was a different bartender; it was pleasant. We chatted—that's how I like her, cheerful and serious and concerned about herself—because basically she is positive, even hard, and occupied more than anything with her success in life. I explained to her how it was important for her to always "take advantage," to "invest well," but that in the end life can only be of advantage to life itself, that one should not take everything out of life under the pretext of getting more out of it. We discussed this idea of obtaining a return from life, which is linked to that of serious-mindedness. I need to question myself more on the subject. On the whole I know that the highest priority for me is having as complete a grasp on the world as possible. And I have learned that such a grasp is only possible through *one* life. And I'm demanding of myself only things that are a function of this life, which is itself a function of the world—but that's not precise enough. Védrine is interested only in personal gain without really knowing what it means to be a person; if one cares to explain it at the lowest level, there is social success on the horizon. But in a sense, social approval is for her a guarantee of the metaphysical objectivity of realities and values. In any case, it was interesting to talk with her about all this. I was disappointed, on the other hand, in Kos. this afternoon because when I tried to talk with her, as I do with Védrine, about the representation of the self, etc., we didn't get anywhere; she is interested exclusively in her own self in the strictest sense of the word, like in an important person, really a fragment of the world. Védrine has the same liking for totality as Sartre and I do.

How amusing that Védrine is upset at the idea that in ten years we'll be too old for her to love us. In short, she freely wants to stop her love, she will be free in stopping it, and she is free in its anticipation. She admits it and finds it amusing. That's precisely the kind of pathos she has, and this mix of desperate outburst and solidity: because she cries before a wailing wall that she is building with her own busy hands, that she often builds in order to protect the positive riches she fiercely wants to defend. Something of the old Jewish usurer in her, who cries out of pity for the client he is driving to suicide. She is terribly "self-interested"—with generous ideas that she feels passionate about and that exclude the interests to which she clings. But, such as she is, with the unpleasant quality of a Jewish businesswoman, I like her and find her interesting.

We returned home and for part of the passionate night I was a bit carried away, body and soul.

Monday, December 11

I left Védrine—I read a little in the *Carnets de moleskine* while eating break-fast at the Dupont—lycée—letters. A letter from Bost that made my blood run cold. One may have thought it was a letter from a ghost or a crazed man, that's how strongly it suggested that he is beyond everything. He is almost at the front, in the mud, the cold, reduced to the life of an animal and unable even to feel regret. The tone and even the handwriting of the letter seemed to come from another world. I also was sad because Sartre could not help me, and I was almost sure to not be able to go to Morsbronn. There was a white fog in the streets that penetrated your eyes, the pores of your skin, and which was depressing. I went to the Dôme to write Sartre and Bost. I was caught up again by the war, ill at ease and extremely sad. I had lunch and saw Tyssen. She told me that Madeleine Robinson had beaten her up and kicked her in the stomach in the village of Cantal, where both had been living to-gether since the beginning of the war. She moved back to Paris, but without any big plans. "I don't have any luck," she told me, which is rather true.

Lycée Henri IV. Sorokine was waiting at the gate, ready to argue with me, but nice; she accompanied me home. Two hours and a half of excellent work without fatigue, it was going well. Védrine came by, and we went to the Vikings. She plans to come back to Paris but will have a job and does not expect to see too much of me. I rather like the idea.

I went back to my hotel. There, I was handed a package with the address in Sartre's handwriting. Seltzer must have left it. Two black notebooks and a short note that hardly left me any hope. It really depressed me. Kos. came over, especially charming—we went to eat at Pagès; she had a toothache and we went home early. She was depressed and I, worn out and exhausted; we were hanging about listlessly. She left and I read Sartre's notebooks in bed, skimming through them and choosing the easiest one.

Tuesday, December 12

The weather was extremely cold and a fog thick as cotton was covering Paris. I crossed the Luxembourg Gardens walking next to a group of students who were holding their gas mask containers in their hands. It made them laugh to see me enter the Mahieu, where I read Sartre's notebooks for a moment while drinking a coffee. Lycée, then again at the Mahieu; I brought my note-book up to date, which took me two hours—then lunch at the Capoulade with Sorokine. Camille Sée—post office: nothing from Bost—I wrote my letters rather quickly from the Versailles and at home worked for two and a half hours without even looking up. Then for an hour I read Sartre's note-books, which delighted me. A lively emotional memory came back to me, dating from the period of Guille and That Lady, making me very nostalgic about the time when the world was as uncertain as we were. That was our true youth—now it has taken a turn toward the dark and serious; and I am happy with what we are, but we are beings made with strong backbones—while in the past there was a tender and incomplete halo around us. This intellectual and moral climate of the past came back to me and I could still feel it clearly, very close yet forever gone; I found it heartrending.

Spent the evening with Kos., idyllic. Both of us felt rested. We ate at Pagès, and then went to the College Inn—she was telling me about the rehearsal of *Richard III* at the Atelier; she saw Mayenne Copeau* with her granddaugh-ter, whom she treated with passionate tenderness. We met one of the girls of the Atelier, Braque, whose husband is away at war and who really looked the part of a soldier's wife, half drunk and hanging out with friends of sorts.

Wednesday, December 13

A rather miserable day. Lycée, then to the post office and one hour of work at the Dôme, where the boxer woman† met up with me, very shy, dressed in a shabby plaid coat—we had lunch; she has a tender and delightful shy-ness about her, which makes it almost impossible to get a word out of her—I talked nonstop and didn't really enjoy it. At the police station I was told that without a proper document it was not possible to give me a pass. In any case, it would take a month to get it. Fortunately, Sartre wrote that within two months' time he would almost certainly be posted in a mountainous region at the interior of the country, which made me less disappointed. I spent one hour at the Lutétia with Mme Mancy, I wrote Sartre—and went to Ideal Sport; so I'll be going to Megève, but when walking back to the hotel through the cold and darkness, tears came to my eyes when I thought that I would be alone there or with Kanapa, where I had been with Sartre and Bost—still no letter from Bost, the connection has been cut for a long time, and it saddened me.

I went home and found Sorokine in my room; she had placed two beau-tiful blotters on the table, one red and the other yellow; we were supposed

* Marie-Hélène Dasté, Copeau's daughter.
† Lili Bonafé.

190

to work, but started with embraces, and when I wanted to work she held me tight in her arms; then after five minutes she said, annoyed, "Let's work or talk"; I wanted to get up, but she held me back and kissed me. Finally, though very late, we took up Kant, but without leaving the bed where we were stretched out (she had nervously taken off one of my shoes and also opened a pin of my blouse, as a symbolic undressing). She broke down sobbing and became tense: "we're not working"—followed by a big speech interrupted by sobbing about really having to work for hours—I told her that she wasn't crying because of that, but because our physical relationship doesn't work out, that it would perhaps be better to put a stop to it. She threw herself into my arms saying that that would spoil everything, that she loved me in a physical way and that she did not want to feel ashamed about anything with me—I hesitated, I did not want to sleep with her, but that's what she really wanted—and the situation is disgusting and impossible. She snuggled up to me, very trusting, relaxed and charming—she asked me intimate questions, such as whether I have had any physical relationships—yes, was my answer, with Sartre—whether I had not been ashamed of anything with him—no—It's funny one doesn't feel ashamed doing things, only talking about them, one shouldn't, etc. She was extremely pleasant, a beautiful face overwhelmed with passion, and I was very moved and, really, I'm fond of her without feeling vulgar about it, just tenderness—but it's a big responsibility and scary. "You're the first person I'm in love with," she said. She had never before said that she loved me, assigning this particular quality to the word. She left at half past seven, radiant—and there I was, almost obligated to sleep with her. If she didn't please me physically, would I have reacted differently? I don't know, but it's possible.

I wrote to Bost and made entries into this notebook while waiting for Kos. Reading Sartre's notebooks had filled the last two days, strange long-distance intimacy. Kos. arrived at nine o'clock, on edge because of the Atelier; she didn't know whether she would have a part; she would be staying in Paris while waiting, which is getting me down. We had dinner at Dominique's— and spent the evening in my room, where she stayed on until midnight, so bright and alert she was—and charming as she had never been before with me. She was funny and really seductive, but I was heavy with sleep.

Thursday, December 14

The war is starting again for me—I got up, went to the post office, where I had a letter from Sartre, so tender, but I can't go to see him. Fortunately, it seems that he is soon being sent toward Annecy and that idea sustains me. A letter from Bost: "In ten days Delarue will be proven right.* I wondered whether I should tell you, but I prefer to let you know"; I keep on telling myself: it's not dangerous at the moment—but my soul is transfixed and the feeling won't leave me. All day long it was there, a venomous little anguish that marks everything, and from time to time I told myself: so that's it, and I would like to run out of tears and be done with fear once and for all, but it won't work that way. It was cold; a kind of frozen snow was falling. I read Sartre's notebooks at the Versailles. The place had never been as dead; the floor was soapy, all the chairs put upside down in the dark, and no waiter to serve you; it felt poetic. Sartre's ideas on will and ethics seemed totally satisfying and definitive to me. But I don't know how he is going to give a content to his ethics; I would need to read the rest. Lycée Camille Sée. At half past noon, Sorokine with a stubborn face; and during lunch in the little blue brasserie, she didn't open her mouth. I got annoyed. When we left, she almost broke down in tears claiming that it was because of her work, but that's her usual defense mechanism. I made her admit that it was because of our physical relationship and because I had suggested we put a stop to it and she was desperate that with so little time it wasn't going anywhere. That's why it needed to increase its intensity. She was happy she finally spoke up and became charming and touching again. She would never want to be hypocritical with me, she said; she would like us to have a "complete" relationship and would tell me all her lies, for example, she already had kissed someone on the mouth. When I left Henri IV she was still there, offering her excuses. She accompanied me only to the Mahieu. I worked very well, two and a half hours; it's going well, if only I had more time. I finished my letters, then Kos. arrived, still on edge—we left immediately for the Ursulines—we saw *La Symphonie burlesque* [The Burlesque Symphony] again, which I enjoyed. And we watched *San Francisco,* which was dull, but the earthquake at the end was fabulous. We went home, chatted a while, still very lovingly. And I went to bed dead tired. I'm tired every night now.

Friday, December 15

I woke up with difficulty. I went to the Dôme and fortunately could work well. There I met the Gérassis with their dog. I stayed only fifteen minutes with them—they worried me. Somber information about Russia; it doesn't

---

* Which meant that he was going to the front lines.

seem to be going well at all. The newspapers constantly write about patrols, local activities, and I remembered what Gombrowski said, that for those who are there they die there all right. I was getting ever more demoralized. Letter from Sartre, nothing from Bost. He said that he was concerned, but I didn't think he was happy. I went to the Biarritz where I found Védrine, who is now living in Paris, as I learned. She arrived with Kanapa; she was loud and authoritarian having decided that I won't be going on a ski vacation until Easter—she got on my nerves. What annoyed me most of all was perhaps the fact that she came back because of Kos., who isn't leaving. Kanapa and I decided that we would go on a ski vacation together. The idea of leaving with a young man to go skiing, which would create a distant and yet intimate companionship between us, chilled me. It's a parody of my past, of this precious departure with Bost,* of my old and pleasant relationship with him—I am so sorry that Védrine puts so much energy into worrying about it. Lycée Henri IV. At the Mahieu I wrote my letters and then went by taxi to Camille Sée, where I had a meeting about the student honor roll. Anguish. I arrived two hours early, but it didn't matter for I could read *Les Carnets de moleskine* and even finish them—not that they were interesting or pleasant to read, but I could feel the war in them and that undid me. I got goose bumps from reading them, which never happens to me.

I left by taxi at 7:20 knowing what was waiting for me. I got to rue Malebranche and was wandering about looking for Védrine's hotel, which I had trouble finding in the dark. By chance I went up the stairs of a sordid little hotel, crowded with Chinese people. I found Védrine, who looked pretty in a blue dressing gown and was settled in a little comfortable room. She was "hard-hearted" having waited for half an hour, but I explained and she calmed down. We went for dinner at the Mirov and then she accompanied me almost to my hotel. At half past nine I went up to see Kos.—she was with Mouloudji, who greeted me with an expression both shy and mocking—it's because Kos., following up on my survey, had asked him what impression I made on him. He had at first found me hard and brusque, a woman who goes right to the heart of things, while Poupette had looked to him more like a cleaning lady, which he found more reassuring, and then, at the Rotonde the other day he had noticed that I was interested in the wine I was drinking and was good at telling stories—according to him I looked interesting, rather than pretty.

Kos. and I chatted at the Rotonde, then at my place until about midnight.

---

* Christmas 1937.

Saturday, December 16

Lycée. Work in the restaurant Lumina across from my parents' house.* The Lumina looked depressing and cold with its red tiles and all deserted. The proprietress was talking incessantly with a regular customer. They refused to serve me coffee; it's really getting scarce. Outside it was freezing cold—also at my parents' place where I had lunch—worked at the Versailles some more—no letters. The night before I had noticed a letter to Kos. written by Bost on Monday: "My love, you must write me," still some jealousy in me and a vague satisfaction that she isn't treating him right, but so dulled that I find myself in a state of indifference. I stayed with Kos. for a little while—then wrote my letters—and went to the Vikings to give Sorokine her lesson. She was sitting in a booth in the back with her pupil, who left immediately—her unfortunate friend had her furniture seized by the bailiff; they were going to be evicted. I explained Descartes; she understood easily and behaved well. All the while, in a neighboring booth, Mr. Laporte† was violently embracing some blonde woman in a green dress. Sorokine, embarrassed, asked me to explain a passage from Mac Orlan about some copper wires and that she thought to be very obscene. But they were extensive lyrical comparisons where a woman is compared to an electrical battery, written in a terrible style, I might add. She confessed that the colonel had kissed her twice on the mouth and after that he had broken off with her. I left her and took a taxi to rue Malebranche. Védrine greeted me passionately—we dined at the Knam,‡ bad music—I focused all my attention on her and on the whole was in a good mood; perhaps my gaiety was a little put on. We returned home early, went to bed, chatted a while, embraced, and went to sleep. I hated her a little during the night because she was tossing and turning and puffing, which is very much like her. But she was really nice.

Sunday, December 17

Pleasant Sunday that reminded me of other poetic Sundays except that I didn't love Védrine then and they remain like a poetic abstract—those Sunday mornings in the Latin Quarter or at Montmartre with Bost, how precious they were! We dozed until nine o'clock, almost like sleeping in, which I hadn't done for a long time. I felt like a fat man who had had his fill because

---

* Her parents' house was at 71, rue de Rennes.
† A philosophy professor at the Sorbonne.
‡ A Polish restaurant that her friend Stépha had introduced to her a long time ago.

I eluded the caresses and thought only of breakfast and getting to my work. Looking out the window, I felt slightly disoriented; it was a snowy morning. That was it, the altered look of the street, which evoked mornings with Bost, but without warmth; this one is not going to be engraved in my heart. We went to the post office; two letters from Sartre, making me very happy— feeling of leisure, almost like a vacation with time for work ahead of me. It also brought back to mind certain mornings with Sartre in Rouen. We went to the Mahieu, sitting next to each other, eating our breakfast and working. It was pleasant. Védrine was wearing her Cossack hat, a blouse with a tie, and if she hadn't been wearing makeup she could've been mistaken for a charming young boy. We had lunch at the Capoulade. We were comfortably seated and talked—then we went to the Danton, where we worked some more until half past four. I went to meet Kos.—I felt a little anxious as I always do when I have been in a situation that I kept secret. It seems to me that it leaves a trace behind, that it is visible—but no, not at all; she was a little morose but only because of her natural sullenness. We took the metro. She told me that Mouloudji was beginning to be a nuisance because he was too clingy. Concert: the Eroica, which I didn't listen to very attentively, I was a little tired—then *Rhapsodie espagnole* by Ravel, which one just has to listen to in spite of oneself—without a beginning like an obsession, or an obstinate reappearance—it's really great—then a piece by Roussel that was unremarkable, and finally the pleasant *Sorcerer's Apprentice*. We went home and then to Dominique's and the terrace of the Dôme, where we saw the Mage* in uniform with a red cross band on his arm: "So, you're not mobilized" he said affably. He works with public health statistics in the Moselle region. It was cold and we went home early. Kos. was somewhat frustrated seeing that it was only half past ten, but left me nevertheless and I wrote my letters. I read *Le Moine* [The Monk] to fall asleep. Artaud arranged it beautifully for the stage; it's really terribly amusing.

Monday, December 18

Lycée. I went to the Biarritz feeling sad and worked for an hour and a half— a bunch of uninteresting students were sitting in pairs in the little booths. There was a lot of pinching going on. The *Graf Von Spee* was blown up and the newspapers deplored the lack of heroism. If a man gets killed unexpectedly he is a superhuman hero, but if he doesn't get killed he is the worst of

---

* A regular at the Dôme.

cowards; there is no middle ground, as if the superhuman was the average level of man during wartime. True, they were Germans and the enemy; like the communists who for Guille are redeemed only by the exceptional, only a minimum of correction is due—a young student defended this point of view held by *Paris-Midi,* but the waiter put him in his place: What about the sailors who got blown up for nothing? He said this loud and clear, which seems to me a sign of this war, namely the open solidarity with the enemy soldiers, who are considered the proletariat of the armies.

Védrine showed up in a friendly mood. She told me that she was [afraid] of being boring and there was a little bit of truth to it. I had shocked her the night before concerning Sartre's theories. She said that she was bothered when he changed theories and I had said, "That's funny because I too change theories, it changes my outlook on the world."—So that made her think about her own seriousness. I went to Henri IV—faculty meeting, I was commended. Passed by the Gérassis to get an address of a seamstress for Kos.; they had gotten drunk the night before at the Jockey. Went to say hello to Kos., who gossiped about A. Ménard. Worked. In the meantime I had passed by the post office and it put me in a state of bliss that will not leave me for a long time to come. Two long letters from Sartre, so moving and intimate. Without this war I would have never really known his love for me—nor would I have given in to mine with such sweetness. I was becoming hard. He would like to leave Védrine gradually—I don't think he will be able to, but no longer will I have those futile worries and bitterness. I'm not afraid of anything; once again I'm one with him, alone with him as I was at the time in Le Havre or Rouen before Kos. I also had a huge letter from Bost explaining how much the war interested him and that he was neither a ghost nor to be pitied. I'd never appreciated him so much. He is more and more intelligent and shows character. I feel a tremendous friendship for him—for him as he is at present, dirty, muddy, and stupid—and when I think of how he was, of his sweetness, his beauty, his tenderness, it all seems to be in the distant past—as if I were really *living with* him as a soldier.

So, I'm happy. I wrote to Sartre, then to Bost, but the Moon Woman showed up, as always imposing, pleasant to look at and be with. She told me some stories: she didn't see Youki again—she goes drinking with Therese and the exhibitionist, who want to sell her to some Argentineans, but she remained faithful to her Polish lover. I showed her the letter from her husband that I found rather charming and amusing. She left to sober up at the Dôme, dizzy with leisure and freedom. I worked for a little while, then Kos. came by. We went to the Milk Bar to eat; afterward we worked on her weekly assignment. She hadn't worked on it at all and the idea of having to improvise everything scared me. But then I threw myself into it and enjoyed it. I also enjoyed realizing that I was still capable of such an intellectual effort after a day's work. I have a vague idea of myself as being generous and full of vitality, etc. Kos. was delighted: "Not only are you doing it, but you also enjoy it; you're so nice!" Funny, because what she is grateful for is the fact that I did it *spontaneously*—if I had to force myself, she would hold it against me thinking that I felt I had to do her a favor. She was amazed when it was finished: "It's entertaining," she said—and I felt how lucky one is to be an intellectual whose own thinking is always interesting and for whom everything turns into thought, even a calamity that provides thought on the calamity. We discussed some ideas on rancor: the paradox, for example, that it is directed at the other's freedom in its spontaneity of the moment—but affirming the other's constancy in time beyond the freedom of the moment. The other always feels the unjust rancor and defends himself in turn either by invoking the constancy of his character: I'm like that, it's not my fault— or his freedom: I'm no longer the person who did that. We returned home toward eleven o'clock. I finished my letter to Bost, and *Le Moine* by Matthew Lewis, which I enjoyed down to the last page.

Tuesday, December 19

I slept a little less than seven and a half hours, but in general it's enough for me. At eight o'clock I was at the Mahieu drinking hot chocolate and bringing this notebook up to date. It was a very pleasant moment, a gratuitous benefit. I'm happy because of yesterday's letters. Lycée. Then two hours of good work at the Mahieu. I finished chapter 2. Sorokine had lunch with me at the Capoulade. She was a little sad but not demanding. Poor thing, it's really sad, her life. Three hours of teaching. At the post office I had very pleasant letters from Sartre and Bost. I read them at the Versailles, quickly answered them, and worked another hour. Then I met Védrine at the Mahieu at half past six. She was charming and I enjoyed seeing her. We dined at the Batik while telling each other the stories of our lives. She was supposed to see her father at nine o'clock and left me at half past eight. Since Kos. didn't show up I had the advantage of a long, happy moment for myself, which is extremely precious to me regardless of how I may spend it: long entries into this notebook and grading papers. I'm beginning to look forward to my winter ski vacation. Kos. arrived at half past ten—she was depressed even though she had done a good improvisation in Dullin's class—we went for a drink at the Milk Bar—

she had not received a letter from Bost since Monday—but that didn't give me even an ounce of pleasure, these jealous feelings are after all too empty. We chatted more or less until midnight and I fell asleep. The night before I dreamt that I was looking at my head, holding it in my hands; this in itself didn't surprise me; however, the fact that I still felt it on my shoulders did. I thought that it was like the "ghost member" felt by an amputee.

Wednesday, December 20

This morning the alarm clock tore me out of my dreams. I noticed that in dreams one utters completely inarticulate sounds; I remembered just enough to be aware of it but was unable to finish. Got up earlier than usual. I had breakfast at the Dupont while starting a letter to Bost, a pleasant moment. Two hours of private tutoring at Camille Sée—I finished the letter to Bost, and then went to the Balzar, where I met Védrine. Work—I am redoing chapter 3 now; it's going well. Two distinguished and mature men next to me were talking about elegant parties with ladies. We took half an hour for lunch at the Capoulade. Then more work upstairs at the Mahieu. The place was almost empty; from there we could see the Luxembourg Gardens below looking very wintry, a beautiful sight. Védrine felt important: "Sartre *wants* me to write him everything I think about the *Journal* by Dabit"; angry without really meaning it and flattered by this request, which clearly shows the need the man has for her and the averred nature of a relationship that allows for a tender authority: this often came up in discussions with Sartre. She read the second chapter and found it too exaggerated, which I don't believe it is, but she made a detailed and very accurate critique. I worked until I had a headache. At half past four we went out, prepared a package for Bost— paper, tobacco, smoked bacon—post office. I had a letter from Sartre. Then I went to my place for a ten-minute respite to look at *Le Canard* and read my letter. Afterward I went to the Vikings and found Sorokine at the door; she hadn't dared enter. We sat down in a small booth and as she had a headache we didn't work. We began evoking memories of July and she asked me what I had thought the first time I kissed her. She talked without embarrassment about the time we were "chaste and pure," and without embarrassment and in a charming way she told me every so often that she loved me with all her might, or she put her head on my shoulder, or held her lips out to be kissed. She told me how last year she and the students in her class thought that I was shameless and she showed me her notebooks where she wrote down little tidbits of information on the second trimester philosophy and the dawn of her relationship with me—it's dry and pleasant. In turn I read her passages of this notebook and was touched by the extent of her interest in everything and how much she tried to know *me,* how I am in my private life, and not only as an object of her love. That's a concern Védrine doesn't have at all. Then I gave her a long lecture on whores and bordellos, which interested her enormously. I'm on the best terms with her; there's nothing about her that I don't like, and I almost feel like having a real love affair with her; all evening I was thinking ever so slightly of her charming tenderness.

I got home at eight o'clock and met up with Kos., still just as morose—went to dinner at Pagès, then to the College Inn. Kos. could hardly get a word out, yet she was still pleasant despite her gloominess. We spent the evening in silence but without sadness. The College Inn was also pleasant because in addition to their woman pianist they had a pianist in uniform who was just passing by. She welcomed him warmly, but he acted rather coldly. The pianist was with a gang that included two other musicians, and they played with five or seven hands, just having fun, a noisy and healthy merriment because it expressed itself in their art. The place felt like war; the evening felt like war, however, it was not at all unpleasant; one could feel the austere but not the cruel aspect of it. We returned home at eleven o'clock. I wrote Sartre a long letter, performed some minor tasks, and then graded papers etc. until half past midnight for the pleasure of taking advantage of my vitality.

Thursday, December 21

Got up at eight o'clock. At the Dôme at half past eight. One hour and a half of good work. Lycée—lunch with Sorokine at the blue brasserie. I explained Descartes to her and got almost annoyed, because understanding an author for her means to reconstruct him from two sentences out of the totality of his system. I begged her to read him first—I often get annoyed at her, but it's an honest and respectful annoyance, never an aggravation—she is gauche, but graceful in her language and her looks. Last night she gave me a charming little drawing of myself as a bird with beautiful earrings. She accompanied me to Henri IV—teaching—post office—letter from Sartre and Bost, which I answered—worked at home; I revised chapter 2, I think this time it's the definitive version. I ran to meet Védrine at the Mahieu. The evening was ice cold, moonlight, mixture of cold and light. The Luxembourg Gardens looked bewitched with their white statues behind the railings. Védrine was at the Mahieu, tired, morose, and dressed in a beautiful red dress. We ate very well at the little Alsatian restaurant while talking about Kant. Then to the Ursulines to watch *The Petrified Forest* with Bette Davis, H. Bogart, L. Howard, an absolutely fabulous movie. Védrine annoyed me by painfully pressing my hand and passionately nodding her head, which distracted me from the movie. We went home and I bristled listening to her graceless chatter: "We're going camping in Arizona, all three of us," etc. Annoyed, I protested: "But Sartre doesn't like nature." Védrine in an authoritarian tone: "He'll get to like it."—I, stubborn: "No, certainly not." "We'll leave him in New York with some American girl," she answered with the mawkish smile of an accomplice. It seemed like schoolgirl banter, to pass the time, and vulgar. There's fecal vulgarity under Védrine's mawkish smiles—all this incidentally makes for a rather strong personality and an interesting one, but I could see her in the future like a Louise Weiss, except more intelligent. We went home; I was tense and frigid like a petrified forest—she spread out on the bed naked, explaining, "I find that ridiculous," emphasizing "ridiculous" by moving her lips forward, "putting on a shirt just to take it off." That's economical, rational, sensible, and it immediately lends the physical relationship a staid and organized character that gives you a chill—we could have the worst passionate excesses, but the passion would not be a revelation, a new and unexpected understanding of things; it would not be spontaneity, it would be as expected and classified like a mechanical reaction. I felt this mechanical side during all our embraces and I *hated* Védrine fiercely and enjoyed hating her, yet she was in ecstasy over my caresses. Nervous relaxation, feelings of disgrace, nervous caresses that were not meant for me, but as a release of too much passion—awkward caresses whose awkwardness gave me malicious pleasure. When feeling her hurtful hands I was amazed at the awkwardness of women where men are experts. Is it because, like the fellow in Gide's *Journal,* "women put themselves in your place, but it's themselves that they put there," while a man is incapable of this substituting for a person and seeks to give you pleasure? Perhaps that's why? But P., Kos. and Védrine, how many indiscrete small torments.

We went to sleep. Good night.

Friday, December 22

We got up at around half past eight—getting ready with Védrine—indifference. I worked at the Mahieu a good three hours. Then I met Lévy, Kanapa, and Védrine at the Biarritz. Kanapa had the train ticket and I had the joyous feeling that I was really going to leave. I now like the idea. Lycée—saw Sorokine—post office—letters from Sartre and Bost—correspondence—a quick visit with the Gérassis, who had nothing amusing to tell—the White Russians were delighted with Stalin's policies, the communists too. A package with *marrons glacés* from Metzger: another unhappy passion (last year Goetschel told Sorokine that she loved me "as passionately as a man would"); all that doesn't flatter me. It seems to me that I lend my face to a myth that is adored by girls because it's typical for their age. It fits Védrine, but Sorokine less so. She resists, critiques, and can give reasons for her esteem.

I went home before seven o'clock and worked for an additional hour. Kos. didn't come by and I made entries in this notebook having fun doing so.

She finally arrived at a quarter past eight. She didn't get the role of Tyrval and felt disconsolate about it last night, but she got over it and now felt rather relaxed at not having this maddening hope any more. She was only furious with Toulouse and would one day tell me her theory on it. We chatted in my room and had a drink at the College Inn—returned at eleven o'clock—and went to bed around midnight.

Saturday, December 23

Day of departure, spent running errands and saying goodbyes. Lycée, then to the Hotel Mistral where I picked up my skis. The owners were there and welcomed me with demonstrations of friendship. I was moved to see the hotel again and to leave Sartre's skis behind in the cellar while taking mine— passed by Gégé's and Pardo's place to get my clothes, but alas! Gégé and Pardo had left. "Not only that, but we heard very bad things about them," the concierge told me stiffly. I had lunch with my mother, we organized my affairs in a manner of speaking—at my place suitcases, then I met Kos. at two o'clock. She wanted to stay with me until four o'clock. I phoned Védrine to cancel, feeling neither regret nor remorse—conversation with Kos. at the Rotonde. I then met Sorokine at the Vikings. She brought *Le Mur* so I could explain the obscenities to her, and I began an entire course in obscene physiology— but a fellow nearby overheard us and we went to my room. Kisses, but chaste ones—I felt like having a passionate affair with her, a love affair, because she completely charmed me. She showed me a passage from her journal about me: she called me Ossotchka, which means little wasp—she explained that she had everything to gain by associating with me while I had nothing to gain from associating with her and for me to get attached to her she just had to count on her "personal charm"; that was lucid and pleasant. I was as tender with her as I could possibly be, and she with me. She left at half past six and I immediately passed into Védrine's hands. She was very nice and her little face touched me. But I was insensitive to her story about her pathetic crisis of last night concerning my departure; pathos is her daily bread. I went to the post office with her to send packages to Sartre and Bost, then I got dressed and we took a taxi to the station. I was beginning to get into a departure mood, which I found extremely pleasant. There were few people in the train. I met Kanapa and we each had a corner near the window in an empty compartment. A young member of the Youth Hostel Association was the only other person to join us. He wasn't bothersome; he offered me tea and some spice cake. We chatted a while with Kanapa; God, how dry he can be! I had nothing to say to him—this going away together didn't create the least bit of friendly camaraderie between us. Behind the windows, the suburbs were drowned in fog and flooded with moonlight—deserted and sinister-looking roads. At times the fog was so dense that one could see absolutely nothing at all, only the light of invisible cars. The train stopped during the night while the alarm signal sounded endlessly. We inquired about it and heard that it was a drunken fireman who had sounded the alarm. The train stopped at twenty stations and was a good two hours late, which it couldn't possibly make up, but I didn't care. I stretched out on the empty seats, and in this warm and comfortable compartment I felt very much at ease and on vacation. For a long while I was thinking of Bost—I became aware of how much tenderness there had been in our relationship, from the very beginning, perhaps even from our first meeting. I loved to talk with him, tell him things; I always felt a rapport between us, and the moments spent with him never seemed contingent to me. I fell asleep remembering him as he was in the past, at Tignes, on our first night and many others—and it was cruel yet sweet.

Stereotypical dream: it's strange, because God knows Kanapa inspires me with no lustful or tender thoughts—as with Bost in the barn where I dreamed that in that very barn he was taking me in his arms, I dreamed lying on these seats, just as I was, Kanapa also, and he was caressing my hand—and that later he lay down next to me without his glasses, half undressed and looking at me with the strange face of a crazed man and also full of desire, and this face was beautiful while still his; he moved me but as the youth hostel fellow seemed to want to leave discretely, I motioned him to stay; I didn't want any emotional demonstrations—that's the difference with dreams I had about Bost, where I wanted them to be true—in this case I also wondered for a long time in my dream whether it really was a dream and I concluded that it wasn't. I should mention that upon awakening I didn't feel the slightest trace of sentimentality for Kanapa, which often follows an erotic or tender dream.

Sunday, December 24

I woke up at seven o'clock and looked at the Jura Mountains toward Culoz and the route along the Rhone River until Bellegarde. It was rather pleasant, a beautiful blue day was rising, but there was very little snow. I read *Miss Denion* by Wallace, then the latest *Empreinte*, somewhat funny. We got to Sallanches; I was very moved. I had the impression that something was waiting for me in this part of the country, and all day long it seemed to me that I found Sartre's memory there, wrapped in misty cold, all intact and alive—five years of skiing vacations spent with him, I remembered everything and was consumed by tenderness, choking back my tears. We took the bus to Megève; there were people, beautiful people with leather suitcases and women dressed in furs—the bus almost burned down on the way—no snow in Combloux, almost none in Megève—I crossed town to get to the post office: it looked very shabby and the place smelled of death—half the hotels and boutiques were closed, the advertising posters torn up, an air of abandonment everywhere and the streets almost deserted. I got emotional passing by the pastry shops and the newspaper vendor; all these places have a history for me. We took the blue train, then the cable car—the prices had gone down slightly and I was amazed at how few people there were. We got to the summit at half past eleven; glorious weather, snow, but no snow on the pine trees. The small path was filled with golden sunlight. But I had a heavy suitcase and a difficult time climbing up to the chalet; I was so out of breath that I thought I'd die. The chalet had just opened. We were not expected and at least for a while would be the only residents, which was absolutely fantastic. We were able to choose our rooms; mine was minuscule but charming with wood paneling, a small bed, a corner sink, and a panoramic view of the mountains. I put my things away and felt in heaven. We quickly went downstairs for lunch. It was excellent; there were a few other people, residents of Megève on an outing. Our lunch was not very exciting. Kanapa is exactly neutral; nothing about him that would shock you, nothing pleasant either. But it's precisely what I needed. I won't be skiing alone and afterward I can enjoy solitude, no need putting up a façade, and no constraints whatsoever. And at the same time it prevents me from feeling a pang of anguish at being isolated, a feeling I might have at night in this deserted chalet.

We left immediately after two o'clock—we went to Montjoux, a mere ten minutes away, and the ski lift was working; it was sheer joy. I crashed two times while taking off—the slope covered with frozen snow was the worst and the descent was awful, but for a start, it wasn't too bad. We returned at four o'clock and had some tea. There was a good concert on the radio that was all ours to control: Beethoven's Fifth Symphony, two Polonaises, and Franck's Oratorio. It was sheer enjoyment sitting there, writing letters and listening to music while outside the sky took on all the colors of the rainbow with big gray clouds passing across it. We were alone; Kanapa worked on Epicurus while I was writing. The room was charming, all done in wood and small windows. It was warm and felt cozy. I wrote only two voluminous letters to Sartre and Bost—then I finished my detective story and continued reading Kafka's *Trial*. We ate dinner, very delicious. We stayed up only a short while, as we were dead tired. But in bed I continued reading until a quarter to ten. I lifted the curtain and could see the mountains as clearly as in daylight, but a sad daylight—it was the moon illuminating them; the sky was a deep blue and starless. It was beautiful and delighted me. A warm room, a hot water bottle in my bed, comfort, solitude, and my heart at peace.

Monday, December 25

Dreamed a little about Sartre, the kind of dream I had about Zaza: sorrowfully I reproached him for no longer seeing me. Dreamed about the snow, which had completely melted, and in the morning there was nothing but grass. I woke up at daylight, a little before seven o'clock, wonderfully rested, and cozy warm in my sheets I watched the sunrise. Then I got up, eager to test the snow. Succulent breakfast. At eight o'clock I was outside and as the weather was mild I was just wearing Sartre's little white sweatshirt. I went up Montjoux and carefully practiced descending on skis, but I still needed more practice. I met Kanapa at half past nine. We skied twice down to Megève—back up by lift—after the second time we went back to the chalet, all tired out and content. The lunch was copious—then I read for three quarters of an hour *Prélude à Verdun* [Prelude to Verdun] by Romains, which I found very interesting—but until now I have not found more on the 1914 war than in my readings of September: boredom, the duration, etc. I already knew all that. Ski again on the slope of Montjoux—I'm constantly improving—and return to the chalet for tea and entries into this notebook. I don't think I could really work here.

Written to Sorokine—Védrine—Poupette—and Kos. I wasn't able to do anything else. Excellent dinner—correspondence until nine o'clock and reading of Jules Romains. I was amazed at how few people there were this year on the lifts and on the slopes; it lends a pleasant aspect to the countryside, an out-of-season look.

Gob. 71–42 (Gérassi)
Sécretan Palace: *Disparus de St Agil* [The Lost Souls of St. Agil]

Billfold
Bœuf clandestin   Restif de la Bretonne
Batteries   Armandy
Salted lard
Tobacco and cigarettes
Alcohol

4,350 francs	2,300 francs	3,550 francs	10,200 francs

January	Kos.	2,500 francs	
	Sartre	500 francs	
	Myself	2,000 francs	
		5,000 francs	
Drycleaner		550 francs	
Sartre's leave		1,500 francs	10.200
End of the month—winter holiday		650 francs	7.700
		2,700 francs	2,500

Remain—taxes   1,500 francs
1,000 francs: Kos.—diverse—winter holiday—Poupette

NOTES

1. Défense Contre Avions were antiaircraft guns.

2. In *L'Invitée*, Françoise fears that Pierre's love for her is aging ("en train de vieillir" [Beauvoir 1943, 198]), and she calls his love for her a "whited sepulcher": "Tu as besoin que tes sentiments gardent toujours la même figure, il faut qu'ils soient autour de toi, bien rangés, immuables et même s'il ne reste plus rien dedans, ce t'est bien égal. C'est comme les sépulchres blanchis de l'Évangile, ça flamboie à l'extérieur, c'est solide, c'est fidèle, on peut même périodiquement les recrépir avec de belles paroles. . . . Seulement il ne faut jamais les ouvrir, on n'y trouverait que cendre et poussière" (199).

3. A political antidemocratic, right-wing, and nationalist movement.

4. In response to Wahl's suggestion, which Beauvoir presented to Sartre in a letter of December 3, 1939 (Beauvoir 1990, 1:322), Sartre replied in his December 5, 1939, letter, "Pour l'idée de Wahl, elle est parfaitement irréalisable: on doit faire des thèses rigoureusement inédites et les cent premières pages de *L'Imaginaire* ont déjà paru dans la *Revue de Méta*" (Sartre 1983, 1:460).

NOTEBOOK 4

December 26, 1939 – January 19, 1940

Tuesday, December 26

Watched another beautiful sunrise this morning from my bed—breakfast, read in *Verdun*—the whole beginning of the book, the start of the offensive and the move of the men toward Verdun, is excellent. We left at half past eight for the Montjoux, from where we took the ski lift, then down the slopes to Megève until the cable car, from there on foot to the Tour. Skied down the Tour. It was all very mediocre skiing, true, the snow was hard, but it was still a far cry from what it was last year. We walked through Megève. There were quite a few people at the Megève ski lift and on the streets; it seemed that it was mostly the mature and potbellied gentlemen who had been eliminated. We had a drink in a little brasserie, and then on foot went up the Calvaire path that I remembered so well from having walked it with Bost. Cable car. Return. It was one o'clock already before we got back to the chalet. So much sun gave me a headache, and the sun continued beating down on my head through the window all through lunch. The terrace was crowded with people picnicking; they were loud and bothersome.

Read *Verdun*. Then at a quarter past two we left toward St. Gervais—
mediocre descent—halfway down the second part we had to take off our
skis and walk down; there was no more snow. We took the ski lift going back
up and returned just at nightfall. Tea. Work. I was dead tired, my head was
buzzing, my body aching, and I felt weak all over. I started rereading my
notebooks. There isn't much to be said about them; the September one is
interesting because of the events, and also because it was carefully written.
Then they become less and less so because my life has become so sensible.
I had thought that I would rethink things concerning myself by rereading
them, but I didn't think anything at all. Finally they brought me my mail:
letters from Sartre, but not very long ones, and one got lost—a letter from
Bost, who was going to be moved toward the front—a charming letter from
Sorokine and a short note from Kos. I was in such a daze that all that hardly
affected me; it just gave me a vague impression of anguish. Dinner, letters to
Sartre and Bost and entries into my notebook made in bed, and then I fell
asleep at about ten o'clock. There were now people in this chalet: a woman
alone who seemed to be a teacher, decked out in brightly colored sweaters,
and a group of students who were not loud but talked a lot. Kanapa doesn't
seem very intelligent to me. A lot of show in what he told me about the revolution and the war.

Wednesday, December 27

A good day of skiing. Skied down well to Megève without falling—skied
down the trail of the Tour correctly and the slope of the Rochebrune ski lift
so that I had fun being back there. In the afternoon a good descent toward
the Bettex despite a dense fog. We got back at four o'clock and I felt so fresh
that I was able to get back to my novel, which gave me enormous pleasure.
Two long letters from Sartre, one from Bost. Dinner. Spent the evening writing letters.

Thursday, December 28

I got up early to take a lesson at half past eight, but the instructor didn't
arrive until half past nine. I had much time to read: I finished *Verdun,* the
beginning of which I had found excellent, but the end I found much more
mediocre. And I read Dabit's *Journal.* It's often boring, not too bad as far
as the populist descriptions are concerned; at least he knows to create an

atmosphere, but he comes through as a pathetic guy and such a damn fool it's hard to believe. His sentimental stories are comical in a discreet way. I wrote letters and read the *Journal* and then, finally, when I was about to blow my top, the instructor arrived, very nice. He was on leave and put on his skis for the first time in a long time—he was stationed in St. Veran. He made me work on sideslipping and christies going uphill. It didn't go too well. Then while working on those techniques I skied down to Megève. I was terribly tired; I didn't do too well. Descent of the Tour, endless walking up again to the cable car. Return to Ideal Sport. Bad descent to the Bettex, and then some practice of christies. Work from four to seven o'clock. Dinner. Correspondence.

These days have been extremely pleasant. It's difficult to render what's pleasant about them. While rereading my first notebooks I realized how the sense of a day could become distorted when told in the present; what constitutes its worth and significance is often its relationship to the future. The present days focus first of all on Sartre's leave, which, I now feel, is quite close. Then, during the day, all along the descents on the slopes, there is the appeal of that moment at four o'clock when I can get back to my work and I experience the anticipated pleasure of this work. And in the evenings, the memory of the daylong skiing in the snow, and all this intimately intertwined in order to make each moment heavy and full. Solitude, possibility of thinking, remembering, making plans, and entertaining some useless ideas. All this is so rare and so precious for me.

Unfortunately, the chalet was now crowded in the evenings. There was a woman alone, apparently a teacher, always dressed in yellow or light blue bulky wool sweaters, and a group of students, not too loud, among them a girl, probably a sister of one of them and not too bad looking. But there was also an awful little redhead, who was preparing his PMS,* Catholic, rightwing, incredibly stupid and even more incredibly self-important. His self-importance didn't make him brag, but made him talk about himself with meticulous precision. He admitted to all his blunders and, incidentally, got some funny reactions; everything seemed exceedingly interesting to him at the very moment these things happened to him. He continuously crashed on his skis and even broke them in the process, commenting on the fact with curiosity. He wrote a letter in verse, seventy verses in all, to a female friend from his university; his tongue was hanging out while he was searching for rhymes and everyone was bored to tears with it. "Something that rhymes with 'neige'

---

* Préparation militaire supérieure [officers training].

but not Megève," he said in all sincerity.[1] He quoted Hugo and Marot in the most pedantic but ignorant way for he mixed everything up. He confused Jules Romains with Romain Rolland, which didn't prevent him from hating Barbusse[2] "and all those deserters," he said with much authority. He wanted to run the whole show; he explained the poker rules—incidentally, he was wrong there too, he played stupid card tricks and annoyed the others, but he had nevertheless some prestige in their eyes. I found him horrible. Kanapa protested, but he protests out of principle; he refuses to judge, to write, and to go into depth of whatever it may be. There's nothing he finds funny; how unattractive he is. He is all tied up in knots and gives the impression that if he were to be untied, we wouldn't find anything very interesting either.

Friday, December 29

A pleasant day among all the others. I got up at seven o'clock as I do every morning. I quickly ate breakfast as I had an appointment with the ski instructor at nine o'clock at the ski lift of Rochebrune. It was snowing. I dressed warmly and at a quarter after eight started the descent toward Megève. It gave me a pleasant feeling since it wasn't gratuitous this morning; it was really a necessary means of communication. There was white fog, white under my feet with the gentle swishing sound of freshly fallen snow when the skis tore through it; the sky was white and white was all around me. Not a living soul; it was a silent, muffled world in a subdued light; hurried little snowflakes were blinding me, and fog was swallowing up the relief of the terrain; it was impossible to distinguish the hollows from the moguls. It always comes as a surprise to be suddenly lifted up into the air or precipitated into the void. Only once was I so surprised that I fell down on my side. I walked toward the village of Tour. It no longer looked like a ski resort, but like a winter morning in the country: an old woman with her umbrella, a motorcyclist with a backpack. The descent of the Tour was easy and pleasant. I brought along, stuck to my body and held in place by my belt, Fabre-Luce's book on Munich. While waiting for the instructor I read it in the house of the Indian, where it was ice cold. Memories. Pleasant thoughts, happiness in this cold hut where the old people were moving about, numbed by the cold. The instructor was waiting for me too. Twice we went up by ski lift and skied down just doing christies. I was making progress. Afterward I went up to Rochebrune and mistakenly skied down the A trail; more wonderful moments of solitude in the snow. Good descent. I wandered around Megève for a while; I felt so blissfully happy and my life, so wonderful, all around me.

Saw a female dog with a chastity belt: a small metal instrument pierced like a sieve, intended to defend the animal's virtue and make her unassailable. Two male dogs were fiercely fighting over her, but when the winner mounted his conquest, he got quite confused and furious and so surprised that he barked while knocking himself out in vain.

A lot of people in Megève, some are stylish, but life is lived as in slow motion. I bought some chocolate as I was starving. The blue train left very late and was crowded. Cable car. I got to the chalet at a quarter after one. Lunch. At two o'clock we left for the Bettex. It was too easy, given the fresh snow, but it was a charming outing. I went again up the Montjoux, same weather as when I skied there with Sartre last year. But the snow was sticky, impossible to reach some speed or even take off with élan. It mattered little, I liked returning on foot, alone under a gray sky. I suddenly thought of Guille and thought that I would like to write a novel about an entire life so as to trace the pattern of a life. I would need to invent the entire technique. Perhaps I'll do it after I finish this novel.

At four o'clock I returned to work on chapter 3 in its definitive version. I worked from four to seven o'clock—it was going well. Dinner. Correspondence and this notebook. All the small windowpanes in the room were covered with ice. Outside fresh snow coming down in flakes; warmth, in the heart of the mountains in the heart of winter. Almost no one there: Kanapa was working—the redhead was chatting with his friend but without causing a commotion. Then no one at all. Impression of a retreat, alone in this room—the leisure—feeling of well-being—it was precious. Vacation. I was searching for music on the radio: de Falla, Granados, a little Debussy, but it was difficult to capture and incoherent. Then the radio fell silent. The humming of voices from people on the staff who were going upstairs to sleep. Smoked cigarettes. Sleep drawing near. But regret to let go of this day already. Wish for a long retreat, alone, without any pretext but work and reading and without the temptation of outside activities.

Saturday, December 30

Another pleasant day. With Kanapa I skied down to the cable car and then up to the Tour. Then we bought tickets for Rochebrune. It was the same elevator car as last year: memories. We stood in line and had to wait for a hundred numbers to be called. I waited in the cafeteria, where Sartre began his explanations with Védrine. How used she seems to me, the poor little girl. I bought a coffee and began writing letters to Sartre and Bost. I had a backpack with a cold lunch and a biography of Heinrich Heine;* I was counting on eating lunch on top of the mountain, but for the moment I left all that at the cafeteria—the place was bustling with people, very young boys, very pretty girls—it was pleasant. We took the cable car. Kanapa, meanwhile, had waited the entire half hour in the waiting room, standing. I believe that he is a little on the cheap side, but most of all he is terribly indifferent. Wherever he is left, he waits—he waited while I read, or worked—in the evenings, he halfway pretended to open Meyerson, but in fact he kept his eyes riveted on the clock. What is it: poverty, emptiness, or rich inner resources? Poverty for sure and total indifference.

We took the lift and I shook him off. He skied down I don't know what trail. I skied carefully down the A trail, which was great fun. I got one more ticket: another half an hour of exercise on the cable car slope and at noon again to Rochebrune. Brilliant sunshine. I went to the chalet to eat my cold meal. The room was pleasant: the floor was laid out in brick, a large beamed ceiling, a kind of hostel but with fewer visitors because of the altitude—there were a few other guests. I ate while I began reading the biography of Heine. Then at one o'clock alone on the slopes, a charming descent. At the foot of the slope I found the instructor, who made me work for one hour. I was able to do christies on the uphill slope. Return to Megève on the little path I used to take in the past, full of memories. Return to the chalet. Work, started chapter 4. At six o'clock the delivery boy returned from Megève; it caused a little stir in the house and they brought me my letters from Sartre, Bost, and Sorokine—a very pleasant moment. Dinner, correspondence, sleep.

Sunday, December 31

A long and tiring day. Kanapa's departure. I graded a whole pile of papers while having breakfast. It's amazing how much one can accomplish when people leave you alone. Too many charming little "pests" in Paris. They eat up your time. We left at half past eight, Kanapa being very worried about his luggage, and he'll be that way all day; it's one of his mannerisms to lose himself in practical worries. Total lack of generosity, no inclination for comfort or streamlining his efforts. We skied down to St. Gervais easily and quite well even though the trail was hard. Then we went to look for the little train that climbs up the Voza pass; a little wooden wagon with compartments where they locked us inside, and a charming locomotive that pushed

---

* Probably the biography by Antonina Vallentin (1934) [Paris: Gallimard].

the wagon—it looks so beautiful on posters amidst impressive snowy landscapes. The landscapes were indeed as depicted—and as the train was gradually climbing higher and higher we ate our cold lunch. We arrived at the
pass around midday and had coffee at the beautiful hotel that impressed
us so much when I was there with Sartre three years ago: an American bar,
straw matting on the walls, and a large dining room, which was really pleasant. We had a coffee and left for the blue trail. This one I also remembered
and all the details of our descent; and I felt so strongly united with Sartre
through all these adventures we had together, and so much of our lives we
already have spent together—each curve and turn on the descent came back
to me. It was a real little pilgrimage. I skied down well, then we went back
up by cable car, and then by ski lift to the summit of the Prarion. Vast landscapes, sumptuous, snowy solitude. We skied toward St. Gervais over totally
pristine snowfields. I was much better at this than Kanapa. How fast we
were going—in the sunshine the snow took on all colors of the rainbow; it
looked like a dusting of precious stones. An absolute delight. It gave me the
desire to go to the mountains for some big excursions. The path was poorly
outlined; we got lost and had to go back up for a quarter of an hour. The end
of the descent, where there wasn't any snow, was rather awful. We had to
take our skis off and even though we ran, we missed the last cable car and
had to take the bus to Megève. I left Kanapa without shaking hands or making plans to meet in the future. He was the one to exaggerate the coldness,
whereas I was only looking for convenience.

Bus—then the blue train. I got there just in time for the last ski lift at six
o'clock. They let us get on without the attendant in the cable car, myself and the
young delivery boy, who didn't have any letters for me tonight, and a young
ski instructor—somewhat tubercular looking, Catholic, and very handsome
of a wide-eyed Merleau-Ponty kind. Ice-cold night: –18° C. We groped along
on the road under a starry sky, and despite the cold it was extremely poetic
walking in single file to the little chalet shining brightly in the night.

The evening was astonishing poetry. I settled in the first room next to
the radio with a pack of Cravens—there was a rather handsome young man
who had arrived the evening before and taken up with the single woman;
she was quite titillated by it. I was shamelessly hogging the radio: beginning
of the Fifth Symphony and a Bach Prelude—then during dinner an excellent
concert: Ravel's *Pavane* and Debussy's *Children's Corner,* de Falla's *Danses de
la vie brève* and Stravinsky's *Firebird.* Afterward some more Borodine and
Lulli. The instructor was repairing skis in the hall; the girls of the household
in pretty white jackets were going out through the snow to I don't know what

New Year's Eve party, and soon after, the waitress also left with a white kerchief tied around her big head, accompanied by her husband, the chef. The atmosphere of a festive evening came through very strongly. We, the single people, were left behind—for there were only single persons left in the chalet. And there was a poetic person, a musician, who had arrived the evening before offering his services for all sorts of tasks in exchange for room and board. He was dressed in black, with a black tie and a collar, a beard along the jawline, and a violin, which he played. He asked me what kind of music I liked and he approved: "I see, you love real music!" As the radio was playing Gounod's *Ave Maria*, I suddenly heard the violin accompaniment; it was the musician. By request of the solitary woman, who, in the company of the young man, had rediscovered a youthful soul, he played gypsy airs and bourrés, poorly. Then he made conversation while I continued fiddling with the radio, which became increasingly difficult to understand clearly. I felt I was in a storybook as the whole evening had been like fiction, a novel that might be continued as a detective novel or whatever. And I felt like a character in the novel (without a representation of *myself*; just the place that I was occupying with the radio next to me). I didn't want the evening to end and didn't even have the courage to write my letters, that's how involved I was. Kanapa's absence even heightened this feeling, as I was alone among others. A very remarkable evening of the kind I don't often have, and spent authentically. It was eleven o'clock before I went upstairs and to bed.

Monday, January 1

As a result of that beautiful day and the long evening I felt rather exhausted in the morning. I wrote Sartre while eating breakfast. Then I went skiing to Mount Arbois, the Tour, and Rochebrune. It didn't go very well. I'm doing pretty much what I want to do now, but don't know how to want, as Gandillac* would say. And fatigue. What is fatigue? It's not so much a consciousness of the tired body but the very way of becoming aware and acting accordingly. Yet this posits once again the consciousness-body relationship—one is not physically tired, it's always a weakness of the heart as well as a state of the conditioned body. I felt meditative and languid. I missed Sartre and all seemed futile without him.

---

* Clairaut in *Memoirs of a Dutiful Daughter*, a co-disciple of Sartre and his "buddies" at the École Normale and their whipping boy. He was also the subject of one of Sartre's poems: "De Gandillac Le Patronier, / Est le dernier des niais, des niais" (De Gandillac Le Patronier is the last of the simpletons, the simpletons).

I returned to the chalet for lunch. I didn't know what to do with the excess of freedom—the same on the trails; I lacked constraint that the presence of another person would have imposed on me. I went to Montjoux—then I had the great idea to make the descent to Combloux. I left on the St. Gervais trail, which I could do very well because I was going fast and felt too lazy to crash, so I didn't. Then pristine snowfields, delightful—it was so easy that it was no longer a sport, but it was charming, as speed didn't make me afraid here—ease. Sun, pine trees, and the impression of a delightful outing. And enchantment. On the road the return was icy and tiresome, but a car gave me a ride back to Megève. The blue train. From five to six o'clock I waited for the cable car while writing to Bost in the little café used by the guides. Cable car and return with the ski instructor. The evening was milder than the previous evening and the return under a starry sky was as poetic as it could possibly be. The handsome young man was hogging the radio but let me have it while making conversation with me. The radio was rebellious. I listened to some Chopin, Brahms, and the Eighth Symphony broadcast from Budapest—but it was annoying to think that this box had something inside; I felt the crazy need to squeeze it. At nine o'clock, however, I gave up and went to bed, dead tired. All evening the musician played various background music on his violin.

Tuesday, January 2

Last day. I got up early and entrusted my suitcase to the musician so he could send it by cable car while I descended toward St. Gervais; my descent wasn't brilliant. Solitude gives rise to timidity as does the too complete absence of instruction. In the time it takes to impose an instruction on oneself, the descent is already over and poorly done. But the weather was so nice that the morning turned out to be pleasant. At half past nine I was sitting in a bistro at the side of the road. It was wonderful to be able to sit outside in the sun—I read the Henri Heine[3] that I had the foresight to take along, strapped to my belt. Bus to Le Fayet, where I left my suitcase, and on to Houches. I had been looking forward to eating at the hotel at the Voza pass, but the food wasn't too good. Left for the blue trail—sluggish descent—intimidated at being alone, I was so careful that it bordered on cowardice. I arrived at the foot of the slope tired and with such low morale that instead of going back up as I had promised myself, I sat down in a café. How cold this Chamonix valley is! From Mount Arbois one can see a dense and impenetrable fog covering it in the morning and at night. And when you come down into the valley from the top of the mountains, an icy sadness takes hold of you. I read the end of the life of Heine—it interested me because it is impossible to be more "in situation"[4] than this man, a Jew and German refugee, living in solidarity with other exiles in France, etc.—and it's strange, the German immigration of a hundred years ago, analogous to the one of today, and all the people he knew—this hellish Proust-like love, and this horrible end. I read and went to still another bistro to wait for the bus and from where I wrote to Sartre and Bost. Bus, vague daydreaming, the enjoyment of these daydreams; that's so rare for me. Memories from a year ago, walking the same roads with Sartre while waiting for the train and talking about Védrine.

Le Fayet. A small, warm café divided in two by large screens. Behind the screens were soldiers saying good-bye to their captain: "You have been a father to us," etc. I did my diary entries and corrected papers. I really liked this long afternoon of departure, the leisure time and the focus on the trip. I bought some food and books, *Le Bœuf clandestin** and *Gilles* by Drieu La Rochelle.

Around eight o'clock I was at the train, which was completely empty; it had a blue light where the blue paint was ever so slightly scratched so that I could read a little in *Le Bœuf clandestin.* Then I fell asleep. Some soldiers came on board in Bellegarde. There were four going to Bourg; they were from Savoy, big eaters and heavy drinkers who spoke with a thick accent. One of them pretended to be polite. "I'm going to barf," said his buddy. "Don't use that kind of language," said the other—out of respect for me; he wanted the light turned off, but a little soldier in a corner sighed, "I don't like that, it makes me feel weird." Another was talking about his old mother. "My mother is going to have a hard time," he said, "as for the rest of us, we don't care because we never give a damn," then he got emotional: "My little brother is twenty years younger than I; he won't know me when I get back." They finally went to sleep and so did I.

Wednesday, January 3

I woke up at about seven o'clock. Snow in the flat countryside. I read *Le Bœuf clandestin,* which was really not so funny—and *Gilles,* which was not so boring. Arrival at nine o'clock. I was happy for no one knew of my return; I had a long free day ahead of me. Paris was deserted, the weather mild. Had to wait a long moment in front of the station waiting for a taxi. Hotel. Kos. wasn't in

---

* By Marcel Aymé

and I was glad about it, this great freedom. Washed up, put my things away, and went to the hairdresser. At the post office a two-day-old letter from Sartre and from Bost. But I felt vaguely disappointed; it almost seemed to me that I was going to find him again. I was annoyed that the Shakespeare wasn't there, the notebooks weren't there, and the letters from Megève were still missing, but it was a more absurd and deeper disappointment. Then to Neuilly to collect the money and home for lunch. Afterward I worked at the Dôme for four hours, putting my heart and soul into it. This, I really liked doing. Once more I went to the post office: sent a package and the money to Sartre. A letter from him sent the evening before; I was happy. I went for dinner at the Coupole and sitting right across from me was Gérassi, who said hello. He was with two Spaniards, the poet Alberti and the journalist Borca, who admires Sartre. I was going to meet up with him at his place at eight o'clock. They were eating a pork loin that Unamuno's son was to share with them, but he left them in the lurch. The studio was cold and full of smoke from the iron stove. They were morose. The police had searched the premises of the Republican (?) Center and taken one and a half million used to pay pensions to the Spanish veterans. And now Fernand no longer gets anything. Sarraut promised that the money would be returned, but the right wing is opposed to it. Incidentally, Pétain asked that as a gesture of friendship for Franco, the Republicans be fired from the radio service where they were employed. They were disgusted. Stépha doesn't have a work permit and has a great many problems with her identity card. They believe, of course, in a ten-year war. They want to get the hell out of here. Fernand is dreaming of being a fisherman in Santo Domingo and other niceties and calls Stépha a coward for not wanting to embark with him on those escapades. They are mad at each other at the moment; Fernand makes two thousand francs for working all day at a radio station.

I left them early in the evening and went home to sleep; I was tired. In bed I read *Gilles* for a while and found it entertaining.

Thursday, January 4

It's awful to wake up in the dark and the humidity. At seven o'clock it was still completely dark and my beautiful daily sunrise so far away. As always when I return from vacation I dressed up with care: my blue turquoise blouse and turban; it looked beautiful together with my earrings and my black and white overcoat, which looked like new again. I worked at the Dôme for a while, from half past eight to ten o'clock. It was going so well, I wish I had more time. Saw Stépha. Went to the post office; letter from Sartre and a short note from Bost. Lycée. Sorokine was waiting at the door after class, all pleasant and friendly. We had lunch at the blue brasserie telling each other our lives' stories. It made me so happy to see her again that I promised her the evening with me if Kos. wasn't coming. Still more teaching at Henry IV. At four o'clock I met Védrine at the Mahieu. I felt an icy chill as I always do when I first see her again. She was acting like a spoiled child and was on edge because of annoying problems with her parents, and complaining that they may perhaps stay on in Paris. We talked but I had nothing to tell her, nor she to tell me. We made plans about seeing each other this trimester. We agreed on two evenings a week plus some moments snatched here and there, which won't eat up too much of my time. Ran some errands together and passed by the post office again. Letters from Sartre sent last night and from Bost. We said goodbye. I considered keeping the evening for myself but a charmingly simple note from Kos. announced her return for the next day. So I won't have a free evening anymore. I called Sorokine and went to the Dôme to work on my correspondence while waiting for her. She arrived at eight o'clock, being her charming self. Instead of going to any "cabaret" she preferred going to my place to show me all her secrets that she was carrying in a little suitcase. She showed me letters from the colonel and from her girlfriend, photos, poems, and drawings about "moods, working, and time schedules" in purple and red on a purple background; they really jump out at you—she told me about her shoplifting at the Uniprix du Printemps:[5] for a month she and her girlfriend were stealing fountain pen sets that they would resell at the lycée for a couple of quarters—wool and sewing material for which they made their parents pay half price. "My mother is so poor I can't make her pay department store prices." With the money they had an orgy of roller coaster rides at the fair. However, one day, an inspector picked them up; they were taken to jail, the parents were called in—a terrible drama. What is worse, the parents were suspected of being accomplices and were subjected to having their homes searched. She made me swear never to tell this story.

We started kissing. I asked her—I had to, after our last conversations: "Do you want our relationship to be really complete or should it remain this way?" "As you wish." So I didn't go any further—but soon afterward she got upset, looked at me with hate in her eyes, lashing out with her fists and burying her head in the pillow. It was almost eleven o'clock; it was crazy to let her leave like that. I explained. "You said: 'as you wish,' but since I asked the question, it meant that I wanted to." She relaxed: "I would like so much for us not to be hypocritical!" I said that I wasn't, that I would like to go further. Still somewhat hostile, she asked me to be precise and I was embarrassed and said that, for example, it wouldn't be the same to be dressed or undressed. "Oh, I see," she got annoyed again. "It's no good to do things halfway." I then started to undress her a little and she told me, "Turn the light off." I protested, "but if it bothers you . . ." "Not if you turn the light off." So I turned the light off and suggested, "Do you want to take it all off?" A shocked laugh: "No, not all." A moment later and very politely: "Would it bother you to undress?" "No, not at all." I took off my blouse. After another moment she said that she was cold, then resolutely, "Oh, well, might as well go all the way—but don't turn on the light!" We lay down on the bed. It was strange and pleasant to hold her in my arms all wrapped up in her nakedness and curious about the experience. I caressed her a little but briefly. No sensuality. She didn't seem to feel sensual either, I think, since she tensed up because of her shyness, but she was content as "we are not hypocrites" and "we are intimate." We chatted. In the dark she asked some questions, if I slept this way with Sartre, whether he had hair on his chest, and whether he walks around naked in front of me. Horror a virgin feels for the male. She really came across as a typical virgin, not in the moral sense, but because of her rebellious body and her concerns about being ridiculous and embarrassed. "It's ridiculous to undress and then get dressed again." We stayed this way for a while, talking; the strangeness and sleepiness gave this hour a dreamlike quality that I could not easily fit into our day time relationships. At midnight she got dressed in the dark, kissed me without embarrassment when the light was turned on again, and left. I felt relieved. I knew I had to sleep with her and feared outbursts of passions, but she was really pleasant and lighthearted and unpredictable as her usual self.

Friday, January 5

I got up at eight o'clock and worked from half past eight to noon at the Dôme—almost finished chapter 4, it was going well. Saw Stépha, and around noon Wanda, who was pleasant and talked charmingly about the Moon Woman and L'Aigle. Had lunch at the Biarritz with Védrine, Kanapa, and Lévy. Védrine was wearing a gorgeous seal fur coat. She gave me a little note that I read as I left and in which she complained about our disagreements the night before. But she thought that it was because of her being on edge. I'm afraid that if her parents don't return she will be awfully free and feel my coldness toward her. However, they'll probably return, which makes her feel depressed.

Three hours of teaching. Sorokine, charming, was waiting for me after class and accompanied me to the post office. Three letters from Sartre and just as many from Bost, who is at the front but getting along spendidly. I read the letters at the Versailles and felt profoundly happy. Sartre will come on leave on the twenty-fifth and I'll work uninterruptedly for three weeks with the idea of showing him my work. I like this idea very much. I returned to my room; I was expecting Merleau-Ponty and Kos. but neither one showed up, and so between five o'clock and half past seven I wrote my letters and entries into this notebook, which really needed updating. Unexpected windfall. I felt happy and fresh and all ready to work tonight.

I was still able to correct a tall stack of papers. Merleau-Ponty came by at a quarter past nine but only to make another appointment, then Wanda came and both of us went to the College Inn. The place was rather depressing; not even the woman pianist was there anymore. But we had a friendly talk. Stories about the Moon Woman, who, when the war is over, wants to become a celebrity. Among other things I also talked to her about Sorokine. I very much like Wanda's face and voice and the way she tells stories. She was very engaging and charming.

Saturday, January 6

Worked little but don't feel bad about it since the last few days have been filled with study. Two hours of teaching and one and a half hours of work at the Dôme. Then Védrine arrived and we had lunch—she was relaxed and friendly, and it was pleasant. When she is this way, familiar, friendly, and easy-going, I like talking with her. It doesn't draw me out of myself, but it doesn't bother me either. After lunch we went to work. At that moment a certain student of Merleau-Ponty showed up, sent to me for I'm not sure what reason. I left her in Védrine's hands and continued my work. Then Merleau-Ponty came by and Védrine left. He thought she was too sure of herself and too rational, to which there is some truth. He talked, not too much, about his daily life as an intelligence officer at the Luxembourg border. He was stationed in a rich industrial region—behind him were evacuated villages, but there were lots of civilians in the rather wealthy area where he was stationed. He was billeted at the house of a midwife, where he slept on a hard bed used in deliveries, in a room with blood splatters on the walls. He was working very hard, taking his meals with the officers, whose intellectual level was, he said, unimaginable. He was telling me that they had arrested the madam of a bistro-bordello in Luxembourg where the soldiers used to go drinking even though it was off-limits, and who was getting information out of them for Germany. And he told me about a night of high alert one October eighteenth when they expected a German attack and the men had holed up in the trenches, and he was in his observation post looking at the Luxembourg plain and the long, straight roads by which the Germans were going to march in, and the kind of disappointment the guys felt, who were still very much "involved." And (just as it happened in *Verdun*) the colonel—because they were in front of the Maginot Line—had to fight to get artillery support for the infantry because they wouldn't let him have any at all, fearing they might lose some guns. He asked me to check out his student. She had thin lips, an interesting and hard face, but not at all ugly. I was slightly interested but had to turn it down for lack of time.

Afterward I stopped at the post office—at my place I had a huge package of letters, many from Sartre that had been forwarded from Megève. I read them at the Vikings in front of Sorokine. Lesson on Leibnitz; I found it a little amusing to have to plunge myself into this strange kind of thinking, especially since I had to explain everything very thoroughly. We talked. She told me some more stories about the colonel, how she had stolen a picture of him, etc. We took a taxi to the Hoggar, where she left me, and I wrote to Sartre and Bost while waiting for Védrine. We had a pleasant and light conversation. I ate a *salade algérienne,* some pastries at the Alsatian pastry shop, and went to sleep at her place. Little ado; it was really the old serious liaison with its monotony but convenience. The only thing that bothered me was the profound disgust I have of her body, but we didn't tarry much. Sleep.

Sunday, January 7

A pleasant, studious day. I stopped at the hotel, feeling somewhat adulterous, but Kos. hadn't shown up yet and my offense won't be discovered. I got ready, and at nine o'clock went to the Dôme and didn't leave there until half past four. I had some coffee and *suisses,* smoked a few cigarettes, and worked. At half past noon I ate some beef while reading *Gilles.* From one to four o'clock I worked some more. From four to half past four I wrote to Sartre. And I wasn't tired, it was great. I wrote close to twenty-five pages: copied on the typewriter, I mean; they will constitute the entire beginning of chapter 5; I was thrilled about it. I thought that Kos. had perhaps come back, but a whole day of solitude was too good to give up and I felt like going to a concert. So I didn't go back to the hotel, but went out on the boulevards. The Conservatory was closed—I went to the Opéra Comique on foot. There was a dirty layer of fog and crowds of people in the streets, but I like the boulevards on a Sunday in the humidity and the dark—street vendors with their torches, lighting their stalls and wares in the dark, just like in Venice. Even though I felt a little tired, it was pleasant. Went by taxi to Gaveau Hall; took a loge like the time when they played the quartets and Bost was acting like Zuorro's mistress. I wrote him a little note from there—Berlioz, *Pelléas et Mélisande* by Fauré, a terribly boring *Symphonie espagnole* by Lalo. Not knowing how to analyze why some music is bad, I often think that I'm the one who is disgusted with music, that's the effect it has on me, so I was happy I liked the *Nocturne* by Debussy. The concert finished with Ravel's *Rhapsodie espagnole* that I had enjoyed so much when I was with Kos. My main reason for going there had been to hear the piece again, and I was right.

I returned on the U* bus. At the hotel, there was light in Kos.'s room. It always gives me a little shock and a vague apprehension. A friendly note under my door, and in her room a charming Kos., dressed in a blue print blouse just like in her big photo. We talked while dining upstairs at the Rotonde. She told me about her stay at L'Aigle—the visit of the Moon Woman and the horrible story of A. Ménard's abortion: the screaming girl in her hotel room and the crowd gathered on the stair landing; the doctor, who was asleep; two panic-stricken friends, begging her to be quiet; and suddenly, as she stood up, a blonde head between her legs and a kid falling to the floor. Halfway unconscious, she suddenly heard a moaning. At once the doctor woke up, the kid was alive, consternation: it was difficult at seven months, infanticide, jail or hard labor—she begged them to kill the child, they refused, she then dragged herself to the child and broke its neck, then passed out. A while later she screamed again while spilling her insides. The guys took off, leaving her with the kid, which she wrapped in newspaper and stuffed in a suitcase. Horrible hemorrhaging. Luckily the people in the hotel promised silence and washed the sheets. But when the Moon Woman showed up three days later, she noticed a terrible cadaver stench in the room; the sink and bidet were stopped up from coagulated blood. Ménard told her the story and opened a suitcase: she saw the baby, her neck broken, her face very serene. The Moon Woman didn't say a word, but when Ménard started whimpering, "My poor little daughter, she looked like me," etc., she cut her off, disgusted, and said, "Shut up or I'm leaving immediately." "Yes, you're right," Ménard said, blowing her nose and hiding her tears. She asked the Moon Woman to throw the cadaver and the linens in the sewer; the Moon

---

* At that time the buses had letters, not numbers like today.

Woman accepted only the cadaver; the package was too large. Thereupon Ménard, quite naturally, squeezed the suitcase shut, making the little bones crack. The Moon Woman took it away and threw it in the sewer, almost under the eyes of a policeman. Afterward, all shaken up, she told her Polish lover about it, who was outraged: "You French bitch," etc., and threatened to leave her.

We talked about this until midnight. I went to bed and to sleep.

Monday, January 8

Two hours of teaching—worked at the Source—at a quarter to one Védrine came by; she was very nice, we had lunch, and I explained some mathematics to her. Lycée Henri IV—at the door when I left, Sorokine, all charm, who had finally decided to approach the girl she had been stalking in the library. It took all her courage: "I would like to speak with you"; the other had smiled, being greatly surprised. Sorokine, her knees shaking, squirmed without finding anything to say. Finally she blurted out, "We've got to meet, just for an hour in case we don't like each other," and they agreed on a date. She told me that while we were in a taxi on the way to the post office, and she accompanied me to the Dôme. I sat down in the back of the restaurant. I read my letters, a long tender one from Bost, a long charming one from Sartre. I worked. Adamov stopped by, rolling his eyes, asking me for a date, which I refused. Ménard was there, looking gorgeous, her face hard; she was flirting with the guys. It was strange seeing her there after listening to the Moon Woman's story. Work, then home to write my letters. Kos. came at half past seven, and we went out to dinner at Pagès; afterward we went to the terrace of the Dôme. We saw Y. Morineau, all alone and shabby-looking, like some time ago at the Brasserie Paul in Rouen. She gave the impression of a decent whore or a peddler from Burma who had traveled as a stowaway—our conversation languished. Y. Remade is a real hooker, who has had run-ins with the police. We dropped her and went inside the Dôme—I go there so rarely these days that I found it poetic. We talked, in fact, I was the one to talk about my winter vacation, Sorokine, etc. Kos. was animated and seductive; pleasant company. I went home and went to sleep around midnight.

Tuesday, January 9

This morning I crossed the gray Luxembourg Gardens and had breakfast at the Mahieu; I always find it delightful. Henri IV—I have teaching interns* to whom I passed on two stacks of papers. Work at the Mahieu—ate lunch with Sorokine at the Milk Bar blvd. St. Germain—very pleasant, but while entering the metro station, she explained that I wasn't ranking my friends correctly: instead of granting them time in my schedule according to how long I have known them, the ranking should be according to the degree of affection I have for them; I protested. She told me, like Védrine, that one should not consider oneself obligated to people or feel that one owes them something—which doesn't prevent them from making demands. Lycée. At a quarter past three I went to the Versailles—work—post office, then on the AF, where I read my letters, to the Dauphin on the Théatre Français square, where I wrote my letters. We had fixed a date for seven o'clock to see *Chacun sa vérité* [To Each His Own Truth]. They arrived at half past seven; as a result I could make headway in this notebook. It's no longer very interesting, but I like to profile an entire year. When they arrived, we went for some ice cream and then to a small bar, where I had been before with Poupette and Gégé, and which looked like the Cintra, a mountain chalet, or a hunting lodge. I drank some Xérès and ate long sandwiches. We chatted. Kos. was in a feverish rage because she just came from Dullin's class. She had recited poetry quite well; he had caressed her hair, but it drove her crazy, consciousnesses being focused on her; she was beside herself. More interesting than Wanda, but Wanda is more pleasant to look at—a limited charm, but less bland, a little rough and harsh. We got to our loge in time for the end of the curtain rise: *12 Louis*—terrible; we wandered around the foyer. Wanda was delighted because it was so vast. Kos. started to have a toothache. The performance of *Chacun sa vérité* with Ledoux, Bovy, Debucourt was excellent and the staging done extremely well. A pleasant evening. But upon leaving the theater, Kos.'s toothache became worse—no taxi; we went home on the metro, where she collapsed—tantrum and sobbing on the way home, which annoyed me since it's up to her to see a dentist. Went to bed at midnight.

---

* Candidates for the *agrégation* who were spending a few weeks as interns in a graduating class, which was to prepare them for the teaching profession.

Wednesday, January 10

No teaching and a great day of work. Since my return, I've retyped sixty pages in one week, well done. I was at the Dôme before nine o'clock with *Le Canard enchaîné* and *La Semaine à Paris,* which I perused to check the attractions of the week. But there weren't many. Worked from nine o'clock to a quarter past twelve, interrupted by a short conversation with Stépha—Gérassi was furious that he had to work—and by the arrival of Védrine, who worked next to me. Lunch at my parents' home—my father seemed somewhat less senile—he had his friends from the Versailles read *Le Mur;* they admired it and understood that the moral of *L'Enfance d'un chef*[6] is the idea "that a leader must be not only forceful but also ruthless." I went to the Versailles, where I worked from two to five o'clock, sitting next to Védrine, who read my third chapter and made some sound critical remarks. There was a gang of horrible and housewifely whores—one of them accused me of making her reek of smoke and called me "a crazy old nutcase." At five o'clock I met up with Sorokine. "It will give you some material for your novel," said Védrine with a superior look; she never inquired whether I liked Sorokine, nor did she ever think that she might have some worth—as if she alone held the interest of the entire world. A funny kind of blind self-importance, which isn't a preference for the self, or for anything at all, only shortsightedness. Spent the rest of a charming afternoon with Sorokine; we studied Descartes—then she threw herself in my arms, said that she had been frantic yesterday because of me, but I assured her of my affection, and she was passionately happy—she knows how to turn passion into grace—she whispered her outbursts of anger, her worries, her love, while holding me tightly in her arms, and I was touched. So as not to be a hypocrite and out of tenderness, she forced herself to say, "I love it when you caress me, I love to be in your arms." She doesn't really believe me when I tell her this, but I like to spend the evening this way with her.

Kos. didn't come and I had one hour to write my letters. I was the one who went upstairs to see her. She had her new coat, which is not that pretty. Wanda was there. We said hello, and I went to the Milk Bar with Kos., informing her that I was once again going to spend some evenings with Védrine and she let it go. We went home at half past ten because she was afraid of getting a toothache, and I wrote to Poupette and made entries into this diary before going to sleep.

Thursday, January 11

At half past eight I was at work at the Dôme and stayed until ten o'clock—lycée—lunch with Sorokine. She charmed me with her scorn for my literary work: "you, you *invent* things to write," she said with scandalized irony at the little blue brasserie while eating the ritual Thursday *salade niçoise*. I explained a few things about abortion and condoms, which interested her very much. Lycée Henri IV. Worked upstairs at the Mahieu, sitting near the window, from where you could see student couples in the bare Luxembourg Gardens. Védrine arrived at half past five and we took a taxi to the Opéra Comique. We had an excellent loge and from six to ten o'clock we listened to *The Marriage of Figaro,* performed by Calanel, Bourdin, and Delprat—a great pleasure. With easy music and a lighthearted theme, the inconveniences of the Opéra disappeared; nothing is meant to be taken seriously anymore, the plot and scenery are like cardboard cutouts. On the way back we stopped to eat at the Capoulade, then I wrote to Sartre from the Mahieu. I slept at Védrine's place. Physical disgust, disgust of her skin, especially of her odor, a fecal odor and her mawkish face. We talked a while about how she lets herself get carried away by her jokes and shocks me. "I'm not authentic," she correctly concluded. She kissed me during the night, which woke me up, startled and annoyed.

Friday, January 12

Six and a half hours of work. I got up at eight and ran to my hotel, washed up, then went to the Dôme, where I worked from nine to noon. Gérassi came by to tell me that Stépha had said I wouldn't go to see them because I found him too awful, which I vigorously denied. A quick lunch with Védrine and her sister at Mirov's—then at the lycée I had my students take an exam while I worked for three and a half hours. In one day I revised the entire sixth chapter, on Elisabeth. True, there wasn't much to be redone. On the way out, a former student, Nicole Berman, was waiting for me. In a frivolous mood, I invited her for coffee at the Capoulade—she was rather pretty, not too dull, but not very entertaining either. Then an hour with Gégé, who told me about her meeting with Poupette and about a dream, a kind of "charming fantasy," suggesting that Sartre make it into a short story. Afterward to the post office; two letters from Sartre—correspondence at the Versailles. I met up with Kos.; we had dinner at the Dôme, returned at about eleven o'clock and went to sleep.

Saturday, January 13

A long, long day of work. Two hours' teaching at Camille Sée—as I was leaving I found Sorokine, convinced that I had stood her up on purpose the day before at one o'clock at Henri IV, where she had lunch, and she was furious, and furious that she had come—I told her that I had sent a pneumatic dispatch, which calmed her down. She accompanied me to the Latin Quarter and I gave her some money for book rentals at Monnier's.* I then went to the Source, where I worked sitting in a draft. Védrine came and read chapters 4 and 5 of my novel, which she found flawless and which made me happy nonetheless. After having lunch together at the little Alsatian restaurant, we went to Monnier's to see the photos of Sartre, but we were out of luck. I bought the latest Jules Romains. Afterward we went to sit in the back of the Sorbonne,[7] where disgusting young students were playing cards—I worked until past half past six. Took a taxi to the post office and sent Bost a big package of sausages, etc. A letter from Sartre. At seven o'clock I went to the Coupole to dine, write my letters, and work on this notebook. I bought some envelopes for the letters and when I left the stationery shop there was Sorokine, very friendly, her plaid scarf around her head and posted there like a reproach: she had just come out of the metro, saw me go into the shop, and figured that I would be late. We went to my place; I noticed with some apprehension that I had left my notebook at the Coupole. We rushed back and, fortunately, found it. We returned to my room; it was nine o'clock—we chatted for a very, very brief moment, sitting next to each other, then kisses, and very quickly, embraces; we turned the lights off and lay down on the bed—this time she was relaxed and passionately happy and tender, always showing the same restraint in her passionate feelings and the same grace in her tenderness. We turned the lights back on to read the notebooks, but we read very little. She asked me questions: "what's the worst thing one can do between women?" and "what if we were criminals, what if we deserved to go to prison?" an idea that would delight her—I had the definite impression of an "initiation," which I would feel ashamed of had I not been so profoundly caught up in the moment. As for her, not a shade of passion, only an immense tenderness and esteem, for nothing in the world would I want to hurt her—such a touching face when she smiles with all the abandon of which she is capable, an abandon freely consented to and over which

---

* Adrienne Monnier was the driving force behind the famous bookstore of 7, rue de l'Odéon, la Maison des Amis des Livres, frequented by many writers, among them Joyce and Gide. Gisèle Freund's photos of Sartre were on display there.

she never loses control. More embraces that are reciprocated, shyly, but not awkwardly—physical tenderness, also for her. An altogether pleasant evening. She left a little before midnight, leaving behind her watch, eyeglasses, combs—and as for me, I went to sleep.

Sunday, January 14

At nine o'clock I was already at the Dôme, from where I didn't budge until half past four—working steadily. I need to invent an entirely new chapter, I started the continuation; it requires more effort than the previous work. Breakfast—lunch, during which I read a little in Jules Romains—shook hands with Gérassi—and a half hour of insignificant conversation with Védrine barely took an hour away from my work. Letter to Sartre, then I met up with Kos. I found her in the company of Wanda, who had just returned a little disheveled from the flea market—as for Kos., she had a toothache all day, and the evening before, in a fit of pique, she had cried right in the middle of class because of a role that was too easy and that she played with too much ease. Incidentally, she looked charming in her plaid hood when she was telling me all that. Went by U-bus to Salle Gaveau, where we couldn't find any more seats; we persisted obstinately but finally had to give up. We took a taxi to the movie theater Boul' Mich, where we saw *Les Disparus de Saint-Agil* [The Lost Souls of Saint-Agil] with Michel Simon and Von Stroheim, both excellent, and Mouloudji, who amused us—they also showed a charming cartoon in color, *Le Rat de ville et le rat des champs* [The City Mouse and the Country Mouse] and during the newsreel, they showed terrible cannons, such beautiful, noble machines that looked as if they should be intended for other things than crushing poor human flesh to a pulp—trenches, mud, it made my blood run cold with horror. From there we went to the upstairs of the Rotonde where we spent a rather depressing moment because Kos. had a toothache. We returned home, and I still had time to write to Bost before I fell asleep.

Monday, January 15

Lycée. Work at the Sorbonne,[8] next to Védrine—had sauerkraut while reading Jules Romains: that made two and a half hours of work—lycée Henri IV—at the gate, Metzger,* whom I dismissed, and Védrine, who accompa-

---

* A former student of Beauvoir.

nied me as I went to pay Poupette's rent and then to pick up a record player at Florès's studio on rue Broca. The weather was nice, that means gray and mild, and sad; a wintry day in Paris in the more pleasant but somewhat deserted neighborhoods—Florès's studio is located at the end of a charming cul-de-sac where there are nothing but studios on both sides of the street and at the very end an enormous plaster statue of a man. We climbed a little staircase and there we were in his studio. He showed us some paintings, somewhat sentimental, yet sober, in the style of Watteau, but revised and made obtuse by cubism. We took the record player with us, left it at my place, and then went to the Versailles after having picked up my letters—two long and pleasant letters from Sartre, who seemed so alive to me, so lively that it made me cheerful again. I answered him and after Védrine had left, I read the three short letters from Bost, who had not been relieved for twenty-five days and was freezing and beginning to complain. I wrote to him and worked for another two hours. Near me, a meeting, which intrigued me, was taking place between a captain and his wife, whom he called Minette and whose back he was stroking—she was dressed in black and mauve, proper, but not "attractive"—a fellow from the *NRF* whom I had seen before—another couple of officers—some sort of intellectual women from the Dôme, but well-to-do—and all those people were talking about a banquet and aperitifs for all. Toward the end of the evening, Carteret showed up with his long beard and dirty hair. They were all discussing anthropology; I didn't understand the relationship between these different people, but it was entertaining listening to them.

I returned just after eight o'clock and found Gérassi at the Kos.'s place. We couldn't go out together—so after a bit of hesitation, we decided that Kos. and I would go and eat at Dominique's, then would meet up with Wanda at the Jockey. At Dominique's Kos. had a mild toothache, but it went away. At the Jockey we had great seats; I drank an Alexander, I already had drunk Kos.'s vodka at Dominique's, but it had no effect on me—they, on the other hand, were animated immediately after having had one martini; they danced together quite nicely—we chatted a while—there were many people: young officers, done up in their uniforms, feeling quite heroic and handsome and dancing with rather elegant whores—a drunken woman fell flat on her face in the middle of the dance floor; she was dragging a dog behind her, systematically preventing him from sleeping—she wanted a man badly and finally took up with an obese man. Bad attractions: a singer from Marseilles in a white dress, looking altogether shabby, and the impersonator, Rue/doux, who wasn't impersonating anything. The drunken woman at least contributed something unexpected to the act. I felt very good being with Wanda. We returned home at eleven o'clock, and I read for a while.

Tuesday, January 16

At the Mahieu at eight o'clock after having crossed the Luxembourg Gardens. I read a while and then ran to Henri IV. I felt a little depressed; last evening I shed a few tears thinking of Sartre in a fit of real sad weariness [*ennui*]—I felt nothing passionate, but this weariness was killing me. Fortunately, I've got my work to hold on to. Worked from ten o'clock to noon. Lunch at the Milk Bar in St. Germain with Sorokine, always so pleasant and sweet. Then four hours of written exams during which I worked on my novel. I stopped at the post office; had a letter from Sartre, whose leave has been postponed—I went to place Pigalle and in a red brasserie wrote to Sartre and Bost. Then I left for place Dancourt to watch the dress rehearsal of *Richard III*.* At the Touraine I met Wanda, who had been asked to wait for me; from there she took me to the theater, crossing the stage behind the set. We sat close to Kos.—I was delighted to be there. First of all because it seemed my private property since I described it in my novel, and I think that I rendered it very well—and then, it recalled the past; it was also quite pleasant in itself even though it didn't have the impact on me that it once had; it's familiar to me now. Beautiful decors, beautiful costumes, Mayenne Copeau looking gorgeous in her black dress and the white headdress; Blin looking splendid in his white Buckingham outfit. Only Dullin was wearing a light jacket with a Basque beret that gave him a mischievous look. The women were playing well, and Dullin was fantastic; the men played less well, even Blin, who looked like a disturbing angel, but much too angelic and not disturbing enough, except in the death scene, where he was fantastic. Mouloudji, after his short performance, walked around the theater in a phantom's nightgown. I said hello to Kéchélévitch, who looked rather beautiful. Dullin did a series of his little "sketches"† as Mouloudji so charmingly called them—the one from the balcony, where he was to harangue the crowd, was especially well done. He said hello to me: "*She* has bronchitis," he said in a ceremonious and sly way as he does whenever he speaks of Toulouse.

---

* At Dullin's Atelier.

† Ritual attacks of rage and pretend despair accompanied by curses and imprecations—very entertaining for the informed public.

Kos. was hungry like a bear—at half past nine I decided to follow her, being starved too, and so I missed the last act. We ate at Touraine, which was really pleasant with people from the neighborhood playing cards and the owner's wife, who discussed the rehearsal with Kos., and the electrician, who had left at nine o'clock. We got home at eleven o'clock; Kos. was exhausted and I had enough time to write letters, bring the notebook up to date, and sleep for a long time.

Wednesday, January 17

From half past eight on I worked at the Dôme—that made a good three hours, still working on the new chapter 7 that's coming along all right. Lunch at home where it was icy cold, with the Cordonnier cousins—one more hour at the Lutétia, where I met with the neurasthenic Mme Mancy—then to the post office, no letters. I went to my place to write my letters, and Sorokine came by. Leibniz, conversation—she admitted having lied to me about the blond girl, who had laughed at her and didn't show up at all at the date. She told me her big secret: a short story with the title "Le râtelier" she was writing with her friend. She was charming, but nervous when she arrived, and furious, just because she had to leave. I had a half hour to write to Bost.

At eight o'clock, Védrine. She irritated me right away, because she was standing in the doorway striking a pose like a star, brimming over with joy she was going to bring me; nothing puts me off more than this attitude of certitude lined with demands. I put on makeup and did my nails while she was all over me giving me little kisses, which continued to annoy me—we went to Dominique's for dinner—then because I felt an inner need to be distracted, I took her to Betty Hoop's, on the former site of Mirages—it was soberly decorated, blue and deep pink, and cold. A good orchestra, beautiful dance floor, good lighting; shabby clientele. Betty Hoop appeared all in pink, pink hair, an ugly old hat, dancing and singing without charm—a raconteur telling Marseilles[9] stories, not funny—an excellent tap dancer, who did some very good numbers, one as Professor Nimbus—in between performances, people danced. Védrine constantly stole some tender glances at me, trying to be overly discreet, but with a terrible smile that set my nerves on edge. She told me that she had been jealous of Kos. when I offered her only two evenings compared to Kos.'s five—and little by little she explained "that it wasn't fair," "that they [the Kos. sisters] didn't deserve," etc. I explained a little the morose Kos. and the courage of inertia they have, which disgusts her—she accepted a dance, to be polite. She dances well, but without feeling, like a fashionable girl—then I demolished her idea of "merit" and "moral effort" and talked a little too much on the subject so that she got quite thrown off track. She admitted that she was only moral for me, so that I'd esteem her more, and she used this naive phrase: "So, as Elisabeth says in your novel, all that for nothing?"[10] "Of course, not!" I told her. She came back up to my room with me, a little confused, kissed me, and left.

Thursday, January 18

In the morning I worked for only one hour at the Dôme—lycée—lunch at the blue brasserie with Sorokine, who again got annoyed when she left me. I have a cold; the intern fortunately returned the homework on "mathematic intuition"—Sorokine was waiting at the gate with some chocolate by way of reconciliation. At the Mahieu, Védrine, in a friendly mood; she hadn't even thought further about the moral problem we raised the previous evening. We were thrown out. Worked at my place and wrote letters. At eight o'clock, Kos. knocked; she was in her robe, very morose, she had such a toothache that she didn't even want to see me, but I kindly insisted. I went to buy some smoked salmon and some Vichy bottled water and we ate in her room—she put on a record, a tune from *The Three Penny Opera*, and "my" record that the Moon Woman had given me: *40 hommes, huit chevaux* [Forty Men, Eight Horses], sung by Gilles and Julien;* it was an antiwar song, rather beautiful. At that very moment the Moon Woman knocked on the door: she was looking for Wanda, who was in bed, freezing. They don't want to heat their rooms in order to punish the owner, who has the effrontery to make residents pay for it. The Moon Woman left with Wanda; the vague echoes of their lives that come down to me through Kos. amuse me: the Moon Woman, Dominguez, Florès, *bal nègre*, etc. The conversation got bogged down, and at half past nine Kos. wanted to sleep. I hesitated and decided to go and see *Cette sacrée vérité* [The Awful Truth] with Irene Dunne, playing right next door—not very funny. Amazing, listed in the cast and credits of *Le Congrès s'amuse* [The Congress Is Having Fun]: "London is having fun, Paris is having fun. All of Europe is having fun." The entire audience was a little shocked. Got back at eleven o'clock, with enough time to write Poupette and finish Jules Romains, about whom I have nothing good to say.

---

* Anarchist and antimilitaristic singers, well known since 1932.

Friday, January 19

I worked at the Dôme from half past eight to half past eleven—shivering there from the cold—post office—a long, sweet letter from Bost, letters from Sartre as usual—by metro to the Sorbonne where I met Védrine, who, while we were eating omelets Parmentier, really gave me an earful: for two hours she had shaken and sobbed in bed thinking that my life was like a mosaic with me in the center and that I *wasn't giving* of myself, that she wasn't *my* life, etc. All that is jealousy of Kos.—she is half within and half outside this craziness, which is exasperating and must not be taken seriously. I wasn't very kind and told her curtly some reasonable things: "Love isn't a symbiosis." "That's what really gets me," she said, standing in front of the lycée Henri IV, her teeth chattering. Three hours of classes—half an hour with Metzger—then work at home. A note from Kos., saying that she woke up all lopsided because of an abscessed tooth. I stopped in to say hello and worked. At eight o'clock I went to get some food, and we gorged ourselves on jams and cakes in her room—I still have a bad cold, but we chatted quite amicably until eleven o'clock. I finished my letters, went to bed and slept.

NOTES

1. *Neige* means "snow."
2. Henri Barbusse, French author (1873–1935). His most successful novel was *Feu*.
3. A biography of Heinrich Heine by Vallentin.
4. "In situation" is from Marcel 1936–37.
5. A discount department store.
6. *L'Enfance d'un chef* is a short story from Sartre's collection *Le Mur*.
7. A restaurant called the Sorbonne, not the university.
8. The restaurant.
9. The city and the people of Marseilles are often the butt of jokes.
10. Elisabeth's remark, in anguished reflection on her "struggles and hatreds" with her beloved brother, Pierre, as he prepares to leave for war, comes in chapter 9 of Beauvoir's published novel; "Pour rien, murmura-t-elle. Tout cela pour rien" (Beauvoir 1943, 473); "'For nothing,' she murmured. 'All that for nothing'" (Beauvoir 1984, 380).

NOTEBOOK 5

January 20 – February 23, 1940

Saturday, January 20, 1940

Lycée—at the Dôme from eleven to a quarter past one, but the cold was so intense that I ate lunch and continued to work at the Coupole. I returned to the Dôme for a hot toddy and to wait for Sorokine, who showed up at five o'clock sharp and immediately tensed up, tapping her glass, because the moments when we are not definitively settled in seem lost to her. We went to the Nordland. It was cold on the streets, a damp and gray cold—I was tired and felt a cold coming on. I drank a punch and she ate little anchovy sandwiches while we discussed Proust, art, and life. I left her, went home to write for half an hour and wait for Védrine. She arrived, all smiles; her delirium was over. She brought me records, and we listened to a bad Schubert trio and some Chopin. We then went to the Select for dinner, trying to sort out her craziness: how she had wanted to imitate Kos. and how, setting it out for me, she had forced herself to stay within this madness just to impress me even though she no longer felt like doing it. We discussed love, morality, and everything. I was rather taken by her again; I found her engaging. After returning home I wrote another letter and went to sleep.

Sunday, January 21

Worked at the Dôme all morning; had lunch with Gégé and the Gérassis. I complained and many other clients did likewise, because while pretending to serve us the rationed hundred grams of meat, they served us only some old bones; the manager was besieged with complaints. There was nothing special about the meal. At two o'clock I settled into my corner in order to work and write letters. I also corrected some papers. Then at five o'clock Kos. and I took the metro and went to a concert at the Conservatory, where we listened to a rather beautiful Adagio and Fugue by Mozart, and a very beautiful *Requiem*. She was still all wrapped up in her scarves, but the swelling on her cheek had gone down; it had almost stopped hurting and she was very pleasant. We had dinner at Pagès, and together with Wanda we listened to music on her record player in her room: the Appassionata Sonata[1]—Concert and Fugue by Bach—Beethoven's Variations on a theme by Mozart. At eleven o'clock I left to write my letters and sleep.

Saturday [sic], January 22

Lycée Camille Sée—work—but first I took the metro to the Madeleine to buy tickets for the Ravel festival on Saturday—I returned by bus. It was snowing, the air was mild, and rue Royale looked delightful in the snow; the cars had slowed down, everything had taken on an old-fashioned look, enveloping the scene in a village air. I sat down at the Mont St. Michel, but writers are not welcome there and after eating my egg with tomatoes I settled down at the Mahieu continuing my work. At eight o'clock in the morning when I was going downstairs, Sorokine showed up; her father and mother had been fighting, and she was seeking my support—they were quarreling because they wanted to separate and neither wanted to take her. Her father, however, hugs her from time to time, saying, "Your father is your best friend," and tries to kiss her on the mouth. She was telling me all that on my way to the post office to get Sartre's letters, but the mailbag hadn't been opened yet. We had breakfast in a little café across the street. She made me promise to meet her at two o'clock in the teachers' lounge, which I did, but I got there late and she didn't even look up; she was sulking.

Lycée—then, as I had an appointment with Kos. for a movie at St. Germain-des-Prés, I sat down at Lipp's, where I felt wonderfully comfortable because of the large tables and the warm and quiet room. I worked, wrote my letters, and met up with Kos. at the Deux Magots, which was crowded. I had a hot chocolate with fruitcake and bought some dates to eat at the movies. The movie played at the Récamier, where I had been as a child, as I remembered. The movie house had the air of an entertainment hall about it. It still had an orchestra pit. We watched a bad gangster movie with Humphrey Bogart, *Menaces sur la ville* [A Beleaguered City], a propaganda movie, and a slightly bungled, yet pleasant film with Bette Davis, *Nuits de bal* [Dancing Nights]. On our way home it was bitter cold and dark. In bed I read a little in *The Castle*. I found it superior by far to *The Trial* and was quite captivated by it.

A dark and rather unsettled day.

Tuesday, January 23

Lycée Henri IV, where we were shivering—the students had red noses, we could only think about the best way to use our coats; fortunately an intern returned the homework.

Worked at the Mahieu on chapter 8, which I didn't really enjoy. Last night I had letters from Sartre announcing his leave as definite, but it rather disoriented me. I don't believe in it, but am unable to get interested in other things. And then I started work on another chapter, which is unrewarding; I felt ill at ease.

Sorokine came by at noon; we had lunch at the Milk Bar, but she was sulking, and I let her know that it annoyed me. Suddenly, at three o'clock, as I was leaving Camille Sée, she showed up, full of hate, but unable to resist the need to see me. She accompanied me to Montparnasse. I had two letters from Sartre that made me feel a little better, and others from Bost, so sweet. I worked at the Versailles. Védrine came by, but read my novel and so didn't bother me at all. We went on foot back to my place. I worked some more and Kos. came to get me. She was depressed, but nevertheless quite pleasant. We spent the evening at the Dôme, where we ate dinner while she talked to me at length about her work from a technical point of view, which amused me. We returned at ten o'clock to listen to Bach and the Appassionata. I finished my letters and went to sleep.

Wednesday, January 24

At a quarter past nine I was already at the Dôme, but Stépha ruined a quarter of an hour for me with problems concerning her apartment. It annoyed me. I worked for three hours, still on chapter 8, which is drawing to a close.

Post office: two letters from Sartre, two from Bost. I read them on my way to my parents'. Meal with my family; we compared K. Mansfield and Maupassant, I corrected some papers. Again to the Dôme to work all afternoon. At five o'clock I went home and saw Sorokine. Our little session gave me quite a turn: she threw herself into my arms telling me without getting emotional or upbraiding me, but with a touching face and in a moving voice, that she loved me "so much, so much" and that it weighed on her, keeping her tense. Embraces and kisses that, however, couldn't go very far today—I had to explain it to her discreetly because she was getting agitated. In the end I gave myself over to her and was extremely rough with her; it was amazing how in a second she became calm, all smiling and happy. We talked pleasantly—she didn't ask me to love her passionately and I took care this time not to let her think that, but she would like me to be fond of her. I really am fond of her and after she left I remained very shaken.

Védrine came by; she was neither bothersome nor interesting. We went out to eat broiled beef at the Nordland; it was mildly boring. Afterward we went to the Dôme, where I drank a brandy—she felt a little melancholic, we discussed science and politics—there wasn't anything in it for me, her intelligence being moderate and inferior to mine. I felt bored with her.

I wrote to Sartre, reread his letters, read *Le Canard enchaîné,* and went to sleep.

Thursday, January 25

I lingered a while in bed until past eight o'clock. As I had so much catching up to do in my notebook, I decided not to work on the novel this morning but go to the Dupont instead and bring it up to date. The cold had abated. I passed by the post office—nothing from Sartre—two letters from Bost. I went to the Dupont to read them while surrounded by warmth, red tables, and music. I was gripped by a fit of melancholy such as I hadn't experienced for a long time. He first wrote about some guys in his company who had seen combat and that scared me, and then, the more I rediscovered him alive and charming, the greater the tenderness I felt for him and the more his fate seemed unfair to me, and the more afraid I became. These home leaves seemed to me more like taking leave of someone condemned to die. What will happen afterward? It will be that famous spring, so greatly feared. Will it come to battles? These home leaves, which mark the end of a waiting period, now that they are at hand, make me think already of the undefined "thereafter" that's going to follow. I felt a tremendous need to cry—this morning was as dark as night. And I wanted so much for Sartre to come.

Lycée. I had a twenty-minute godsend, because my students, wearing hats and gloves and carrying their gasmasks at their sides, left for an air raid drill in the building across the street. I read *The Castle* sitting in one of the deep armchairs in the teachers' lounge. Then class. When I left, a beaming Sorokine was waiting for me. We had lunch together while once more discussing Proust. Lycée. I saw Védrine very briefly and went to pick up my letter, and this time Sartre's leave seemed certain, he would really be coming. Worked at the Dôme—wrote letters to Sartre and Bost in my room—my fountain pen lost its cap. I bought a bottle of ink so I could dunk my pen in it like a crude penholder.

Kos., dispirited but charming as usual, came to pick me up, and we went to eat at the Dôme where she talked to me about diction and breathing. We went home rather early, and I corrected some papers.

Friday, January 26

I got up very early and was at the Dôme before half past eight. I was furious with Stépha, who told me about her reconciliation with Fernand. When he learned that she had found a job in Paris, he, who had wanted to leave for Santo Domingo, had jumped at the opportunity and declared his passionate love for her, backing up his words with heroic nightly exploits. Her eyes clouded with tears as she meditated on the complexity of human nature. I nevertheless worked extremely well until noon. Then I went to the Biarritz; they were all there: Kanapa, Lévy, Besse, and Ramblin. After they left I ate an omelet and potatoes with the others who had stayed. Of course, Védrine was there too. Lycée. Sorokine came by, but I dropped her because Védrine was waiting for me at the Mahieu. She showed me a short and touching list of all the observations she had made about herself. We went to the post office—letter from Sartre—then to the brasserie Lutétia, where I worked another hour and a half on my novel and my letters, and since Kos. didn't show up I corrected papers. Because of the icy streets she didn't arrive until after eight o'clock. At the Atelier they thought they should reimburse the customers because at half past seven, Blin, who couldn't get a taxi, was absent, as was old Marthe Mollot, who was seen walking up rue Dancourt helped along by two children. Besides, only thirty-eight people had come for the performance. We went to the Récamier to watch *Les Pillards des mers* [Pirates of the Seas] with George O'Brien, which was somewhat funny, and *La Grande*

Farandole [The Story of Vernon and Irene Castle] with Ginger Rogers and Fred Astaire. In their first two sketches they were absolutely charming, as good as in their best movies, then it became tedious.

When we left the cinema the ice was thawing, but there were still some dangerous spots—we took the metro to Montparnasse and at the Milk Bar bought some toast that we ate at the counter of the Rotonde—the cafés close at midnight now, it's nice.

Saturday, January 27

Got up at half past seven, a little fatigued. Lycée—then to the Dôme, where I worked after having received my letter from Sartre. Stépha—with her dog—was sitting close by, which exasperated me; she was muttering a word from time to time, staring at me intensely while I was writing. Florès stopped by and talked to her, which caused some noise. I wound up inviting her to lunch with Boubou and then was furious with myself for having done so. I felt tense. I had slept poorly for sheer joy in anticipation of Sartre's arrival. Last night his mother dropped off his clothes at my place; it's beginning to look real and it causes me anxiety. I got back to work after lunch—but it was noisy, my head felt heavy, and I was fatigued. Kos. came by; now she wanted to go to the concert, but yesterday she didn't want to and I gave the ticket to Stépha—and it was she I took to Gaveau Hall instead; I was still furious. Elegant people, a good program, on the light side: a quartet, some piano pieces, and mostly very beautiful cantatas sung magnificently by an amazing woman by the name of Madeleine Grey. Unfortunately, we had to sit through Pierre Bertin's lecture and an endless auction where the Baroness de Rothschild and the Count de Polignac and others were fighting over some handwritten pages by Duhamel, Claudel, and Valéry for two thousand francs—I was flabbergasted to see those people spit out money by the thousands. In the metro, on the way to Sorokine's, I met Védrine and her mother—then I read *The Castle*—it gripped me—at the end, Amalia's relationship with the castle made me think of Zaza.* I think it does have a special meaning that can be understood only if one has experienced—in one form or another—this kind of relationship with a personal God—this story had a strong emotional impact on me; it weighed heavily on me all day, intertwined with all kinds of anguish. During the concert I felt a moment of deep anguish, due in large part to my fatigue.

---

* Her best childhood friend. See *Memoirs of a Dutiful Daughter.*

Sorokine was charming—we talked about Proust—she explained how she saw my feelings for her, and she was right on the mark: that I would gladly spend ten days traveling with her, but no more; that I would freely see her for three hours three times a week, but no more; that I had moments of "exaltation," but which quickly dissipate. The only thing she can't feel is this very strong "intention" of being good to her and this deep and tender consideration I have for her. It's slight but consistent with my feelings for her, and I shouldn't be irritated that she doesn't feel it or appreciate as precious the little I do give her—which seems to me already quite considerable but which obviously cannot satisfy her. With her long straight hair and her face peeking out from under it, I like her physically more and more.

I took a taxi home and went to the Dôme to write Sartre my last letter—then at home I spent a long time on my personal care before going to sleep. A letter from Mops,* who is in Paris.

Sunday, January 28

I slept badly, feeling anguished. I saw Sartre and felt nothing when looking at him, because he sometimes had the features of Dullin and then in turn those of one of my students; and I became indignant that he had been replaced by someone else, and I was disconsolate at the idea of never again finding the emotional warmth of before—it was unbearable. I slept until nine o'clock, left a word at Mops's, wrote to Bost, and updated this notebook. Yesterday I had noticed Kos. holding Bost's notebooks, and it was difficult for me; that was part of my anguish. I anticipate some very painful jealousy when he's on leave and right after Sartre's departure. I was going to work, but Stépha was next to me again with her dog and her presence was enough to irritate me.

Stépha behaved, and so I could work well; I almost finished everything. In between I had a bite to eat. Then I took the metro after buying a detective novel that bored me to tears. I met up with Védrine at the Cintra on rue du Faubourg Montmartre, which was rather pleasant; she looked cute in her black velvet suit with a pretty blue blouse. She told me that she had been a little depressed because of those ideas on morality and didn't know what to do anymore. I encouraged her tenderly. We spent an hour together and then went separately to the concert. I met Wanda in the concert hall; we were waiting for Kos., who arrived at the last minute, just when they were about to close the loge doors. Bach's five Brandenburg Concertos, beautiful—the

---

* Mme Morel's daughter.

hall was packed, it was hot, but I felt cool, I listened well and enjoyed it to the fullest; I was completely fulfilled.

We went home, then ate at Pagès; Kos. was tired and almost on edge—we went back to her place early, chatted languidly, and listened to a record by Sophie Tucker.* I left at half past ten, wrote to Bost and Poupette, and went to bed. Slept well.

Monday, January 29

I had a hard time waking up; I am beginning to feel a little tired. Last night Védrine told me that she and her mother had noticed how totally exhausted I looked last Saturday. But soon I'll rest up; already I felt relaxed having almost finished all I wanted to show Sartre of my novel. It gave me an impression of leisure the moment I woke up.

Black ice on the streets—I made my way to the metro taking tiny little steps. Lycée Camille Sée—then post office. I had a short letter from Bost, who wrote little because he would be coming here soon. Two letters from Sartre: his leave was still not certain. Worked at the Dôme, corrected papers, ate some salted pork, then on foot to Henri IV, crossing the Luxembourg Gardens, which were a sea of frozen mud. Two hours of teaching, then returned on foot. I worked for an hour at the Dôme, then Mops, with whom I had a two-hour-long conversation of no interest, showed up. I learned that Zuorro had lost his brother-in-law—Guille was depressed and wanted to leave for the front, God knows why. Then I wrote to Bost and updated this notebook. At present there is some faint music at the Dôme coming from I don't know where.

At eight o'clock I met up with Védrine at the Deux Magots, which was crowded for a change—we had dinner at Lipp, seated toward the back, and I found it pleasant to be there—I was very friendly and feeling in sync with her. We discussed philosophy; the problem is that I can barely talk with her because she never contributes anything of her own; all I can do is explain things to her—unless we talk about her, that's the only subject on which she has something new to offer. We talked about Einstein and non-Euclidian geometries. A gentleman with a rosette in his lapel[2] who had scrupulously been following our discussion intervened to explain Lobatchevski's parallels; he even made a little drawing for me. Then we went to a crowded Flore,

---

* The interpreter of, among others, the jazz tune "Some of These Days" that Roquentin listened to at the end of *Nausea*.

where we ran into Gégé. We chatted some more, then went to the Odéon metro station, and I went home.

Tuesday, January 30

This was a transitional period for me as I was no longer working, just waiting for Sartre without really believing that he'd be coming—and once more, with leisure time to look at the situation instead of keeping my nose in my papers, I was feeling ill at ease. I was afraid of the spring, that war would start for good and days like last September would return. In all, I was able to bear it when I was in the thick of it, but from afar those hours of fear seemed unbearable to me.

I walked to my classes crossing the Luxembourg Gardens, which were like a skating rink; on the place du Panthéon the students were taking tiny steps like little old ladies. Everything was covered with ice, creating a great natural disaster—silence, a country-like calm this morning, all in white. When I got out, big city trucks were spewing sand on the roadway and the concierges were cleaning the sidewalks—during the day it changed into vile slush—but the restroom attendant at the Mahieu said that people had gotten killed last night. I worked two hours at the Mahieu correcting papers. Then Sorokine arrived, she was happy with me and therefore charming; we ate at the Mont St. Michel—she told me about her problems in Chemistry, how she breaks the stills and makes herself hated by the assistant. Three hours of teaching at Camille Sée on rancor and timidity. At the post office I had a letter from Sartre—it seemed certain now that he'd be here in two or three days. I went to the Sorbonne, where Lévy, Kanapa, and Védrine were working, spread out in a circle at the back of the room. I sat down near Védrine, corrected some papers, and wrote to Bost until half past seven.

At half past seven I met Kos. at the Mahieu—we went to see *La Kermesse funèbre* [The Funereal Fair] by Eisenstein at the Ursulines; the movie was very short but interesting and the photography was truly wonderful. They also showed a short retrospective of talkies from 1900 on. We walked to the Milk Bar for a light supper and went home. I spent a long time on personal care and preparations and went to bed.

Wednesday, January 31

I slept for nine hours, less from inclination than because I had explicitly decided on sleeping late since I needed to rest up a bit. I went to the Dôme with

Le Canard, La Semaine à Paris and *L'Œuvre* that I perused before working on this notebook. Stépha, of course, sat down across from me while I began rereading the draft of the second part of my novel; but I didn't look up and almost went so far as to be rude; I found her impossible. I'll have my work cut out for me in the next one hundred fifty pages, but I had already been mulling it over and even so, felt almost tempted to start on it the next day. I spent two hours in the morning reading it. Then I went to have lunch with my family—afterward by taxi to Neuilly and Rys to buy some sewing material with the money I just collected, but didn't find anything. I went home and wrote to Bost. My mother gave me a beautiful lavender-blue sweater with a turban to match. I put it on and found myself very beautiful.

Sorokine arrived at four o'clock. I gave her a lesson, then took her with me to the post office and to pick up a record player that I had taken to be repaired. I came back with her, and we played the Quartet No. 16 by Beethoven, which is beautiful but difficult, so I listened attentively—it infuriated her, and she threw herself in a corner of the couch. "Ten after six, already," she said, and I sensed that she was calculating the time left for embraces—that annoyed me. I had proposed to her an extra hour for listening to music and there she was grumbling. I know I'm unfair; she sees so little of me, she can't bear being in the same room with me and not being in my arms. But I gave way to some sulkiness myself; I put on another record since she didn't want to talk to me, until she was on the verge of tears and begged me to stop. For my part I was nervous because in Sartre's letters he said that he didn't know yet the exact date of his leave. I regretted having stopped writing to him; I wasn't happy and my rather cold behavior toward Sorokine was a reflection of it. Finally I took her in my arms and five minutes later we were in bed. Embraces. But right afterward she wriggled about and half moaned, "We spoiled it, there's nothing we can do about it," etc., then she grew languid again under my caresses. We turned the light on, got dressed, and as she tried again to jostle me, I had a fit of temper that brought her near tears and for which I humbly asked for forgiveness. But she left me, her eyes brimming with tears, saying, "It's going to be so unpleasant," and there was nothing I could do to console her. Besides, she uses those tears as blackmail, thinking that if I can be convinced that she's suffering, I'll grant her more time. She's so interesting even though at the moment she's unbearable because of her caprices and demands. It has a strange effect on me, and the same goes for Védrine: when I see them very upset because of me, I feel that I'm under attack.

She left showing me a clenched fist. As Kos. wasn't coming, I played some more records: *Prince Igor;* Ballade and Nocturne by Chopin; *La Cathédrale engloutie* and *The Afternoon of a Faun* by Debussy, all while finishing a stack of papers and writing in this notebook.

Kos. arrived a little before nine o'clock; it took her an hour, she said, to make her face look human again; she was depressed and wanted some outside distraction. We went to Pagès for dinner, then to the Jockey for a drink. They gave us a table in the back near some men who were out looking for women and seemed disgusted with the near decency of the Jockey. They complained, "I'm happy to have seen that!" they said ironically and suggested going to the Sphinx.* The club had a female singer and a dancer, both cute but quite incompetent—it was crowded, the jazz was better, the place was swarming with people, and that was not unpleasant. We chatted very amicably. Kos. talked a little about Bost: she was afraid that he might show up unexpectedly; she said that that would be too dramatic, and I thought it strange, this kind of distant relationship where one has to prepare for having a fellow stay with you—I would be in a tizzy for a moment, but I'm sure it would be simple right away. I didn't mind hearing this, as always, since it showed a flaw in their relationship—she hadn't had a letter for five days; that too I liked to hear since I received one on Wednesday. All this goes only skin deep; it remains in the abstract, which is not even half passionate,[3] only an indication of possible jealous feelings. She spoke of Bost's notebooks and told me lots of interesting things. But she was annoyed at what she called Bost's "modesty," which I myself find so attractive; she said that it had to do with the timidity of his thought and the awkwardness of his expression, but it goes deeper than that; besides, on another occasion she told me in an irritated voice that it would be better for him to be with his own kind of people than with oafish peasants—that was the Russian aristocrat coming out in her and the taste for dashing officers. I don't like her when she acts this way, even though she was charming toward me all evening.

The alarm went off at midnight; we really felt like lingering a little longer in the cafés but were turned back everywhere. We went home, talked vaguely about the books she could read but won't, and went to bed.

Thursday, February 1

Once more I forced myself to sleep until half past eight, and once more it gave me a headache. I went to the Dôme and finished rereading the draft of my novel, which gave me the desire to continue working on it—Stépha

---

* A famous bordello.

stopped by, of course. I went to Camille Sée—two hours of classes. When I left, Sorokine was waiting for me with a wry expression, but I softened her up quickly—we went to lunch where she told me how she had hated me until midnight and had written a long letter cursing me, but mixed with remorse. We agreed that she was wrong to want to spend the time with me solely by looking into my eyes. I talked to her a little about her short story *Le Râtelier* [The Rake]; she was all loving, and we were on the best of terms. At Henri IV the intern gave a two-hour lecture on evolution—I was so bored that I simply corrected a stack of papers; I was now rid of this task for almost a month. I took a taxi to the post office and returned to the Latin Quarter. Sartre still didn't know when he'd be arriving. I wanted to see him so badly that tears came to my eyes while reading his short letter. But I could wait another three days or so, that wasn't so bad; I felt in a strange vacant state of mind and everything I did had a gratuitous air about it.

I met Védrine at the bar of the Sorbonne and worked next to her. I was dreaming about chapter 10 and had a number of felicitous new ideas and a plan for an entirely new beginning, which needed reworking the most. I worked indolently, having fun as always when I'm inventing. Afterward I worked on this notebook.

Everyone said I looked very beautiful in my new blue sweater. During the intern's lecture I became vaguely conscious of my looks, myself, and my (past) life and was satisfied with all of them.

At half past seven we left the Sorbonne to go to dinner at the Bortch. We ate and had another long conversation on the subject of authenticity because of a letter Védrine had received from Sartre. Suddenly I was struck by Védrine's character of "a pious Jewish woman," and the fact that she had never been a child but always a little adult—from childhood she had always been carried along by the social current, living *with* the social and not *against* it as children traditionally do—partly because of her education but mostly because of her somewhat formidable intelligence, which from the start allowed her to have a technique of thinking that allowed her to manage in this constructed world. And so it continued: with Sartre and myself she immediately had access to an adult's love life. She only cared to create for herself an increasingly rich existence in the world of "das man,"* and after all, it's easy to understand; she can't very well live simultaneously both on this plane and the existentiel one; she is more authentic at the moment

---

* Heidegger's neutral "one" that lives inauthentically since it lives according to the opinions of the other.

in living in that sense than in seeking authenticity: I told her so, and she looked greatly vexed, which made me laugh, thinking that the very riches of her life cut her off from a certain authenticity. She wants to have it both ways—she also admitted that she wanted to be authentic so that she could be our equal within the trio. I told her not to imitate Poupette and de Roulet, and in a sense not to trust us; that one was always a charlatan when *speaking* about morality to others, that one could only be serious for oneself. She understood and it satisfied her a little—even though she was bothered by this vicious circle that makes her very desire of authenticity inauthentic.

We went to the former Gypsy on rue Cujas. We were seated in the back, which was not unpleasant: blue and pink grottoes amidst greenery—rather good jazz—not such good singers. A fighter pilot sang songs of inimitable obscenity. I was gentle with Védrine. I gave her red carnations; she was happy. But my heart felt heavy as lead. I was thinking of Sartre and Bost, whom I would like to see. I felt the war all around me, and my nerves were so on edge that I was close to tears.

We went to the Odéon metro station where I left her at half past eleven. Kos. had left in my box one of Bost's notebooks, which I looked at before going to sleep. Nightmare.

Friday, February 2nd

All in all, I had not had an inner life for a long time. I was working too much and felt stifled, and most important, there was nothing around me worth desire or anguish—a calm and desiccated world—it seemed strange to me this morning at the Versailles to find within me an expectation, an emotion and peacetime values. A strange day. Sartre would perhaps arrive today or tomorrow, but Sunday for certain. I just returned from the post office where I had nothing; I won't know anything before four o'clock. I did have a letter from Bost, who wrote of his home leave as a real thing. He would first go to see P. Bost,* then see me, and I think he'll give me twenty-four hours at a stretch—but I'm not sure; I'm afraid that it won't work out, I'm afraid that this leave will be difficult; I don't know—but just *believing* in it makes me feel anguished. I don't know what to do with myself; I don't really feel like working. I felt a vague need to cry, uncertainty, and my throat was dry.

I got up after eight o'clock with a strange impression of contingency. I went to the Dôme and read Bost's notebook, the second one about the front

---

* Pierre Bost, his older brother.

lines; it conveyed a good idea of his life over there, his daily routine. The strange impression of a Kafkaesque war was everywhere, when, for example, he wrote, "They said that on that farm there were Germans, but no one has ever seen them"—some guys told about having seen them, even up close, and that they were daring like anything—and upon inquiry, it was pure hallucination; some guys got killed by them, but upon inquiry, they killed one another—their entire life turned around them, and they were not to be seen anymore than the high judges of *The Trial* and the masters of *The Castle*. It seemed that if everyone suddenly stopped believing in them, there would be peace as before, and that war was a destiny one created for oneself from a combination of inner fatality and distorted freedom.

I passed by the post office—nothing from Sartre, a short letter from Bost. I came here to write him and finish this notebook.

Lunch with Védrine at the St. Michel, but my mind was not on the conversation; I was turned inward and terribly on edge, more so than I had been in a long time. At the lycée I returned the compositions; the students were taken to a room with formalin in order to test their gas masks, and during that time I wrote this. There was really no joy in me, only anguish that was choking me, no living image—empty tension, extremely unpleasant and on a background of depression so that as a result I was on the verge of tears. Outside it was damp and gray. Desire for solitude, malaise.

Sorokine was at the door when I left—I went to the post office, where I had no letter. Then in my nervous state I went to the Gare de l'Est on the off chance and sat down in the dark café. I wrote there for two hours—not expecting anything; I firmly believed that Sartre would not come—I had the vague impression that he existed only in my dreams, or if not that, at least this story of the home leave only existed in my dreams, that I was a mythomaniac who invented waiting and despair. I took a taxi to the Hotel Mistral on the off chance there was a message. I recovered my serenity and relaxed a little.

I was happy to see that Kos. did not question my account of last night or my project of going on a trip.* We went to the Dôme, where we had dinner and spent the evening—she had a toothache but was nice. She told me that Bost was planning to see her for five days, after Taverny,† and that satisfied me; she also said that he intended to spend some nights, but she couldn't do that. She was definitely morose concerning Bost, and I knew it would pass but, nevertheless, it was also a satisfaction for me.

---

* The purpose of this fictitious tale was to explain her absence during Sartre's leave.
† The place of residence of Bost's parents.

I went to sleep in this nervous state—a bedbug walking across my face woke me at half past three in the morning.

Saturday, February 3

Taught my classes at Lycée Camille Sée while waiting in a state of nervousness. I've been reading these last few days; during breakfast I finished *L'Envoyé de l'archange* [The Archangel's Messenger] by the Tharauds on Codreanu,* head of the Rumanian fascists—it was somewhat funny, as was the embarrassed attitude of the authors. Sorokine was waiting for me at the gate of the lycée; her presence weighed heavily on me, but I mentioned nothing to her about it—to the post office—had a letter from Sartre, who'd be arriving in ten days. Disappointment nevertheless, but I hadn't put my hopes up too high—I went to the Dôme; what annoyed me most was the fact that I spent all of this time without writing to him. Had a letter from Bost, who'd be arriving either Wednesday or Thursday and who seemed clearly determined to see me and quite happy at the idea—a definite impression that I count for him and that satisfied me. But I was getting lost in schemes to make these two home leaves work out with reference to each other. A short letter for Bost, a huge one for Sartre. Lunch. I didn't work until one o'clock. At two I saw Kos. and told her that I wasn't leaving. Telephoned Védrine and made a date for Monday. Then back to work at the Dôme. As I was sending off some money and books to Sartre, I found his letter at General Delivery: he would be coming after all. I shuddered at the idea that he could have arrived tomorrow without my knowing it; the post office would be closed the following day. I went to notify the Hotel Mistral that a telegram might be forwarded to me there. Then I went home, where Sorokine was waiting. Afternoon of embraces: I told her Kos.'s story—she was happy and delighted and charming, but again when leaving she showed me a clenched fist—it irritated me a little.

While waiting an hour for Kos. I read Rauschning's† *Hitler m'a dit* [What Hitler Told Me]. I started feeling happy even though I was still annoyed about the uncertainty. We went to the Milk Bar for a light meal, then to the Bal Nègre—she had the preposterous idea to drag me there—I did have fun though. We saw Wanda, charming in a new skirt with a beautiful white

---

* Founder of the "Garde de fer" [Iron Guard] in 1931.

† Hermann Rauschning also authored *La Révolution du nihilisme* [The Revolution of Nihilism]. He was a former member of the Nazi party, having broken off with it before 1939. The work mentioned here appeared a few days before the outbreak of the war and caused a stir.

blouse and hair in her face, who was dancing with a black man in uniform. We sat at her table—it was crowded but not overly, it wasn't tiring. I had fun watching again young black women dancing beguines[4] with shameless obscenity. The Kos. sisters danced marvelously well, together and separately, but the true Kos. felt sick, which discouraged her and made her totally miserable. Around eleven o'clock Mouloudji showed up, in a very angry and belligerent state; with him were Youki and a handsome Abyssinian, Youki's lover whom we had often seen at the Dôme; we had even shared the same table with him, Gérassi, and Florès; he invited Kos. to dance, he was graceful.

We got home around midnight and once in my room, Kos. broke down in tears; such was her distaste for this kind of evening: her future was screwed up, etc., she lamented. I comforted her a little and went to sleep.

Sunday, February 4. Sartre's Arrival.

In the morning I went to work at the Dôme and toward noon brought Sartre's suitcases to Hotel Mistral. The telegram was there. Shock, that was something concrete and real, and finally I had a true belief that brought tears of joy to my eyes. I didn't know quite what to do with myself; I felt like walking through Paris thinking about tonight, but the weather was bad—I went to the Coupole for lunch while reading *Hitler m'a dit* by Rauschning. Then I packed my own suitcase and met Kos. at two o'clock, telling her that I was definitely leaving. I also phoned Védrine to cancel, and she sounded very sad at the news. Kos. was as nice as she could be; we chatted amicably at the Rotonde, even making plans for going on a trip together. She had bought herself a beautiful blouse at the flea market—she was still depressed.

I left her at half past four and took a taxi to the Gare de l'Est; I went to an old brasserie with black wood paneling and lots of old mirrors where Sartre and I often went during the Laon period;* I sat in the room downstairs, all dark and poetic. I tried writing in this notebook but was too nervous; I barely managed to read *48* by Cassou. Waiting—waiting but also believing this time. I thought back to so many waits I have known, of how at first, one would like to hurry up time to have the moment arrive faster, and then little by little slow it down because when the moment seems to be gone, one has lost one's chances. I tried to catch Sartre's appearance at the top of the stairs, but he arrived before I had time to get there. He was easily the dirtiest soldier in France with his frayed greatcoat, his huge shoes, size 44,† and his

---

* Sartre was professor in Laon from 1936 to 1937.
† His normal shoe size was 38–39 [8–8½]!

filthy outfit. He put down his numerous bags and sat down beside me; we found each other again just as easily as in Brumath, perhaps even more so as I felt less separated from him these last three months than during the first three, exactly because of Brumath, where our life together had been taken up again. We left quickly for Hotel Mistral, where he changed into civilian clothes, and we walked down to Ducotet.* We had dinner there—then went back to have a drink at Rey's; we went to bed at midnight and talked until past one o'clock. Sartre told me about his trip, showed me his notebooks, and started expounding his theories for me. It was all so precious to me but all so familiar, I didn't seem to have been separated from him; there was absolutely nothing between us that needed to be rebuilt.

Monday, February 5

We spent the morning at Rey's. I began reading Sartre's notebooks and he my novel. He left me to visit his parents and I had lunch at Mont St. Michel while I continued reading his notebooks. Lycée. At four o'clock when I was leaving the building I saw Védrine dressed in a sad little raincoat, with a headscarf, looking pathetic in the rain—she was sorry I left her—supposedly for Bost, and with eyes that broke my heart she watched me getting into a taxi. I went to the Cadran Bleu, at the Gobelins, and waited for Sartre. We read again sitting side by side. He found some good things in my novel but also criticized the first chapter. We went for dinner at the Louis XIV,† completely deserted, then in the dark we went for a walk on the boulevards. We went back to Rey's and afterward to our place.

Tuesday, February 6

Impression of plenitude, comfort of head and heart. That's what predominated; I even felt it at night and seemed to wake up much better rested than before. Neither excitement nor amazement, but an overflow of riches; everything could go on, thoughts, tenderness, walks, and we would never find anything but fullness—and that seemed so natural.

That day we spent the morning again at Rey's, still reading notebooks and novel, and this time Sartre told me that he found it very good, only the beginning needed to be changed. It gave me enormous pleasure. I left him

---

* On rue Fossés-Saint-Bernard.
† At the place des Victoires.

at the last minute; I just had a quarter of an hour to eat at the blue brasserie and then to go to the lycée. At three o'clock I met Védrine at the Biarritz; she was not as sad as the previous night, though still nervous, and I promised to have lunch with her the next day. I took a taxi to the Acropole, where Sartre joined me soon afterward—we talked—we walked down avenue d'Orleans and the boulevard Arago while discussing authenticity; it was quite romantic and intense how we felt united in Paris beyond Paris, separation, and departure. It was dark and the weather was mild; we walked along the quay and in the end took a taxi to the Brasserie Lipp. Dinner at Lipp, as in the past. Sartre continued reading my novel and paid me lots of compliments. A short stop at Rey's, to bed, and again conversation.

Wednesday, February 7

Morning at Rey's, reading the notebooks and the novel—we stopped at the post office; I had two long letters from Bost, both loving; he would be arriving soon and promised to see me three days in a row. I stopped at my mother's place, rue de Rennes, for a letter and continued walking down to the quay. The weather was good, mild springtime temperatures, sunshine, and while crossing place St. Germain-des-Prés I felt happy as I hadn't been in months. Sartre was here, Bost almost, my year's work had been really good, Paris was beautiful—an intense and full moment and free, to be joyfully prolonged.

We took a taxi to Passy: he took another taxi and we changed taxis on the way. I was going to meet Védrine, and as I saw her in the street, I got out of the taxi and took her to the Maisonnette de Passy; it was depressing and the waiter looked disgusted to see the customers stoop so low as to eat there. Védrine was less unhappy but somewhat reserved and tense—and it was boring as it so often is.

I went by taxi to Marignan, where I wrote a long letter to Bost—then I met up again with Sartre and his mother in front of the cinema Biarritz. We watched *Mr. Smith Goes to Washington,* with James Stewart, very funny, so charming—the station at Marignan was damned annoying. Then we left, Sartre and I for the Champs-Élysées, rue de Rivoli, the Opéra, and the boulevards. We started talking about simultaneity, time, the consciousness of the other and got all worked up. We had dinner at Kuntz, where I ate a delicious foie gras while the discussion continued. I realized that I had a certain philosophical bad faith that made me readily confuse being and value. It's nothing new; in my youth I knowingly used Nietzsche for this purpose, whom I didn't understand very well. That's why I contended that the other's consciousness *did not exist* for me under the pretext that I did not valorize it—and in a sense I deeply felt the contrary. We returned along the Boulevard Sebastopol, walking almost the entire way to our place all the while keeping up our debate.

Thursday, February 8

We had a great moment at Rey's when Sartre nearly finished my novel and I finished reading his,* which I found delightful. Then lycée. Sorokine was waiting for me when I left; she gave me a letter in which she explained that I should not fix my hair when she is about to leave nor look happy to put her out, that it spoils everything; I promised whatever she asked for and took a taxi to stay longer with her; she was very happy about it. Lycée. I met Sartre at the Closerie des Lilas—we stayed a while, then took a taxi to the *NRF;* he dropped me off at a little café on rue de l'Université where I wrote to Bost while Sartre was meeting with Brice Parain—both of them came to join me—boring conversation about Drieu La Rochelle, Parain defining everything in terms of "generations" and apologizing for everything in his generation.† Sartre and I chatted a while in a café on rue du Bac, then we went to see Toulouse. She received us in her spacious studio, which looked as though a move was imminent; a screen behind which all sorts of old things were piled up divided it in half—she was wearing short sleeves, a pleated skirt, all in black with a velvet ribbon in her hair; she looked pretty. The table was set: wine, port wine, pâté, and delicious fruit salad—but the conversation dragged a little since Sartre was uptight, not wanting to bore her with his talk about the war and thinking that Toulouse acted cold. It was nevertheless pleasant. We left at eleven o'clock, went home and to bed at once.

Friday, February 9

We spent the morning at Rey's reading our novels—we again debated about the consciousness of the "other," then Sartre left to spend time with his family; I went to the post office, where I had a very short note from Bost, whose leave had again been delayed and who was totally disgusted—I was too—I quickly ate at the Capoulade. Then three hours of teaching. Afterward I met

---

* *The Age of Reason.*

† This conversation prompted Sartre's letter to Brice Parain (February 20, 1940) and the latter's answer (March 2) (see the Correspondence).

Sartre at Café Rey, where we stayed until seven o'clock. He left to be with Wanda, which didn't bother me because I didn't have the impression that those three days were taken away from me; they'd remain part of a home leave that I was living with him in its totality. As for me, I met up with Védrine, whom I took to dinner at the Alsatian restaurant on blvd. St. Michel. It was sweet and went without any incident—we drank some linden tea at the Biarritz and I got a little annoyed because, in social terms, she completely misunderstood Sartre's theory of authenticity—she thought that one had "to imagine oneself in a situation"—irritating to admire so passionately theories she doesn't understand.

Saturday, February 10

About seven o'clock in the morning I woke up happy in my room at Hotel Mistral. I was alone but would see Sartre in the afternoon; our schedule would follow along the same pattern and I didn't feel I had left him—this way I'd have time to think of him again, of myself, and enjoy these days. From half past seven on I was at Rey's; it was a poetic godsend for me— almost the impression of an adventure in our café from last year, alone, and yet hidden in complicity with Sartre. I read his notebooks while having breakfast; then lycée, which didn't bore me; post office, no letter from Bost—back again at Rey's where I finished reading the notebooks—lunch with my parents. I returned to the Mistral to pack my suitcase and, barely feeling anxious, went to the hotel. I knocked at the door of Kos., who answered in a welcoming voice. She came down to my room and we chatted for an hour. She had been in a depressed mood all week and didn't show her face at the Atelier, etc.—she told me about the party Sunday evening in Florès's studio where Florès went straight for her and kissed her on the mouth. She was still with me when Sorokine knocked and then ran off in disarray; I told her to come back in five minutes, and then Kos. also ran off. Sorokine soon returned; she had been at the Mistral and was convinced I wanted to play a trick on her; I explained that that was stupid, and she fell passionately into my arms. Embraces—she was charming, especially after she had carefully covered herself with the sheets and read me all her papers on Proust, on art and life. We discussed and I explained some things to her; I was all loving affection with her. I would have been completely taken by this girl if only I had given of myself a little—but I had absolutely no desire to give of myself; I even felt somewhat bad about it. She was finishing combing her hair when Sartre came; again she fled.

I went to the Vikings with Sartre—he told me about his evening, his day. I had no passionate feelings at all, only the impression that was again so very difficult for me, that the Kos. sisters existed. They existed little for me, I had no love for them, but through Sartre's and Bost's affection they took on value and life again, and that has always been hard on me. And then, it has always been unpleasant to hear a third party speak about the Kos. sisters because they could never be trusted even when they were on good terms with you: a slight complicity between Kos. and Wanda, etc. Perhaps what was so hard to bear was the image they had of me: this austere relationship with Sartre, this blind generosity, and this somewhat detestable power that I represented in their lives. Sartre was busy with his consciousness, and that too, his situation, was hard on me, for him and therefore also for me—there was something tense in his way of speaking and in himself.

At the Dôme I wrote a letter to Bost; I met Kos., and we went to Vadja and the College Inn. But I was a little tense in her company even though she was very nice—I was also tired and the evening turned out rather dull. The thought that we would start again seeing each other regularly like this and that this would be my life again was difficult for me to bear. I went to bed feeling rather out of sorts.

Sunday, February 11

The day was hard to get through—great fatigue for lack of sleep. I tried in vain to sleep a little later; I was awake at half past eight; I was bored in bed and when the alarm rang at nine o'clock I got up. Right away I felt sick at heart; I already felt this way during my sleep. It had nothing to do with passionate feelings; it wasn't Sartre being with Wanda that weighed so heavily on me; it would have been the same if he had been with his family—full suffering at not seeing him. And it wasn't only today's emptiness; I was already experiencing his departure, all those days when I could no longer tell myself: in two days. I had difficulty understanding how I had been able to put up so well with his absence; I felt abandoned in an indifferent and hostile world; perhaps it's because I was barely aware of other people's consciousness that his consciousness was such an absolute for me and that this morning the world seemed absolutely empty to me, as if I had been thrown into a mineral solitude. When I thought of the substitutes, Kos. and Védrine, I felt nauseated; I would've preferred (at that moment) to think of myself as absolutely isolated; having to see them today weighed on me.

It seemed a little strange to rediscover a full love, the kind I inspire in

Védrine and Sorokine; it seemed a silly illusion; I don't sympathize with the need they have of me. The heartrending feeling I'm familiar with concerns above all passion for Bost and even Sartre. That's really a shortcoming, a wrong. It's without rebellion, without despair, but I cannot tell myself, "four months like this"; I was on the verge of tears. And I knew that the four months wouldn't be like this, but then I would have to forgo any sweetness and affection, become hard again and lose Sartre in thought and image, after having lost him in the flesh. I went to the Dôme, worked for three hours with a slight headache, keeping busy with my work like a good student with a page of writing but without any tomorrow. Then I ate a little and worked on this notebook. My sorrow has not let up since this morning—it's a comfort to think that it is still part of my life with Sartre; I shall tell him about it on Tuesday. However, I fear what will come afterward, not fear of myself, of suffering, etc., but rather refusal per se, refusal of this life without him, even if I have to accommodate myself to it in a less painful way than today.

It was a day that stood out, a day when time could be marked; the dull gloom of the morning turning into something more dreadful, I was closer to tears but it felt almost more bearable because of the depth of my fatigue. I stopped off at the Deux Magots to drop off Sartre's notebooks. I was tempted to stay; I understood (it was my turn) the intolerable need that Sorokine or Védrine might have to see the beloved person, be it only for five minutes—but to see the beloved. I understood the absolutely dire distress about someone's absence. I went to the Dôme, wrote in this notebook I had abandoned for a week and worked. Around three o'clock Cl. Chonez arrived with a young fellow. They sat down at my table; it was obvious that she wanted to introduce me to this guy of whom she was proud. She loved him, she wanted to show him off; he discreetly refused to let her—I thought of Bost and was very pleased, because there was nothing scandalous about this couple, only the fact that she was so stupid. He was a soldier, stationed in Orléans, only twenty-one years old, but looking older because of his light blond beard— his name was George L.—I liked him—it was the first time in a long while that I was physically attracted to a fellow—he was rather handsome with a charming smile, and a face that made you want to be affectionate with him, like Bost's face. He wasn't shy, but reserved and discreet; impossible to judge whether he was intelligent, but he behaved tactfully even though she made his situation difficult. And it seemed funny to me to experience what Poupette would call "a sentimental fantasy," to think that an affair with him could (perhaps) seduce me, that in general there were fellows in the world with whom a new affair would be possible for me. Right away the fantasy itself was prevented from going any further because of the war; even if I saw him again, in a few months he would leave Orléans, from where he visited only on Sundays, etc. I had the impression that he liked me very much because when I mentioned casually "I hope we'll see each other again," he said openly and directly, "I hope so too," and he took a piece of paper with my name on it when I gave it to Cl. Chonez. They surprised me by speaking admiringly of Adamov, as well as the surrealists and Berger; I found it amusing. However, they scared me with their news about five hundred company leaders being rushed to the front, of natives[5] landing, and the rumor about a possible attack. It distressed me. Suddenly I realized I had mentioned Sartre's being here on leave, that Védrine was going to come and Cl. Chonez would commit a blunder; embarrassed, I cautioned her. And she did put her foot in it, but she managed to get out of it. Védrine spent an hour with me; I was nice, somewhat as a reaction against the Kos. sisters, because I considered it a little mean of Sartre and myself to have thrown her to the wolves.

I met up with Kos.; I was feeling low with a terrible headache and my throat so tight that I was unable to speak, etc. She told me that Bost would arrive Thursday and was counting on seeing her Sunday; I suddenly felt dizzy, which reminded me of last year, when I was near fainting out of sheer confusion. It was idiotic; he wrote me that he'd see me first for three days; but I imagined a discontinuity between the Bost who wrote to me and the Bost who wrote to her. And anyway, I remained dispirited until we got to the movies. I was thinking that I would be unhappy as a dog during this home leave. I had a craving to see a movie, as an excuse and perhaps even a distraction. We watched *Les Trois Loufquetaires*[6] [The Three Daffies] at the Cluny theater, and it worked; after the movie, at the Hoggar, I was able to be cheerful and at ease—in fact, my spirits were raised so much that while I was writing this tonight in bed I was in a good mood again and even felt a real affectionate gladness for Sartre, whom I'd see again on Tuesday; for Bost, whom I'd see in a week, and for the world, which was really not so barren.

Monday, February 12

I slept well and calmly—dreamt of Zuorro, who wore lipstick and, incidentally, was very nice looking, and whom [I] saw again with much emotion. It was because of Daniel in Sartre's novel and the young man I met yesterday and whose lips I found charming. I got up without gaiety or sadness, with a headache but no more dark anguish. Only a slightly painful memory remained that made me sensitive to the sadness that Védrine and Sorokine might experience because of me. Dupont. Lycée, while reading *Tandis que j'agonise* [As I Lay Dying][7]—then post office. Bost would arrive Friday and be with me until Monday, and in the meantime would see a little of Kos.; but I felt nothing concerning passion in me. It was again going to be complicated to arrange all that; what a headache my life has become! I went to work and worked well, my head rested. Slowly but surely I was emerging from my depressed state and turning again toward happiness; however, by accepting absence, a certain form of affection gets lost.

Lunch, lycée, I returned to the Dôme feeling serene and a growing joy based on the certainty of seeing Sartre again tomorrow.

Two hours of good work. Then Kos. came by, mournful but very amiable, and we chatted from six to eight o'clock. Then I went home to meet with Védrine.

A tiresome evening with Védrine—she arrived, too radiant as usual, and passionately threw herself on me—right away she sighed and dug her nails into my shoulder. We had to get into bed and embrace each other—embraces interrupted by sentimental banter and passionate questions: Do you love me? Are you happy? repeated insistently. I was tense and she felt it—she also spoke of Easter vacation, but there I was definitely on the defensive. She could see that I didn't want to spend it with her. We got up, went to dinner at Lipp, where we were again seated next to A. Parodi.* We discussed Kant, about whom she uttered inanities, and at eleven o'clock I accompanied her to the Odéon. When I told her that Poupette was coming this week, she sighed, "You are besieged," and left, feeling very sad. I returned by metro where I noticed Lexia looking pretty and sad in her blue headscarf.

Tuesday, February 13

I wanted to sleep well but hardly slept a wink, that's how nervous I was at the idea of seeing Sartre again. I thought about Védrine and Kos. etc., I tossed and turned and awoke terribly fatigued and anxious. Lycée Henri IV. I took a taxi to the Dôme, where Sartre had not yet arrived, but he showed up a moment later and we talked first there, then at the Closerie des Lilas—he explained how he had felt morally ill at ease with Wanda, especially since she was so nice to him, and he wondered whether it wouldn't be better to be

---

* Inspector general.

faithful to one person for one's entire life. It was somewhat unpleasant for me to think of the superiorities that Wanda takes over me and the strange idea that Kos. must have of me. But that's minor. Both of us felt a little dispirited at leading such complicated and burdensome lives.

At 12:25 I met Sorokine—she was about to sulk because I was ten minutes late but I yelled at her so loud that she quickly shut up, and in fact, when I talked to her about the conversation I had with Sartre, we spent a charming half hour with her quite affectionate and happy. Lycée. The three hours were not as long as I had feared they would be. I met Sartre at four o'clock in the little blue brasserie near the lycée. The restaurant was dark and deserted, and we chatted affectionately and pleasantly about Sorokine, Védrine, Wanda, etc., for quite a while. We went to dinner at Lipp, where once more we were seated next to A. Parodi—we spent the evening at the Vikings, where they made us leave at midnight, and we talked for another great while before going to sleep.

Wednesday, February 14

We went back to our pleasant mornings at Rey's. I discussed Sartre's notebooks with him; he read the last chapter of my novel, which I had started over again these last few days, and we discussed it. He paid me compliments that were very encouraging to me. We discussed whether he could or could not break up with Védrine, and he had almost decided to do so, saying that the war had hardened him and that he had to wait for the war to end before seeing each other again. He left and I went for lunch at the Dôme. I hadn't quite finished when Sorokine arrived and from a distance I gestured my excuses, which made her laugh; I distracted her by ordering her a tart. We started with my explanations of Descartes and then went to my place, where we worked for an hour, after which she stopped dead in her tracks wanting to go on to embraces—which we did. Then we talked about friendship, fidelity, etc. She was quite cheerful; she would make a charming companion if I had the time to see more of her and in a more relaxed way. She brought me a drawing of Sartre that we pinned to the wall.

Sartre arrived and we went to the Vikings, and from four to seven o'clock we talked once more intensively about Védrine. Then I saw Kos. from seven to nine o'clock, as always charming but pathetic.

At nine o'clock I met up with Sartre; he was very tired. We went to the Coupole and for one hour we had a difficult time because he felt empty and distraught and I was sad thinking that it was our last evening. But I had the good idea to get him away from there and take him to the O.K.,* which was warm, filled with people but not crowded, and which he liked. There was a door at our back that bothered us, but we changed tables. The radio was playing soft music, and we felt very much at ease. We talked again, about this leave, about our lives, about the two of us, and it was so strong and full that nothing could ever top those moments—we regretted having to leave at midnight. We went home, talking for a long while in our hotel room at the Mistral without going to bed for fear of being overtaken by sleep. Then we did go to bed and fell asleep, without feeling sad.

Thursday, February 15. Sartre's Departure.†

We got up at seven o'clock, had breakfast at Rey's without feeling sad—it seemed normal to see this leave coming to an end and life continuing with this precious period taking its place as part of our past. We went to pick up Sartre's military uniform that he had left at the Coupole. He changed at my place, and we took a taxi. He looked quite handsome and clean now, for his mother had everything freshly cleaned. We arrived in front of the station at around a quarter past nine; a large notice was posted there: "Return of military personnel. All trains depart at 9:15." A crowd of soldiers with their women streamed down the passage leading to the lower levels of the station. That moment, realizing how calm I was leaving Sartre and looking at it as a collective event, brought tears to my eyes. The same was true for the scene on the platform: seeing men and women awkwardly shaking hands brought a lump to my throat. There were two trains on either side of the platform, both crowded. The one on the left pulled out first, and a stream of women— in a crowd of two hundred women there were barely ten men, elderly fathers for the most part—among them mothers, but mostly wives and girlfriends were leaving, eyes red-rimmed, with a vacant look, or some even sobbing—it was also moving and primitive, this elementary separation of the sexes with the men being carried off and the women returning toward the city. Only a few were crying before the train left; there were a few, nevertheless, clinging to their men. You could sense a hot night behind them, and the lack of sleep and the nervous exhaustion of the morning. Some soldiers looked at them, gently teasing, "Well, look at this flood of tears!"—but there was solidarity among the men who all wanted to be each with his own woman; that was

---

* A bar at the Vavin crossroads.

† This passage was quoted in *La Force de l'âge*, p. 443 [*The Prime of Life*] in the *NRF* edition, and in the Folio edition, p. 493.

rather pleasant. An example may prove the point: when the train was about to pull out, the door was blocked by some soldiers, I could only see Sartre's cap in the dark of the compartment, his glasses and his hand waving once in a while; the guy in the doorway then stepped aside and yielded his place to someone else who kissed his woman and called out, "Who's next?" The women formed a line and each climbed up on the step to kiss her man—I also climbed up and shook hands with Sartre who disappeared inside again. The air was filled with a collective and enormous tension: This train, about to depart—it was really like a physical tearing away, something a train's departure had never meant to me before—it was going to happen, it was unbearable, it seemed that everything was going to crack—and it did happen, the train pulled out. I was the first to leave for I could no longer see Sartre, and I left running fast, my tears hesitated, there were a few, but I held them back, and when I got outside and stopped a taxi, it was over, really it was like after a surgical operation.

A damp and nauseating cold over Paris—the taxi took me to the post office. Nothing from Bost—lycée—I managed to teach my class well, I wasn't too tired—Sorokine was waiting for me when I left, she looked charming in her plaid hood and wearing a little lipstick. We went to eat; I was on the same level as she, that's what was so pleasant. I told her about Sartre's departure and some things about Védrine and also about Sartre; she was delighted and when I told her that Sartre was underhanded, she shook with laughter. She cheered me up. I was somewhat entertained expecting a bullfight with Védrine; I found it less insipid than our usual get-togethers. Two hours of student presentations on history, which was really a godsend, for after all, I was not inspired. Afterward Sorokine accompanied me to the Sorbonne, where I met Védrine, a little distrustful but already smiling. I started explaining myself right there, then continued at the Hoggar. It didn't pay off, for right away she contradicted me and accused herself; I broke her down without resistance. She moved me when I looked at her serious face, with its reserved smile or on the verge of tears in a restrained way—and she was beautiful today. I felt a little uneasy when I thought of what was awaiting her, but I firmly repeated to her that she would never have a greater part of my life, that I hadn't promised more, that I treasured my solitude and my freedom. She reproached me for not having any "life in common" with her, which is really a superficial view; she is haunted by my relationship with Sartre and wants to copy it exactly.

We parted at seven o'clock and this time I met with Kos.; we went to the O.K.; Kos. was very friendly and so was I—she was making plans to embellish my looks and scolded me affectionately as she hadn't done in a long time, telling me that she found my travels on foot "adventurous," etc. I was wondering whether this wasn't against Wanda, perhaps forming a couple with me against the Wanda-Sartre couple. She left me at ten o'clock and I read a few pages in *Le Diable amoureux** [The Devil in Love] before I fell asleep dead tired. Excellent night.

Friday, February 16. Bost's Arrival.

I woke up well rested after ten hours of sleep. No sadness. I didn't feel like working but had a thousand things to do. Among others, write a long letter to Sartre, cash the check from the baccalaureate, and go to the hairdresser. I received no word from Bost, which annoyed me a little. I was however supported by the idea of seeing him soon. His last letters were so affectionate that I was hardly worried. Lunch with a reticent but pleasant Védrine. Lycée.

It was already a quarter to four when a woman employee dressed in black and with a mysterious and almost somber look came to tell me that a certain M. Bost was waiting downstairs in the visitors' lounge—my hands started to shake, my face was flushed and my throat dry. Yet, I had to continue the class and I carried on with sociology, but with some emotional breaks. I quickly went downstairs. In a large parlor filled with mirrors and green furniture I saw Bost, alone and quite like himself, and I was back with him in the blink of an eye—and he with me—right away we felt at ease and happy—we left by rue Clovis and as by a miracle the weather was good, we went for a long walk on the quays, to the Bastille, place de la République, the St. Martin canal, Jaurès, and the Gare de l'Est. Looking at Paris so pleasant under the blue sky and in the snow, a host of memories of walks along the quays with him last year came back to me. All that was most precious in our relationship last year was given back to me. But above all we talked; Bost talked endlessly; he told of his outposts, the return trip, his officers, and his comrades. He said little about himself, and I, I hardly said a thing, but we felt at leisure with the days ahead of us where we could share these six months of war. We stopped at the Gare de l'Est, in the dark brasserie where I had waited for Sartre, and Bost continued talking, looking up every once in a while amazed and surprised to have found me again, which I felt so strongly. I phoned Kos. that Poupette had just arrived in town; she was quite curt on the other end of the line—for a minute it was unpleasant. We

---

* By De Cazotte (1772).

stayed until eight o'clock and then went to Kuntz, where the dinner was excellent, all the while talking and happy. I was profoundly happy; this love seems to me as strong and full as possible and I was overjoyed to feel it as profoundly important in Bost's life. I consider Kos. as a thing *in* Bost's existence, next to him—and myself, with Sartre, as constituting the very world where Bost lives, just as Sartre and he constitute the world for me, so that this war is really lived by us together, and that together we are awaiting *our* future, and not just each his own.

We took a taxi to the hotel so I could get my luggage; he remained hidden in the night on rue Vavin—it was night in the taxi, night in Paris, night of peace and the future, while I was so overwhelmed that I kissed him again. We got off on place D. Rochereau at the Oriental, which was luxurious and warm. Everything was so familiar that I couldn't believe six months separated me from his kisses, his looks. I remembered everything so strongly. It gave me courage for the future—it would remain continuous and become exactly the same again, despite the times passing.

Saturday, February 17

We slept very badly; it was too hot and I was feverish. Waking up was pleasant; we lingered a long time just talking and being quiet. We went downstairs for breakfast at the Oriental and I told Bost everything I remembered about Sartre since September. The weather in Paris was catastrophic, everything buried under snow and mud; you had to negotiate snowdrifts to step from the sidewalk onto the street—the taxis bespattered you up to your eyebrows. I went to see Zébuth* to get Sartre's manuscript. I found her at the Petite Chocolatière, avenue d'Orléans—she seemed to be prospering. She gave me the packet sealed with two big red stamps, which I handed to Bost to read while I went to see Kos. She was in her room at the Hotel Albret, looking rather depressed—I stayed for half an hour, then did some shopping for Sartre and went back to Bost, who had started reading the novel with satisfaction. We went to the Ducotet, where it was very pleasant this early afternoon with men in leather aprons drinking their beer at the bar. It was already four o'clock when we left. I talked to Bost about Sorokine; he was delighted by the fact that she shakes her fist at me and hits me. We left, roaming the quays in this disastrous weather, looking for a taxi to take us along the boulevards. There we wandered about again looking for a pipe for

---

* A cousin of the Morels.

Sartre and some "Seltona Paper,"* which we were unable to find. Then we went to the cinema Vivienne to watch *La Baronne de minuit* [The Midnight Baroness] with Claudette Colbert and Don Ameche; it was entertaining. From there we went just next door, to the Cintra on rue du Faubourg Montmartre, where we had such a wonderful conversation that three hours went by without our noticing it. I wrote a short letter to Sartre, and Bost started reading the chapter on Sumatra†—he found it so gripping that he insisted on finishing it; we went to a café across the street where we read it together. This was a romantic and emotional moment such as I had rarely lived, a necessary moment. Jazz playing on the radio, this chapter that overwhelmed both of us, the idea of Sartre being far away, back in his solitude and yet able to move us as if he were some stranger we had invoked through a beautiful book, and all these impressions received through Bost, and his precious, miraculous, and fragile presence—all that brought me almost to the verge of tears and left a lump in my throat. Bost felt quite emotional when we left there, and in the taxi he deeply regretted the loss of his civilian life; he had a moment of gloom, but he had it *with* me.

We went to the Nox—he talked for two hours, softly, by fits and starts, not feverishly like last night. This time he spoke for and about himself, about the war, the future, his regrets, and his hopes—it made me feel united with him almost more than ever before, and more than once I came close to tears. It was the same Nox as before: same women, same décor, same light, and yet completely changed, because instead of being part of our present world, it was a memory, a pilgrimage, and also an artificial décor.

We were thrown out at midnight—the sidewalks of the boulevard St. Michel were covered with packed snow; as if we were in the countryside, in Paris. We went to the same hotel as in the past;‡ a most tender and passionate night—and I slept like an angel.

Sunday, February 18

A pleasant morning at the Dupont St. Michel—we read a little in Sartre's notebooks; Bost found them marvelously funny. We talked; I was moved seeing how he was interested in everything about my life, how it remained present for him even though he followed it from afar. He left to have lunch

---

* Paper for photographic prints; Sartre had several portraits made of himself as [a military] meteorologist.
† In *The Age of Reason*.
‡ In October 1938, at the Hotel Porc-Lion, in the Latin Quarter.

with Pierre Bost and I went to the Flore to write to Sartre while waiting for Védrine. She came at half past eleven—we ate lunch at the Petit St. Benoît and had coffee at the Deux Magots—our discussion touched on her shamelessness concerning a dirty dream that she told to her friends.

I went to the Dôme and continued my letter to Sartre. Kos. came by and we spent a miserable day together despite her goodwill. I just couldn't find the button that would trigger "the putting between parentheses"[8]—feeling of inner tension. We went upstairs at the Rotonde where it was steaming hot and I was feverish and exhausted—I feared that she might notice how bored I was with her.

I waited for Bost at the Source while reading one of his notebooks. He arrived at half past seven, quite cheerful after having lunched with Lafaurie,* and looking very happy and totally charming. He took me to the Maison Rouge, where we spent one of the most wonderful evenings I ever spent with him; it was very intimate and gay, also lighthearted and united—he made me talk about Védrine and Sorokine, and what I especially appreciated was the deep feeling of friendship he exuded and conveyed to me through his eyes and smiles. We talked again about our past and our whole affair. I felt that he *wanted* it as much as ever. That's what made me totally happy. Marseilles† had left me with the painful impression of being for him *an* affair, one that was very pleasant, but at times embarrassing and somewhat *accidental*. That's why I cried so much in Juan-les-Pins and the reason for the disappointment, which for the entire vacation had left me despondent. Since the war the situation had improved because of the letters, but it was only in the course of this evening that everything was restored in a way that seems definitive to me—it's of the essential and not the accidental; he wants it as much as I do; it's really a way of being together in this world. We finished the evening upstairs at the Dupont, where Bost spoke of the men he was living with, of peasants and Malfilâtre,[9] the peasant, according to Alain, of humanism, and what one can and must do for people—we were wholly caught up in our conversation; it was wonderful; that's what it means to be bound by a shared engagement in the same things.

We left at midnight and despite the cold and the mud we walked all the way to the hotel, on place Goudeau‡—the woman recognized us and went upstairs to prepare a room for us. We talked for a long while, and I cried my

---

* His brother-in-law.
† At the end of July 1939.
‡ The Hotel du Poirier on Montmartre.

heart out because it was intolerable to me, the idea that he would be leaving again and that this peacetime life wouldn't return until how long?

People kill each other at night—some drunkards came to "annoy" a woman—did they rape her? She hollered, called the manager of the hotel; it caused a terrible ruckus—so much so that even Bost woke up.

Monday, February 19

Waking up was so pleasant. We took a long, leisurely moment before going to the Dupont on place Blanche for breakfast; the weather was mild. I felt so united with Bost. For the first time we had talked a little about Kos. the night before, and we talked again about her and Wanda—he said that her letters didn't tell him anything and that they were completely superficial—which amazed me since she was very pretentious about them. Once more, a de-romanticizing of their relationship, which sometimes makes me feel almost like Wanda, only a little less fantastic. We went for a walk. Paris was sweet— we went toward the Bourse and drank some white wine at the Dufour across from *Paris-Soir;* it's a bistro all in green and dark, extremely pleasant. Bost was very cheerful and came up with a host of little charming inventions, as only he knows how to do. We lunched at the Louis XIV—I don't remember why I talked about "when I'm old" but he said, "You are going to be a charming old lady" with a rush of affection that overwhelmed me—he also said with obvious delight, "You are a brain, I'm thrilled at the thought!" Pierre Bost was there, too, having lunch with St. Exupéry; it amused me to see them, but I couldn't make them out too well. We had a drink at Benjamin's in Les Halles[10]—it was crowded with women selling butter and who were adding up their receipts, playing cards, and having a drink—it was nice. We took a taxi to the post office. I had three letters from Sartre—they were so affectionate, I was very moved by them—I read them at Lipp, sitting next to Bost; I felt totally fulfilled. Bost talked again about Kos. and her egoistic way of loving. He seemed to hold a bit of a grudge against her because of the letters—I told him that I really thought her to be superficial despite her subtleties and her depression. I thought it was because she was always cut off from the situation, or simply stated, that she never ever thought of anything but women's stories.

We chatted leisurely; we went for a walk through the streets around St. Germain-des-Prés—I wasn't too emotional about leaving Bost. Because he gave me something so solid these last four days, such a certitude—because regrets, like empty rancor, are especially painful when there hasn't been plenitude—because I'd see him again once more and I didn't think it would create a break—because he was seriously thinking of having me come to Charmont or somewhere in Oise. He left me in front of Pierre Bost's, and I went away, tired, but not at all confused.

I went home. I reread Sartre's letters and wept; I wept over Sartre and over Bost, but it was with tenderness and affection. I wrote to Sartre. Bost came back for a second, more gracious than ever, to ask for some money—he disappeared—I finished my letter, lay down for a moment to rest; I could think of nothing but sleep.

I met up with Védrine at the Deux Magots. I was nice to her but exhausted. I was really afraid that I was sick and went home to bed; she stayed with me; it was rather pleasant. I know well this physical and sentimental mournfulness that follows these extraordinary days; I let myself go, I was in a daze and a cocoon-like state.

She left—I remembered—no other sadness than seeing the memories already fading, all those precious smiles, expressions, and kisses becoming part of the past. I fell asleep.

Tuesday, February 20

At a quarter to seven I was already awake. That too, I recognized, the emptiness, the listlessness, the desire to remain wrapped up in the past and not wanting to budge, not wanting to create a new present that would push everything back into the distance. A weariness stemming from fatigue or sadness, I'm not sure which. I stayed in bed for a long while; one has the impression that one could find this plenitude again, that one has come away with so many riches, but it's forever evading us; it's only in the present, in their presence or in present action and present thought, that one can find people again.

I got up. The Luxembourg Gardens were rain soaked. Lycée—I was tired—I met Sorokine on my way out. I had behaved scandalously toward her—last night she wrote me a short letter that moved me, because she didn't even bawl me out; and now she had a beautiful expression on her face, quivering with despair. We went to a sad Viennese pastry shop. I told her I was sorry, I explained and blamed myself—she remained sad, she only said, "I looked desperately for you yesterday, I looked for you everywhere!" She came looking for me at eight o'clock in the morning, and then went to Camille Sée and twice again to the hotel, and finally she approached Védrine—and her pain tugged at my heartstrings. But I couldn't do much about it, which weighed on me. And how appropriate, in an almost necessary fashion, this horrible weather outside and this sad silence in the sad Viennese pastry shop. We went to my place, I kissed her, and her hardness gave way. We had lunch at the Milk Bar. Lycée—she was again waiting when I left there. I went home.

I spent a difficult moment. I was tired. I wanted to see Bost very badly, a simple desire, without anguish, not heartrending, but it created a void around me. I had a short note from him suggesting we meet. I went up to my room, lay down and dozed—memories, tenderness, and fatigue—at the moment I felt no jealousy of Kos., only envy that she was seeing Bost for such a long stretch of time, but I knew it was fair. I knew that they would indeed get back together again; it would be a little painful for me when Kos. told me about it, but really, it's all the same to me, it would take nothing away. I shook off this feeling, went to the post office, where I had a letter from Sartre—I was still on the verge of tears; it was because of my state of fatigue and helpless affection. I went to the Versailles, where I worked on this notebook for over an hour. It made me feel happy and full because it was like being with Bost still.

Wrote a letter to Sartre—took bus 91 to the Austerlitz train station to pick up Poupette. I waited for half an hour in a café while reading Bost's notebook. Poupette arrived at the station; she looked fresh under a horrible black hat and was angry that I had used her,* already stating her claims—all of a sudden I woke up and was back in reality; I took her to the Select, where we chatted until midnight. Nothing bored me, just as nothing amused me. I killed time using simple pretexts, but what counted was this vague feeling inside me in which I remained immersed.

Wednesday, February 21

The long night was filled with dreams of Bost, tender and painful dreams, for he told me sententiously, "He who doesn't know what he loves, doesn't know how he lives" and concluded, "We shouldn't have seen each other except on the roads"—yet there was a sweet air about it, for he told me that he loved me. I woke up in an awful, sentimental and vulnerable state that matched the mild and clement weather—blue sky and gentle breeze. I went to the Dôme and corrected papers. How empty I felt; I could think of nothing but seeing Bost again, that was all. And suddenly, there he was, all

---

* By falsely telling Olga that she already arrived last Friday, which in Olga's view would reduce the time that she, Poupette, was entitled to be with Castor.

smiles; he suggested we go together to see Pierre Bost. I was touched that he came to get me—we talked, feeling a little uneasy because we didn't have enough time to really talk; we could only say insignificant things, but seeing him did me so much good.

I met up with my family: parents, sister, and the Cordonnier cousins at the Relais de Sèvres on rue de Sèvres. I was tense and withdrawn and couldn't get a word out. Took a walk with Poupette and, despite Poupette, I felt springtime very intensely in the Luxembourg Gardens.

At three o'clock I met Kos. at the Dôme—I felt neither jealousy nor remorse; I definitely wanted this affair such as it was. Besides, through Kos.'s words I could recognize Bost's affection for her without feeling pain; I no longer saw their relationship as poetic or sacred; with all my heart I felt that my relationship with Bost was by far the better—complete and sincere. Kos. was quite angry because C. Gibert told Mouloudji all about her intimacy with Sartre, and that disgusted Mouloudji, who got mad at Wanda, who in her turn was furious—the two sisters also seemed to have been very much affected by a passage in Sartre's notebooks about his breakfasts. Kos. spoke to me as though she believed I felt no more solidarity with Sartre.

At five o'clock Sorokine was waiting at my place—she received me by hitting me with her fists because I was five minutes late—I took her with me to the post office to get Sartre's letter; it was a sad letter that pained me—I think he is going to have a hell of a problem because of Wanda, and that annoyed me. Sorokine meanwhile was sulking, not very convincingly, and that irritated me even more. We returned to my place; I started to explain the "ontological proof"—she wasn't listening but cried and hit me; I kissed her and again Descartes and tears. I was really fed up; I thought that she was putting me on and that the mixture of philosophy and feelings was absolutely intolerable. She was sobbing, but it was faked, and I didn't fall for it; on the other hand, I was touched when she fell into my arms, admitting that she had done it on purpose and why, trying to be sincere; I kissed her and caressed her to calm her. She did calm herself, but our goodbyes in front of the Dôme were somewhat chilly.

From the Dôme I wrote to Sartre; Poupette met me there. She felt like going to Bobino, and right from the start of the performance I found it was a godsend. The hall was packed—a pleasant show—"Satan's barman" had four soldiers come on the stage and had them taste some Pernod and rum; one of them scored a hit when he shouted, "There is no bromide in it, I hope?" There were two funny clowns, Alan and Porto; a good singer, Fred Maurice; and Edith Piaf, who seemed hunchbacked and hydrocephalic and made me cry. I was in an overly sentimental state and terribly sensitive to songs. A sharp desire to see Bost—feeling somewhat apprehensive about it, for I knew that it was never the same thing when seeing each other again afterward, sandwiched in between. We went to the Dôme, where I finished my letter to Sartre.

Thursday, February 22

Mild springtime weather but with a hint of ocean brine in the air. The day turned around Bost. In the morning I corrected some papers at the Dôme—then lycée. Lunch with Poupette—we walked to the Duroc, where it was warm, cozy, and dull. Lycée. Sorokine was waiting for me in the school-yard with a piece of chocolate and a beautiful colored handkerchief. At four o'clock I jumped into a taxi to hurry home. Bost arrived almost at the same time. We walked a stretch and then went by taxi to the Long Bar at the Palais Royal and sat in an out-of-the-way corner on a low couch; one could have mistaken it for a salon. I brought Sartre's and my notebooks, we talked, he read a little, and it was pleasant, but he was a bit sad; he was beginning to think of his leave drawing to an end and a little embarrassed as usual when he wants to neither talk nor talk about Kos. etc.; as for me, I suffered some-what from suppressed sentimentality, but it was most pleasant. We walked back in the evening, walking through the Carrousel. At the post office I had a letter from Sartre that I read at the Vikings. He explained how moved he was by my relationship with Bost and that tore me out of the slight contin-gent [state] I was in. We spent one very happy and solid hour at the Vikings. I would see Bost again on Saturday.

I met up with Poupette; it bored me to tears. We were walking through the streets in the mild spring weather and she began talking to me about communism, God, morality, assassination, etc.—it was terrible. She told me only this interesting thing about her painting: "I paint so that there are no more holes"—the holes meant the kitchen where laundry is drying; it's a kind of nausea she has of household chores that I once knew in the past. She is inclined to be sincere, but her sincerity doesn't amuse me. I dragged her to watch *Pension Mimosa,* which could not move me despite my sentimen-tal goodwill. I was crushed because Gérassi invited Poupette to extend her visit, but back at my place while writing to Sartre I fiercely decided to make everybody toe the line and get back to my work. If not, I would get myself into a deadly depression.

Friday, February 23

Woke up once again blurry-eyed and fatigued—I went to the Dôme around nine o'clock and tried to work a little, but without much success. Poupette arrived at ten o'clock, looking fresh and almost pretty in her cream-colored blouse—and Stépha turned up. We spent a moment of unbearable boredom chatting about beauty creams, etc. Then Ninouche arrived, a very pretty girl, a friend of Stépha who had been engaged to the painter Bennal, who recently died—it seemed like a novel to me because I remembered him at the Gare d'Orsay when he was leaving with Gérassi to fight in Spain, and they were already saying back then that he had only one lung left. The same girl had lost another fiancé, a Spanish anarchist whom the anarchists shot dead because he wouldn't let them destroy his first communion pictures and other souvenirs of his mother. We talked. Seated next to us, A. Ménard was getting chewed out by the shady character that was pursuing Stépha. I let time go by; it went by slowly, so slowly.

Noon—they left me at my table. I ate some rabbit stew. C. Chonez stopped by to say hello. Lycée Henri IV. Sorokine was there when I left, as usual repentant and charming. Post office, a letter from Sartre. Work, at the Vikings, rather mediocre. As I stopped by my place, I saw Bost, who came by to get books and some money; I was happy to see him for five minutes.

NOTES

1. By Beethoven.
2. An officer of the Légion d'honneur.
3. It seems rather obvious that when the author uses *le passionnel* in the original she means "jealousy," a word she carefully avoids in this context.
4. A rhythmic native dance of Martinique.
5. Natives from the French colonies pressed into military service.
6. An obvious play on *Mousquetaires* ("Musketeers").
7. By William Faulkner (1930).
8. An allusion to Edmund Husserl's method of phenomenological reduction, where reality claims are put between parentheses, or bracketed.
9. Malfilâtre, a French poet (1732–67), born in Caen; the author of Eclogues.
10. Les Halles was the central wholesale food market district of Paris.

NOTEBOOK 6

June 9 – July 18, 1940

S. de Beauvoir
21 rue Vavin, Paris

POW Transit Camp Nr. 1
9ᵉ Cie—Baccarat*

"Inasmuch as it is the other who acts, each consciousness pursues the *death* of the other. . . . The relation of the two self-consciousnesses is therefore determined as follows: They experience themselves and each other through a struggle to death. *They cannot avoid this struggle since they are forced to raise their certainty of self to the level of truth,* their certainty of existing for itself; they each must experience this certainty in themselves and in the other." Hegel.

"Each self consciousness must pursue the death of the other since it risks its own life in the process, since it does not value the other more than itself; the essence of the other appears to self-consciousness as other, as external, and it must surpass this exteriority." Hegel, *Ph*. P. 143–150.[1]†

---

* Sartre's address in June 1940.
† The epigraph of *She Came to Stay* was taken from this passage.

270

June 9 to June 30*

On *June 9*, a Sunday, the news had been bad the previous afternoon around five o'clock: an unspecified retreat in the Aisne region. I had spent the evening with Védrine at the opera; we saw *Ariane and Blue Beard*†—the house was empty—we had the impression of a last show of courage by Paris in the face of the enemy. The weather was stormy, we were both on edge—I can still see the grand staircase and Védrine in her pretty red dress with a red scarf tucked inside; in a pastry shop nearby we had bought some pastries and then settled in our loge. We returned home on foot taking the avenue de l'Opéra; we first discussed the music, which she didn't like and I did—the discussion had been acrimonious—and then we talked about the war, about a possible defeat. I can still see us on place Médicis, where she said that we could just kill ourselves and I replied that we certainly would not. Besides, from a distance it seemed interesting to live through it, that very tragic interest that I had been feeling for a month and that was still with me despite everything. However, even while defending this optimistic thesis I felt tense and all tied in knots—she asked me with some embarrassment to come up to her room, but I took off quickly; I wanted to be alone. I went back to my hotel. I no longer quite know what I did the next morning, but that Sunday was spent the same way I had just spent the last two weeks: I read in the morning, listened to music at Chanteclerc's from one to three o'clock in the afternoon, went to the movies to see *Fantôme à vendre* [A Phantom for Sale] for a second time and also *L'Étrange Visiteur* [The Strange Visitor]. Then I wrote to Sartre from the Mahieu—the air defense was shooting off its guns leaving white puffs of smoke in the sky, and the people sitting on café terraces cleared out. The news in the papers wasn't any better—I felt the German advance as a direct threat and had only one idea: not to be cut off from Sartre and Bost, not to be caught like a rat in occupied Paris. The weather was still stormy—I was nervous, and furious at being so. I thought that it would be great to fear nothing in the world, but that would mean being a complete stoic and no longer caring about anything—but to love people means wanting to love them, hence, I didn't honestly want that kind of independence. I listened to some more music, Mozart, as in the morning. It was pleasant to listen to and required no effort, which suited me just fine. Then I walked back to the hotel; it must have been ten o'clock when I got there. I found a

---

* This part has been used, though not entirely, in *The Prime of Life*.
† By Paul Dukas.

frantic note from Védrine saying that she had been looking for me all day, that she would be at the Café Flore, that she had some very serious news for me, and that she might be leaving during the night. That really made me feel nervous; I looked around for a taxi, but there were already none to be found. I took the metro and arrived at St. German-des-Prés. Védrine was sitting outside on the terrace of the Flore, with the Swiss friends and a few others. I grabbed her and we left. She told me that she knew from someone at headquarters that a retreat was planned for the next day along the Melun Line—north of St. Dizier—and incidentally, all exams had been canceled and professors released from duty—my heart froze. It was definitive and hopeless; the Germans would be in Paris in two days; there was nothing for me to do but leave with her for Angers. I went up to my parents' place to let them know that I was leaving; for financial reasons they could not leave for the next two days. My mother for once showed herself to be heroic—I was filled with emotion as I went downstairs. It seemed to me that, in any case, it was the most definitive break and that I would never see Paris again. At that point, on rue Cassette, Védrine told me that obviously the Maginot Line would be taken from the rear; that was only common sense, of course, and I understood that Sartre would be a prisoner indefinitely, that he would have a horrible life and I wouldn't have any news from him. Considering the state I was in, this idea was unbearable to me and for the first time in my life I had a kind of nervous fit. I think this was the most awful moment of the entire war. We walked all the way back to my place—I packed my suitcases taking only the essentials; I left all my books, papers, and old clothes. I took manuscripts, notebooks, and clothes I liked—all this was rather heavy and we had a hard time dragging ourselves to Védrine's hotel.* I made up my face, and we went to see Posi, a Swiss. Lévy, Ramblin, and a bunch of other Swiss were there; we drank and smoked—I can't remember what we talked about. Posi explained to me the difference between a piano and a harpsichord, but we mostly discussed the war. We still believed in victory, thinking it would be a matter of holding out long enough behind the Paris Line for American reinforcements to arrive. The hours went by; it was comforting to be surrounded by people and noisy talk—around four in the morning we went to sleep but I hardly slept a wink.

On Monday, *June 10*, I got up around seven o'clock and while I was getting dressed, there was a knock at the door. It was Sorokine, for whom I had left a note at the hotel. The poor girl, quite content not to have an exam

---

* On rue Royer-Collard.

that day, had come to ask me to spend the day strolling about with her. She had been shattered to see me at Védrine's and when, after quickly getting dressed, I went out with her, she looked somber. She wanted me to persuade her mother to let her leave with me; I was annoyed because I wanted to be back at nine o'clock so as not to miss M. Védrine—luckily I found a taxi, which took me to Camille Sée—there were a few students who had come on the off chance that the baccalaureate exams would be held after all. The principal handed me evacuation orders; I went to the teachers' lounge to collect Bost's and Sartre's letters* and some notebooks—I got back into the same taxi, which then took me to Sorokine's, where I had a brief talk with her mother. I persuaded her to let me take her daughter along. She would see whether she could have a safe-conduct pass since that was required for foreigners, and I stopped by my hotel, where I had a cheerful letter from Sartre, which I couldn't even read for the mist in my eyes. I returned to rue Royer-Collard, where the car and M. Védrine were waiting. He didn't seem enthusiastic about taking me along because he was already taking one of his women employees and was loaded down with accounting books and cases, but in the end he promised to get me out of Paris. At that point Sorokine showed up; she had hitched a ride on a truck to let me know that it would take at least a week for her to get a safe-conduct pass and even then she needed to come up with a certificate of residence. I was aghast at the idea of leaving her alone like that in Paris. We went for a melancholic walk in the Luxembourg Gardens; we were again on good terms, and I was upset about leaving her. She accompanied me back to the Mahieu; I met some students who were all smiles because they had been acting like queens strolling around the lycée Fénelon; for many young people this exam day without exams felt like a holiday, a disorganized day and a day of leisure. They were walking about happily on the boulevards and seemed to be having great fun. However, the café terraces already looked rather deserted and on boulevard St. Michel the heavy stream of traffic had begun. I talked with the students and made arrangements to see them in the Angers area, as I had done with Lévy and the Swiss. At that point we all thought of an exile

---

* Castor believed for a long time that she had lost Sartre's letters. In *The Prime of Life* ([1960] p. 440 in the *NRF* edition; p. 489 in the Folio Edition) she wrote: "He wrote to me almost every day, but I lost this correspondence during the exodus," and in a note a few pages further on: "I had taken all of Sartre's letters with me. I don't know where or when they were lost." Fortunately, this was not the case—since she herself edited the two volumes (extensively expurgated) of *Letters to Castor* in 1983. However, while the war letters have been saved, Sartre's very first letters to her, from 1929 on, during his military service in Saint-Cyr and Saint-Symphorien and even those dating from a later period when she was appointed to a position in Marseilles, as well as those written during the very first years of their relationship, are quite definitely lost.

rather than a defeat. We were mentally preparing ourselves for a life in the provinces with the least possible boredom.

Afterward I went to the Mahieu to write to Sartre and Bost—perhaps these letters would still reach them, they would have been the last ones—I sobbed while writing and had only one thought: "We're going to be separated." I could see us, as we were, each of us stuck in some corner of France, without news, without letters, alone, and each feeling twice the anguish by imagining that of the other. I couldn't bear the idea—the moment of breaking away, of renunciation is always hard—as long as one resists, says no and doesn't want to. And then, once the break has occurred, there's no longer even any cause for suffering; there is simply nothing left at all.

I returned to the hotel, devastated—the Swiss were hanging around and I composed my face to go out and join them in drinking some bad champagne left behind by an Austrian woman who had been sent to a concentration camp. That made me feel a little better. Then I went for lunch with Védrine at a Savoyard restaurant—the proprietor told us he was leaving that very evening—everyone was leaving; the restroom attendant of the Mahieu was packing her bags, the grocer on the rue Claude Bernard was closing up shop, the entire neighborhood was emptying. After the meal we went to wait for M. Védrine outside the Mahieu. It was a long and nerve-wracking wait; he had said he would be there between two and five o'clock and we were wondering whether or not he would be coming, whether it would not be too late to leave after all, but we were mostly eager to get it over with; this interminable farewell to Paris was unbearable—we remained sitting there without saying a word. The Swiss came by, as did Lévy and Ramblin; the stream of traffic never let up; people were looking for taxis, but there were scarcely any left on the streets and as soon as one did stop, it was taken by storm. Toward midday we saw for the first time those large cartloads of refugees that I was to see so often afterward: there were about ten large wagons, each one harnessed to four or five horses and loaded with hay, over which a green tarpaulin was fastened on one side—bicycles and mattresses were stacked at either end and in the middle people were grouped together, huddling motionless under large umbrellas. The whole was composed with the precision of a painting—it reminded me of Breughel's paintings. Later I saw them again, undone, in disarray, but here they were perfect and dignified like a procession on a feast day. It was extremely moving, precisely because they weren't shabby-looking but beautiful. Védrine started to cry, and I understood her so well; I myself had tears in my eyes. The weather was hot and humid; we hadn't slept, our eyes were stinging, and we ached from head to toe. We were waiting for the car that would take us away, deliver us, but it wouldn't arrive. We went to buy some food: fruit, brioches, and chocolate. Looking once more at these streets where we had been so happy: rue Royer-Collard, rue St. Jacques, I had my last bout of sentimentality. There were too many memories everywhere and I remembered, as something real, Sartre coming toward me on these streets, smiling. This was the last time that the past was brought back to my mind in such a vivid and unbearable fashion.

The car finally arrived. Védrine and I sat in front, the employee with the piles of suitcases in the back—I was glad to finally have done with waiting, to move, to go away. Just as we were leaving the hotel, the proprietress, quite elated, called out to us, "The Russians and the English have just landed in Hamburg!"—a soldier arriving from Val-de-Grace was spreading this news. I have since learned that the rumor of Russia's entering the war had gone insistently around Paris in the days that followed. The news left me stunned, but I quickly understood that the story was false; otherwise the radio would have broadcast it immediately on the four thirty news. Védrine clung stubbornly to this hope that slowly died during the course of the trip, as the seven thirty broadcast did not mention a word about this extravagant news. So we left with the vague idea that in any case all was not lost, things could still happen. We arrived at the Porte d'Orléans, where there was heavy traffic but no real congestion, only a few bicycles and no pedestrians as yet. We were leaving before the large crowds. I felt a kind of wrenching heartbreak at the idea of Paris that I was leaving behind me, of Paris full of Germans. At the Croix de Berny we stopped for a quarter of an hour watching truckloads of exhausted-looking young soldiers pass by; it was a distressing sight. I was thinking of the trucks that had transported Bost and his comrades to the front lines; I didn't know whether these soldiers were going to or returning from the front, but in any case it upset me terribly. We went on the highway again and soon veered off onto small roads, passing through Orsay, headed toward the Chevreuse valley. It was beautiful weather, and there was little traffic. We saw small villas with flowering gardens; it was as if we were starting off on a weekend outing. In the vicinity of Chartres we were rerouted and began to encounter various roadblocks that created traffic jams. At one point we sat in a long line of cars stopped on the highway, their passengers spread out across the fields. It took us a while to understand what was going on, but a soldier running from car to car shouted that there was an air raid warning—so we got out too, M. Védrine carrying a precious case that contained all his pearls,* and we sat down to eat something at the edge of a little wood—the situation had just a hint of adventure about it and made us feel that it wasn't quite a normal trip. For an hour afterward we sat in a long line of cars hardly making any headway; then we took off. As we were passing through a small village, we saw a soldier blowing a little trumpet; he called out to us: "Air raid warning! Take cover outside the village!"—we drove on and continued along the highway. We had encountered many soldiers in those villages, one village in particular where the soldiers were all young and almost all charming—at in intersection one of them informed us of Italy's entry into the war; we couldn't have cared less since we had anticipated it. We continued on our way as night fell. A bicycle was strapped to the front of our car blocking the headlights, so it was pointless turning them on, and M. Védrine had to make out the road in increasing darkness. Finally we stopped in Illiers, a tiny village. We were lucky enough to find two rooms right away at the home of an old man suffering from goiter. Before going to bed we looked for a café where we could have a drink. We found one with its metal shutters almost closed. People were discussing the issue of streetlights and the municipality. They were distrustful and asked from what area of Paris we came. We went back to our rooms to sleep. Védrine slept on a mattress in her father's room and I shared a double bed with the employee. There was a large eloquent clock that threatened to keep us awake, but we carefully stopped its pendulum.

The next morning, on *Tuesday, June 11,* I woke up at eight o'clock and immediately jumped out of bed. A hellish sadness was choking me. I went to the window; I can still see the gray sky, the rectangular garden with a horrible flat countryside stretching out behind it. I got dressed and hurried down to last night's café to write to Sartre. I wrote a short letter and couldn't help crying; I don't think he ever received it. At half past eight the radio brought news—I was in the back of the shop with another woman who sobbed while listening to the communiqué; I cried too. The stench of defeat had begun the night before, and that morning it was impossible to not begin to believe in it; you came up against it everywhere: in the announcer's voice and in the words he spoke, in the face of the woman who was listening, and in my own tears—it was also everywhere in the village, and all day long in all the villages we were greeted with these words: "So, that's it. We are done for? Paris has been taken?" The Védrines came in; we quickly ate something and then left. Some-

---

* He was in the pearl business.

body was putting up posters about the Italians; the women were calling to each other in a somber mood. At every street corner we saw refugees' cars.

We left around nine o'clock. The drive was very easy; from time to time we saw large carts, similar to those I had seen on blvd. St. Michel, but already half undone, the hay half eaten and the people trudging alongside. We had seen encampments the night before, where the horses were unhitched and people eating on the side of the road; it didn't look too sad because there weren't too many of them yet, but mostly because the weather was beautiful. We drove along without any trouble until Le Mans, which was swarming with British troops, and Laval—where it began crawling with refugees. We came across a car with flat tires; it had driven through the town of Evreux in flames; I began to tremble with fear for the Kos. There were many people turning up from Normandy. Laval itself was one huge traffic jam. One could still get a sense of the small peaceful river town it must have been before, but now all the sidewalks were lined with cars and all the bridges and squares crowded with refugees, the wealthy seated at tables in cafés that had extended their terraces endlessly, and the poor sitting on the ground or their suitcases. We went first to the train station—the rumor was spreading that the trains from Paris had gotten lost on the way—we got some information about the bus schedule, and I found out that I had a bus for Angers at half past five; that was perfect. After that we looked for a restaurant; at the town's grand hotel they laughed in our faces, they had nothing left, not even a scrap of ham. So we went to a brasserie with tile-covered walls, which must have been quite a peaceful place in normal times with its backgammon and checkers game table set against a window, but now it resembled a huge railroad station buffet with all its tables put together in a row and all being served the same dish: veal with peas. I felt terribly tired. We found a table and I was also very happy to eat veal with peas while drinking a little wine. Afterward we took my luggage from the car and I said goodbye to the Védrines. I took my suitcases to the bus depot and went to the post office to try to phone La Pouèze. I waited more than an hour for the connection. There was a huge crowd, the heat thick with humidity; from time to time I collapsed on a chair in a corner thinking I was going to get sick. I remember a pathetic-looking refugee woman who approached the telephone operator asking her, "Would you make a call for me?"—the other laughed out loud. Just to have something to do I took care of the woman; she told me what locality she wanted to telephone, and I named all the subscribers, but none would do for her: this one had left, that one must be out working in the fields—finally

I just walked off. I was so tired and nervous that my heart began to pound and my voice trembled when I had Mops* on the telephone; That Lady also came to the phone and told me that the house was turned upside down and crowded with people but that they would welcome me with open arms and would come by car after dinner and pick me up at Angers—it was wonderful news. I had just enough time to pick up my luggage and jump into the crammed-full bus—I had to stand. I met C. Neveu, a former student from Rouen, whom I used to like a little. She was with her husband, fleeing from Rouen, carrying only a backpack and taking one bus after another. She had become quite drab, but it gave me something to do, talking about C. Audry, Collinet, and Mme Feldman,† of whom she didn't seem to be very fond. At Château-Gontier I found a seat and about eight o'clock I arrived in Angers.

I sat down at a café terrace on station square—it was crowded with refugees who didn't know what to do with themselves since there were no accommodations at all to be found. I can still see a kind of crazy woman, wrapped in a blanket, pushing a stroller loaded with suitcases, who kept endlessly and desperately turning round and round about the square. That Lady told me later that Angers was always overflowing with refugees and that those coming from the North came with their cars riddled with bullet holes and their dead strapped to the top of the cars between two mattresses.

I was very tired—time went by, night fell and a little rain with it, and I was wondering what would become of me when finally a car showed up: it was Mops [and] her sister-in-law Lili, a tall, beautiful woman of German origin and looking the type, who had married J. Isorni after the divorce from a husband who left her with a blond son, good looking and stupid, who had come along too. I got into the car. At La Pouèze I found That Lady, who gave me hard-boiled eggs and a salad to eat. I was delighted to see her and would have loved to talk with her if Lili hadn't stayed around ranting against the lack of idealism in today's French soldiers. She did finally leave. I chatted a little with That Lady and went upstairs to sleep. For the first three nights I slept in the very bedroom of That Lady. The bed was pleasant because they had taken out the box springs and the mattress sank way down between the slats so that I could imagine myself on the bottom of a boat. That Lady slept in the room next to That Gentleman's bedroom so she would be able to respond to the slightest sound of the bell, considering that he was suffering from acute anxiety. A poodle slept in my room; he was a little too friendly, especially in the morning, but he didn't bother me too much.

---

* Jacqueline, daughter of Mme Morel, "That Lady," married to an Isorni.
† Friends and colleagues from Rouen.

Wednesday, June 12—I woke up after a good night. Lea brought me tea and some plum jam—every morning I had the same breakfast at half past eight. My first disappointment was that I had no letters and I was sure that they had forwarded letters from Sartre and Bost from Paris—there was only a telegram from Sorokine requesting an authorization from the prefect of Maine-et-Loire so that she could join me. I had a heavy heart. I wrote letters from the dining room, which I was unable to do without shedding tears; then I threw myself on some detective novels and for three days I couldn't read anything else; they were stupid, but I didn't care. The days were spent reading in my room or the dining room without my even bothering to stick my nose outside. Around one o'clock we ate and chatted a little, and about half past eight we had dinner and talked until ten o'clock. But I scarcely saw That Lady, who almost never left That Gentleman's bedside:* not only was his bedroom hermetically closed and kept in darkness, but it seemed that he also had drapes around his bed, which was so elevated that he could not see anyone unless the person was standing right at his bedside. That Lady and Mops would remain standing there for three hours. By the end they were so exhausted that they had mattresses placed on the floor where they stretched out during That Gentleman's somnolence.

He would call them almost every night, and they had to watch over him while he, bathed in sweat, spent himself in horrible nightmares of the war. That Lady literally did not sleep; I wonder how she was able to hold up.

The village was full of people: the Isorni family had come from Villers after watching from a distance the gasoline tanks in Le Havre explode and burn. It seemed that the sky was pitch black and the sea covered with oil. The family consisted of the father; the mother, who, from morning till night bemoaned her four sons on the front lines; and the daughter Helene with her little girl—there was also Lili and her son, who didn't get along with the rest and were treated like strangers. At times she would decide to live on her own, then again she would come back to live with the others. The question of where to room at La Pouèze had caused a drama the first day with Mme Isorni fighting over the lodging with another woman, each throwing the number of their drafted sons into each other's face. That Lady, who felt responsible, was very indignant. Besides the Isornis there was the Nissim family, which had arrived two days earlier from Rambouillet. Nissim was a doctor and horticulturist who in this capacity had corresponded for years with That Gentleman without ever meeting him in person. He wrote beauti-

---

* He had been sequestered from the world since his return from the war of 1914–18.

ful stoic exhortations to life and hope, and That Lady had suggested he come with his family to take refuge at her home. They had come by train and been given the bungalow. The family consisted of an unassuming wife; a completely dazed young woman, with wide and shiny eyes, who had had marital misfortunes; and her two children, terribly Jewish, self-important and conceited. As for him, he was a miserable little man, humiliated and offended. He was practically the only person of the family one would get to see; in the most tragic moments he would show up with pencil sketches of rose bushes or an ingenious way of drawing water, inspired by Hindu fellahs. He would take That Lady botanizing and once she was frantic because she couldn't locate a blue cedar that Nissim had given to That Gentleman. When you asked him, "How are your women?" he would always reply, "They are shattered!" and then with raised arms would say, "Let's hope, let's hope."

Also in the village were Marie-Noelle and Martine de Quayla, but we almost never saw them. In the house across lived an old senile woman, Mme Mairelle, the former governess of Mops's cousin,* who ate her meals with us. She was all shriveled up and hunchbacked, her eyes almost swallowed up by pink skin; it seemed that before my arrival she would talk nonstop like a broken record, but I must have intimidated her, for in my presence she hardly opened her mouth.

Finally, the large room, across from the dining room, was occupied by the Russian princess, more hard of hearing than ever and fallen into disgrace. She worried about only two things, which were enough to cause her to fill the house with her shrieks: her dog Capri, who had an infected nail, and her identity papers, for which she wanted an extension from the mayor. She hardly left her room, except during the news broadcast; then she would show up, haggard looking, asking that someone write down a summary for her. She lived in terror of being abandoned by everyone and shot.

The first day passed somberly—we listened to every news broadcast: at half past eight, half past eleven, half past four, half past six, and at half past eleven at night; the wait in between marked the rhythm of the day, and so it went every day until there was silence—I don't quite remember what the announcement was that particular Wednesday; in any case, more retreats; it wasn't good. L'Aiglet† was very much in danger; the pressure was increasing toward Reims, which is what I feared most because of Sartre and because I understood quite well that it was even more serious than Paris, that it was there that everything would break down. Around nine o'clock in the evening the

---

* The cousin called "Zébuth."
† Olga had gone back there to her parents' home.

doorbell rang—strangers were asking for Mme Mairelle. We looked at them askance. At dinner time there had indeed been an air raid warning: mysteriously someone had come to alert That Lady and while Boudy* trembled with fright, That Lady and Mops hastily disappeared. Parachutists had been seen and That Lady was to alert the gendarmerie five kilometers from there, and in order to do that she had armed herself with a gun. In fact, the next day we learned that the parachutists had been only small balloons, but that evening That Lady was very nervous and when the people knocked at the door, she was almost ready to believe that they were the parachutists themselves even though Mme Mairelle knew them. She was especially suspicious of the man because he was Dutch. In fact, they were the daughter of a dry cleaner in Paris and her husband; they had left Tuesday night and had had a difficult trip, for Tuesday the crush had already started and they had been shot at by machine guns. They stayed in Mme Mairelle's house where the woman who owned the dry-cleaning business joined them three days later.

The following day, *Thursday, June 13,* there was again no letter—I sent telegrams and for the last time wrote letters, without any hope.

June 30†

For five days now my entire life has been dominated by opposite certainties: they'll be coming home—they won't be coming home. When I arrived in Paris last night I experienced the depth of despair—there was talk about huge prison camps in Garches and Antony where they were "fed dead dogs," and my parents claimed that they would be kept there until war's end. The armistice stipulated that those who were "prisoners in Germany" would be kept until the end of the war—but my father argued that occupied France was considered to be Germany. This morning, after having thought about it, I could scarcely believe it any longer, and then there was this comforting note in *Le Matin*: the issue was raised whether the families shouldn't be allowed to communicate with the soldiers while waiting for them to be demobilized—so I thought that these camps detained perhaps soldiers who were then going to be released in stages. It was an idea that occurred to me during the night. And then this morning at the Dôme, as some old woman was bemoaning the fact that she was without news, that "his" room was ready and waiting for him, the cashier reassured her that they would arrive one fine morning. I can't help but hope.

---

* Mops's seven-year-old daughter.
† From June 30 to July 14, part of the journal appears again in *The Prime of Life*.

As a result I recovered a kind of gaiety this morning after feeling more miserable last night than I ever had in my entire life. The weather was lovely. I took my usual place at the Dôme, near the terrace; the place was almost empty with the exception of three couples with women who seemed rather young. I recognized the cashier, the waiters, and the décor. The specials of the day were posted, and I saw open grocery stores displaying magnificent fruits and fresh ham. Compared to the empty stores of Le Mans or Chartres, they looked downright prosperous. Hardly a soul on the boulevard. I saw two trucks filled with young Germans in light gray uniforms drive past, but I've seen so many Germans these last days that it scarcely struck me as odd. Suddenly, with all the strength I could muster I believed in an "afterward"—sad or cheerful, whatever, an afterward where we would live together; the proof of this is the fact that I purchased this notebook and a bottle of ink with the intention of untangling the history, the story of these last three weeks, and writing everything down for Sartre and Bost and, for the future. It was the first day that I came out of my shell and stopped living like a "crushed bug" and tried to become a person again. Those last three weeks I was nowhere—there were big collective events or a particular physiological anguish and neither past, nor future, nor anybody. I would like to find myself again as in September and think that all of that forms part of my history, my story. Perhaps it would be possible in Paris—I thought that if I could draw my salary, I would stay here for quite a while. Certainly, difficult moments would become even more so, but there would be times where one could leave them behind—while at La Pouèze one lived in a polite environment and it was unseemly to be occupied with oneself—a constant flight.

I got up around half past eight. I was in a somber mood while getting dressed, but the sweetness of the morning overwhelmed me. Last night Paris was "somewhere on earth" and I felt completely lost in the world—this morning the Montparnasse intersection had regained its individuality and had become a refuge for me. I bought the German *Le Matin,* where I found nothing worth reading. I sat down at the Dôme, rediscovered the café and the Swiss from a month ago, and wrote the first pages of this notebook. Around ten o'clock I began my rounds in Paris: I was unable to reach Mme Mancy by telephone, went on foot and by metro to her place, tried calling Taverny,* to no avail, went on foot to see Sorokine, who wasn't home, to Colette Audry, who wasn't home, back again to see Mme Mancy, where I left a note for Sartre, just in case, and returned to the Latin Quarter by metro, and settled

---

* At the home of Bost's parents, "the pastor and his wife."

at the Mahieu, where I was going to write for a while. I ate some currants and butter cookies on the way and just had freshly squeezed lemonade to drink.

Paris was remarkably empty, even more so than last September. We had about the same good weather, the same calm; we didn't see many Germans: a few motorcycles and cars, a few on foot or in the metro—and a few barracks occupied by them. Another difference from September were the long lines at the rare food stores that had remained open. But the difference was mostly felt inside, not so much on the streets themselves. In September it was a beginning. Something terrible was beginning, but the idea had something adventurous and passionately interesting about it. I was interested in my own self, wondering how I would react, how I would bear hardship; and I, just like Sartre, already saw myself at the end of the war. It wasn't so much that I was making a date with the future, but everything took on meaning in relation to the happy ending that I never doubted. Now it was over—there was no longer a shining moment on the horizon to which one could offer up the present—there was no more waiting, no more future—the time before me was absolutely stagnant; it seemed that all I could do was rot in place for years to come. From time to time I had the pleasant impression that I was living in some Wells novel, being transported into an era and a place totally detached from me, but with the miraculous possibility of watching what was happening to the world—and then I remembered that there was no other world waiting for me, that there would be no awakening, and that that was my own destiny.

Passy and Auteuil looked absolutely dead, smelling of greenery and linden trees, which reminded me of an approaching summer vacation of bygone days. Even the concierges had left. On boulevard de Grenelle I passed in front of the former women's concentration camp—the armistice terms stipulated that all German refugees must be handed over to Germany—few clauses seemed more ominous and implacable.

I returned to the Latin Quarter—it was deserted, but the cafés were nearly all open; there were some people on the terraces—hardly a German around, I only saw two passing by. Just three weeks ago I was writing to Sartre from here—I was in deep anguish; I remembered the humid heat and the puffs of smoke from the antiaircraft guns hanging in the sky. I would like to go back to that moment in time in my account, but instead I'm going to begin with the return trip because it is more recent and the most interesting.

Friday, June 28 I left in the morning—for four days I had been restless—I had convinced myself that Sartre and Bost could have returned to Paris unexpectedly and that in any case I would have news there, and besides I wanted to see Paris again under the Occupation; in short, I was bored reading from morning till night and carefully avoiding the least bit of thinking. There was some talk about a train to Chartres, but the Dutch people were very eager to leave and so decided to return and agreed to take me along—they wanted to leave on the twenty-fifth, but were advised to wait in view of the fact that with heavy traffic they might be stopped twenty-four hours into the trip. From La Pouèze one saw only a small number of cars passing and so this delay disappointed me; besides, they decided to leave anyway three days later. Mops set the alarm for five o'clock in the morning, and a big get-together took place in my room—they brought me my breakfast, That Lady came, and Boudy and Zébuth. I was emotional about my departure, as I felt anguished at the idea of this void awaiting me in Paris, but at the same time I was happy just to try something. We were supposed to leave at seven o'clock; I went downstairs and came up again several times because the car wasn't there, and when it finally arrived, it took at least an hour loading it. The Dutchman moved so placidly that he made me want to kill him—he put a mattress on top and loads of suitcases in the back, and the young woman stacked up all the packages, making sure to take a jar with green beans, leftovers from the dinner of the night before that they did not intend to let go to waste. Then they put the mother-in-law and me in the remaining space of the backseat—the young woman sat in front, next to her husband—the two women wore hats and white satin blouses.

We left taking little side roads—in principle, refugees were told to avoid the big highways, but in fact the big highways were completely jammed with cars. We drove through villages; here and there we saw signs of bombings and also a tank, then a cannon on the side of the road, a church tower shot through, the grave of a German soldier with his helmet slung over a cross—and mostly overturned cars, stuck in the mud; we saw many of them along the road. We were going toward La Flèche to find some gasoline; that's when I found out that we had embarked on our trip with only ten liters of gasoline in all, trusting in the promise by the Germans to distribute the necessary gasoline along the road—in fact, only this Dutchman had believed it; everyone else at La Pouèze had stocked up on it. As for him, he could have had twenty-five liters a few days earlier, but he had gotten tired of standing in line and instead of waiting another half hour had calmly left, something for which we often bitterly and rightfully reproached him later on. We stopped in La Flèche, and he went to the German military headquarters. It was located in a magnificent building on the waterfront with gardens all around it. That's where I saw the first steel-gray uniforms; all the Germans in La

Pouèze had been wearing Italian-green. Those in La Flèche, in their beautiful uniforms and their beautiful cars of the same color, had an elegant look about them; they were not blond as were the Germans in La Pouèze. There were many different kinds of them, and of all I saw afterward these showed the greatest diversity.

While our driver was half-heartedly waiting his turn, I, flanked by the two women, looked around in the city; we bought a newspaper, *La Sarthe,* where we read the armistice conditions from beginning to end. I knew almost all of them from the radio, except the clause about the extradition of German refugees—and I read attentively the paragraph concerning prisoners, and it seemed certain to me then that only those already in Germany would be held there. This certainty brightened these two days, valorizing my entire journey and making it possible for me to take an interest in things around me. Rarely had I spent more interesting and intense days than those two. We returned to the car and the Dutchman announced that we would have only five liters and not before two o'clock in the afternoon. It was eleven o'clock; we hesitated about what to do and decided to drive on to Le Mans; he "believed" he had enough gasoline to get us there—in fact, he didn't have nearly enough. We left—at ten kilometers from Le Mans we were rerouted and told that there wasn't any gasoline in Le Mans and that three hundred cars were already waiting. As we only had a drop left, we just had to go there anyway—we therefore tried to rejoin the road to Le Mans and five kilometers further down the road the car stopped. The Dutchman had the extraordinary luck of finding in a farmhouse five liters of reddish gasoline that had been left by the English (there were people who made their entire trip on gasoline abandoned by the English, who had been in such a hurry to flee that they left everything behind: cigarettes, gasoline, etc. etc.). We put the gas in the tank and drove on to Le Mans.

That was the beginning of an amazing afternoon. It was noontime; the car stopped on a wide street, between two squares. On one of these was the German military headquarters and on the other the prefecture. We waited for the Dutchman to get information, and then went first to the prefecture— it was still closed—between a hundred and two hundred persons carrying gasoline containers, pitchers, and watering cans thronged at the gates. And around a statue of a ridiculously small man, a delegate to the Convention [of 1793] with a large plumed hat (Levasseur, I suppose), was a large number of cars and trucks, overloaded with mattresses, kitchen utensils, and refugees who were just waiting and eating, dirty and shabby-looking refugees with kids and bundles as I was to see by the thousands during the rest of the trip.

The crowd was grumbling with discontent; they were saying that some people had not budged from there for a week without getting gasoline and that people were sent from prefecture to headquarters, back and forth, endlessly. A rumor was also spread about Paris that they had run out of food supplies. A blazing sun; the Dutchman stood there grinning in that idiotic way of his, and annoyed at seeing such a throng he stepped back, reluctant to get into the fray, but his wife, with me supporting her, had made him stay. She told him that she was h-u-n-g-r-y in a disgusting, low voice, such as one could imagine Mrs. Bloom in *Ulysses* might have had, and she complained that the populace smelled bad—she fashioned a paper hat to protect her husband's precious head. They were saying that you needed a number that would allow you to get a voucher, which in turn would allow you to get gasoline the day the gasoline arrived. When finally, toward a quarter past two, the gates opened, there was a stampede, but the employee chased everyone out, shouting that a gasoline tank truck was on its way with ten thousand liters and that at three o'clock it would be distributed on the square without a coupon to anyone who showed up. Nobody believed it, but they left anyway. In fact, if the Dutchman had persevered, he would have had a number and would have found out that one kilometer further down the road a garage would have sold him five liters of gasoline—but he only thought of going to eat— in all my life I have never seen anyone as indolent and stupid as that man. So we went to the main square—there we witnessed an extraordinary spectacle. What it mostly brought to mind was the atmosphere of large Parisian expositions, with crowds milling about, scorched by the sun. On the grassy area in the center were throngs and throngs of German cars and soldiers in gray, also hundreds of refugee trucks, people, and broken-down cars. All the cafés were crowded, inside as well as on the terraces, and were almost exclusively occupied by Germans. Many of them were young and pleasant looking. The officers, done up snug in their uniforms, wearing gloves and conscious of their gloves, their beautiful uniforms, their distinction, their courtesy, displayed a thick-headed and despicable haughtiness, but there were many soldiers who were smiling, happy, young, and often rather good looking. All those I now have seen in Paris with their cameras and their pink faces looked so stupid that I wondered—but two days ago in Le Mans, they seemed to be of another species, and I could feel what a terrific adventure it must be for a young German to find himself victorious in France, to have made it out alive after one month of war, to be well dressed, well nourished, and to feel himself part of a chosen race. It was overwhelming to see them with their beautiful ambulances, their neat appearance, and their friendly courtesy, while France was represented by hundreds of timorous and miserable refugees. Only these handsome soldiers could be expected to provide them with food, gasoline, transport, and a remedy for their immediate misfortune. And above the whole crowd, amidst the comings and goings of army trucks, radio cars, and motorcycles, a huge loudspeaker was blaring out a deafening military music and also the news in both French and German. It was hell with the sun, the hunger and the fatigue of a day that had begun early. But it was also passionately interesting. Nowhere did I get a better feel for what victory must have meant for the Germans; you could touch it with your finger; each look, each smile expressed victory, and there was not a French face that wasn't a living defeat—it showed in the servility of the café waiters, in the misery of the refugees who were going from one place to the other, carrying empty gasoline cans.

We went to a café that had nothing left to eat; we went to get our own food that served as our lunch. With the exception of four brightly dressed, energetic women cyclists, there were only the Germans and us. They entered and left clicking their heels when saluting, and they drank and laughed. I dropped I don't know what object and they hastened to pick it up for me. For this very overzealousness Von Salomon reproached the French occupation forces in *Les Réprouvés* [The Reprobates],[2] and it was often marked by a hint of disgust because it was so very self-conscious and compliant. But often it was also gracious; even from soldiers (especially the following day from the truck drivers) there was a completely spontaneous, friendly, and straightforward kindness. (I think they must have left the "elite" troops in Paris, because all the ugly German faces that have been invading the Dôme at present have been awful—blond, pink, with glasses, student faces, but of the worst kind.)

So we ate, urging the Dutchman to go to the promised distribution at three o'clock. He finally made up his mind to go and we sat pathetically on some steps across from the car. I was so tired that I didn't care and besides, the atmosphere was so charged that it was impossible to be bored. The spectacle continued, comings and goings, over and over, gasoline cans, pitchers and water cans, always empty. Some people, tired of it all, sat on their gasoline cans and waited for the miracle: that giant gasoline tanker truck with its ten thousand liters. They assailed headquarters, vigorously guarded by both French and Germans. I watched them and I watched the Germans tirelessly; one or two hours passed. The Dutchman returned; he had started to stand in line at the garage and then gotten tired of it. He told me that some German trucks would take people to Paris, and I jumped at it, resolved to get back on my own, if possible. I ran through town as far as the place de la Cathédrale; everywhere the same spectacle of refugees and soldiers. On the place de la Cathédrale, people were sitting on the ground, just waiting, but nobody knew whether trucks would pass and when. I went back to the people [with the car]; we had a drink in another large café crowded with soldiers and then convinced the Dutchman to return to the garage and try to get some gasoline. We all went there, in a procession, the mother-in-law groaning and apologizing to me for her son-in-law's incompetence. In front of the garage an impossible line—we stood about for a while, then I suggested that the mother-in-law and I go and get some food, which we did. I passed by the train station and was told that there would be a train for Paris the next morning at half past eight and to be there at six if I wanted a ticket. We bought some bread and cold cuts—in the pastry shops young Germans were gorging themselves on ice cream and candies. Always this tremendous impression of youth and happiness; I didn't know the difference between the green uniforms and those beautiful, sharp gray ones that left the neck free and were of an infinitely more elegant cut—but in Le Mans the soldiers were almost all in gray.[3]

Again we went to a sidewalk café where we waited until eight o'clock. Finally the Dutchman came back with his wife and five liters of gasoline. We took off. I couldn't describe the relief I felt leaving that torrid caravanserary. Driving through open countryside we began to wonder where we would sleep. Then around nine o'clock we veered off the main road toward a farmhouse. We were told that the night before, ten cars with refugees had stopped there, but this night we and a carload of Belgians were the only ones. We ate a little and slept in the straw.

I am now at the Dôme. It is close to four o'clock; there are some customers on the terrace, among them the Swiss sculptor,* the woman from the Hoggar, the once beautiful woman who was wearing strange golf pants and a small hood, but on the whole few familiar faces. And starting an hour ago there has been a constant stream of Germans. In the abstract it feels strange thinking: the Germans at the Dôme, but it remained abstract. There are lots of them, but scattered nevertheless; their faces are so completely dull that I feel nothing looking at them. It amazes me a little because for the last two days I have been filled with a host of violent impressions. I must say that they were much closer to us then, our lives were mingled with theirs, we felt solidarity; and besides, they were in action. Here, they were tourists,

---

* Giacometti.

reserved, foreigners. We don't feel their collective force and as individuals they are of no interest to me. Generally speaking, I don't feel anything today about all those great cataclysms—was it because I was tired from being in it up to my neck these last two days?

All day long, airplanes have been flying over low, skimming the rooftops, with huge crosses painted under their shiny wings.

Half past five—I stayed at the Dôme reading *Le Drageoir d'Or* [The Golden Drageoir]—the place is now full, both inside and on the terrace—a few whores, three or four looking for German customers and scoring some success.

On *Saturday, June 29,* I woke up in a stable where we had spent the night. It was a little cool, but I had slept rather well. The other women woke up moaning and groaning, especially the old woman whose rheumatism and sciatic nerve bothered her—and the young woman said in her obnoxious voice, "Those naughty Germans—ah, if we had those little Krauts right here, we would whack them!"—her husband remarked drearily that the straw had pricked his knees during the night. We went to have a bite to eat—the farmer's wife made us pay for the eggs and milk, but very tactfully. It was seven o'clock; the ground was covered with dew—the countryside, the barnyard, and the sense of adventure—all this was pleasant. But I was beginning to get exasperated from being with these people and I wondered anxiously if we would find gasoline at La Ferté-Bernard. There were refugees at the farm, people from Pontoise who had fled haphazardly and ended up stopping there—they said that the towns in the area, La Ferté, Nogent, etc., had been pillaged, not by the Germans, but by the retreating French soldiers.

We took off; the main highway was already terribly crowded—the cars with their inevitable mattress strapped to the roof, trucks, and especially carts that I had seen for the first time on blvd. St. Michel and that had wrung my heart. They had been loaded once more with hay, and the women, with blank stares and white kerchiefs tied around their heads, were sitting among the bicycles and mattresses while the men were walking alongside the horses. Many bicycles were on the road as well, and some pedestrians, but few.

At eight o'clock we arrived at La Ferté-Bernard—again broken-down cars on the square, refugees sitting on their suitcases, children, bundles. The German trucks that had brought them from Le Mans had left them there for the night. They were hoping that other trucks would pass. And again, people were uselessly carrying empty gasoline cans around and rumor had it that there wouldn't be any gasoline that day. I therefore decided to get home on my own. I ran all the way to the railroad station, two kilometers from there. As I arrived at half past eight, I saw a train pulling into the station. I thought it was the one coming from Le Mans and going to Paris and I wanted to rush to it, but was held back. They were railroad employees who were being taken back to Paris. There were many empty coaches, but they wouldn't let anyone on board. Besides, there was a sudden order that no passengers bound for Paris would be allowed to board; paying customers only would be taken as far as Chartres, and even for Chartres you had to prove that you were domiciled there. I waited a while—some people had been coming there every morning for several days now and leaving again disappointed. The employees were saying that Paris had no food supplies and that this was the reason for refusing to repatriate the refugees. It seemed strange considering that the newspapers and the radio told everyone to go back home, that German trucks did not hesitate to take people back, and that, moreover, the cities between Angers and Paris were without any food supplies so that people would be much more likely to die there than in Paris. The rumor spread at the station that the British had bombed Le Mans during the night. Strange. What was certain, however, was that I was decisively refused any ticket whatsoever. I went back to the city, feeling disheartened. I sat on the car's running board; the sun was beginning to beat down. I wanted to buy something to eat, but all the shops were completely bare; I found only some coarse and overly salted bread of which I ate a huge piece in a melancholic mood. The [Dutch] people returned. They had been told that for the next three days there wouldn't be any gasoline—my heart sank—I again told the old dry-cleaner woman that I would entrust my suitcase to her and decided to leave no matter how. The only way, in fact, was to find a vehicle. I was 170 km from Paris—it's easy to say, "I'll walk there if I have to," but 170 km on a blacktop road with the sun beating down is a discouraging distance and it seems awfully futile to put one foot in front of the other. And yet, there were crowds of refugees who did 400 km on foot. For a moment I remained stupidly seated, afraid of not being able to get back home, yet somewhat content to be thrown into a common adventure as a result, almost without any privilege—in fact, I did have the great privilege of having 1,000 francs in my purse, which made it possible for me to remain there without harm—but to get anywhere, money was useless. The day before, people had been asked to pay 1,500 francs to be repatriated, and I think that on this day even for that price you wouldn't have found a vehicle. In that sense I was really on an equal footing. So I waited; two volunteers, with armbands over their sleeves, stood in the middle of the road. They stopped all cars that seemed to have some room, but in fact, none had any to spare. Finally a German truck stopped; two women made a dash for it, and so did I. The German laughed and said that there was only room for three more, and as the two women had gotten on, I also climbed on board. The truck was headed for Mantes and I was so exhausted that the name no longer meant anything to me—but they said that it was forty kilometers from Paris and that was a lot closer. I was quite content, alone, and without luggage in this German truck that was speeding down the road. However, the truck was covered with a heavy tarpaulin and loaded with gasoline cans, a crowd of people, and stifling hot. I was sitting on a suitcase in the back of the truck facing backward and jolted by the bumps in the road. Soon I felt terribly sick and somewhat anxious, because it was impossible to get out from under the tarpaulin to an opening—I decided to vomit in the space between my feet among the gasoline containers. It's amazing, by the way, how it relieves the unpleasantness of a situation when there are no longer any social constraints at all, nor any inhibitions, and people consider vomiting a natural function—in four or five painful heaves I vomited up all the heavy bread I had eaten—thank heavens, the truck stopped half an hour later—I sat and even stretched out at the side of the road while the other people ate. A German tapped me on the shoulder, asking me if I wanted to eat something. Since I said I wouldn't he didn't insist and an hour later was kind enough to wake me up. There was an old woman refugee who said that for two days those truck drivers had showered them with cigarettes, food, and champagne; and the fact was that they were as nice as they could be, polite and discreet, eager to be of service while being completely unaware that they were personifying German generosity.

I had the bright idea of asking the next truck, which was not covered, if I could get on. At first I was facing backward and everything went well as long as the truck was moving, but when it stopped I felt funny—then I sat facing forward and I had a beautiful sunny ride all the way to Mantes. There was a pleasant Tunisian woman with gorgeous black hair riding in the truck with me. We passed Nogent-le-Rotrou, which had been heavily damaged; Chartres, where only a few streets had been affected; and Dreux, almost intact. The roads were pockmarked with large shell holes—and everywhere German trucks that merrily passed us; I remember one in particular where the soldiers, dressed in gray, wore sumptuous red roses; they often shouted, "Heil!" in passing—and everywhere, endlessly, a procession of refugees and hay carts, broken-down cars, upturned or burned-out vehicles—it offered a gripping overall view of France after the battle, at least of a certain corner of France. We arrived in Mantes around four o'clock and the Germans helped us get down from the truck. I turned around, somewhat bewildered, and had the good fortune of noticing a Red Cross car that seemed ready to leave—I asked whether there were any trains for Paris, and they offered me a ride. I got in and sat in the back between a particularly fashionable nurse, a certain Miss de Hérédia, who wouldn't let you forget it, and a large bespectacled boss lady. In front sat another nurse and the driver, a certain Mr. de ... I don't know what, with uncertain attributes. All through the trip they discussed with an idiotic seriousness the merits of amateur and professional nurses, but I learned several interesting things: First they discussed the crazy panic that had taken hold of all military medical officers; it seemed that all over France they were fleeing days ahead of everyone else, leaving the nurses in the lurch. The flight of the British and the French: one of them said that for three weeks she had never let go of her revolver because soldiers had mobbed her car in order to commandeer it and get away faster—everywhere the same tune about this extraordinary and frenzied debacle. They also described the fires around Paris and in Etampes, where two lines of cars caught in a traffic jam had gone up in flames; and the exodus of refugees and inadequate emergency relief services; and about the ridiculous civil defense: it appeared that the Germans laughed at the sight of our trenches, which had been dug as shelters with only a few centimeters of soil covering them. They were fanatically Anglophobe.

We made a stop at St. Germain. I was exhausted, my mind in pieces—I saw myself in a mirror and noticed that I looked frightfully dirty. We had peppermint drinks on the terrace of a small café-tabac. The town was completely dead, all shutters closed—this impression of death that gripped me did not leave me until Paris. I saw blown-up bridges over the Seine, signs of bombs, collapsed houses, and everywhere a desert-like silence. Driving up avenue de la Grande Armée I felt like crying. We passed rue François 1er and noticed people lined up in front of the Red Cross office for news about prisoners—I also saw several lines in front of butcher shops, but almost all the shops were closed; I had never expected to find such emptiness; it was appalling.

They let me off on rue Vavin—my landlady* let out cries of despair because she had thrown out all my belongings—she gave me a letter from Sartre dated June 9. I went to my room and had a long crying spell. For three weeks I hadn't looked at his photos or his handwriting. This old letter of another time was still optimistic—it was the last echo; after that there was only silence. I realized how strongly I had hoped to find Sartre, all smiles, waiting for me at the Dôme as soon as I arrived—it was sheer folly—but there were all these nerve-wracking stories about soldiers, dressed in civilian clothes,

---

* The owner of her hotel.

who were coming home when least expected. But nothing was waiting for me; it was the same solitude as in La Pouèze, only more irreparable. Somehow I composed myself and went out to try to phone from the post office. On the way I met my father on the terrace of the Daumesnil. I was completely bewildered and my eyes were burning. I had a sandwich and a glass of beer—there were a few Germans on the terrace, but all in all they were few; they were far less close than at La Pouèze. My father agreed that they were very polite; he said that naturally Paris had only German news—and also that all foreign currencies were frozen and everything was at a standstill. Also that the prisoners would surely not be released, that they would be held in huge camps where they would starve to death. I felt myself caught in a trap, tossed about in space and time, without a future, without hope. I left him. The post office was closed—I went to see the Bosts.* The Flore was closed; there were a few customers on the terrace of the Deux Magots. The Bosts had left, but I was told that the pastor and his wife were at Taverny and I decided that, too bad, I would courageously go there. Then I went to see my mother, who sobbed when she saw me. They woke my old grandmother. They were so shattered that their hatred of the Krauts no longer worked, no longer even existed: my father even tried to understand—they were wild with anger at the British. However, they told stories, certainly false, about people loitering in the streets being shot at, but there was no more question of "standing up to them." On the contrary, people who didn't observe the utmost care were treated as imbeciles. They told about the endless stream of refugees, and of the Germans who followed, also endlessly.

At half past nine they asked me to leave, telling me to hurry.[4] I don't believe that I have ever felt so depressed as during my walk back through the empty streets, under a stormy sky, overexcited and exhausted as I was and sure of not seeing Sartre or Bost again for a long time to come, if they hadn't starved to death along the way. I didn't even think of them anymore—but I felt so totally alone and desperate, without an objective or hope. A great cataclysm had passed through, not one that devastates the earth and leaves everything to be rebuilt, but on the contrary, one that leaves the world intact but destroys humanity. Everything was there: houses, shops, the trees in the Luxembourg Gardens, but there were no more men, there wouldn't ever be any—no one to reopen the closed-up shops, no one to walk in the streets, to rethink the past, to rebuild a future. I was there, me, an absurd survivor.

I went to bed. Fortunately I found a detective novel and managed to sleep.

---

* Pierre Bost's family, on rue de l'Abbaye.

It went better the following day. I waited for Sorokine at the Dôme until six o'clock. Afterward I went to see Zébuth just to do something, to talk to someone. I found her in her candy store, which she had just reopened, serving hot chocolate to two Germans—she had just come back; she had left in the morning and had an uneventful return, as she had been able to get gasoline. It seems that the evening of my departure three Germans soldiers had visited La Pouèze again; one of them had wanted to kiss Mops. We talked, about the prisoners essentially—in Angers she had seen a camp with twelve thousand of them; they said that they were starving to death, that they ate solely what civilians were bringing them. But I convinced myself that Sartre, being thirty-five years of age, was going to be released. I took some books with me and went to have dinner with my parents. When I returned at half past nine, I found Sorokine at my door; she had been waiting for hours. We chatted; I kept her for the night—she was so happy, so overwhelmed, and so charming that I was very touched. But she decided right away that she was going to move in with me, and she felt clingy and since I didn't sleep all night because I was on edge and because she moved too much, I hated her a little.

July 1

I am at the Dôme, tired after my return from Taverny—there are four whores who are chatting, one being almost in tears—just as in the past, they have taken over the entire front part of the café so that one has the impression of entering a bordello. They console the one who is crying, "He didn't write, but nobody writes, don't worry about it"—it's the same refrain everywhere—women in the metro, women on their doorsteps: "Do you have any news?—No, he's surely been taken prisoner—When can we see the lists?" etc. Once more I am convinced that no one would be released before the end of the war; that's all too certain. But the stories continue to circulate: "He had gotten all the way to the entrance of Paris when he was arrested—the Germans are giving them civilian clothes." So there's always the possibility of a miracle and in looking up I was expecting any minute to see Sartre or Bost, all smiles, walking across the Vavin intersection. It's as illusory as a lottery ticket and just as nerve-wracking and irresistible. It's the obsession of every woman in Paris. I had thought that this uncertainty would be unbearable, that one would go mad—but no, even here patience takes hold. Perhaps in a week we will have news and there will be lists and letters—we will wait for a week; time doesn't cost much, we are not waiting *for* something, we are just waiting for a new reason for waiting—everything is at a standstill, finished, indifferent. The weather is sultry. I am tired out and no longer want to do anything but sleep; that is the best one could wish for.

July 2nd

Every morning upon awakening, the devastating surprise of finding myself once again faced with the situation: where was Sartre? And I would remain so several minutes before comprehending how I could have lived through the previous day. I got up, got dressed, and went back to the Dôme—the weather was gray and a little chilly, everything was deserted—there were only six persons at the newsstand in the metro. I bought two of those newspapers—it's miraculous how empty they can be—always that sentimental propaganda in favor of the Germans, a tone of distressed compassion, superior, fraternal for the poor French people—and promises: the railroads would run and the postal service resume again. If at least we would receive mail. Yesterday I had a short letter from Bost* sent from Avignon—he seemed very tired, but finally he had been evacuated to Avignon, that was a tremendous relief; he would remain there for a long time of convalescence, I thought, and then would be sent home; I could expect to see him in about two weeks or a month and he wouldn't have been mistreated. In fact, I was not so much worried about him; I had figured that he must have been evacuated from Beaune very quickly.

So, yesterday, *July 1,* I had decided to go to Taverny to get news of him—the idea had occurred to me that he might already be there. It sufficed to get me going, not enough to make my heart beat faster. I hardly slept that night because of Sorokine and woke up at six o'clock, nervous and out of sorts on a gray morning like today. She insisted on coming with me and that annoyed me; she had me sit on the back of her bicycle and took me through a gray and empty Paris up to her place. It didn't work too well and I finally got off. She started to complain about a backache and I told her that I wanted to go there without her. She protested by stomping her feet the way she usually does and I got so annoyed that I broke an ink bottle that had slipped out of a package I was carrying; it shattered and stained my hands. She then became very sweet, put her bicycle down, and accompanied me on the metro only as far as Porte de la Chapelle.

I arrived there at eight o'clock. A group of refugees was waiting for trucks at the metro exit. I hesitated, wondering whether I should join them, but

---

* Wounded on May 23, he had been taken to the hospital in Beaune, then from there to Avignon.

in the end I decided to walk. I was happy to find myself alone again. This large, endless, straight avenue was not totally deserted; some refugees were following it and a few cars, but very few. Very quickly I no longer thought of anything. I followed the banks of the Seine; after St. Denis I went through Epinay. I was not too familiar with the outskirts of Paris. The area interested me all the more since I considered it a historic place as it was here that the Germans had arrived, a thoroughfare for refugees, coming and going—besides, all along the road one would hear: "We are coming from Montauban, if only we had known, we wouldn't have left, etc." People recognized and greeted each other—I saw someone on a bicycle stopping a group of people, telling them, "Your mother has already returned," and people soon gathered around him for news about the house and the mother. After Epinay I stupidly veered off toward Argenteuil; it turned into the green outskirts; soon nothing else existed but my somewhat worrisome task of walking to Taverny. It was an obstinately long-distance walk but a peaceful one, allowing me to enjoy the sun, the smell of greenery and yellow melilots. At Argenteuil it started to get very hot and I discovered that I had taken the wrong road. I had to go back to Sannois and get to Ermont. I stopped for a quarter of an hour in a bistro to eat some petits-beurre, drink a glass of lemonade, and write a note to Bost. A woman was talking about her husband, a prisoner; two women were begging a fellow to sell them potatoes, but he obstinately refused. I read *Le Matin*. I took up my walk again, following the railroad tracks—it was rather pleasant, these gardens with an abundance of roses and red currants alternating with a few meadows and wheat fields with poppies. What was strange was this blossoming life of the countryside surrounding lifeless villas—some of them having small signs posted: "Occupied Residence" or more often: "Bewohnt."

I arrived at the railway stop in Vaucelles. I was rather moved, I clearly recognized the place.* It was raining when I was here before, the cafés were crowded and it had been a pleasant adventure for me. I stopped in front of No. 32: there was "Bewohnt" written at the door and the windows were open. I went to a café to tidy up a little and write in this notebook while finishing my petits-beurre. Then, somewhat intimidated, I went to the house— I saw only an old housekeeper who said that the pastor and his wife had left for Paris to see their children. I therefore phoned the Pierre Bosts in the evening, but they weren't home; they must have been at the house of one of

---

* She had been there with Bost on Sunday, December 4, 1938, when he was on leave (during his military service in Amiens).

their sisters. I left a note: I had found out what I wanted to know, namely, that Bost wasn't there.

I took off again, this time taking the blacktop highway, hot from the sun. I was happy because I had walked twenty-five kilometers one way and was bravely walking back despite my ill-fitting shoes—but I was hot and was looking for a ride. Two refused to take me, but the third one, a small open jalopy, driven by a fellow alone, stopped eagerly. It was someone from St. Leu who had left the city and gone to Montauban on a motorcycle and had just returned: "If only we had known!" he said it too; that was the phrase one heard everywhere. He explained how difficult those seven hundred kilometers on a motorcycle had been for his wife, who had a curvature of the spine, and for him as well. "I can tell you because you are of age, but there, around my private parts, I hurt, Madame, I hurt!" He said that in the non-occupied *départements*[5] the mayors forbade people to leave, saying that they would be arrested in Vierzon and that at the border of the non-occupied *départements* they had police barricades, but people would wait for nightfall and then leave. Anyway, in Vierzon, no one had been arrested. He took me back to Paris, driving along all the banks of the Seine that I didn't know and toward the Isle of the Grande Jatte, which I beheld in amazement. It was one of those legendary places that I had thought existed nowhere. There were people canoeing and swimming; it smelled oddly of vacation time. Furthermore the season, people's nonchalance and free time, all that gave life an air of a dubious vacation, something gratuitous and unusual. As the car was stopped near a bridge, a package fell from a German truck: a big package of chocolate. The soldier smiled at us and we smiled back. On the road I saw some soldiers blithely talking with some very pretty girls and the guy said, "It looks as if there will be some little Germans in the works"—a statement I also heard ten times over and always without a tone of blame. "It's nature's way," the guy said, "there's no need to speak the same language for that." I did not see hate in anyone, only panicked and stupid fear among villagers, or my mother, for example, and when fear dissipated, people remained wide-eyed and thankful.

I got off at Pont de Neuilly and became painfully aware that I was aching all over. I went to the Dôme after leaving the metro to write a little in this notebook, then went home to sleep a while. Sorokine arrived at six o'clock, sobbing because her mother threw her out. She was counting on me to take care of her, but the idea bothered me since I didn't have any money and didn't know whether I would have any. I told her that if I received my pay I would give her five hundred francs a month for the next three months, which would be enough for her to live on, but then in October, she would go back to her mother. She stopped crying and told me lots of stories about her life in Paris since my departure. She had tried to leave Paris and convinced the student she was tutoring to have a truck chartered by her mother, but when everything was ready on Wednesday, Sorokine had moral scruples and didn't follow through because her mother was in great despair about her leaving—only after a new scene on Thursday did she decide to go ahead with it. The Germans were already at Porte de St. Cloud; they did not prevent people from getting out of Paris; she left on bicycle. For a long while she had walked on the road, alongside a German division, then she had been caught up in a long convoy of trucks and enjoined to disappear. And a little while later, she was picked up, shoved into a truck, and taken back to Paris. Germans on motorcycles were going after the refugees and forcing them to return, and taking them back home in trucks if necessary.

She also told me how for a week she had earned her living by selling newspapers—she said one could make forty-three francs a day, but that it was terribly tiring and she managed to make only twenty-five francs—there was a policeman who had befriended her and would let her buy the papers without a permit, but he disappeared, another took his place, and she had to stop. The situation in which she found herself was terrible, without a work permit, with a mother who could think of nothing but getting rid of her in order to head for Germany and find work. She also told me how she stole a beautiful bicycle, which she would give me. We were planning bicycle lessons and long rides to the outskirts of Paris.

Dinner at my parents' house—they told me, as had Zébuth, that something must have blown up Tuesday, covering all of Paris with a layer of black soot for twenty-four hours, adding still more to the appalling heavy gunfire. Naturally, the conversation turned around the dearth of any food: we had nothing but soup and macaroni for dinner. For days now I had not had a real meal. It seemed that Paris was indeed poorly supplied: neither butter nor milk, nor eggs or potatoes, often neither meat nor pork products. My father listed the menu items of the famous restaurant Gaillon: cucumber salad, 8 fr.—cheese omelet, 12 fr.—crabmeat pilaf, 20 fr.—noodles, 8 fr.—raspberries, 18 fr. And nothing else. It reminded me somewhat of the Goncourt dinners at Braibant's during the Siege of Paris.[6]

I went home with Sorokine, who was waiting for me at the door. We made two beds out of one. We spent one tender hour together—and I fell asleep dead tired.

At half past five, still at the Dôme, with some whores, Germans, and a few other people. I called Toulouse and had Mme Jollivet on the phone, who told me that Toulouse had left on foot, carrying a backpack, in the company of Zina:* that was so much like her. They had no news from her. It seemed that Dullin also had met with some misadventures, having to sleep in the open, etc. I'll go see them tomorrow.

I wrote in this notebook this morning at the Dôme—and then Sorokine showed up—in a sense she rescued me from myself and prevented me from thinking; it was a good thing, but it also weighed on me; I did not feel like making any effort—she was as nice as she could be, but already she was wearing me down. I told her that I did not want to keep her in my room and it made her sad, but things could go on like that for a month or two and I would like to regain my normal equilibrium and for that I need first and foremost my independence. We went to City Hall to find out about my salary; from there they sent me to the Sorbonne. As I was filling out some papers at the administrative office of the school district, some fellow wearing the Legion of Honor, who was, I believe, an inspector, grabbed me: "Professor of philosophy? That's just what we need!" He called Duruy[7] and I'm supposed to go there tomorrow. He promised me an advance on my salary in case I don't get paid until the end of the month and needed the money. In a way I was upset that I had let myself be caught in a trap, but then again, I did not dislike the idea entirely, eight hours of work per week, especially since it would not be tiresome. And so, I was settled in Paris at least for the month; I felt stabilized. I therefore went to the hairdresser and bought stockings and beautiful white sandals. Sorokine's company was a little depressing; she was sad that I wouldn't keep her, sad to see me being also a little glum myself. We ate at the Capoulade; it was terribly expensive: at the bar a scanty dish of ravioli cost ten francs. She told me some more things about herself—also that she knew a Jewish woman, director of seven movie houses, who was not allowed to reopen them. She was told to sell her enterprise if she could, but Jews would not be allowed to invest their capital. I went to the Dôme to find Zébuth and we talked for two hours about That Lady, Guille, and the past, and I felt that diving into all this again was something precious. Then I read the papers. It seemed that Reynaud wanted to defend Paris at all cost; Mandel and General Ruhr wanted to take the war to the colonies if necessary, but Lebrun threatened to resign if they did not follow Pétain, and Mandel

---

* Toulouse's friend and slave since childhood, her lackey.

and Ruhr were arrested. The newspapers are scandalous, urging the French to morality and to imitate Germany, etc.

A kind of life was again taking shape around me—it was interesting to see how one lived a separation like this one. At first there was a kind of suspension; the world and the entire present were put between parentheses. One is in a life with some "preferables," but against a background of total indifference—almost no living image of Sartre; a vague, stereotypical image and the very word "Sartre" reappeared without being called forth whenever I stopped being active or thinking precisely. It's somewhat like the idea one has of one's own body, for example, familiar, dull, and constant, even though often covered up by something else. Almost never evoking a possible return or reunion—often a precise idea of the ordeal he is going through, still more often a map of France, the Morsbronn area, with a vague picture of barbed-wire fences with soldiers on the inside. I see them all dressed in blue like him, but I don't picture him any more clearly than the others. All in all, what I'm waiting for most precisely, when despite everything I grasp an orientation in time, is a letter. When I feel that the week is headed for something, it's toward a letter or news. Whenever I hear people ask, where are they? when will we know? there's a lump in my throat and the desire to cry. But all this is in black and white, toneless—to me it's like having tetanus, when one is paralyzed from excessive muscle contractions. Sometimes I tell myself that I am avoiding thinking and that I should try to think, but it's like an illusion; it's not that I'm avoiding thinking, it's because there is no object to grasp; it's like sand—absence has nothing positive about it, that I knew already—and the other's misfortune is unimaginable and even less possible to grasp when it is total. As for memories, I can evoke them as much as I like; there's something like a belief in memories, an impression of belonging that has vanished; it is no longer my past, it does not touch me—this past is definitively buried, once and for all; it does not have that touching characteristic of something that might be reborn—nothing behind me, nothing in front of me—nothing on the horizon, nothing in me. The word "obsession" is absolutely inappropriate; the thought of Sartre is not obsessive at all— he is not an incessantly repeated figure, but stands out from an unfamiliar ground. There is no longer either figure or ground, only a neutral confusion; misfortune is everywhere and nowhere, there are only some physiological consciousnesses dependent mostly on fatigue and sleep: at times it may be the sun and well being, then it may be despondency, or an anguished tension. In a sense I can't even say that I'm unhappy. At the very bottom of this calmness there is still some optimism, despite everything: Sartre is alive, I don't doubt it for a second—one day I'll have news from him (I have a vague idea it'll be in two weeks, a month)—one day I'll see him again (basically, I don't think it'll go beyond a few months). Of all that I'm *sure;* if I should waver in that certainty I would be left where I was on certain days at La Pouèze. But I'm stubborn in my confidence as well as in the certainty that misfortune, fatigue, and constraints will not have harmed him a bit and that whatever the future may bring, he will always be himself. Hence, despite everything, I am at peace.

Sorokine came by at about half past six—we took the metro to the Gare de Lyon in order to pick up my suitcase at the dry-cleaning woman's place: she had not yet returned; they must have been left stranded on the road all these days. It made me shudder. We walked back on foot, chatting. I had dinner with my family and returned to my place, where Sorokine was waiting for me.

July 5

I am sitting on the terrace of the Dôme—the waiter made me leave, saying that single ladies would no longer be seated inside the restaurant; is it the start of the morality wave that is going to engulf Paris? The weather is not bad—a violinist is scratching out a waltz. The newspapers reported that diplomatic relations with England had been broken off. I have taken up my correspondence again. I wrote to Kos.; I am going to write Védrine and That Lady. I don't feel any less desperately isolated for it. Yesterday there was talk about getting the Antony barracks ready. So it seems they intend to keep the prisoners for a long time—I have unlimited time to wait. It works this way: one day after another I manage to get to the end of the day—and the days will then have made up weeks and months.

Wednesday, *July 3,* I went to the lycée Duruy after I had taken a bicycle lesson with Sorokine in the quiet back streets around rue Vavin—on the first try I stayed on the seat and even learned to get on alone and make turns. I was very proud and it was fun. I spent an hour like this and then she accompanied me to Duruy—I taught a course on mathematics, neither interesting nor boring. At noon I met up with Sorokine and we went back to Montparnasse; we discussed bicycle matters and her moving out. We spent half an hour looking for a restaurant and ended up at Rougeot, place Montparnasse, where we ate eggs and potatoes—then we talked a while on the terrace of the Dupont. And at half past two I left to see Dullin at the Atelier. I found Montmartre terribly dead. The concierge refused to let me in: "Monsieur Dullin is in no condition to receive visitors," and then she returned quite amazed, saying that I was lucky, he was waiting for me. I found him in shirtsleeves, an apron tied around his stomach, in a pile of old papers and torn-up photos and looking rather haggard. He shook my hands effusively and said how worried he was about Toulouse. He himself had left on that Tuesday heading toward Crécy-en-Brie to get old Mme Jollivet, and during that time, Toulouse, loaded with luggage, had left with Zina by taxi to the Ivry railroad station, where she caught a train. They had agreed to meet in Tours, but Dullin, not being able to get to Tours, didn't know whether she had stayed there or gone on toward Toulouse; he didn't know a thing. His own flight had been extremely difficult. Crécy had already been almost entirely evacuated when he arrived. He took the old woman with her old maid and left for the Loire. Right off they had joined the endless stream of cars, where they could barely move more than six kilometers per hour, and for thirteen days they drove around in circles without being able to cross the Loire, sleeping in the car, often shot at by machine guns, and scarcely eating. The maid went crazy; one day she was rambling on about food and wound up going into the woods saying she was going to get eggs; she was never seen again. Finally, the Germans caught up with them and made them go back. He said that people were in abject terror, and he also described, like everyone else, the pillaging committed by fleeing civilians. He himself seemed to have been rather fearful; he was convinced that the Germans would harm him if they knew who he was, and he tried to pass himself off as a peasant. It had bothered him terribly when, driving along a convoy of prisoners, he had heard them occasionally call "Dullin!" Afterward, I left him and came to the Dôme to read *Le Moulin de la Sourdine* [The Mill of the Sourdine] by Marcel Aymé, which is only slightly funny. Sorokine picked me up at six o'clock and we went in the direction of the Lion de Belfort, to look for a room for her. We found her one at 160 francs in a sordid and somewhat attractive hotel. I rode my bicycle again for a while. Then dinner at my parents' and last night with Sorokine in my hotel.

Yesterday, *Thursday, July 4,* I taught at the lycée from nine to eleven o'clock; afterward I sat on the terrace of the Deux Magots and read *Gone with the Wind,* which I found quite delightful. Lunch with the family: we had a cheese soufflé and beef and potatoes; it was wonderful. I went back to the Deux Magots to read and write to Kos.; then from five to six I rode my bicycle with fun, fatigue and success. I read the newspaper at the Dôme, which plunged me into a dark mood. I would have wanted to be alone, and the idea of having to spend four hours with Sorokine made me feel sick— and yet, she was very nice—we left on foot heading toward the Palais Royal, where I had the faint idea of checking the list of prisoners. On the way we had quarreled a little because I refused to go with her to steal a bicycle and I used this incident to shroud myself in dark silence. The Palais Royal was closed; there was a terribly long line and people had news mostly about the camps located around Paris—besides, I *knew* that Sartre was a prisoner, but I was interested only in knowing when he would be released. We headed toward the boulevard and ate a sorbet at the Café de la Paix. It was crowded with very elegant-looking German officers, but otherwise empty and totally depressing. We returned by way of place de la Concorde and the Tuileries, where we saw a crazy old woman pulling down her panties. Sorokine and I reconciled, but the mood remained somber. We took my things to my grandmother's place and dined on hard salami we had bought on the way. I went to bed, finished reading *Le Moulin de la Sourdine,* and started a detective novel. I slept almost eleven hours—in the morning I dreamt of Sartre— he was dressed as a soldier; he wanted to strangle me, and then he became gentler and I stroked his hair. I told myself, "Such a dream is too cruel at the moment" and I woke up with a terrible feeling of sorrow. It was close to eleven o'clock and I just had time to get dressed before Sorokine arrived. She told me she wasn't too delighted with the way she spent her days; she thought that she clung too much to me and felt filthy. We went out shopping for bread, apple turnovers, etc., and ate some salami and rice that she had cooked, but half of which she had spilled on the floor. ("Do you have news from your fiancé?" "No, like everybody else." "Did you go check the list of prisoners?" "There are two hundred names, it's not worth the bother." That's all you hear, and it's true, it's much less painful to think that it is a common fate—it suppresses worries, provides the certainty that it will change, and helps to be patient. But as the woman said, it's when the first letters start to arrive that it will be terrible.)

After lunch we went to the library of the Sorbonne, where I read a voluminous and interesting work on Debussy. Then I came here—I have a headache from hunger, I think. I'll go to dinner shortly—I had dinner on the terrace of the Dôme, some lamb and a glass of wine—then I went home without my headache letting up. Sorokine came over around nine o'clock and stayed an hour. I went to sleep almost immediately, and slept like a log.

Saturday, July 6

Single ladies are indeed welcome at the Dôme; what happened was that the waiter had taken me for a whore—on the other hand, a notice in German declared the establishment off-limits to Germans; I was wondering why; in any case, I was glad not to see those uniforms anymore.

I slept heavily this morning; I got up at eight o'clock, limp and terribly sad. I walked down rue Froidevaux; I remembered when during Sartre's last home leave we were walking down the same street and I told him that by his presence alone he was returning to me the view of the entire world—I drank a coffee at Rey's and walked all the way to the lycée Duruy, where I taught two classes. From there I walked to the Deux Magots, where I began to pick up my story, my history since June 10. I tried to read Aldanov's book *Le 9 Thermidor,* but it was unreadable. Lunch at home where I had a postcard from Kos. from June 30, a little terse, perhaps because it was sent without an envelope—it gave me a little shock to have regained contact with her—there was also a long letter from Poupette addressed to Mom, rather ridiculous, but I was nevertheless pleased that she had received news from us; I felt a little less imprisoned. Boring lunch—I walked to the Bibiothèque Nationale, where I got a reader's card and read for a while in Rabelais, who amused me while I was waiting for books on Hegel. I worked for two hours on Hegel with Wahl's book on the unhappy consciousness and the *Phenomenology of Spirit;* at the moment I understand almost nothing. I decided to go to the Bibliothèque Nationale every day from two to five o'clock and work on Hegel. It's the most soothing activity I could find. First of all the very setting reminded me in a poetic way of the year of my *agrégation.*[8] Then there's the reality of books, of the ideas in the books and about human history of which this is only a moment—I felt more assured in the world than I had for a long time.

I returned home on foot and by metro—at rue Vavin I found two old letters from Kos., one dated June 10 and one from June 11; she was depressed, living in the midst of people crushed by fear—and I had a letter from Bost, from Thursday, the thirteenth, which really shook me up—he still believed in victory, as I did that day; it was in the evening that Reynaud gave his foreboding speech that killed any hope. But even so, he talked chillingly about a potential defeat and long separations to envision. Alas! As far as Bost was concerned, I still felt him near; he was surely going to be sent home soon. But Sartre, how far away he was—there were moments when it seemed that the only fitting behavior for me was to throw myself on the bed and remain there crying until his return or until death. Ever since this year the idea of dying no longer seems at all outrageous to me. What is especially terrible when looking at death is its reflection on life, the desolation, the abandonment in which life seems shrouded then—it causes such disgust that living and dying seem to be exactly the same thing, that in any case one is never more than a corpse in waiting.

I couldn't even say that I desire or need to see Sartre. In the state I find myself, there isn't even room for desiring other things. What I envision is a total world revolution—so brutal that my mind is almost too sluggish to even imagine it—the idea may be hard to take both because it boggles my mind and because we don't believe in it enough.

I wrote the continuation of the story, the history of June 10; I started *L'Imaginaire** and telephoned Dullin; he had gone to Crécy, which had been horribly sacked by the French. He had heard about Toulouse's presence in the Tours area and wanted to head out there, catching a ride in a truck.

Sorokine arrived at seven o'clock, a bit morose. We studied math for one hour, which amused both of us. I noticed that I still could remember many things. Afterward we went home; we ate a little pâté and settled down in my room, where I told her stories about my youth. We went to bed at ten o'clock and spent two pleasant hours together—she said that she still dreaded the future but was happy seeing that I truly liked being with her for several hours each day without getting annoyed. I slept poorly, having many dreams involving Sartre; they weren't exactly nightmares, but they were definitely unpleasant.

Sunday, July 7

Always the feeling of distress upon awakening—I slept as late as possible; I got up at half past nine; Sorokine and I went to have coffee on the avenue d'Orléans. Afterward I went to get her bicycle and for an hour I rode it around, to the Parc Montsouris and back, then to the Closerie des Lilas and back. I really handled it with ease, except one time I crashed into a dog and another time I collided with two women, and I was very happy. Afterward I walked to the Dôme—I passed a convoy of armored vehicles loaded with Germans dressed in black whose large berets fluttered in the wind—it was rather beautiful and sinister. Then here, on the terrace, I read some Hegel.[9]

---

* [A book by Jean-Paul Sartre] published in April 1940.

I found a passage that I copied and that would work marvelously as the epigraph for my novel.* I still have great difficulties understanding, especially when reading selected passages, but I'm beginning to see something emerging. As a result I felt the desire to study philosophy, to finish my novel, and the desire also, alas, to talk with Sartre.

I went back inside the Dôme for lunch, to write to Kos. and write in this notebook.

Potatoes in unlimited quantities are again available in Paris, also meat and, often, even butter—and at the Dôme dining has returned to normal. One is no longer aware of any food shortages. What I really would like is to see a good movie, but those being shown now are impossible.

I spent the afternoon reading and around five o'clock left again on bicycle. I went by rue de Charenton to see if the dry cleaner had finally returned— she was back, but not at home. I returned exhausted because the little back streets are very badly paved and the larger ones too. I found Sorokine at my place making fried potatoes; I also found a pile of letters: one from Védrine, who was wondering whether or not she should return to Paris—and six from Bost, all written in Avignon and Carpentras; until the seventeenth or eighteenth they were sent through. It was painful to see the range of his off-duty travel shrinking:† at first Angers and L'Aigle, then Angers alone, then Marseilles and finally there was no more off-duty travel at all. It made me feel very tender and sad; and the separation swept down on me worse than ever before. This, added to my state of fatigue, made me awfully edgy. I was annoyed with Sorokine because she herself had looked annoyed because of the letters and didn't breathe a word to me about them, because I knew that she required smiles and a good mood from me and, more to the point, because I had to see her while I wanted to be alone. That caused a huge and absurd scene lasting four hours, which for me was also somewhat a way of filling the time. First we ate the fried potatoes while stewing in our anger. Then I explained *Eupalinos* by Valéry; she had her pouting and stubborn look while I was scornful and ironic; we kept this up for one hour with rage in our hearts. It came to a blow because of one of my letters that I wanted to reread, and that she prevented me from rereading out of argumentativeness, and that I then tore up into little pieces. Afterward a sort of reconciliation, but we could no longer find any conversation topic. I finally shook myself out of it a bit, but she refused to talk; she held my hands and rubbed her

---

* The one quoted in the beginning of this notebook 6.
† Progressively, as the Germans advanced.

head while I was knotted up with fury; from which came a thousand little bursts of rage. In the end, as she was saying that I disgusted her spread out in my easy chair as I was, I just yelled at her at the top of my voice. She left the room and for half an hour I read my detective novel. After that it was a quarter to eleven and it was time for her to leave; I looked for her in the apartment without being able to find her at first; then I discovered her sitting all hunched up in a corner of the kitchen, shaking with rage. I told her to leave; she said she would stay there and she almost pummeled me with her fists. I managed to throw her out, saying that I wouldn't see her for a week if she didn't leave—she left saying she would sleep on the stairs. I went to bed; I read and after half an hour she rang the bell—she wanted "to talk," but I fiercely refused; I gave her a mattress, first in my room, then in the anteroom, and went to sleep.

Monday, July 8

The next morning we greeted each other amiably—she accompanied me to Rey's, where I had breakfast before going to Duruy—three hours of classes— she met me afterward, we had lunch together at the Milk Bar and I started to explain to her the reason for my rage of the previous day; her total indifference with respect to my own life added to an infantile tyranny. She accompanied me to the Bibliothèque Nationale, a little despondent, which I didn't mind at all, but nevertheless full of goodwill, which touched me.

I read Hegel's *Phenomenology* and Wahl's book; I still didn't understand much—afterward I went back to get the bicycle and went for a two-hour ride in the rue des Francs-Bourgeois area—it went well. It was pleasant to ride around Paris in this way; the city is beginning to be full of people again. I stopped for an hour to finish reading a detective novel and drink a Xerès at the Deux Magots. Dinner at my parents' home. Returned on foot with Sorokine and pleasant conversation in a café on avenue d'Orléans.

Thursday, July 11

A penciled note from Sartre in an open envelope with a postmark from the postal service and a stamp from the Paris government—for a moment I didn't recognize the handwriting—and then I looked without understanding at the letter itself that seemed to have been placed there: as if I were giving myself time for understanding before letting the emotion itself rise up. And then the emotion didn't come—I had the happy feeling of presence: the presence of paper, of the handwriting and an abstract joy, like a coupon to cash in for joy without it's being born exactly. He said that perhaps he would be home before the end of the month, but it remains a maybe—he said for me to write, but I'm not sure the letter will reach him—he said that he wasn't unhappy, but that's natural; basically, I don't know how he is. This letter is so much, and it is nothing—it's an affirmation, a positive reality, but I don't know what reality, a something that is there, but without determination. I turned it over in my hands, indefinitely; it seemed to me that other riches ought to come out of it, that the world around me ought to have changed, but nothing had moved, to the point that I could signify this change only by a sort of personal ruse, by myself changing the order of my day, by not going to the Bibliothèque Nationale, by planning a walk, a letter, etc. A useless effort to create a revision of the world based on this piece of information: "I am a prisoner, I am not unhappy." Basically, the negative liberation I received from this had been at work for a long time; I knew that Sartre was alive and a prisoner and I trusted in his good health and the solid head on his shoulders. Nevertheless, I was breathing more easily. I could envision more firmly the days ahead.

I couldn't write a long letter, I wasn't sure it would reach him, but I was going to work more arduously on this notebook now that it has a certain future.

Tuesday, July 9—I went to the lycée by bicycle and considered it not a mean feat. Two hours of classes, then by bicycle to the Dôme, where I did some reading, then lunch with Sorokine—I rode the bicycle to the Bibliothèque Nationale to work on Hegel for three hours—then went for a long ride from the library to the place de l'Etoile, to the Pont de Neuilly and all along the quays down to Auteuil; the weather was lovely; I rolled along and was enchanted to be able to go on a real outing. I arrived in Auteuil tired and content. I drank lemonade and met Sorokine at the home of one of her pupils to listen to some music: *Quartet* by Debussy, Concerto No. 2 by Bach, Concerto for Bassoon by Mozart, the *Fidelio Overture,* and some Strauss. I loved hearing music and the entire afternoon made up a happy whole: Hegel, bicycle, music—but interrupted by frightening German chatter (against foreigners, Jews, in favor of work, etc.).

I walked back with Sorokine taking the long rue de la Convention, completely deserted—it would have been quite pleasant, this solitude in the early evening, if we hadn't had to hurry so much. We ended up on avenue d'Orléans, I on bicycle and she trotting alongside, pursued by the voice of loudspeakers. She slept at my place: tender conversations, tender embraces—she was really charming and I was indeed fond of her. The following day,

Wednesday, *July 10,* I woke up at eight o'clock, still a little sleepy, but I got up because I wanted to go on a long bicycle ride. I left in the direction of Porte de Vanves, then toward Clamart: the woods were full of Germans doing their drills; it's true it seemed as if they were automatons made of steel. The weather was lovely, but the terrain had too many ups and downs, too many narrow paths in bad condition—it was exhausting and not too interesting. I returned by way of Chaville, Porte de St. Cloud, from where I reached home in twenty-five minutes. Lunch—went with Sorokine on foot to the Bibliothèque Nationale—reading of Hegel—return on foot. Two hours of reading at the Dôme, dinner. I read *Dieu est-il français?* [Is God French?] by Sieburg—it seems that Sieburg is among those who are holding sway over Paris at the moment—the book is not very interesting, but it was amusing to see that he praises France for precisely the attributes for which *Le Matin* pedantically criticizes the country—amusing also to see him write in 1930 that only after anti-Semitism had disappeared from Germany would that country gain consciousness of itself as a nation. Sorokine showed up at half past eight—even though I had a headache, I managed to be nice to her. We stayed for a while, then went up to her little room where we talked tenderly. I went home and very voluptuously read a detective novel in bed.

This morning I got up in a very melancholy mood and went to the lycée—last night too, I was so sad that I was near tears. I had breakfast at Rey's—emptiness, contingence—two hours of classes, then went back to the hotel where I read Sartre's letter. I started a reply when Sorokine came by—we went to lunch together and she started to sulk because I refused to show her Védrine's letter—as she was pouting I took up my book and she left like a fury. I finished my meal and my detective novel and wrote in this notebook.

Thursday, July 25

I stopped writing in this notebook for a long time—I'll try to retrace chronologically the events of the month.

On *Thursday, July 11,* I received Sartre's letter—and had a quarrel with Sorokine at lunch. I remember well the exciting, almost happy, tense day that I had: I had been at the post office of rue du Louvre asking whether I could write to Sartre; they said that I could and I sent a card and two letters, one after the other, written in the green café that I like so much, near the place des Victoires—then I walked about in the streets. I can still see the place de la Concorde crowded with German sailors and soldiers in black uniforms.

I walked up the Champs-Élysées. I wrote another letter from the Deux Magots. I believe it was that evening that I had dinner with my parents and listened to some music: a symphony by Schumann, amazingly mundane; the *Pathétique*; *Le Coq d'Or* by Rimsky-Korsakoff, which was pleasant; and *The Firebird*. Of course, it was extremely difficult to get a little silence: my mother beat time with her head or her hand—Papa gave commentaries or talked with Grandma. What's charming is that my mother, when she wants to talk to me, speaks in a low voice to respect my concentration. I returned to my place rather late, around half past ten, sure of finding Sorokine there and determined to quickly settle the explanation. When I rang, she opened the door, her head all soapy (the keys were under the door, she had taken them); wild with anger at having to wait for me, she had found nothing better to do than shampooing her hair in the bathroom. I told her to hurry in order to be ready on time and that I didn't want to keep her there. She hurried, full of anger, but at the last minute she no longer wanted to leave and I had to shove her bodily out the door. Ten minutes later she started to ring the bell while the renter below, outraged by all the noise we made, hollered that I had absolutely no manners. I wasn't angry, but I felt mean, and to infuriate Sorokine further I left her on the doorstep, where she rang the bell for half an hour while I was reading my detective novel—when I opened the door for her, her face was still smudged and teary, she was touching, but really too hard to handle. I threw her the bedding in the anteroom and gave her a speech in a dry and dignified tone of voice that left her speechless and overcome with rage—all night long she wandered about in the apartment. I hardly slept. At half past seven she woke me "to bury the hatchet" and that exasperated me so much that I threw her out by force—she ran off terror-stricken.

That was *Friday, July 12*—I slept, went to the Dôme to write to Sartre again, and went to the Bibliothèque Nationale to work on Hegel. I don't remember what I did in the meantime, but I met Sorokine at the Dôme rather late; we talked in a depressed mood. I had become friends with her again, but she was crushed and slightly dignified, and I was on the defensive. Dinner and music at my parents' house (Jannequin, Gabrielli, Bach, and Debussy's *Nocturne*)—afterward I met Sorokine, who accompanied me on foot to my apartment, still depressed.

On *Saturday, July 13*, lycée until noon—then to the Bibliothèque Nationale; I wrote to Sartre, and in the evening Sorokine and I reconciled and had a talk, but I don't remember where nor how. I think we went for a short walk.

On *Sunday, July 14*, Paris was depressing, I remember—it was raining—I spent part of a miserable morning at the Dôme, but like a good student I

wrote up my notes on Hegel—that interested me more and more. I telephoned Dullin—I felt such a great need to talk to someone, to do something, to change. I was astonished to hear Toulouse's voice; we agreed to
see each other at six o'clock the very same day. I lunched with my parents
and wrote to Sartre at the Deux Magots. I went home, took a nap, did my
nails, and picked up Sorokine at five o'clock. She was meek as a lamb, really
charming, and together we went to Montmartre.

At six o'clock I was at Toulouse's. She was in a house robe, looking puffy
but rather healthy. Dullin, in an all-silk robe and looking radiant, was there
along with Mme Jollivet and Vandéric. Vandéric had been in the Belgian
army and he told us how they were sent to the front lines, with no weap-
ons at all, how they were left there, and how after three days they were told
to leave again, still without being armed. Toulouse told me about her trip:
on Tuesday she had the bright idea of sending her packages to Tours. They
probably have been lost; they contained a pile of manuscripts and notes—for
her. She left with Zina, each with a backpack and carrying the suitcase with
Friedrich and Albrecht.* They headed first toward Melun, and then toward
Nevers, all by train in two days without much trouble. Then they wanted to
go up to Châteauroux, from there to Tours; they managed to get there by
truck, but it was already getting more difficult. Tours was almost deserted;
the bridges were being mined, and every night the city was bombed. They
were able to get rooms in a big hotel and found a restaurant—but the post
office was closed and there was no way to contact Dullin, the meeting place
being at the *poste restante* window, and they finally left the city. They found a
train somewhere outside the city, a train without an engine that had arrived
from Juvisy from time immemorial and where people were slowly rotting
on the spot. They got on the train. The Germans were expected during the
night and people were shaking with fright. Several hours later, Toulouse,
disgusted, left the train and asked the railroad crossing guard for shelter; he
put them in the woodshed. The next day they found a room and stayed there
for quite a while, sewing peasant dresses for themselves and being bored to
death. Meanwhile the train's occupants gradually drifted away. One night a
colonel arrived to alert them that there would be "a brief artillery battle" the
following day and advised them to seek shelter. So they all went to sleep in
a cave and when the brief battle was finished the next day, they went home.
Toulouse thought she should pass herself off as the railroad crossing guard's
sister-in-law (Védrine had the same concern in Quimper), harboring the

---

* Toulouse's mascot puppets.

strange idea that the Germans had who knows what dark future in store for them. And so she lived there—when she wanted to get back to Paris, she was told that it was impossible because the main body of the German army, after having moved down toward Bordeaux as if on parade grounds, was moving back to Paris and occupying the entire road—she was nevertheless able to send a letter and then get back home on a truck. It seemed that when Dullin learned that there was a letter, he dropped all the packages he was carrying and started shaking so hard that Mme Jollivet thought he was going to faint—as she was telling this, she added rancorously that during the preceding days "they had been like animals sick with the plague," avoiding talking to and even looking at each other.

I stayed only until half past eight—I met up with Sorokine; we were hungry and I would have liked to eat something, but we found that the boulevards, the place du Tertre, and all the restaurants were jam-packed with Germans. So we went back on foot while eating only some rolls.

On *Monday, July 15,* I taught my classes, then worked on Hegel. I was thinking that Védrine might come; I telephoned several times; I felt a little like seeing her and Kos. also, the desire for people, for changes—it was raining mercilessly. I had to eat at my parents' home—perhaps it was there that I listened to Debussy (*Pagode, L'Ile enchantée, Arabesques,* and the Sonata for harp, oboe, and flute). I must have gone home with Sorokine and spent a tender evening with her.

Tuesday, July 16—Lycée, Hegel—I had made a date with Sorokine at the Dôme for a quarter past five (I had used the bicycle all day, and had fun) and when I arrived she told me that Védrine had been looking for me everywhere, but she had put her on the wrong track by sending her to my grandmother. That annoyed me because I had wanted to see Védrine. I finally found her at the Dôme and we spent a moment together. She told me that she had spent ten days with a peasant woman gathering green peas covered with fleas (in order to get out of Quimper and avoid the Germans). I was disappointed seeing her again, as I always am when I have expected from people I don't know what plenitude that only Sartre or Bost could give me. I had also been disappointed at Toulouse's the evening before.

I went home to listen to the Ravel *Quartet* and a very beautiful Mozart festival (Concerto for Bassoon, Symphony in G, *The Magic Flute,* Concerto for Piano)—but I didn't listen very well, excited as I was by the immense bundle of letters that was forwarded to me from La Pouèze—letters from Kos., Sorokine, Poupette, Bost, and even Sartre: an old letter, but one in which he envisioned the defeat with a kind of serenity. As a result I found myself very serene also and, thanks to this note coming from so far, more confident than I had been in a long time. I wrote to him from the Dôme after leaving my parents' place.

On *Wednesday, July 17,* I wrote letters and wrote up my notes at the Dôme, then went to the Bibliothèque Nationale, which now opens at ten in the morning. Hegel. I started on the *Logic.* I met Védrine at place du Trocadéro and we returned on foot to St. Germain-des-Prés—we had dinner at the Casque and a drink at the Deux Magots. Long conversation in which I expounded to her a lot of ideas inspired by Hegel that helped me to accept without distress the present situation—she annoyed me a little as she always does with her bias for despair and her sensitivity to purely social appearances (that she was capable of crying because the British fired at the fleet at Oran, etc.). I met Sorokine at ten o'clock at the Dôme and took her home with me; she was a little upset that my red-haired friend was there and at first we talked in slightly caustic terms, but in the end everything ended tenderly.

On *Thursday, July 18,* I went to the lycée on bicycle and returned the same way in a heavy rain. At the hotel I had a note from Kos. announcing her return. She quickly came down from her room; we went to the Dôme. She was wearing a beautiful new raincoat and a red kerchief; she looked very pleasant and I was happy to see her—she narrated the events in her childlike and unexpected manner. But as soon as I started commenting, it was easy to detect a stubborn antagonism between us. She had a terrible trip, six hours' standing room only in a train where even the restrooms were crowded with people so that the children relieved themselves through the door and the old ladies right on the floor. We went to the Deux Magots, then to the Palais Royal, where I was to meet Védrine at five o'clock—I stayed for only half an hour with her. I also saw Sorokine, who, seeing me with Kos. at the Dôme at eleven this morning, had taken her bicycle back without breathing a word about it and left very dignified in her awful black oilskin raincape. She found malicious pleasure in announcing Kos.'s presence in Paris to Védrine and sending her some poisonous barbs. I met Kos. in a driving rain. We stayed in a café for a while—we returned to Montparnasse, then to my place where we had some tea. We went to sleep in the same bed, but each of us had great difficulty sleeping.

Friday, July 19*

---

* The notebook stops here.

NOTES

1. The passages are from Hegel 1939b. The passages are translated from the German by A. V. Miller as follows: "In so far as it is the action of the *other,* each seeks the death of the other. . . . Thus the relation of the two self-conscious individuals is such that they prove themselves and each other through a life-and-death struggle. They must engage in this struggle, for they must raise their certainty of being *for themselves* to truth, both in the case of the other and in their own case. . . . Similarly, just as each stakes his own life, so each must seek the other's death, for it values the other no more than itself; its essential being is present to it in the form of an 'other,' it is outside of itself and must rid itself of its self-externality" (Hegel 1977, 113–14).

2. Ernst von Salomon, born in 1902, was only sixteen years old at the end of the First World War. But as an aspiring officer, trained in the harsh Prussian school, he was disgusted by the scorn that the populace showed for the soldiers at the front and by the occupation of his country by the allied—often colonial—troops.

3. The regular German army had green uniforms and the German air force wore gray ones.

4. There was a curfew.

5. Administrative divisions of France.

6. Reference to the Franco-Prussian War, 1870–71, when Prussian troops laid siege to Paris, which capitulated after the long siege. The insurrection of the Commune followed.

7. The lycée-collège Victor Duruy, which was from 1820 to 1905 a girls' school directed by the Congrégation des Dames du Sacré-Cœur, became in 1912 a public lycée for girls, and in 1970, a co-ed school.

8. Beauvoir passed this prestigious and competitive graduate teaching exam in philosophy in March 1929.

9. Hegel 1939a, a volume of selected passages.

NOTEBOOK 7

September 20, 1940 – January 29, 1941

Friday, September 20, 1940

This is a letter that I'm starting for you—perhaps you'll have it a year from now. I'm writing to you because I'm finished waiting for you—now I know that you won't appear from behind Balzac's statue.* I waited so long for you—you would wear your blue uniform[1] and your soldier's cap, a haversack across your shoulders, and often, I don't know why, you would appear on a bicycle. I would look so intensely that once or twice I truly *believed* that you were going to materialize and cross the square, in flesh and blood. It even happened one day that I met you twice—on the place du Panthéon; I had such a shock that I thought I was going to vomit.

Now I know that I'll have to live without you—I still have no idea how I'll be able to do that. It's not at all like last year when we had started out together and I knew everything about you every day. You are in an abyss—your love for me, it exists, I know it to be alive, I can feel it—but there's absolutely nothing left that I can touch. I don't even have the desire; I'm afraid

---

* At the Vavin intersection. Sartre had promised he would show up there unexpectedly.

to see your handwriting again because it will be on a card from Germany saying "I'm well" with a sinister return address.

This time I'm unhappy. Last year I was wondering whether I could ever be unhappy—the world around me had become a tragic one, and I lived my life in accordance with this world; that wasn't unhappiness. I remember well how in September I felt just like a fragment in a large collective event—what interested me was the event and my facing it. But for a week now things have been different. I'm not connected to the world, which besides, is entirely shapeless around me. The unhappiness is within me like an intimate and specific illness. A real illness—it's not the grasping of an object, either from my life or yours. It's nothing but a series of insomnia, nightmares, tears, and headaches. Sometimes, as a reward, you appear to me on the horizon with a smile more defined than you have shown me in a long time. Those are moments when I cry hot tears; but most often I spend the morning without thought, going from nightmare to tears and in the evening from fatigue to sobbing. And my head is so empty, my dear. I vaguely see a map of Germany with a heavy barbed-wire border, and then somewhere there is the word Silesia, and then phrases I have heard, such as "they are starving to death"—and nothing else. It's raining this morning, I'm at the Dôme; it's ten o'clock and I'm sitting with coffee and *suisses** in front of me like last year. I find everything as it used to be, even the smell of those austere but hopeful mornings when I would start my work feeling completely united with you. I would like to be capable of starting work again, but I need to have at least a sign from you, a reference point to anchor my life.

Zuorro returned home yesterday morning; he'll be coming by shortly. Bost is with Kos., and I'll see him this afternoon. We're lucky to all meet again alive, you wrote to me. And it's you who aren't there, you who are everything to me.

Drieu La Rochelle told Brice Parain that Nizan had been killed—it upset me—it seems absurd to me and at the moment it confirms my strong impression of the end of a world, of an era.

I don't know which of my last letters you have received. I'm going to try to summarize these last weeks so that I'll be able to remember them and tell you about them one day.

---

* Brioches.

October 1

My sweet darling—I did not continue this little notebook—I haven't the courage for it—each time I stop talking to you I start crying. I'm unstable with lots of anguished and nervous moments. And even when I'm calm, even when several rather full and tranquil days go by, it's against a backdrop of nothingness; it stifles my soul. As if my entire life were between parentheses, it flows by like this, and it doesn't affirm itself as existent, it is suspended outside of time and the world. The result is that I feel nothing, think nothing, and nothing inside me goes anywhere.

I tried to work these last days, all in vain. This afternoon I sat upstairs at the Mahieu. At first I was in despair; you will remember, my sweet darling, our great moral debates in one of those small booths? And then my courage came back a little. I want to work. It seems like a small homage to you—an act of faith in you, our future and our destiny.

I think you haven't forgotten how much I love you—I think you know that I am absolutely nothing more than waiting for you. It gives me strength. Since you know that I'm with you, you're still with me—you, my only absolute.

(Written in pencil)*

"I've found a cushy job here. At first I was sick with 'weakness in the head' (a friendly joke) in the infirmary. I felt very well. A German doctor, a friend of literature, who wanted me to have the opportunity to write, had placed me there. I had a tiny room that I shared with two comrades. I was working a great deal and then some obscure intrigues had me *kicked out* of the infirmary, and I expected the time had come when I would be sent to work on some farm or autobahn. The worst thing was that they took *all* my writing, promising, however, to return it to me. But thanks to a swift recovery I enrolled right away in the Artists, a group of about thirty singers and musicians who perform in the camp to entertain their comrades. Like Captain Fracasse[2] I'm writing and staging sketches for them. We're very well regarded. Sunday, they're putting on a detective play by me, and that'll be my theatrical debut. My comrades are charming and very lively. We're twenty-five in the room and as a result of this captivity I'll be a very able bridge

---

* Written in Simone de Beauvoir's handwriting, copying a clandestine letter she received from Sartre, prisoner at Stalag 12. She was able to start writing to him again over there from October 17 on, using only official German forms.

player for our evenings later on. I'm not cold (we have coal—100 kg for ten days)—I'm not hungry (some good soul gives me bread). I have warm clothing and blankets. I would greatly appreciate if you could send me one or two pairs of socks. A bar of soap would also be a top priority as would some shaving cream. I can do very well without smoking—of which I'm proud, but it also happens that I do smoke and then I miss French tobacco. I have a pipe with a skull and cross bones. *I'm never bored.* I'm teaching some philosophy courses on freedom, a melancholic and timely subject, to some priests (a Jesuit, a Dominican, and a country priest). Like you, I have many grounds for sadness, but they go far beyond myself. Most of all I would like to see you again. Do you know that I'm high on a mountaintop from where we enjoy a splendid view of a large city (Trier)[3] and surrounding hills? You can't imagine how important this site and view are for keeping up our morale. So far I haven't felt depressed for a minute. Pieter[4] is in the hospital and tries to have himself declared incurable, which would ensure him an immediate release. Alas, I'm enjoying an iron constitution, leaving me no hope of returning home by this means. There are others.

"Write me as often as you can through official channels. I haven't received anything yet, neither packages nor letters, but surely it won't be long. Tell me everything . . .

"It seems that Nizan has passed through this camp, but I didn't see him. However, I ran into Mogader here; and since I once did him a favor, he did everything for me when I arrived here in a state of total destitution. It was thanks to him that I was sent to the infirmary, two hours before my entire group left for an *Arbeitskommando.*[5] Unfortunately, he is a Breton and was removed from the camp. I don't know where he is . . ."

November 19

Gloom—days of dark depression because after much hope I'm again aware that I won't see you for a long time.[6] If that meant forever, really, I'd kill myself. But if I live I must not flee. The best time was in July–August when I tried *to think* the situation. Now I flee among people (and so I'm disappointed because Bost is not you and I look for you everywhere while finding you nowhere)[7]—in my work (which often seems outdated and obstinate)—in music that only fills time. I should no longer flee but try to think. Now would be the time to write real memoirs or do philosophy again with Hegel, who brought me so much. But that requires such courage! At this very instant I feel some courage in reaction against the sticky melancholy of these last days and because it's the only way left for me to be united with you. Trying to remember you is futile and depressing. I must try to live in the present in a world where you are.

November 21

By dint of unhappiness, being tired of crying and headaches, I felt a vague desire to take hold of myself and find myself again in the metaphysical solitude of my youth—so much so that the diary of the boxer's friend brought tears to my eyes. But that isn't a firm-enough will—I don't want to stop waiting—I can't want it. I shall continue to drag myself from one day to the next, from music to work, from work to conversations—even if it should last four years. I would like to be really sick. At the moment images are incessantly and insistently coming back to me. And yet, I had tried hard to defend myself; I'm stuck up to my neck.

January 9, 1941

One idea that struck me so strongly in Hegel is the exigency of mutual *recognition* of consciousnesses—it can serve as a foundation for a social view of the world—the only absolute being this human consciousness, exigency of *freedom* of each consciousness in order for the recognition to be valid and free: recognition in love, artistic expression, action, etc. At the same time, the existentiel idea that human reality *is* nothing other than what it *makes itself* be, that toward which it transcends itself. This brings about the metaphysical tragedy of a fascism—it is not just a matter of stifling an expression but of absolutely denying a certain being, a matter, really, of confusing the human with its animal, biological aspect. And according to the other idea of Heidegger that the human species and I are the same thing, it's really *I* that am at stake. After reading a ridiculous and despicable issue of the *NRF,* I experienced this to the extent of feeling anguished. I am far from the Hegelian point of view that was so helpful to me in August. I have become conscious again of my individuality and of the metaphysical being that is opposed to this historical infinity where Hegel optimistically dilutes all things. Anguish. I have finally realized the state that I nostalgically longed for last year: solitude, as complete as when facing death. Last year I was still with Sartre— now I live in a world from which Sartre is absent, gagged. Psychologically I was at times stupidly proud to feel so solid and to get on so well. But today, those superficial defenses are no longer of any help to me. I have vertigo.

The hope of maintaining one's very *being* is the only reason for which I think it is worth accepting death. It's not a matter of having "reasons for living"—it's not a matter of life, but of something more than that. To make oneself an ant among ants, or a free consciousness facing other consciousnesses. *Metaphysical* solidarity that I newly discovered, I, who was a solipsist. I cannot be consciousness, spirit, among ants. I understand what was wanting in our antihumanism. To admire man as given (a beautiful intelligent animal etc.) is idiotic—but there is no other reality than human reality—all values are founded on it. And that "toward which it transcends itself" is what has always moved us and orients the destiny of each one of us.

Since November 21 I have sought only to flee—because this solitary return to work seemed almost a betrayal to me. Now it has come about on its own. And yet, I seem to work in his name as much as in mine. More than ever I feel (while being inconsistent) that I would kill myself if I were never to see him again.

January 21

Hegel or Heidegger? Why would my individual destiny be so precious if consciousness can transcend itself? I can't decide. At times it seems to me that the Hegelian-Marxist universal point of view deprives life of all meaning. Then again I think that perhaps individuality as such has no meaning and that wanting to give it one is a delusion. The idea of personal *salvation*—but why that idea? (Kierkegaard, Jaspers, Kafka, etc.)[8] Does it have meaning? Where is the truth and where is the delusion? Do we need only *to think* that it has meaning? But how could the universal have meaning if the individual has none? That could be the subject of my next novel; it has preoccupied me constantly for a year. The idea of happiness that I used to entertain, how much it seems wanting! It dominated ten years of my life, but I believe that I have almost entirely left it behind. (Happiness linked to a contemplative thought of the world.)

My novel.* I'm eager to finish it. It rests on a philosophical attitude that is already no longer mine. My next novel will be about *the individual situation*, its moral significance and its relation to the social. The importance of this metaphysical dimension.† It seems to me that people who lack it are badly *wanting!* There is no living attitude that doesn't have a metaphysical *meaning*,

---

* *She Came to Stay.*

† The theme was taken up again and developed in [1946] in the author's "Literature and Metaphysics," [reprinted as] chapter 3 in *Existentialism and the Wisdom of Nations* (1948) [and published in English translation in Beauvoir 2004, 269–77].

often ignored, but for me so present that, on the contrary, my psychological reactions are modeled on it. Even so, there's an impression of domination over those who do not know how to extract this meaning on their own.

Have read Scheler[9] (*L'Homme du ressentiment* [The Resentful Man]). There are passages on genius and the average man that express my feelings precisely when comparing Sartre (or even myself) to someone like Bost or Kos. or others. For the "genius," apprehension of values is initially not comparative—for others, yes.

January 29

On the subject of *Banjo* by Mac Kay: Mouloudji criticizes him for romanticizing the workers' existence and for taking the point of view of a guy who has come out of it (since he writes). I thought again of the boxer, who maintains that every *individual* can do so. Sophism. In a sense, certainly, only the individual point of view is true: but with respect to my individuality alone, and only as I *experience* it, not as I think it. I cannot think the masses and claim to think them as *subject*—that's the error Lévy makes when he says that one dead or a million dead is the same. Only *my* death is unique, and I cannot really live the death of *an* other as *my* death. That's the false Kantian universalism of the subject. A social thought must deliberately take men as object. (Consciousness being in this object, but as rendered passive.) I can always save myself; that doesn't give me the right to contend that an other ought to be able to save himself. For this salvation is (yes or no) carried out by my freedom—therefore, it is unpredictable and cannot be assigned to the other as *Sollen*.*

I would like my next novel to illustrate this relation to the other in its existentiel complexity. It's a beautiful subject. *To suppress* the other's consciousness is a bit puerile. The problem gets back to the social, etc., but must start off from an individual case. I must find a subject-object relationship; perhaps simply a case of unrequited love.

ON MY NOVEL

It is perhaps a mistake to have mixed two themes: (a) the rationalization of the world by happiness, (b) the irrational of the consciousness of the other. The second theme has been well treated, but not the first.†

---

* German word for *devoir* [here, "having the duty of obligation"].
† Reflection on *She Came to Stay*.

Another aspect of the consciousness of the other: in a sense it is the enemy. But then again, nothing has value except through it (Hegel). The only absolute is the consciousness of the other, whether embodied (as Sartre is for me), or indistinctly denied. If the meaning of the value of these consciousnesses disappears, then the value of mine does not exist either. A profound Hegelian idea on the *mutual recognition of consciousnesses*. This could be the theme of a new novel that would be more intimately linked to the social than the first novel.*

Historicity linked to this problem: transcendental and yet temporal consciousness—the passage from youth to adulthood, etc.

Perhaps the following simple construction: two heroes, a man and a woman, with the point of view of each one (totally adopted each time). In the man's character, the theme of *fault*—in the woman's, the illusion of the recognition of consciousnesses through love—hence ordeal and solitude (something like Sorokine facing Guille). It's a novelistic subject about an effort at *moral integrity* (in the sense of total assumption and reconstruction of the world) leading to the failure of facticity. That would be the essential subject—the flaw of the other theme is that it recalls a theme of the first novel, namely the disclosure of solitude. Relation of the *social and the metaphysical* (after the relation of the psychological and the metaphysical, which would be an excellent subject). I would have to end with a *social act* (less difficult to invent).

Temptation to merge with the universal (for example when returning to Paris in June, when Germany has won)—then conquering individual existence again. Search for *conciliation*.

ON THE NOVEL

Relationships between people—how each one can be only exteriority, facticity for the other—and is, therefore, in the wrong and overrun by his being for others—and can never reach the other except in his exteriority. This precludes him from taking a *moral* point of view on the other in his actions (from the other's point of view), but only the point of view of facticity. Hence also the character of *struggle* comprising people's relationships, each seeking to realize his being, even in the most generous love (like Sorokine), each fighting and having to fight for his being.

---

* It was to become *The Blood of Others*, a novel on which Simone de Beauvoir worked from 1941 to 1943 and which was published in 1945.

Probably describe a love affair in this perspective.

Several stages—Youth—(2) [*sic*] the individualistic idea: if *I* do not prefer *myself,* then who will prefer me?—(1) [*sic*] the relationship with God, understood as consciousness by whom my being is recognized—and the collapse when the belief in God ceases. Sudden nakedness of the world, and man is no longer anything but an ant. Then attempt to resort to oneself.

(3) Sad hardness of heart—inability to found oneself alone.

(4) A love affair—unhappy.

(5) Consciousness that this love was yet another means of saving oneself. Broadened individualism and transition to the social.

At the same time, history of this love from the point of view of the man, who lets himself be loved without loving but seeks to be moral and regrets that he is unable to be, posing the problem of the relation with the other in facticity. (The heroine being the relation to the other in freedom.) How can I *choose for the other?* (For example, not seeing or seeing someone. One can imagine Sorokine running after Guille, who wonders what right he has to choose—and claims to leave her free, which creates yet another situation).

(It would be preferable to complicate the situation a little.)

A possible scene: the exodus (as seen by the woman) along with the temptation to renounce herself. At that moment she would have lost her love; she would be devastated. And then taking a corrective course, holding on to her individual value—a destiny linked to that of the world. She throws herself into an antifascist action.

(But how unrewarding it is to write about social matters, and how can I avoid sounding edifying and moralizing?)

I should be able to handle social subjects (strikes, riots, the action of a leader) in order to mark the relation to the other: freedom and facticity. Perhaps I would choose a man who is much older than the woman and thrust into an action: a newspaper, a [political] party. A man having much influence (a man like Garric of the Équipes Sociales, a leftist and powerful man).* The man's fault is that he doesn't love the woman and creates a false happiness for her. His anguish when faced with his action. Because of her individualism the woman is not interested. Then ten years later, the man is dead or in prison—she takes up his work again as clandestine action. Or

---

* This theme will be taken up again in *The Mandarins.* As for Garric, see *Memoirs of a Dutiful Daughter.* The young Simone greatly admired this professor of French literature at the Institut Sainte-Marie in Neuilly, who was a practicing Catholic but held liberal social beliefs.

they meet again in this common work, which goes beyond love. (There's something moral and stupid about this subject.)

A beautiful case of conscience: should he or should he not push for war? (It would suffice if this were a man whose voice is heard: Malraux, Gide, or Alain.)

Blomart* refuses to play the demiurge, to take an intermonadic point of view on men: because the point of view is false, there are only *separate* lives—because he will reach only the outside, the facticity—because the relation to facticity is *absurd* as is facticity itself, and because he himself becomes a mechanical and absurd power.[10]

Mind (esprit) and Reality

The Cartesian *cogito* leads to an idealism with respect to the self, insofar as the self overflows the moment. The confusion of the affirming and affirmed term[11] is realized only in the moment, given the temporal nature of the "I think"—the *cogito* does not give consciousness of the eternal [self] since time is thrown back to the exterior of the mind, giving rise to idealism of the eternal, and thus of truth, which requires a recourse to God even for mathematical truths. The relation of thought with its past and its future appears as suggested from the outside, and thought, therefore, loses all autonomy—

Descartes considers thought as the translation of a reality while according to Kant it is a constructive power.

The principle of connecting representations can be grasped only in its immanence in representation. It's a dynamic factor that cannot be represented and has nothing in common with representation: there we have the ultimate term of the mind, an originating pure reason [*naturant*] that translates into an infinity of natural representations [*natures*].[12]

"Spontaneity and autonomy of thought can reside only in this fundamental consciousness of the relation of interiority that unites representation of nature [*naturé*] to the representative power of reason [*naturante*]—consciousness in which mental activity, far from being informed by its own representation, appears to itself, on the contrary, as having given birth to it and as being able to reproduce it indefinitely, identical to itself" (Lachièze-Rey).[13] But in Kant's work this transcendental consciousness is a pure nothingness, qua self-consciousness, that which entails the negation of all metaphysics. If, on the contrary, one acknowledges in thought a mode of relation

---

* Blomart, hero of *The Blood of Others*.

of self to self that is not reducible to either the passive or the constructive type,[14] a metaphysics becomes possible that would translate consciousness into knowledge and would make possible a philosophy of the subject (Hegel and Husserl).

To sum up: For Kant the "I" is the supreme law of synthesis, a timeless law in itself and in its active representations. The event is nothing but the aftermath of its action, but the "I," being unable to engender its own content, is often viewed by Kant as a simple reference point: it appears as posited, and not as positing. But the necessity of maintaining the mind's autonomy leads Kant in the end to posit a self positing [*autoposition*] of the "I," and this interior connection that links the combinatory act to its law and makes of it truly an act entails the admission of a direct consciousness of this relation, which orients us toward a philosophy of the subject.

Descartes posits that the presupposed object can be affirmed only if it merges with the affirming subject. Kant shows that there exists only one, unique act of the determinant consciousness that posits the spatial-temporal Universe: he therefore condemns the problematic idealism of Descartes.

In his refutation of idealism what Kant posits is the impossibility of constituting the objective self [*moi*] solely by using the action of self [*soi*] to self, Being [*Sein*] and the form of time. The constitutive act of objective succession must be integrated with the totality of its conditions (Husserl, on the contrary, *first* posits transcendence, then shows that it presupposes time).

[The following is written in pencil on the manuscript]

Can an *order* exist that is not constructed and empirically observable? Not for *succession*—any association presupposes an activity (p. 254)—for *simultaneity* there is *one* sort of apprehension of the simultaneous which is the spatial form itself (not derived from succession, but, like it, immediate).

The synthesis of apperception is not an autonomous operation but it has as analytical factors the synthesis of the imagination and the conceptual synthesis, the latter being essential and leading to the category (p. 279). The association of ideas presupposes concepts—the association presupposes a priori rule of apprehension that is presupposed by apprehension itself, so the act of connection appears as indefinitely reproducible—

Is there consciousness without concept ? (p. 282)

For B.
The Possessed—The Brothers Karamazov
For Mouloudji

Dostoyevsky
John Dos Passos—*The 42nd Parallel* plus *1919*
Proust—*Du côté de chez Swann* [Swann's Way]

(p. 20)
Bennert (in 2 vols.)—
Maugham—*Of Human Bondage*
Dane—*Legend, A Regiment of Women*
Kennedy—*Together and Apart*
Woolf—*Orlando*—*The Years* (1937), *The Waves, Flush* (1933)
Lawrence—Lawrence in Mexico
Letters from L.—Life of Lawrence, etc.
Sarn
Pepys—Proust since *Sodome et Gomorrhe* [Sodom and Gomorrah]
Dreiser—*An American Tragedy*
Sherwood Anderson
Sinclair Lewis—*The Prodigal Parents*

[p. 16+]

Notes on Labor Unions

Authority lies with a general assembly that meets every three months. In between times, it is assumed by a union council that is elected by the assembly to which any member can be appointed unless he holds a political mandate. The council meets once a month, and all members may attend its proceedings.

The unions are members of the Bourse de Travail in the Democratic Union. The authority of the Democratic Union lies with the central committee, consisting of one delegate from each member union. This committee elects an executive commission.

In a Fédération du Livre[15] the federation was centralized, its committee holding almost all power—each delegate represented four hundred union members—most often federations were decentralized—each local union could decide on a strike. In 1922, the CGTU[16] was founded.

In 1932 founding of the Institut supérieur ouvrier—reformist attitude of the CGT.

The CGTU, on the contrary, is a member of the International and pursues aggressive policies. At the St. Etienne congresses, there were three tendencies: communists, anarchistic revolutionaries, moderates—in fact, labor union autonomy was not respected.

Dissension in the CGTU: the radical unionist CT tries to return to the prewar individualistic tradition—the minority members join the CGTRS or the CGT—decline of the movement in 1932.

Idea of rebuilding unity. Workers are forbidden by law to take any kind of *threatening measures*, such as intimidation through gatherings, demonstrations, etc. The Unification Congress was held in Toulouse in the fall of 1935 and in February 1936—the CGT remains a member of the International of Amsterdam while keeping a presence at the SDN[17] in Geneva and the International Workers Bureau—affirming the independence of the Labor Unions vis-à-vis the political parties.

NOTES

1. Though Sartre was stationed with the artillery division, whose members were clad in khaki, he wore the blue uniform of the meteorological unit of the air force division.

2. Fracasse is the hero in *Le Capitaine Fracasse,* a cloak-and-dagger novel by Théophile Gautier (1863).

3. A city in Germany on the Moselle River.

4. Pieter, a businessman in civilian life, was a private in the meteorological service, like Sartre, and roomed with him during the early months of the war.

5. German military term for *fatigue detail.*

6. In Beauvoir's original manuscript, this sentence opens with "Sombre—jours de noire dépression," instead of "Sombre—jours de sombre dépression," as in *Journal de guerre* (360).

7. This sentence begins as follows in the original manuscript: "Maintenant je fuis dans les gens (d'où déceptions car Bost n'est pas vous, et partout je vous cherche . . .)" instead of: "Maintenant je fuis dans les gens, et partout . . . " as in *Journal de guerre* (360).

8. The name in the original manuscript is "Jaspers," not "Jacques," as in *Journal de guerre* (362).

9. Max Scheler, a German philosopher (1874–1928), was the author of several important phenomenological essays.

10. The published edition of Beauvoir's wartime diary ends at this point with this editorial note: "In this Notebook 7, one also finds, not transcribed here: —philosophical exposés (intended as course material); —notes on philosophical readings; —lists of diverse readings to do (in particular, philosophical and musical, and English novels); —lists of readings intended for various friends (Vedrine, Mouloudji); —notes on readings on the Beethoven Quartets; —accounts of chess games; —accounts; —schedules (*hypokhâgne* and *khâgne*); —notes on the history of labor unions between 1922 and 1936." The following pages are a translation of the final pages of notebook 7 of Beauvoir's handwritten diary, transcribed by Sylvie Le Bon de Beauvoir.

11. Beauvoir may mean that Descartes confuses the self that does the affirming (says "I exist") and the one that is actually affirmed, which is something that exists only in the moment during what it is affirmed; so that the term in question here is "self."

12. *Naturant* refers to reason, that is, thought that is generated spontaneously; "nature" refers to mental impressions generated in our minds by what is coming, as it were, "from the outside."

13. Pierre Lachièze-Rey (1885–1957) was a scholar of modern philosophy and author of *L'Idéalisme kantien* (1931) and *Les Origines cartésiennes de Dieu de Spinoza* (1932).

14. That is, where "passive" alludes to *naturé* and "constructive" to *naturant*.

15. Loosely translated as a labor union for writers.

16. The Confédération Générale du Travail Unitaire (CGTU) was a communist-oriented labor union that broke off from the French labor union federation, Conféderation Générale du Travail (CGT). The CGTU reunited with the CGT in 1936 under the Popular Front.

17. A Socialist party.

Works Cited

Arp, Kristana. 2001. *Bonds of Freedom: Simone de Beauvoir's Existentialist Ethics*. Chicago: Open Court.

Bair, Deirdre. 1990. *Simone de Beauvoir: A Biography*. New York: Summit.

Barnes, Hazel. 1959. *Humanistic Existentialism: The Literature of Possibility*. Lincoln: University of Nebraska Press.

Beauvoir, Simone de. [1926–27]. Carnets. Holograph manuscripts. Bibliothèque Nationale, Paris.

———. 1943. *L'Invitée*. Folio. Paris: Gallimard..

———. [1944] 2004. *Pyrrhus et Cinéas*. Trans. Marybeth Timmermann. In Beauvoir 2004, 89–149.

———. 1945. *Le Sang des autres*. Folio ed. Paris: Gallimard.

———. [1947] 1948. *The Ethics of Ambiguity*. Trans. Bernard Frechtman. Secaucus, N.J.: Citadel Press.

———. 1948. *The Blood of Others*. Trans. Roger Senhouse and Yvonne Moyse. New York: Pantheon.

———. 1949. *Le Deuxième Sexe*. 2 vols. Paris: Gallimard.

———. 1958. *Mémoires d'une jeune fille rangée*. Paris: Gallimard.

———. 1959. *Memoirs of a Dutiful Daughter*. Trans. James Kirkup. New York: Harper and Row. Originally published as *Mémoires d'une jeune fille rangée* (Beauvoir 1958).

———. 1960. *La Force de l'âge*. Folio ed. Paris: Gallimard. Also published in an NRF edition in 1960. All references are to the Folio edition unless otherwise indicated.

——. 1968. *The Second Sex*. Trans. H. M. Parshley. New York: Knopf. Originally published as *Le Deuxième Sexe* (Beauvoir 1949).

——. 1973. *The Prime of Life*. Trans. Peter Green. New York: Lancer Books. Originally published as *La Force de l'âge* (Beauvoir 1960).

——. 1984. *She Came to Stay*. Trans. Yvonne Moyse and Roger Senhouse. London: Fontana. Originally published as *L'Invitée* (Beauvoir 1943).

——. 1990. *Lettres à Sartre*. 2 vols. Ed. Sylvie Le Bon de Beauvoir. Paris: Gallimard.

——. 1992. *Letters to Sartre*. Trans. Quintin Hoare. New York: Arcade. Originally published as *Lettres à Sartres* (Beauvoir 1990).

——. 2004. *Philosophical Writings*. Ed. Margaret A. Simons with Marybeth Timmermann and Mary Beth Mader. Urbana: University of Illinois Press.

——. 2006. *Diary of a Philosophy Student: Volume 1, 1926–27*. Ed. Barbara Klaw, Sylvie Le Bon de Beauvoir, and Margaret A. Simons, with Marybeth Timmermann. Trans. Barbara Klaw. Transcribed by Barbara Klaw and Sylvie Le Bon de Beauvoir. Urbana: University of Illinois Press.

Bergoffen, Debra B. 1997. *The Philosophy of Simone de Beauvoir: Gendered Phenomenologies, Erotic Generosities*. Albany: State University of New York Press.

Chapsal, Madeleine. [1960] 1979. "Une interview de Simone de Beauvoir." In *Les Écrits de Simone de Beauvoir*, ed. Claude Francis and Fernande Gontier, 381–96. Paris: Gallimard.

Delacampagne, Christian. 2006. "Heidegger in France." In *The Columbia History of Twentieth-Century French Thought*, ed. Lawrence D. Kritzman, 251–55. New York: Columbia University Press.

Fabre-Luce, Alfred. 1940. "Lettre à un Américain." *La Nouvelle Revue Française*, December 1, 68.

Frasier, Miriam. 1999. *Identity without Selfhood: Simone de Beauvoir and Bisexuality*. Cambridge: Cambridge University Press.

Fullbrook, Edward. 1999. "*She Came to Stay* and *Being and Nothingness*." *Hypatia* 14:4 (Fall 1999): 50–69; reprinted in Simons 2006b, 42–64.

Fullbrook, Kate, and Edward Fullbrook. 1993. *Simone de Beauvoir and Jean-Paul Sartre: The remaking of a twentieth-century legend*. London: Harvester.

——. 1998. *Simone de Beauvoir: A Critical Introduction*. Cambridge: Polity Press.

Galster, Ingrid. 1996a. "Simone de Beauvoir and Radio-Vichy: About Some Rediscovered Radio Scripts." *Simone de Beauvoir Studies* 13:103–13. (Abridged English version of Galster 1996b.)

——. 1996b. "Simone de Beauvoir et Radio-Vichy: A propos de quelques scénarios retrouvés." *Romanische Forschungen* 108 (no. 1/2): 112–32.

Gheerbrant, Jacqueline, and Ingrid Galster. 1999. "Nous sentions un petit parfum de soufre . . .'" *Lendemains* 94:38–47.

Gothlin, Eva. 2006. "Beauvoir and Sartre on Appeal, Desire and Ambiguity." In Simons 2006b, 132–45.

Hegel, G. W. F. 1939a. *Morceaux Choisis*. Trans. Norbert Guterman and Henri Lefebvre. Paris: Gallimard.

——. 1939b. *La Phénoménologie de l'esprit*. Vol. 1. Trans. Jean Hyppolite. Paris: Aubier-Montaigne.

——. 1977. *The Phenomenology of Spirit*. Trans. A. V. Miller. Oxford: Oxford University Press.

Heidegger, Martin. [1927] 1962. *Being and Time*. Trans. John Macquarrie and Edward Robinson. New York: Harper and Row.

Keller, Catherine. 1986. *From a Broken Web: Separation, Sexism, and Self.* Boston: Beacon.

Kruks, Sonia. 1990. *Situation and Human Existence: Freedom, Subjectivity, and Society*. London: Unwin Hyman.

Lamblin, Bianca. 1993. *Mémoires d'une jeune fille derangée*. Paris: Balland. Trans. Julie Plovnick, as *A Disgraceful Affair: Simone De Beauvoir, Jean-Paul Sartre, and Bianca Lamblin* (Boston: Northeastern University Press, 1996).

Marcel, Gabriel. 1936–37. "Aperçus phénoménologiques sur l'être en situation." *Recherches philosophiques* 6:1–21.

———. 2002. *Awakenings: A Translation of Marcel's Autobiography, "En chemin, vers quel éveil?"* Trans. Peter S. Rogers. Intro. Patrick Bourgeois. Milwaukee: Marquette University Press.

Rowley, Hazel. 2005. *Tête-à-Tête: Simone de Beauvoir and Jean-Paul Sartre*. New York: HarperCollins.

Sartre, Jean-Paul. [1943] 1953. *Being and Nothingness*. Trans. H. Barnes. New York: Philosophical Library.

———. 1983. *Lettres au Castor et à quelques autres*. 2 vols. Ed. Simone de Beauvoir. Paris: Gallimard.

———. 1984. *The War Diaries of Jean-Paul Sartre*. Trans. Quintin Hoare. New York: Pantheon. Translation of *Les Carnets de la drôle de guerre: Novembre 1939–Mars 1940*, ed. Arlette Elkaïm-Sartre (Paris: Gallimard, 1983).

———. 1993. *Quiet Moments in a War: The Letters of Jean-Paul Sartre to Simone de Beauvoir, 1940–1963*. Trans. Lee Fahnestock and Norman McAfee. New York: Macmillan. Translation of Sartre 1983, vol. 2.

Sevel, Geneviève. 1999. "'Je considère comme une grande chance d'avoir pu recevoir son enseignement.'" *Lendemains* 94:48–49.

Simons, Margaret A. 1999a. *Beauvoir and* The Second Sex: *Feminism, Race, and the Origins of Existentialism*. Lanham, Md.: Rowman and Littlefield.

———. 1999b. "From Murder to Morality." *International Studies in Philosophy* 31 (no. 2): 1–20.

———. 2000. "Beauvoir's Philosophical Independence in a Dialogue with Sartre." *Journal of Speculative Philosophy* 14 (no. 2): 87–103.

———. 2002. "Beauvoir and the Problem of Racism." In *Philosophers on Race: Critical Essays*, ed. Julie K. Ward and Tommy L. Lott, 260–84. Oxford: Blackwell.

———. 2003. "Bergson's Influence on Beauvoir's Philosophical Methodology." In *The Cambridge Companion to Simone de Beauvoir*, ed. Claudia Card, 107–28. Cambridge: Cambridge University Press.

———. 2006a. "Beauvoir's Early Philosophy: 1926–27." In Beauvoir 2006, 29–50.

———, ed. 2006b. *The Philosophy of Simone de Beauvoir: Critical Essays*. Bloomington: Indiana University Press.

Suleiman, Susan Rubin. 1992. "Life-Story, History, Fiction: Reflections on Simone de Beauvoir's Wartime Writings." *Contention: Debates in Society, Culture, and Science* 1, no. 2 (Winter): 1–21.

Vintges, Karen. 1996. *Philosophy as Passion*. Trans. Anne Lavelle. Bloomington: Indiana University Press.

Index

abortion, 221–22, 225

absence, 163, 253, 256

absolute(s), 13, 17, 18, 19, 150

action(s), 23, 31, 323. *See also* political action

Adamov, Arthur, 52, 53, 97, 171, 222, 255

adaptation, 178, 184

L'Adolescent [The Adolescent], 45

Adventures of John N (Stevenson), 85

affection, 104, 148, 160, 223, 252, 253, 256, 264, 265

The Afternoon of a Faun (Debussy), 243

L'Age de raison [The Age of Reason] (Sartre), 129, 251, 262

Aida (Verdi opera), 166

air raid alerts: Beauvoir's writings in Notebook 1 about, 47, 49, 51, 57; Beauvoir's writings in Notebook 2 about, 106, 123, 145, 148, 150; Beauvoir's writings in Notebook 3 about, 163, 167; Beauvoir's writings in Notebook 5 about, 237; Beauvoir's writings in Notebook 6 about, 275, 276, 281

Alain, 76, 161, 324

A l'angle du monde [At the Edge of the World] (movie), 169

Alceste (Gluck opera), 166

aloneness: Beauvoir's writings in Notebook 1 about, 63; Beauvoir's writings in Notebook 2 about, 110, 117; Beauvoir's writings in Notebook 4 about, 210, 211, 213; Beauvoir's writings in Notebook 6 about, 271, 274, 293, 296, 306

Ameche, Don, 262

America Day by Day (Beauvoir): and anti-black racism, 21; and blacks, 12; and consciousness as shaped by society, 21; and shame, 29

Les Ames mortes [Dead Souls] (Gogol), 91, 95

Anderson, Sherwood, 326

Anges aux figures sales [Angels with Dirty Faces] (movie), 95

anguish: and Beauvoir reading *The Castle*, 238; Beauvoir's anguish over Bost's

military leave, 245; Beauvoir's anguish for Sartre, 27, 317; and evacuation, 282; and war, 86, 112, 319
appeal, 30
appearance. *See* beauty
apperception, 325
apprehending [*saisir*] the world, 72
Ariane and Blue Beard (Dukas opera), 271
Art of the Fugue (Bach), 172
art of living, 15
asceticism, 10
As I Lay Dying (Faulkner), 256
Astaire, Fred, 238
Au Bord du fleuve [At the River's End] (Curwood), 85
Audry, Colette, 70, 94, 160, 173, 176
Audry, Minder, 70, 161, 174, 177
authenticity, 23, 143, 168, 213, 225, 244, 245, 250, 251
Ava Maria (Gounod), 213
Les Aventures de Jack London [The Adventures of Jack London], 84
Aventures du Saint [The Saint's Adventures] (Leslie Charteris), 84
Aymé, Marcel, 215, 302, 303

Bach, Johann Sebastian, 52, 169, 172, 212, 234, 235, 239, 308
bad faith, 3, 23, 250
Bair, Deirdre, 1, 3, 4, 6, 31, 32, 34*n*7, 34*n*9
Banjo (Mac Kay), 321
Barbusse, Henri, 209
Barnaby Rudge (Dickens), 122, 123
Barnes, Hazel, 3
La Baronne de minuit [The Midnight Baroness] (movie), 262
Barrès, Maurice, 123
Baxter, Warner, 160
beauty: and Beauvoir's view of herself, 117, 119, 160, 166, 184, 185, 216, 242; and others' views of Beauvoir, 187, 193, 244
Beauvoir, Georges Bertrand de (father), 185, 224, 281, 293, 310
Beauvoir, Françoise Brasseur de (mother), 170, 201, 272, 293, 297, 304, 310
Beauvoir, Henriette de (sister). *See* Poupette

Beauvoir, Simone de: affair with Bost, 6, 20, 119, 132, 157–58, 163, 262, 263; affair with female student, 31–32; anguish for Sartre, 27; aspirations, 15; Bost's passionate effect on, 11, 132; charges of collaboration by, 31–32; death of, 1, 3; and defeat of France, 283; devotion to Sartre, 17; first meeting with Sartre, 2; as former lover of Kos., 4; lies about influence on Sartre, 1; lies about sexual affairs with women, 1; lies about work in philosophy, 1, 2, 6, 8; lies about writing *She Came to Stay*, 4, 6; loss of self, 25; as lover of Lamblin, 21; mutual dependency with Sartre, 17; part of "couple" with Sartre, 7; philosophical transformation, 2, 8, 9, 10, 13, 17, 23, 28, 29, 30, 31, 33, 320; political transformation, 24; as refugee (*see* refugees); relationship with Sartre, 19; remorse for Bost, 24, 62–63; renunciation of religious faith, 18; Sartre's use of Beauvoir's philosophy, 7, 8; self-representation as Sartre's follower, 8; as teacher (*see* teaching); visit to Sartre, 20 (*see also* visit to Sartre). *See also* evacuation of Paris; return to Paris
becoming, as German philosophy, 71
Beethoven, Ludwig van, 59, 60, 120, 185, 195, 204, 212, 234, 235, 308
being, 250, 319
Being and Nothingness (Sartre): influence of Beauvoir's philosophy on, 6, 8; influence of *She Came to Stay* on, 2, 6, 7, 8; philosophical similarities to *She Came to Stay*, 3; predated by *She Came to Stay*, 2; and solipsism, 15
Being and Time (Heidegger), 9
Bergoffen, Debra, 8
Bergson, Henri: and Beauvoir as teacher, 9, 34*n*6; and body and freedom, 20; and *élan vital*, 18; and freedom, 10, 18; and the self, 10
Berlioz, Hector, 181
Bessie Cutter, 82
bicycling, 298, 301, 303, 305, 307, 308, 309
Bienenfeld, Bianca. *See* Lamblin, Bianca; *see also* Védrine, Louise

black(s): and racism, 21; soldiers, 56; and solidarity, 12; stereotype of, 122; women in Paris, 117, 248

Blood of Others (Beauvoir): and conflict between individual and universal, 28–29; and consciousness as freedom, 13; and death, 13; and facticity, 324; and History, 26; and personal history, 26; and political action, 29; and shame, 29; and situated subjectivity, 10

body, 10, 12, 20, 213

Le B<oe>uf clandestin (Aymé), 215

Bogart, Humphrey, 200, 235

boredom, 112, 182, 236, 268, 269, 284, 318

Bost, Jacques: affair with Beauvoir, 6, 20, 119, 132, 157–58, 163, 262, 263; affair with Kos., 6, 120, 132, 157, 164, 194, 267; and Beauvoir's political transformation, 24; Beauvoir's remorse for, 24, 62–63; Beauvoir's writings in Notebook 1 about, 40, 41, 42, 43, 44, 45, 46, 49, 59, 63, 68; Beauvoir's writings in Notebook 2 about, 91, 131, 132, 148, 152; Beauvoir's writings in Notebook 3 about, 157, 178; Beauvoir's writings in Notebook 5 about, 239, 243, 247, 255, 256, 260, 261, 262, 264, 268; Beauvoir's writings in Notebook 6 about, 304; on front lines, 17, 24, 40n, 196; marriage to Kos., 40n; as model for Gerbert in *She Came to Stay*, 5; passionate effect on Beauvoir, 11, 132; return from front, 316 (*see also* military leave of Bost); wounded, 295

Bost, Pierre, 44, 245, 264, 267

Boubou. *See* Gérassi, Fernand

Bourla (friend): and Beauvoir's inspiration for political engagement, 33; murder by Nazis, 13

"the boxer" (Bonafé), 57, 80, 97, 101, 321

"the boxer's wife" (Lili), 57, 190

bracketing (*époché*), of existential claims, 27. *See also* "put in parentheses"

Brandenburg Concertos (Bach), 172, 239, 308

break, 55, 274

Breton, André, 47, 53

Brontë, Charlotte, 63, 64, 68

Buck, Pearl, 57, 97

Le Cabaret de la derniére chance [The Last Chance Saloon] (Jack London), 88

cafés and restaurants, effect of war on, 41, 55, 90, 113, 193, 234, 277, 282, 301, 303

Le Canard enchaîné (magazine), 51, 108, 115, 157, 164, 198, 224, 236, 242

Capri, Agnes, 9, 49, 57, 143

The Castle (Kafka), 235, 238

Catholicism, 18

censorship: Beauvoir's writing under, 26, 31; and collaboration, 27

certainty: and Beauvoir's reaction to Sartre in prison, 301; opposite certainties, 281

Cette sacrée vérité [The Awful Truth] (movie), 231

Chacun sa vérité [To Each His Own Truth], 223

Champigneulles, Jacques (cousin), 15–16

Chapsal, Madeleine, 8

Charteris, Leslie, 84

La Chasse au renard [The Fox Hunt] (movie), 101

Chekov, Anton (aka Tchekov), 159

Chevalier, Maurice, 160

Children's Corner (Debussy), 212

choice(s): and freedom, 11, 30; of women, 132

Chonez, C., 69, 171, 254, 255, 269

Chopin, Frédéric, 242

Christie, Agatha, 94

Claudel, Paul, 18, 74, 75

Le Clavier universel [The Universal Keyboard] (Véry), 84

Colbert, Claudette, 262

collaboration with Occupation: Beauvoir's reaction to, 26, 31; and censorship, 27; and charge against Sartre, 31; and charges against Beauvoir, 31–32; as denial of humanity, 28

Colonel Jack (Defoe), 95

La Comédie de Charleroi [The Comedy of Charleroi] (Drieu de la Rochelle), 79

Comme tu me veux [As You Like Me] (movie), 114

community, connection with, 43

Conan Doyle, Arthur, 69, 159

concentration camp(s): and Austrian

woman, 274; and Gérassi, 71; and Germans living in Paris, 49; and hermaphrodite, 119; women's camps, 283; and women wearing mourning, 64

Concerto for Bassoon (Mozart), 308

Le Congrès s'amuse [The Congress Is Having Fun] (movie), 231

consciousness: Beauvoir's writings in Notebook 1 about, 71, 79; Beauvoir's writings in Notebook 2 about, 103, 150*n*; Beauvoir's writings in Notebook 5 about, 250, 251; Beauvoir's writings in Notebook 7 about, 320, 322; and Beauvoir as teacher, 9, 34*n*6, 109; and body, 12, 213; distinguished from consciousnesses, 2; as embodied, 11, 322; and freedom, 11, 12, 13, 17; of the other as an absolute, 18, 322; and the other in Hegel, 14, 17–18, 250, 251; the other's consciousness, 7; Sartre's consciousness, 253; as shaped by society, 21; transcendental consciousness, 324; women's consciousness as shaped by society, 18

consciousnesses: Beauvoir's views about, 2, 5, 17–18; Beauvoir's writings in Notebook 2 about, 150; Beauvoir's writings in Notebook 4 about, 233; Beauvoir's writings in Notebook 5 about, 251; Beauvoir's writings in Notebook 7 about, 320; Beauvoir's writings in Notebook 6 about, 300; distinguished from consciousness, 2; in Hegel, 17, 28; and recognition, 17–18, 28, 322

confrontation, self-other [*on s'oppose*], 4, 5, 93

consideration of the other, 158

contingent, 69, 110, 111, 132, 149, 245, 268, 309

Cooper, Gary, 105

Le Coq d'Or (Rimsky-Korsakoff), 310

Corbin, Henry, 9

Couperin, François, 68

courage, 318

Coward, Noel, 184

Crapouillot series on war, 83, 84, 94

Curwood, 85

Dabit, 207, 208

The Damnation of Faust (Berlioz opera), 181

Davis, Bette, 200, 235

death: Beauvoir's views about, 13–14, 305, 319, 321; and reality in Heidegger, 30; soldiers' view of, 111

The Death of Sigmund (Lawrence), 58

Debussy, Claude, 212, 243, 303, 307, 310, 312

De Chazotte, Alain-René, 260

Defoe, Daniel, 88, 95

delusion(s), 93, 320

Les Déraciné (Barrès), 123

Descartes, René: and Beauvoir as teacher, 9, 34*n*6; and Cartesian *cogito*, 324, 325; and distinction between freedom and power, 13; and limits of devotion, 18; and thought, 324

desire(s): Beauvoir's abandonment of, 25; Beauvoir's writings in Notebook 1 about, 75, 78, 82; Beauvoir's writings in Notebook 2 about, 105, 112, 113, 117, 120, 131; Beauvoir's writings in Notebook 5 about, 252, 266, 268; Beauvoir's writings in Notebook 6 about, 306, 312; and freedom, 18

despair, 265, 281

destiny, 246, 283, 317, 319, 320

Les Deux Dianes [The Two Dianas], 107

devotion: absolute, Beauvoir's criticism of, 30–31; Beauvoir's, to Sartre, 17; and freedom, 18; Mercier's views about, 15

Le Diable amoureux [The Devil in Love] (De Cazotte), 260

Le Diable boiteux (Lesage), 169

diary: and Beauvoir's anti-Semitic remarks, 21, 22, 188, 244, 280; Beauvoir's bracketing of existential claims, 27; Beauvoir's deletion of her philosophy from diary for *The Prime of Life*, 3; and comments by Sartre, 131; and embodied consciousness, 11; and freedom, 18; and historicity, 130; and humanity as a species, 12; publication, 1, 4; and reality, 12; and situated subjectivity, 10; and time, 24; and transcendence, 12; and writing of *She Came to Stay*, 93, 98 (*see also* writing); written for Bost, 25, 282; written for Sartre, 25, 282

Diary of a Philosophy Student (Beauvoir). *See* student diary

Dickens, Charles, 122, 126, 129
Dieu est-il français? [Is God French?] (Sie-
   burg), 309
disengagement, 27, 147
Les Disparus de Saint-Agil [The Lost Souls of
   Saint-Agil] (movie), 227
distress, 91
Dos Passos, John, 60, 94, 326
Dostoyevsky, Fodor, 326. See also *L'Idiot*
Le Drageoir d'Or [The Golden Drageoir], 289
Dreiser, Theodore, 326
Drieu de la Rochelle, Pierre, 79, 215, 216, 220,
   251, 316
Dukas, Paul, 271
Dullin, Charles: Beauvoir's writings in Note-
   book 1 about, 65, 66, 67, 68; Beauvoir's
   writings in Notebook 2 about, 145; Beau-
   voir's writings in Notebook 3 about, 156,
   179, 197; Beauvoir's writings in Notebook
   4 about, 223, 229; Beauvoir's writings in
   Notebook 6 about, 302, 311
Dunne, Irene, 231

East Wind, West Wind (Pearl Buck), 97
Ehrenbourg, Ilya, 41, 53, 55, 90
élan toward others, 29–30
élan vital, 18
embodiment, 10
emotions, 10, 164, 245, 307
emptiness, 52, 253, 257, 265, 309
Les Enfants du limon [Children of Clay]
   (Queneau), 95
England (British), 61, 275, 277, 285, 290, 293
ennui, 58, 229
entertainment, 117, 120, 143, 170, 185, 199, 228,
   230, 243, 248, 267
L'Envoyé de l'archange [The Archangel's Mes-
   senger] (Tharauds), 247
époché (bracketing), of existential claims, 27
Équipes Sociales (Social Teams), 23, 24, 323
L'Étrange Visiteur [The Strange Visitor]
   (movie), 271
The Ethics of Ambiguity (Beauvoir), 8, 29
Europe (review), 96, 162
evacuation of Paris (Beauvoir's), 272, 273,
   274, 275, 276. *See also* return to Paris

existential claims, and Beauvoir's bracketing
   in diary, 27
expression of self, 158

Fabre-Luce, Albert, 27, 209
facticity, 18, 322, 323, 324
Fantôme à vendre [A Phantom for Sale]
   (movie), 271
fascism, 12, 24, 28, 319
Faulkner, William, 256
Fauré, Gabriel, 59, 185
fear: Beauvoir's writings in Notebook 1
   about, 50, 54, 55, 56, 59, 64, 86; Beauvoir's writings in Notebook 2 about, 91;
   Beauvoir's writings in Notebook 5 about,
   236, 241; Beauvoir's writings in Notebook
   6 about, 277, 297, 304, 311; Beauvoir's writings in Notebook 7 about, 315–16
Fear and Trembling (Kierkegaard), 34*n*13
femininity: of Beauvoir, 20, 133; and
   consciousness shaped by society, 18; as a
   situation, 9, 133
Fermé la nuit [Closed at Night] (Morand),
   175
Fidelio Overture (Beethoven), 308
Fifi peau de pêche [Every Day's a Holiday]
   (movie), 169
film(s). See movies; *see also* specific titles
The Firebird (Stravinsky), 59, 310
Florès, 228, 252
food shortage, 194, 298, 299, 306
La Force de l'âge (Beauvoir). See *The Prime
   of Life*
Foujita, 101
France: and armistice conditions, 281, 285;
   defeat of, 276, 287; German attack on,
   107, 271, 272; and German occupation (*see*
   Occupation); German propaganda in, 71,
   73. *See also* evacuation of Paris
Franck, César, 197, 204
Frasier, Hazel, 33*n*1
freedom: as an absolute, 13, 18, 19; appeal
   to the other's freedom, 30; Beauvoir's
   views about, 10, 18, 19; in Bergson, 10, 18;
   and body in Bergson, 20; and choices, 11,
   30; and collective action of women, 23;

and consciousness, 11, 12, 13, 17, 319; in Descartes, 13; and desires, 18; and devotion, 18; distinguished from power, 13; and embodiment, 10; and loss of freedom of expression, 25; and love, 15; and the other, 321, 323; and reality, 18–19; and rejection of childhood influences, 18; and salvation, 321; and separation of men, 30; and the universal, 25; and violence, 14; of women, through collective action, 23

friendship, 7, 101, 103, 131, 146, 196, 223, 263

Fullbrook, Edward, 1, 7

Fullbrook, Kate, 7

Gable, Clark, 101

Galster, Ingrid, 32, 34n6, 34n7

Garric, Robert, 23, 323

gas masks, 41, 42, 45, 47, 48, 51, 105, 106, 143, 189, 237

gas shortage, 284, 285, 286, 287, 289, 290

Gégé (friend of Poupette): Beauvoir's writings in Notebook 1 about, 42, 43, 44, 46, 47, 48; Beauvoir's writings in Notebook 2 about, 88, 90, 92, 113, 118; Beauvoir's writings in Notebook 4 about, 225

gender, Beauvoir's experience of, 20

Les Généraux meurent dans leur lit [Generals Die in Their Beds] (Charles Harrison), 83

generosity, 8, 18, 31, 211, 291

genius, 321

Gérassi, Fernand (aka Boubou): affair with Beauvoir, 144; Beauvoir's writings in Notebook 1 about, 40, 41, 45, 48, 51, 53, 54, 55, 56, 58, 59, 60, 61, 70, 71; Beauvoir's writings in Notebook 2 about, 89, 91, 92, 108, 116, 118, 144; Beauvoir's writings in Notebook 3 about, 158, 164; Beauvoir's writings in Notebook 4 about, 216; Beauvoir's writings in Notebook 5 about, 237

Gérassi, Stépha (aka Baba): Beauvoir's writings in Notebook 1 about, 40, 61, 70, 71; Beauvoir's writings in Notebook 2 about, 91, 92, 96, 118; Beauvoir's writings in Notebook 4 about, 216; Beauvoir's writings in Notebook 5 about, 237, 239, 269

Germany: and anti-Semitism, 309; and

armistice conditions, 281, 285; army advances, 25, 50, 54, 271, 272; battle with French troops, 107; and German refugees' fate, 283; and German-Soviet Pact, 41; and Hitler's demands, 37; invasion of Western Europe, 4, 8; and meaning of victory, 287; morale in, 177; occupation of France (see Occupation); peace offers, 83, 84, 85; propaganda, 71, 73, 295, 300, 308; restrictions inside of, 61; and Russia's division of Poland, 76; threatens invasion of Holland, 146; treaty with Russia, 83; victory of, 286, 287; war on Poland, 37, 40, 41, 56, 59, 61, 74, 83

Gheerbrant, Jacqueline, 34n6, 34n7

Ghéon, Henri (pseudonym of Henri Vauglon), 68

Giacometti, 288

Gibert, 150, 151, 152, 183, 184

Gide, André, 42, 45, 48, 50, 51, 52, 54, 68, 85, 92, 137, 177, 324

Gilles (Drieu de la Rochelle), 215, 216, 220

Giono, 100

Giraudoux, 65, 101

Gluck, C. W., 166

Gogol, Nikolai, 69, 70, 72, 91, 95

Gone with the Wind (Mitchell), 302

Le Gorille [The Gorilla] (movie), 173

Gothlin, Eva, 14

Le Goujat [The Scoundrel] (movie), 184

Gounod, Charles, 213

Graf von Spee, explosion of, 195

Grand Cap, 69

La Grande Farandole [The Story of Vernon and Irene Castle] (movie), 237–38

Green, Julien, 92, 94

Guerre [War] (L. Renn), 84

Gunga Din (movie), 112

happiness: Beauvoir's writings in Notebook 1 about, 45, 53, 56, 64, 72, 79, 82; Beauvoir's writings in Notebook 2 about, 96, 119, 122, 123, 128, 129, 130, 133, 139, 149; Beauvoir's writings in Notebook 3 about, 158, 163, 178; Beauvoir's writings in Notebook 4 about, 209; Beauvoir's writings in Notebook 5 about, 256, 261; Beauvoir's writings in Notebook 6 about, 307; Beauvoir's writings in Notebook 7 about, 320

Harrison, Charles, 83

Haydn, Franz Josef, 120

Hegel, G. F.: Beauvoir's philosophical turn from, 28, 30; Beauvoir's writings in Notebook 6 about, 304, 307, 308, 309, 312, 313; Beauvoir's writings in Notebook 7 about, 319, 322, 325; and consciousness and the other, 14, 17–18; and epigraph for *She Came to Stay*, 14, 270, 306; and History and Spirit, 25; influence on Beauvoir's attitude toward war, 22, 26; influence on Beauvoir's philosophy, 25; and recognition of consciousnesses, 17, 28; and recognition of self, 30; and the universal, 25, 26

Heidegger, Martin: and Beauvoir as teacher, 9, 34n6; Beauvoir's reading of, 34n8; Beauvoir's writings in Notebook 7 about, 319; and concept of appeal, 30; and death, 30; and historicity, 7; and humanity as a species, 11, 12, 17; and postwar revelations about, 32; and reality, 30

Heine, Heinrich: biography read by Beauvoir, 20, 211, 214; and racism in Heine's situation, 21, 215

Henriot, Phillipe, 32

Henry IV (Shakespeare), 68, 75

heroism, 196–97

historicity: Beauvoir's escape from, 19, 97; in diary, 130, 322; in Heidegger, 7

History (*Histoire*): Beauvoir's criticism of Hegel's views about, 30, 319; distinguished from personal history, 26; experienced by Beauvoir, 24, 25, 26; and Spirit in Hegel, 25

history (*histoire*). *See* personal history

Hitler, 37, 84, 85, 100, 105, 107, 114

Hitler m'a dit [What Hitler Told Me] (Rauschning), 247, 248

Holland, threat of German invasion of, 146

L'Homme du ressentiment [The Resentful Man] (Scheler), 321

hope/no hope: Beauvoir's writings in Notebook 1 about, 41, 42, 55; Beauvoir's writings in Notebook 2 about, 88, 94, 96,

110, 135; Beauvoir's writings in Notebook 6 about, 281, 293, 304; Beauvoir's writings in Notebook 7 about, 320;

The Hound of the Baskervilles (Conan Doyle), 69

Howard, Leslie, 200

humanism: and humanity as a species, 11; and reality, 12, 304; and separation of men, 30

humanity and war, 63, 293

humanity as a species: Beauvoir-Sartre dispute about, 11, 12; Heidegger's views about, 11, 12, 17, 319; and solidarity, 13, 18; and transcendent activities, 13

"the Hungarian": Beauvoir's writings in Notebook 1 about, 44, 47, 50–51, 53, 54; Beauvoir's writings in Notebook 2 about, 101, 104, 139

Husserl, Edmund: and Beauvoir as teacher, 9, 34n6; Beauvoir's writings in Notebook 7 about, 325; childhood memory, 161; and *époché* (bracketing), 27; and solipsism, 7

idealism, 164, 168, 324

L'Idiot [The Idiot] (Dostoyevsky), 91, 133, 134, 136, 164, 166

Idt, Genevieve, 24, 34n12

illness and unhappiness, 316

Les Illuminés (Nerval), 105, 107

illusion and love, 93, 253–54

L'Imaginaire (Sartre), 177

impression(s): Beauvoir's writings in Notebook 2 about, 91, 122, 128, 130, 131, 134, 135, 137, 139; Beauvoir's writings in Notebook 3 about, 156, 159, 171, 178, 181–82, 184; Beauvoir's writings in Notebook 4 about, 207, 210, 226; Beauvoir's writings in Notebook 5 about, 246, 247, 252, 253, 255, 265; Beauvoir's writings in Notebook 6 about, 271, 283, 288, 292, 300; Beauvoir's writings in Notebook 7 about, 316;

independence, 159, 299

Les Indes galantes (Rameau), 120

indifference: Beauvoir's writings in Notebook 1 about, 45, 48, 49, 64, 75–76; Beauvoir's writings in Notebook 2 about, 107;

Beauvoir's writings in Notebook 3 about, 194, 200; Beauvoir's writings in Notebook 4 about, 211; Beauvoir's writings in Notebook 6 about, 300
individual, and conflict with the universal, 28–29, 320
inevitability (*fatalité*), 39
Intempéries (Lehman), 132
intersubjectivity, and situated subjectivity, 14
L'Intransigeant (newspaper), 40
L'Invitée (Beauvoir). See *She Came to Stay*
Italy, 276

Jack le satyre [Jack the Satyr] (movie), 62
Jacques. *See* Champigneulles, Jacques
James, Henry, 61, 62, 63
Jane Eyre (Charlotte Brontë), 63, 64, 68
Jaspers, Karl, 320
jealousy: of Beauvoir, regarding relationship between Bost and Kos., 6, 11, 112, 120, 132, 175, 194, 197, 239; of Beauvoir regarding relationship between Sartre and Lamblin, 21, 117; of Védrine, regarding Kos., 230, 232
La Jeunesse de Théophile [Théophile's Boyhood] (Jouhandeau), 75
Jews: and anti-Semitism in Germany, 309; Beauvoir's anti-Semitic remarks in diary, 21, 22, 188, 244; Beauvoir's concern for, in the Occupation, 23; and Beauvoir's remarks on "Jewishness," 280; and Heine, 20, 215; and Lamblin, 21, 22; and Landau, 70; restrictions against, 299
Joan of Arc (movie), 65
Jollivet, Simone (aka Toulouse). *See* Toulouse
Joseph, Gilbert, 32
Jouhandeau, Marcel, 75
Journal (Dabit), 207, 208
Journal (Gide), 42, 45, 48, 50, 54
Journal (Green), 92, 95
Jouvet, Louis, 65, 151, 183
joy: Beauvoir's writings in Notebook 1 about, 70, 76, 79, 80; Beauvoir's writings in Notebook 2 about, 118, 139; Beauvoir's writings in Notebook 3 about, 163, 170,

203; Beauvoir's writings in Notebook 5 about, 238, 248
Joyce, James, 286

Kafka, Franz, 175, 204, 235, 238
Kanapa: Beauvoir's writings in Notebook 1 about, 71; Beauvoir's writings in Notebook 2 about, 109, 142, 145; Beauvoir's writings in Notebook 3 about, 159, 176, 190, 200, 202; Beauvoir's writings in Notebook 4 about, 207, 211, 212; Beauvoir's writings in Notebook 5 about, 241
Kant, Immanuel, 84, 324, 325
Kautsky, Karl, 84
Keller, Catherine, 34*n*9
La Kermesse funèbre [The Funeral Fair] (movie), 241
Kierkegaard, Søren, 28, 29, 34–35*n*13, 320
Knock (movie), 115
Koestler, Arthur, 109, 111
Kos. (Olga Kosakievitch): affair with Bost, 6, 120, 132, 157, 164, 267; Beauvoir's writings in Notebook 1 about, 40, 41, 55, 57, 58, 59, 60, 61, 62, 63, 77, 85; Beauvoir's writings in Notebook 2 about, 90, 105, 106, 108, 109, 110, 111, 114, 115, 116, 118, 120, 121, 131, 136, 139, 140, 141, 144, 145, 148, 152; Beauvoir's writings in Notebook 3 about, 156, 157, 158, 162, 166, 168, 169, 170, 172, 175, 176, 178, 183, 187, 189, 193, 195, 197, 199; Beauvoir's writings in Notebook 4 about, 221, 223, 227, 228, 229, 231; Beauvoir's writings in Notebook 5 about, 233, 237, 239, 243, 246, 248, 252, 253, 259–60, 263, 264; Beauvoir's writings in Notebook 6 about, 313; and Bost's military leave, 132; as former lover of Beauvoir and Sartre, 4; marriage to Bost, 40*n*; model for Xavière in *She Came to Stay*, 4, 5
Kosakievitch, Olga. *See* Kos.
Kosakievitch, Wanda: affair with Sartre, 52*n*, 57, 116, 256, 260, 267; Beauvoir's writings in Notebook 2 about, 103, 112, 114, 115, 116, 117, 118, 119, 131, 139, 148; Beauvoir's writings in Notebook 4 about, 219, 223, 227, 229, 230;

Beauvoir's writings in Notebook 5 about, 252, 253, 260, 264, 266; letters to Sartre, 131, 136

Kreutzer Sonata (Beethoven), 185

Kruks, Sonia, 9

labor unions, 326–27

Lachièze-Rey, Pierre, 324

Lalo, Édouard, 221

Lamblin, Bianca (aka Bianca Bienenfeld): Beauvoir's anti-Semitic remarks about, 21, 244; Beauvoir's remorse for, 22; and Beauvoir as teacher, 34n6, 34n7; lover of Beauvoir and Sartre, 21; sexual affair with Beauvoir, 33n1. See also Védrine, Louise

Landau, Katia, 70

leave(s). See military leave of Bost; military leave of Sartre

Le Bon de Beauvoir, Sylvie, 1

Lehman, Rosamund, 132

Leibniz, Gottfried, 9

Le 9 Thermidor (Aldanov), 304

Lesage, Renee, 169

"Lesbian Connections" (Simons), 33n1

letters from Beauvoir, in Notebook 1: to Bost, 50, 51, 54, 56, 58, 61, 62, 69, 73, 74, 76, 80, 83, 84; to Kos., 50, 51, 68, 72, 81, 84; to Poupette, 46, 76; to Sartre, 53, 54, 56, 58, 62, 66, 69, 73, 74, 76, 80, 82, 83, 84; to Sorokine, 74, 81, 84; to Védrine, 46, 51, 58, 61, 62, 80, 83, 84

letters from Beauvoir, in Notebook 2: to Bost, 4, 90, 92, 94, 95, 97, 98, 107, 108, 111, 112, 114, 115, 120, 124, 129, 131, 132, 134, 140, 141, 144, 146, 148, 150; to Kos., 91, 129; to Poupette, 91, 101, 134; to Sartre, 91, 94, 95, 98, 104, 106, 107, 109, 111, 112, 113, 114, 115, 117, 120, 139, 140, 141, 146, 148; to Sorokine, 95, 129; to That Lady, 95; to Védrine, 91, 95, 104, 109, 120, 131, 134, 172

letters from Beauvoir, in Notebook 3: to Bost, 159, 161, 163, 168, 169, 175, 180, 182, 187, 191, 196, 197, 198; to Kos., 204; to Poupette, 167, 175, 204; to Sartre, 159, 161, 167, 169, 175, 180, 182, 185, 196, 197; to That Lady, 159;

to Toulouse, 162, 172; to Védrine, 162, 169, 180, 204

letters from Beauvoir, in Notebook 4: to Bost, 210, 214, 215, 220, 227, 228, 229; to Poupette, 224; to Sartre, 210, 213, 215, 220, 229

letters from Beauvoir, in Notebook 5: to Bost, 240, 241, 242, 253; to Sartre, 236, 260, 262, 267

letters from Beauvoir, in Notebook 6: to Bost, 274, 296; to Kos., 301, 302; to Sartre, 271, 274, 276, 310, 311

letters in Notebook 1: from Bost, 41, 56, 57, 58, 59, 62, 69, 72, 80, 82, 83, 84; from Kos., 40, 50, 77, 80; from Sartre, 48, 53, 56, 57, 59, 60, 63, 69, 72, 76, 80, 82, 83, 84; from Sorokine, 40, 57, 69; from Védrine, 59, 63, 69

letters in Notebook 2: from Bost, 89, 90, 91, 93, 95, 105, 107, 108, 110, 112, 114, 117, 118, 119, 121, 139, 145, 149, 152; from the Hungarian, 139; from Kos., 88, 95; from Poupette, 139; from Sartre, 89, 91, 92, 96, 98, 104, 105, 108, 110, 111, 114, 115, 118, 121, 139, 144, 145, 149, 152; from Sorokine, 88, 139; from Védrine, 88, 91, 99, 107, 117, 119, 139

letters in Notebook 3: from Bost, 159, 160, 162, 163, 167, 170, 171, 172, 174, 175, 180, 183, 189, 197, 200; from Sartre, 159, 160, 162, 163, 167, 169, 170, 171, 174, 175, 180, 181, 182, 183, 187, 191, 193, 195, 196, 197, 198, 200; from Védrine, 160, 181

letters in Notebook 4: from Bost, 207, 211, 216, 217, 218, 222, 228; from Kos., 207; from Sartre, 207, 211, 216, 217, 218, 220, 222, 225; from Sorokine, 207, 211

letters in Notebook 5: from Bost, 235, 236, 240, 245, 246, 247, 250, 251; from Sartre, 234, 235, 240, 241, 242, 247, 264, 265, 267, 268, 269

letters in Notebook 6: from Bost, 285, 304, 306, 312; from Kos., 312; from Poupette, 304, 312; from Sartre, 292, 312; from Sorokine, 312; from Védrine, 309

letters in Notebook 7, from Sartre, 317–18

"Letter to an American" (Fabre-Luce), 27
letter writing, importance in wartime, 84, 158–59, 300
Lettres à Sartre [Letters to Sartre] (Beauvoir): and Beauvoir's sexual affairs with women, 1, 33*n*1; mistranslation of, 2; publication of, 1, 4
Levillain (former student), 62
Levinas, Emmanuel, 34*n*9
Lévy, Raoul, 71, 108, 142, 145, 159, 241, 272, 274, 321
Lewis, Matthew, 195, 197
Lewis, Sinclair, 326
life: Beauvoir's rejection of Sartre's view of its completeness, 13; Beauvoir's writings in Notebook 1 about, 45, 56, 63, 83; Beauvoir's writings in Notebook 2 about, 135, 136; Beauvoir's writings in Notebook 3 about, 188; Beauvoir's writings in Notebook 5 about, 254, 261; Beauvoir's writings in Notebook 6 about, 296, 300; Beauvoir's writings in Notebook 7 about, 310, 315
"Literature and Metaphysics" (Beauvoir), 3
Logic (Hegel), 25, 313
London, Jack, 84, 88, 121, 137, 138
Lourdes, France, Beauvoir's pilgrimage to, 15
love: and Beauvoir's idea for future novel, 321; Beauvoir's love for Bost, 82, 120, 148, 159; Beauvoir's love for Sartre, 78, 82, 93, 317; Bost's love for Beauvoir, 139, 264; Bost's love for Beauvoir and Kos., 129; and freedom, 15; and illusion, 93, 253–54, 322; of life, 70; Sartre's love for Beauvoir, 196, 315; and symbiosis, 232
Loy, Myrna, 101

Mac Orlan, Pierre, 83, 180, 181, 194
Mademoiselle Bécut (Véry), 82
Malraux, André, 53, 90, 177, 324
Man, Paul de, 33
Mancy, Mme (Sartre's mother), 45, 49, 96, 139, 173, 190, 230, 238, 250, 258, 282
Mané-Katz, 47
Mansfield, Katherine, 236
Marcel, Gabriel, 9, 34*n*9
Marianne Magazine, 37, 51, 86

Marie-Claire (magazine) 53, 101, 115
La Marie du port [Marie of the Port] (Simeon), 82
Marriage of Figaro (Mozart), 225
Mars, ou la guerre jugée [Mars, or the Truth about War] (Alain), 76
"Marseillaise," 172
Le Matin (German paper), 282, 296
Maugham, W. Somerset, 84, 326
Maupassant, Guy de, 236
Mauriac, François, 18
meaning: disinterested, 68; metaphysical, 320; of war, 85
Les Mémoires de Gramont [Gramont's Memoirs], 79, 80
Mémoires d'une jeune fille rangée [Memoirs of a Dutiful Daughter] (Beauvoir), 2–3, 8
memory(ies): Beauovir's writings in Notebook 1 about, 64; Beauvoir's writings in Notebook 2 about, 108, 130; Beauvoir's writings in notebook 3 about, 157, 164, 190; Beauvoir's writings in Notebook 4 about, 209, 210, 211, 215, 229; Beauvoir's writings in Notebook 5 about, 256, 260, 262, 265; Beauvoir's writings in Notebook 6 about, 275, 300, 303
Menaces sur la ville [A Beleaguered City] (movie), 235
Ménard, Arlette, 119, 144, 148, 164, 196, 221, 222, 269
The Merchant of Venice (Shakespeare), 95
Mercier, Jeanne: attempts to convert Beauvoir, 16; and devotion, 15; and emotions, 10
Merleau-Ponty, Maurice, 11, 44, 140, 219
The Merry Wives of Windsor (Shakespeare), 95
methodology of Beauvoir, in doing philosophy in literature, 3
Meurtre en Mésopotamie [Murder in Mesopotamia] (Christie), 94
Mickey chasseur d'élans [Mickey the Elk Hunter] (movie), 62
Miles, Judy, 34*n*9
military leave of Bost, 239, 246, 255, 256, 260, 261, 262, 263, 268
military leave of Sartre, 4, 7, 19, 23; Beauvoir's writings in Notebook 2 about, 146; Beau-

voir's writings in Notebook 5 about, 237, 249, 250, 251, 253, 254, 255, 257, 258
mind and reality, 324
Miss Denion (Wallace), 203
Mitchell, Margaret, 302
mobilization: of French troops, 8, 17, 18, 41; of Sartre, 38–39
Le Moine [The Monk] (Matthew Lewis), 195, 197
Moll Flanders (Defoe), 88
"Moon Woman": Beauvoir's writings in Notebook 1 about, 59; Beauvoir's writings in Notebook 2 about, 99, 101, 102, 104, 112, 139, 148; Beauvoir's writings in Notebook 3 about, 174, 175, 182, 186; Beauvoir's writings in Notebook 4 about, 219, 221–22, 231
Mops (Mme Morel's daughter Jacqueline), 81, 82, 239, 278, 294
Morand, Paul, 175
Morel family. *See* Mops; "That Gentleman"; "That Lady"
The Mother (Pearl Buck), 57
Le Moulin de la Sourdine [The Mill of the Sourdine] (Aymé), 302
Mouloudji, 181, 193, 195, 267, 321
movies, 60, 62, 65, 94, 101, 105, 111, 116, 160, 241. *See also* specific titles
Mozart, Wolfgang Amadeus, 52, 234, 225, 308, 312
Mr. Smith Goes to Washington (movie), 250
Munch, Charles, 187
Le Mur [The Wall] (Sartre), 98, 201, 224
music, 52, 56, 110, 210, 214, 233, 238, 271, 318. *See also* specific composers/compositions
Les Mutinés de l'Elseneur [The Mutineers of Elsenor] (Jack London), 121, 137, 138

Nanook (movie), 116
Nausea (Sartre), 150
Nazis: and murder of Bourla, 13; and radio broadcasts, 31–32
need for other(s), 2, 15, 30, 254; Beauvoir's need for Sartre, 104, 147
Le Nègre Léonard et maître Jean Mullin [Black Leonard and Master Jean Mullin] (Mac Orlan), 180

Nerval, Gérard de, 105, 107
Nizan, Paul: killing of, 27, 316; as part of "couple" with Sartre, 7; resignation from communist party, 90; in Stalag 12, 318; view of youth, 134
Nocturne (Debussy), 310
nothingness, 60, 300, 317, 324
Les Nourritures terrestres (Gide), 137
Nouvelle Revue Française (NRF) (journal), 27, 28, 49, 92, 98, 177, 178, 319
Nuits de bal [Dancing Nights] (movie), 235

Occupation (of France, by Germany): and Beauvoir as refugee, 21, 22, 25; and Beauvoir's concern for Jews, 23; Beauvoir's idea of freedom as defiance of, 13; Beauvoir's reaction to, 30, 32, 296; and Beauvoir's return to Paris, 22, 282, 293; and first French civilian shot, 28; and Germans, 207, 282, 283, 284, 285, 286, 287, 288, 289, 290, 291, 293, 303, 305, 309; and History, 26, 27; and loss of freedom of expression, 25; as ordeal, 28; and political engagement, 10; and refugees, 284, 285, 286, 287, 288, 289, 296, 297, 298. *See also* collaboration with Occupation; evacuation of Paris; return to Paris
L'Œuvre (newspaper), 48, 51, 157, 242
oppression: Beauvoir's condemnation of, 12; and embodiment, 10; of women, 10, 12
L'Ordre (newspaper), 51
"The Origins of the Music Hall" (Beauvoir's radio scripts), 32
Ossola, Jean, 118
other(s): as an absolute, 18; and appeal from the other, 30; and appeal to the other's freedom, 30; Beauvoir's philosophy in Sartre's diary, 7; Beauvoir's rejection of the other as an absolute, 18; and consciousness in Hegel, 14; and consciousness of the other, 250, 251; and consciousness of the other as an absolute, 18; and duty to self, 15; élan toward, 29–30; and exteriority of, 13, 322; and facticity, 323; and freedom, 321; need for, 2, 15, 30; the other in Beauvoir's views, 2, 3; and the other's conscious-

ness, 7; self-other confrontation, 4, 5, 93; self-other interdependency, 14; self-other opposition, 3, 16; self-other separateness, 14, 16, 17; and solaltrism, 15; and subjectivity, 29; women as the other, 10, 18

Pardo: Beauvoir's writings in Notebook 1 about, 42, 43, 44, 46, 47, 48–49; Beauvoir's writings in Notebook 2 about, 96, 117
Paris: and preparations for war, 42, 44; war damage, 291, 292. *See also* evacuation of Paris; return to Paris
Paris-Midi (newspaper), 37, 38, 45, 51, 196
passion(s): Beauvoir-Sartre dispute about, 11; Beauvoir's passion for Bost, 11, 20, 112, 131, 158, 170, 254, 262; Beauvoir's passion for philosophy, 2, 3; Beauvoir's passions for Sartre, 254; in Bergson, 10; and Kos., 158; and reason, 11; and Sorokine, 191, 218, 224, 226, 227; and Védrine, 158, 200
patience, 80, 294, 303
Pavane (Ravel), 212
Pension Mimosa (movie), 268
The People of the Abyss (Jack London), 84
Pepys, Samuel, 326
personal history (*histoire*): Beauvoir's personal history and wartime events, 25, 282, 304; as distinguished from History, 26
Pétain, Henri Philippe, 216, 299
The Petrified Forest (movie), 200
Petrouchka (Stravinsky), 58, 61
Phèdre (Racine), 151
Phenomenology of Spirit (Hegel), 25, 304, 307
philosophy: authenticity, 23; bad faith, 3, 23; Beauvoir's lies about work in, 1, 2, 6, 8; and Beauvoir's philosophical transformation, 2, 8, 9, 10, 13, 17, 23, 28, 29, 30, 31, 33, 320; and humanism, 12; and literature, 3; situation, 2, 7, 9; solaltrism, 15, 16, 34*n*9; solipsism, 7, 8, 12, 14. *See also* political engagement; situated subjectivity);
Piaf, Edith, 267
Pieter Ibbetson (movie), 105
pillaging: by civilians, 302; by French soldiers, 289

Les Pillards des mers [Pirates of the Seas] (movie), 237
Pilote d'essai [Test Pilot] (movie), 101
plenitude, 265, 312
Plutarque a menti [Plutarch Lied], 84
Poland, 37, 40, 41, 56, 59, 61, 67, 68, 74, 76, 83
political action: and Beauvoir's remorse for Bost, 24; and élan toward others, 29–30; and recognition for one's project (s), 30
political engagement: and action, 23; Beauvoir inspired by Boula's murder, 33; and Beauvoir's philosophy, 8, 10, 28; confrontation between the individual and the universal, 29; effect of abstention from, 24; and first formulation of idea by Beauvoir, 23; and the Occupation, 10; roots in *Équipes Sociales*, 23; and Sartre's views in *The Prime of Life*, 23
political solidarity. *See* solidarity
The Portrait of a Lady (Henry James), 61, 62, 63
Poupette (aka Henriette de Beauvoir): Beauvoir's writings in Notebook 1 about, 43; Beauvoir's writings in Notebook 2 about, 108, 109, 110, 111, 112, 113, 114, 117, 119, 139; Beauvoir's writings in Notebook 3 about, 158; Beauvoir's writings in Notebook 5 about, 266, 268
power: Descartes's views about, 13; as distinguished from freedom, 13
Prélude à Verdun [Prelude to Verdun] (Romains), 204, 206, 207
The Prime of Life (Beauvoir): and Beauvoir's deletion of her philosophy from diary, 3; and Beauvoir's denial of doing philosophy in *She Came to Stay*, 3; and Beauvoir's philosophical transformation, 31; and Beauvoir's relationship with Lamblin, 22; and Beauvoir's views about *She Came to Stay*, 10, 16; and Beauvoir's writings about *The Second Sex*, 9; and confrontation between the individual and universal belittled, 29; and death, 13; and distinction between freedom and power, 13; and driving force of *She Came to Stay*, 5; and

first French civilian shot, 28; and freedom, 19; and Hegel's influence on Beauvoir, 26; and Sartre's views about political engagement, 23

prison camps, 281, 285, 293, 294, 300, 301, 303, 317–18

prisoner(s): lists of, 303; Sartre as, 4, 17, 23, 25, 27, 272, 300, 301, 303, 308, 317–18

project(s), 30

propaganda, 71, 73, 295, 300, 308

prostitutes. *See* whores

Proust, Marcel, 239, 326

psychoanalysis, Beauvoir's teaching about, 114

"put in parentheses," 93, 168, 263, 300, 317. *See also* bracketing

Pyrrhus and Cineas (Beauvoir): and Beauvoir's philosophical transformation, 30, 31; and Beauvoir's rejection of the other as an absolute, 18; and condemnation of oppression, 12; and criticism of absolute devotion, 30; and death, 13; and distinction between freedom and power, 13; and the Occupation, 30; and the other, 29; and political action, 29; and the self and its project(s), 30; and situated subjectivity, 10

Le Quai des Brumes (Mac Orlan), 180, 181

Quartet (Debussy), 307

Quartet (Ravel), 312

Queen, Ellery, 145, 149

Queneau, Raymond, 95

Rabelais, François, 304

Racine, Jean, 151

racism: anti-black, 21; of Beauvoir, 21; in Heine's situation, 21, 215

radio broadcasts, 31–32, 210, 214, 256, 276, 280, 308

Radio-Paris, 32

Radio-Vichy (French National Radio), 32

rage, 165, 305, 306, 310

Rameau, Jean Philippe, 120

rancor, 197, 241, 264

Le Rat de ville et le rat des champs [The City Mouse and the Country Mouse] (movie), 227

Rathenau, Walter, 84

Rauschning, Hermann, 20, 247, 248

Ravel, Maurice, 120, 195, 212, 221, 234, 312

reality: and books, 304; and death, in Heidegger, 30; and freedom, 18–19; and the future, 116; and human history, 304; and humanism, 12, 319, 320; and mind, 324; and transcendence, 12, 28; and war, 135

reason, and passions(s), 11

recognition: of consciousnesses, 17–18, 28, 319, 322; of one's project(s), 30; of self, 30

refugee(s): Alsatian, 108; Beauvoir as, 21, 22, 25; as evacuees, 278, 279, 280, 281; and fleeing civilians, 302, 311–12; German, 285; and Santo Domingo, 118, 237; Spanish, 100. *See also* evacuation of Paris; Occupation; return to Paris

regret(s), 109, 163, 264

relationships between people, 18, 147, 164, 322

remorse: Beauvoir's remorse for Bost, 24, 62–63; Beauvoir's remorse for her country, 31; Beauvoir's remorse for Lamblin, 22; Beauvoir's remorse for Védrine (Lamblin), 148, 149

Renn, L., 84

representations, 324

Les Réprové [The Reprobates] (Von Salomon), 287

Requiem (Mozart), 234

Requiem (Ropartz), 187

Resistance (French), 32

The Return of the Cisco Kid (movie), 160

The Return of Zorro (movie), 180

return to Paris (Beauvoir's), 283, 284, 285, 286, 287, 288, 289, 290, 291, 292

Reynaud, Paul, 299, 304

Rhapsodie espagnole (Ravel), 195, 221

Richard III (Shakespeare), 176, 179, 190, 229

Rilke, Rainer Maria, 150

Rimbaud in Abbyssinia (Starkie), 77

Rogers, Ginger, 237

Romains, Jules, 86n6, 204, 206, 207, 209, 226, 227, 231

Ropartiz, Guy, 187
Roulet (future husband of Poupette), 54
Rowley, Hazel, 33n1
Russia, 41, 67, 68, 76, 83, 275

sadness, 60, 64, 66, 112, 120, 256, 265, 276, 309
Saint-Exupéry, Antoine, 161, 162, 264
Saint Louis Blues (movie), 94
salvation, 320, 321
San Francisco (movie), 192
La Sarthe (newspaper), 285
Sartre, Jean-Paul: L'Age de raison, 129; affair with Wanda Kosakievitch, 52n, 57, 116, 256, 260, 267; as Beauvoir's absolute, 317; Beauvoir's anguish over, 27; Beauvoir's devotion to, 17; Beauvoir's first meeting with, 2; Beauvoir's lies about influence on, 1; Beauvoir's visit to, 20; Beauvoir's writings in Notebook 1 about, 37, 38, 40, 42, 43, 45, 51, 55, 59, 63, 76, 81, 82; Beauvoir's writings in Notebook 2 about, 91, 119, 120, 124, 125, 126, 127, 128, 129, 130, 131, 132, 133, 134, 135, 136; Beauvoir's writings in Notebook 3 about, 178; Beauvoir's writings in Notebook 5 about, 249, 252, 253, 256, 257, 258, 262; Beauvoir's writings in Notebook 6 about, 272, 294, 304, 305; and charge of passive collaboration, 31; and reading draft of She Came to Stay, 7, 249, 250, 251; former lover of Kos., 4; lover of Lamblin, 21; mobilization, 38–39; mutual dependency with Beauvoir, 17; as part of "couple" with Beauvoir, 7; as part of "couple" with Nizan, 7; as prisoner of war (see prisoner[s]); treatise for Beauvoir on prewar events, 6, 165; use of Beauvoir's philosophy from She Came to Stay, 7, 8; and visit by Beauvoir, 20. See also military leave of Sartre; visit to Sartre
Sartre's diary: and Beauvoir's description of love and sadism, 7; Beauvoir's reading of, 130, 131, 189, 190, 192, 249, 262; and embodied consciousness, 11; and friendship, 7; and Husserl, 7; and ideas from She Came to Stay, 7; and influence of Beau-

voir's philosophy on Being and Nothingness, 6; and solaltrism, 15
Scheler, Max, 321
Schumann, Robert, 310
Science and Health, 99
The Second Sex (Beauvoir): Beauvoir's desired interpretation of, 8; Beauvoir's dread of public repudiation of, 8; and Beauvoir's rejection of self-abnegation, 15; and body, 20; and concept of situation, 9; and consciousness as shaped by society, 21; and freedom, 20; and intersubjectivity, 14; and oppression of women, 12; and political engagement, 8; and solidarity of women, 12–13; and women's consciousness as shaped by society, 20; and women's freedom through collective action, 23
The Secret Agent (Maugham), 84
self: and Beauvoir's loss of self, 25; in Bergson, 10; and duty to others, 15; and expression, 158; and its project(s), 30; and recognition, 30; self-other confrontation, 4, 5, 93; self-other interdependency, 14; self-other opposition, 3, 16; self-other separateness, 14; women's loss of, 15
self-abnegation, 15
self-knowing, 132–33, 184
selflessness, 18
self-representation: Beauvoir's self-representation as Sartre's follower, 8; Beauvoir's self-representation to others, 177; and character in novel, 213
La Semaine à Paris (magazine), 224, 242
sentimentality, 93, 292, 268
separation, 112, 131, 249, 271, 306
serenity, 312–13
Sevel, Geneviève, 34n6
sexual affairs with women: Beauvoir's, recounted in Lettres à Sartre, 1; Beauvoir's lies about, 1. See also names of specific women
Shakespeare, William, 68, 75, 95, 176, 179, 190, 229
shame, 7, 29, 33
She Came to Stay (Beauvoir): and action, 23; Beauvoir's criticism of, 17, 321; Beauvoir's

denial of doing philosophy in, 4; and Beauvoir's ideas in Sartre's diary, 7; and Beauvoir's lies about writing, 4, 6; and Beauvoir's philosophy, 2; and Beauvoir's reading of Heidegger, 34n8; Beauvoir's views about, 10, 16, 98; Beauvoir's writings in Notebook 2 about, 93, 98; central subject of, 2; and completion of writing, 3; and consciousnesses, 2, 5, 29; and consciousness and the other, 7, 321; and draft read by Sartre, 7, 249, 250, 251; driving force of, 5; and embodiment, 10; and epigraph by Hegel, 14, 270, 306; and freedom, 10; influence on *Being and Nothingness*, 2, 6, 7, 8; and Jacques Bost as model for Gerbert, 5; and Kos., as model for Xavière, 4, 5; and love triangle, 4, 5; and oppression, 10; and other, 2, 3; philosophical similarities to *Being and Nothingness*, 3; and political engagement, 8; as predating *Being and Nothingness*, 2; and Sartre's use of Beauvoir's philosophy, 7, 8; and self- other confrontation, 4, 5; and self-other interdependency, 14; and self-other separateness, 14, 16; and shame, 29; and situation, 9; and solaltrism, 16; and solipsism, 8, 14, 15, 16, 29; and time schedule of writing, 4–6. *See also* writing

Sieburg, Friedrich, 309

Si j'avais un million [If I Had a Million] (movie), 184

silence, 292

Simeon, 82

Simons, Margaret A., 1, 15, 21, 33n1, 33n5, 34n12

Le Singe d'argile [The Clay Ape], 95

situated subjectivity: and action, 23; in Beauvoir's philosophy, 9, 10; and embodiment, 10; and intersubjectivity, 14; and society, 18

situation: and authenticity, 252; and Beauvoir-Sartre discussions, 2; and Beauvoir-Sartre-Védrine triangle, 147; and body, 2; and femininity, 9, 133; and happiness, 321; in Heidegger, 7, 9; in Marcel, 9; Sartre's, 253; and women, 10

skiing, 203, 204, 206, 207, 208, 212, 213

Snow White (movie), 62

society: and community, 43; shaping Beauvoir's experiences, 19– 20; shaping consciousness, 21; shaping women's consciousness, 18; and situated subjectivity, 18; and suppression of élan toward others, 30

solaltrism, 15, 16, 34n9

soldiers: French, as affected by war, 58, 70, 97, 215, 246, 278; French, pillaging by, 289; German, in France, 282, 283, 284, 285, 286, 287, 288–89, 290, 291, 293, 298, 309; as proletariat of the armies, 196; Spanish, as veterans, 216

solidarity: and blacks, 12; with enemy soldiers, 196; and humanity, 12, 13, 18, 28, 320; and separation of men, 18, 30; and women, 12–13

solipsism: and Beauvoir as a solipsist, 8, 12, 320; Beauvoir's views about, 8, 14, 15, 16, 29; in Husserl, 7; Sartre's recourse to, 7; and theory of time, 33n3

solitude: Beauvoir's writings in Notebook 2 about, 98, 116, 130; Beauvoir's writings in Notebook 3 about, 163, 168, 184, 203, 204; Beauvoir's writings in Notebook 4 about, 208, 209, 214, 220; Beauvoir's writings in Notebook 5 about, 246, 253, 259, 262; Beauvoir's writings in Notebook 6 about, 293, 308; Beauvoir's writings in Notebook 7 about, 319; and theme for new novel, 322

Sonia, 38, 43–44, 49, 57, 61, 108, 143

Sorcerer's Apprentice (Dukas), 195

Sorokine, Nathalie: Beauvoir's affair with, 20, 99, 104, 158, 166, 170, 173, 175, 176, 181, 182, 191, 192, 198–99, 201, 217– 18, 224, 226, 227, 236, 242, 247, 252, 257, 261; Beauvoir's physical fights with, 261, 267, 295, 306; Beauvoir's writings in Notebook 1 about, 31, 38, 40, 84; Beauvoir's writings in Notebook 2 about, 96, 106, 108, 110, 114, 118, 140, 142, 144, 145, 152; Beauvoir's writings in Notebook 3 about, 160, 168, 174, 176, 217, 218; Beauvoir's writings in Notebook 4 about, 217, 218, 220, 222, 223, 225, 231; Beauvoir's writings in Notebook 5 about, 233, 234, 235, 241, 244, 246, 251, 257,

259, 264, 265, 267; Beauvoir's writings in notebook 6 about, 272, 294, 295, 297, 301, 302, 303, 305, 306, 307, 309, 312, 313
sorrow, and Sartre as prisoner, 303
Le Soulier de satin [The Satin Slipper] (movie), 65
Spinoza, Baruch, 26, 45, 144, 145
Spirit and History in Hegel, 25
stability, 52
Stalag 12: Nizan as prisoner in, 318; Sartre as prisoner in, 317n
Stalin, 84, 107, 177
Starkie, Enid, 77
Stevenson, Robert Louis, 85
Stewart, James, 250
Stravinksy, Igor, 59, 310
student diary (Beauvoir): and asceticism, 10; and Beauvoir's aspirations, 15; and Beauvoir's deletion of ideas in diary for *Mémoires d'une jeune fille rangée*, 2–3; and Beauvoir's early philosophy, 33n5; and Beauvoir's religious upbringing, 18; and embodied consciousness, 11; and embodiment, 10, 11; and freedom, 18; and self-abnegation, 15; and self-other opposition, 16; and situated subjectivity, 10
suffering, 65, 101, 118, 119, 253 , 274
suicide, 60, 320
Suleiman, Susan Rubin, 31, 33
sweetness, 67, 68, 91, 196, 254
La Symphonie burlesque [The Burlesque Symphony] (movie), 192
Symphonie espagnole (Lalo), 221

Taras Bulba (Gogol), 69, 70, 72
teaching: Beauvoir's writings in Notebook 2 about, 89, 106, 107, 109, 114, 117, 118, 120, 121, 139, 140, 142, 144, 149, 150, 152; Beauvoir's writings in Notebook 3 about, 160, 162, 163, 164, 167, 169, 172, 173, 175, 176, 181, 182, 189, 196, 197, 198; Beauvoir's writings in Notebook 4 about, 217, 219, 222, 223, 226, 229; Beauvoir's writings in Notebook 5 about, 240, 241, 244, 247, 251, 257, 259, 260; Beauvoir's writings in Notebook 6

about, 271, 272, 299, 301, 303, 307, 309, 310, 312
Temple, Shirley, 160
tenderness: Beauvoir's, for Bost, 236; Beauvoir's, for Kos., 139; Beauvoir's, for Wanda Kosakievitch, 117; Beauvoir's lack of, for Védrine, 144; Bost's, for Beauvoir, 170, 196, 202; Sartre's, for Wanda Kosakievitch, 116; Sorokine's, for Beauvoir, 226–27
Terre des hommes [Wind, Sand, and Stars] (Saint-Exupéry), 161, 162
terror, 302
Testament espagnol [Spanish Testament] (Koestler), 109, 111
Tête d'Or [Golden Head] (Claudel), 74, 75
"That Gentleman" (M. Morel), 83n, 278, 279, 280
"That Lady" (Mme Morel), 46n; Beauvoir's relationship with, 81; Beauvoir's writings in Notebook 1 about, 7, 75, 77, 82, 84; and shelter for evacuees, 278, 279, 280, 281
thought, 197, 324–25
time, 11, 24, 33n1, 111, 135, 136, 172, 248, 250, 254, 283, 300, 324
Time and Free Will (Bergson), 10
Le Tombeau de Couperin (Ravel), 120
Toulouse: Beauvoir's writings in Notebook 1 about, 40, 59, 60, 65, 66, 67, 68, 69, 82, 85; Beauvoir's writings in Notebook 2 about, 97, 101; Beauvoir's writings in Notebook 3 about, 179; Beauvoir's writings in Notebook 5 about, 251; Beauvoir's writings in Notebook 6 about, 299, 302, 311
La Tradition de Minuit [Midnight Tradition] (Mac Orlan), 83
Trafic d'armes [Arms Traffic] (movie), 40
transcendence: and human activity, 13; and reality, 12, 28, 319; and war, 176
translation: of Beauvoir's letters, 1; of Sartre's letters, 1
The Trial (Kafka), 175, 204
Les Trois Lanciers du Bengale [Lives of a Bengal Lancer] (movie), 112
Les Trois Loufquetaires [The Three Daffies] (movie), 255

trust, 148, 168
Tucker, Sophie, 240

Ulysses (Joyce), 286
uncertainty, 49, 60, 126, 163, 176, 245, 247, 294
the universal: and Beauvoir's reconciliation
to events, 26; and conflict with the individual, 28–29, 320; in Hegel, 25, 26; and
individual expression, 25

Valéry, Paul, 306
Védrine, Louise (Bianca Lamblin, aka Bianca
Bienenfeld), 42*n;* Beauvoir's affair with, 18,
75, 98, 143, 144, 145, 146, 158, 182, 184, 194,
200, 201, 225, 256; Beauvoir's anti-Semitic
remarks about, 188, 244; and Beauvoir-
Sartre triangle, 146–47, 245; and Beauvoir's
evacuation of Paris, 274, 275, 276, 277;
Beauvoir's writings in Notebook 1 about,
42, 45, 53, 69, 70, 77, 85; Beauvoir's writings
in Notebook 2 about, 1, 115, 117, 118, 131,
134, 140, 142, 145, 148, 149; Beauvoir's writings in Notebook 3 about, 19, 182, 187, 193,
194, 195, 196, 197, 198; Beauvoir's writings
in Notebook 4 about, 217, 218, 219, 226,
230, 231, 232; Beauvoir's writings in Notebook 5 about, 233, 235, 237, 239, 240, 246,
257, 263, 264, 265; Beauvoir's writings in
Notebook 6 about, 271, 272, 273, 294, 312,
313; conflict with mother over Beauvoir,
73, 74, 75; letters to Sartre, 131, 135; and
Sartre's military leave, 146, 255
Verdi, Giuseppe, 166
Véry, Pierre, 82, 84
Vintges, Karen, 15
violence: as acting on exterior of man, 13;
and freedom, 14
visit to Sartre, by Beauvoir: effect on
Beauvoir's life, 132, 134; and happiness,
128; and meeting with Sartre, 126; and
Sartre's diary, 130, 131; and Sartre's novel,
129; return from, 137–38; and solitude,
30; travel regarding, 122–25; and wartime
existence, 135
Von Salomon, Ernst, 287

Wahl, Jean, 173, 176, 177, 307
waiting: Beauvoir's writings in Notebook
1 about, 49, 85; Beauvoir's writings in
Notebook 2 about, 92; Beauvoir's writings
in Notebook 5 about, 241, 248; Beauvoir's
writings in Notebook 6 about, 275, 294,
300, 305; Beauvoir's writings in Notebook
7 about, 315, 317
war: declaration of, 19; effect on cafés and
restaurants, 41, 55, 90, 113, 193; effect on
civilians, 56, 64, 79, 133, 134, 135, 138, 150,
271, 277, 293; effect on French soldiers,
58, 70, 97, 138, 215, 246; and evacuation of
Paris (*see* evacuation); as everywhere, 137;
and humanity, 63, 293; lived by Beauvoir
with Bost and Sartre, 261; meaning of, 85;
military operations of, 45, 50, 54, 138, 220,
272, 280; and the Occupation (*see* Occupation); preparations in Paris for, 42, 44; and
reality, 135; women's experiences of, 19, 58,
64, 101, 258–59, 294, 295, 296, 303
wedding (morganic) of Beauvoir and Sartre,
104
West, Mae, 148, 169
When Things of the Spirit Come First (Beauvoir), 19, 25
whores, 127, 156, 219–20, 222, 228, 243, 294,
301, 304
women: and choices, 132; consciousness
as shaped by society, 18; and freedom
through collective action, 23; and loss of
self, 15; oppression of, 10, 12; as the other,
10; and societal pressures, 19; and solidarity, 12–13; wartime experiences of, 19, 58,
64, 101, 258–59, 294, 295, 296, 303
Woolf, Virginia, 326
world change (Beauvoir's), 305, 308, 316, 319
World War I (aka war of 1914), 67, 84, 85, 185
World War II. *See* war
Wright, Richard, 12
writing, of *She Came to Stay:* and Beauvoir's
philosophical transformation, 320; chapter
1 work, 182, 183; chapter 2 work, 197, 199;
chapter 3 work, 198, 210; chapter 4 work,
211, 214; chapter 5 work, 220; chapter 6

work, 225; chapter 7 work, 230; chapter
8 work, 235; chapter 9 work, 115, 141, 159,
160; chapter 10 work, 160; and entire novel
in Beauvoir's mind, 170; general work on,
140, 162, 172, 180, 181, 207, 229, 230, 242,
243; and happiness, 119; and need for new
chapter, 227; and new ideas, 244; and plan
for story line, 98, 99; and rough draft, 157;
and Sartre's reading of, 249, 250, 252, 257;
and thoughts of publishing, 176, 177–78;
and wish to show Sartre, 240
writing new novel: and desire to write, 210;
themes in new novel, 322, 323, 324

Zaza (childhood friend), 238
Zuorro, 61, 75, 82, 240, 316

Contributors

ANNE DEING CORDERO is associate professor emerita at George Mason University, where she established and directed the Translation Program. She has published numerous translations from French and German.

SYLVIE LE BON DE BEAUVOIR is the adopted daughter and literary executor of Simone de Beauvoir. She is the editor of *Lettres à Sartre* and many other works of Beauvoir.

MARGARET A. SIMONS is a professor of philosophy at Southern Illinois University Edwardsville. She is the author of *Beauvoir and "The Second Sex"* and editor, most recently, of Beauvoir's *Philosophical Writings* and *The Philosophy of Simone de Beauvoir*. She is also coeditor, with Barbara Klaw, Sylvie Le Bon de Beauvoir, and Marybeth Timmermann, of Beauvoir's *Diary of a Philosophy Student: Volume 1, 1926–27*.

BOOKS IN THE BEAUVOIR SERIES

Series edited by Margaret A. Simons and Sylvie Le Bon de Beauvoir

Philosophical Writings
Edited by Margaret A. Simons
with Marybeth Timmermann
and Mary Beth Mader
and a foreword by
Sylvie Le Bon de Beauvoir

Diary of a Philosophy Student:
Volume 1, 1926–27
Edited by Barbara Klaw,
Sylvie Le Bon de Beauvoir,
and Margaret Simons,
with Marybeth Timmermann
Foreword by Sylvie Le Bon de Beauvoir

Wartime Diary
Translation and Notes by
Anne Deing Cordero
Edited by Margaret A. Simons
and Sylvie Le Bon de Beauvoir
Foreword by Sylvie Le Bon de Beauvoir

The University of Illinois Press
is a founding member of the
Association of American University Presses.

———————————————————————

Composed in 10.25/13 Adobe Minion Pro
with FF Meta display
by Jim Proefrock
at the University of Illinois Press
Designed by Copenhaver Cumpston
Manufactured by Sheridan Books, Inc.

———————————————————————

UNIVERSITY OF ILLINOIS PRESS
1325 South Oak Street　Champaign, IL 61820-6903
www.press.uillinois.edu

FEB   2009